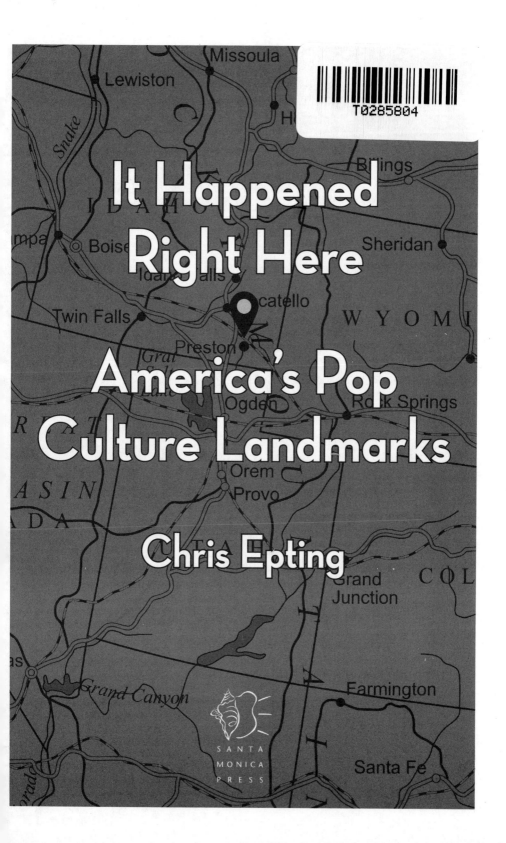

It Happened Right Here

America's Pop Culture Landmarks

Chris Epting

SANTA
MONICA
PRESS

Published by:
Santa Monica Press LLC
P.O. Box 850
Solana Beach, CA 92075
1-800-784-9553
www.santamonicapress.com
books@santamonicapress.com

SANTA
MONICA
PRESS

Printed in China

Santa Monica Press books are available at special quantity discounts when purchased in bulk by corporations, organizations, or groups. Please call our Special Sales department at 1-800-784-9553.

ISBN-13 978-1-59580-1-203 (print)
ISBN 978-1-59580-772-4 (ebook)

Publisher's Cataloging-in-Publication data

Names: Epting, Chris, 1961-, author.
Title: It happened right here : America's pop culture landmarks / by Chris Epting.
Description: Solana Beach, CA: Santa Monica Press, 2023.
Identifiers: ISBN 978-1-59580-120-3 (print) | 978-1-59580-772-4 (ebook)
Subjects: LCSH Historic sites--United States--Guidebooks. | Popular culture--United States--History. | Popular culture--United States--History--21st century. | United States --Guidebooks. | BISAC TRAVEL / Special Interest / Roadside Attractions | SOCIAL SCIENCE / Popular Culture | TRAVEL / Museums, Tours, Points of Interest | TRAVEL / Special Interest / Family | HISTORY / United States / General
Classification: LCC E159 .E69 2023 | DDC 917.304/929--dc23

Cover and interior design and production by Future Studio

Cover photo by Chris Epting
All photos in this book courtesy of the author's private collection.

Contents

INTRODUCTION 5

CHAPTER ONE: **AMERICANA: THE WEIRD AND THE WONDERFUL** 7

CHAPTER TWO: **BORN IN THE USA** 67

CHAPTER THREE: **HISTORY AND TRAGEDY** 91

CHAPTER FOUR: **CRIME, MURDER, AND ASSASSINATION** 141

CHAPTER FIVE: **CELEBRITY DEATHS AND INFAMOUS CELEBRITY EVENTS** . . 193

CHAPTER SIX: **LET'S GO TO THE MOVIES** 241

CHAPTER SEVEN: **LET THERE BE MUSIC** 289

CHAPTER EIGHT: **CHANNEL SURFING** 373

CHAPTER NINE: **ART AND LITERATURE** 407

CHAPTER TEN: **PLAY BALL!** 429

INDEX BY STATE 457

Author Chris Epting in the doorway of the "Gram Parsons Room 8" at the Joshua Tree Inn 2003 (left) and 2023 (right).

Introduction

I find one of the locations in this book to be arguably the most prophetic of them all: The dorm room where Facebook was created. Because just like the first book of this sort I ever wrote, *James Dean Died Here*, that was 20 years ago.

In a world before social media had essentially taken over so many corners and brands, books were where most people went to find places like the ones contained in this book, others that I've written, as well as many other titles written by other authors. But that has all changed today. I marvel at the work that some people do online to document their pop culture journeys.

In documenting the additional content in this new edition, a couple of things jumped out to me in particular. One, in terms of television locations, docuseries programming and bingeable series TV have become firmly entrenched in many of our minds. Thankfully, they have given us many interesting places to visit.

Something else that jumped out, sadly, is the number of mass shootings that have taken place in the last 20 years. Tragically, they have become commonplace, and the locations matter more than ever. That's why you find them included in this book. They are reminders of how much better we can be as a society—and hopefully, these memorials and tributes will last forever, so that those stricken by these senseless tragedies will never be forgotten.

I have often been asked: Why is it so important to you to go stand at the exact location where something happened? I always struggled with the answer; I know what it feels like, but it was hard to put into words.

That was until my friend, writer Warren Beath (*The Death of James Dean*), wrote this: "I like to read and build an architectural structure of the imagination, and the final step is actually to walk into it—to inhabit the same space as the events while experiencing them emotionally. I seem to retain a connection with the event and the place, and I relive it continually. These are the places of my dreams."

I read that years ago, and his words still resonate with me today.

CHAPTER ONE

AMERICANA: THE WEIRD AND THE WONDERFUL

Apple Computer

2066 Crist Drive • Los Altos, California

It was 1975 and the paths of two Bay Area tech-heads, teenagers Steve Jobs and Steve Wozniak, had crossed once again. This time, Wozniak was working on a primitive forerunner of the personal computer. Hewlett-Packard and Atari showed little interest in the invention, but Jobs thought there was something to the device and insisted that he and Woz start a company. In 1977, they wound up here in the Jobs family's garage, where Jobs' father removed his car-restoration gear and helped the boys by hauling home a huge wooden workbench that served as their first manufacturing base. The Apple Computer Company was born.

Area 51

Groom Lake, Nevada

DIRECTIONS: From Las Vegas take I-15 north for 22 miles. At exit 64 take US-93 north. After 85 miles, 12 miles past Alamo, you come to the intersection with Highway 318 on the left. Directly across the road, to your right, you will see the ruins of an old casino. At the intersection, turn left onto Highway 318. After less than a mile turn left again onto Highway 375. At that intersection you will see the "Extra-terrestrial Highway" signs. From the beginning of Highway 375 it is about 15 miles to the beginning of Groom Lake Road, 20 miles to the Black Mailbox and 39 miles to Rachel.

Area 51, also known as Groom Lake, is a top-secret military facility about 90 miles north of Las Vegas. The number "51" refers to a 6-by-10-mile block of land, at the center of which resides a large air base the government keeps under heavy wraps. The site was selected in the mid-1950s for testing of the U-2 spyplane due to its remoteness, proximity to existing facilities, and presence of a dry lake bed for landings. Due to all of the government secrecy, the area is a hotbed of UFO interest. The boundary of the base is patrolled by a high-tech security that can detect movement around the installation. Another 20 miles down Highway 375 is the Black Mailbox, where a former Area 51 worker led groups to view strange aerial displays above the region in the early 1990s. Visitors from all over the world (this world) have left hastily-scrawled thoughts on the box over the years, making it an interesting landmark in an otherwise barren area. Travel another 19 miles and you'll come to the town of Rachel, Nevada. Dubbed the "UFO Capital of the World," Rachel continues to be a popular destination among UFO fans all over the world, especially those who are attracted to Area 51. This is due to the fact that it's the closest town to the Area 51 region, though

"town" seems to be a bit of an over-statement. In Rachel you'll find the Little A'Le'Inn (pronounced "Little Alien"), a casual restaurant and bar that has some fun with its own history, a UFO gift shop, and the Area 51 Research Center.

Arizona Meteor Crater

Located off Interstate 40 at exit 233, 35 miles east of Flagstaff, 20 miles west of Winslow, Arizona • 800-289-5898

Fifty thousand years ago, a huge iron-nickel meteorite, hurtling at about 40,000

miles per hour, struck the rocky plain of Northern Arizona with an explosive force greater than 20 million tons of TNT. In less than a few seconds, the meteorite, estimated to have been about 150 feet across and weighing several hundred thousand tons, left a crater 700 feet deep and over 4,000 feet wide. Large blocks of limestone, some the size of small houses, were heaved onto the rim. Flat-lying beds of rock in the crater walls were overturned in fractions of a second and uplifted permanently as much as 150 feet. Today the crater is 550 feet deep, and 2.4 miles in circumference. Twenty football games could be played simultaneously on its floor, while more than two million spectators could observe from its sloping sides. The topographical terrain of the Arizona Meteor Crater so closely resembles that of the Earth's moon and other planets, that NASA designated it as one of the official training sites for the Apollo Astronauts. The U.S. Government deemed the crater a natural landmark in 1968.

Bigfoot
About one mile upstream from the confluence of Notice Creek and Bluff Creek • Bluff Creek, California (Humboldt County)
Six Rivers National Forest: 707-442-1721

This remote area (about 38 air miles south of the California/Oregon border and 18 air miles inland from the Pacific Ocean) is in the Six Rivers National Forest. Bigfoot footprints had been found there in prior years, which is why Roger Patterson and Robert Gimlin went out there on horseback on October 20, 1967. They were searching for the creature and, as the world would soon learn, they claimed to have found it. At first sight of the beast, Patterson's horse reared and knocked him to the ground, but he was able to get his movie camera out and shoot what has become the most famous Bigfoot footage ever recorded. Though it's never been proven to be authentic, Bigfoot aficionado Al Hodgson spoke to Patterson the night the footage was shot, and Al has said that what he heard in his friend's voice felt like nothing but the truth. Whatever you believe, there is no denying how compelling the image is of the "Bigfoot" calmly walking off into the woods and looking over his shoulder as the camera rolls.

Branch Davidians
Waco, Texas

DIRECTIONS: From the Waco Tourist Information Center (I-35 at University Parks Drive) take IH-35 North just across the river to the Lake Brazos exit. Go right on

Lake Brazos. Just across from the Holiday Inn is Orchard Lane. Turn left on Orchard Lane and go to Loop 340 where you will turn right. A short distance on the left is FM 2491. Turn left onto that road. You will come to a split in the road, but stay on 2491 which bears to the left. About 5 miles from Loop 340, you will see large wavy metal gates (Double E Ranch Road) on the left (not far from the split). Just beyond that property is a gravel road on the left (Double EE Ranch Road). Turn down that gravel road. The Mount Carmel property is a short distance on the right.

On February 28, 1993, a team of agents from the U.S. Bureau of Alcohol, Tobacco, and Firearms (ATF) launched an assault on the premises of a religious community called Mount Carmel, outside Waco, Texas. The community was occupied by a sect called the Branch Davidians, who were led by a man named Vernon Howell, who had assumed the name David Koresh. The raid resulted in a shootout in which four ATF agents and six Davidians were killed. This was followed by a takeover of the operation by the Federal Bureau of Investigation (FBI) Hostage Rescue Team and a 51-day standoff, which ended in an assault on the premises on April 19, 1993, and a fire in which 76 of the occupants died, including many women and children. The circumstances of the assault brought intense criticism of the way government agents handled the situation.

Buffalo Wings
Anchor Bar • 1047 Main Street • Buffalo, New York • 716-886-8920

In 1964, Dominic Bellissimo was tending bar at the now famous Anchor Bar Restaurant in Buffalo, New York. Late that evening a group of Dominic's friends arrived at the bar touting a ravenous appetite. Dominic asked his mother, Teressa, to prepare something for his friends to eat. At about midnight, Teressa brought out two plates she had prepared in the kitchen and placed them on the bar. The aroma from the plates captured the attention of Dom and his friends and everyone asked, "What are these?" They looked like chicken wings, a part of the chicken that usually went into the stock pot for soup. Teressa had deep fried the wings and flavored them with a secret sauce. The wings were an instant hit and it didn't take long for people to flock to the bar to experience this new eating sensation. From that point on, Buffalo Wings became a regular part of the menu at the Anchor Bar. Today, the original restaurant is internationally famous and a tourist destination in Buffalo that serves up over a thousand pounds of wings each day to the likes of famous movie stars, professional athletes, political leaders, and thousands of customers who seek the unique and great taste of their Original Buffalo Wings.

Cell Phone Call (First Wireless)

57th Street and Fifth Avenue (approximate location)
New York City, New York

The first public telephone call was placed on April 4, 1973 on a portable cellular phone by a gentleman named Martin Cooper, then the General Manager of Motorola's Communications Systems Division. It was the incarnation of his vision for personal wireless communication—distinct from cellular car phones—which initially pushed this technology. That first call, placed to Cooper's rival at AT&T Corp.'s Bell Labs, caused a fundamental technology and communications market shift toward the person and away from the place.

Classic Hollywood

Chez Jay

1657 Ocean Avenue • Santa Monica, California • 310-395-1741

The dark and cozy Chez Jay restaurant is a true Hollywood haunt—a place where the likes of Marlon Brando, Johnny Carson, Julia Roberts, Kevin Spacey, Cher, and Madonna have sought refuge. It's where Lee Marvin once rode a motorcycle through the front door and ordered a drink, where Quentin Tarantino has rehearsed actors in the back room, where Ben Affleck and Matt Damon have worked on scripts in the front, where Michelle Pfeiffer and David E. Kelly had their first date, where Angie Dickinson once waited tables, and where Frank Sinatra, Dean

Martin, and Sammy Davis, Jr. were regulars back in the sixties. (In fact, Sinatra inspired the name of the place in the 1957 film *Pal Joey*. Sinatra's character Joey Evans runs a joint called "Chez Joey." Owner Jay Fiondella was a huge Sinatra fan and in a nod to the name in the movie called his joint "Chez Jay" and it stuck.)

It was also where the Pentagon Papers were leaked to the press in the always-dim environs of the bar. And then there's table 10, the infamous tryst table where Warren Beatty got his under-the-table idea for the movie *Shampoo* and where Linda Ronstadt would steal away with then-Governor Jerry Brown, (among many other private arrangements that took place here). Chez Jay is also home to a cocktail peanut that astronaut Alan Shepherd took to the moon (a nut that Steve McQueen nearly ate in the 1970s).

Ciro's
8433 Sunset Boulevard • Hollywood, California

Ciro's was opened in 1939, and for nearly 20 years it was a true Hollywood hotspot. Actress Lana Turner said it was her favorite place, and other regulars included Gary Cooper, Lucille Ball, Desi Arnaz, Betty Grable, and Dean Martin. Ciro's may have been the most famous nightclub in the nation back then, where stars were not only in the audience but on the stage as well. Actor/bandleader Desi Arnaz and his band played there on occasion. Frank Sinatra famously punched out a photographer here, and buxom screen legend Mae West even took the stage at one time to judge a bodybuilder's contest. Today, the building still stands as the famous Comedy Store.

Montmarte Café
6753 Hollywood Boulevard • Hollywood, California

Long considered to be Hollywood's first nightclub, this is actually where actress Joan Crawford was discovered. Located on the second floor of

a financial institution, the Montmarte virtually sparked the nightlife of the Hollywood community in the early 1920s and was regularly frequented by fans and stars alike. The building stands virtually unchanged today, though the Montmarte is long gone.

The Trocadero
8610 Sunset Boulevard • Hollywood, California

During Hollywood's Golden Age, the world-famous Trocadero became synonymous with starlets, movie producers, and big-time nightlife. It was a posh, black-tie, French-inspired supper club as well as the setting for many famous movie premiere parties, notably *Gone with the Wind*. Among the celebrities who were regulars here were Bing Crosby, Myrna Loy, Cary Grant, Fred Astaire and Norma Shearer. The Trocadero was even featured in the film *A Star is Born*. The building was razed in the 1980s and no trace of it remains today.

Clinton, Bill/Paula Jones
The Excelsior Hotel • 3 Statehouse Plaza • Little Rock, Arkansas
501-375-5000

On May 3, 1991, The Excelsior Hotel was the site of a meeting of state employees. The ballroom was swimming in liquor and loud talk. Paula Corbin was a small, dark-haired, state clerical worker. Around 2:30 P.M., Bill Clinton, then age 46 and the governor of Arkansas for the past 12 years, strode into the hotel foyer, surrounded by his entourage of "yes men" and a squad of state trooper bodyguards. He took notice of Miss Corbin and her workmate, Pamela Blackard. Clinton allegedly turned to trooper Danny Lee Ferguson and told him to obtain a key to one of the hotel suites, saying he needed about an hour for some urgent phone calls (he had a phone in his Limousine). After Clinton went up to the room, Ferguson went over to Paula and told her that the Governor wanted to see her in his room. Paula hesitated; Ferguson reassured her, "It's OK, we do this all the time for the Governor." Jones later accused Clinton (after he became President) of sexual harassment and the mega-scandal further crystallized Clinton's reputation as a skirt-chasing good old boy. (Clinton and his lawyers finally reached a financial settlement with Jones though he would admit no wrongdoing.)

Cooper, D.B.
Portland International Airport • Northwest Airlines • Gate 52
7000 NE Airport Way • Portland, Oregon

On November 24, 1971, Dan Cooper boarded a Northwest Airlines flight from Portland to Seattle, demanded and received a $200,000 ransom, and on the return flight parachuted into the forest. He has never been seen again. The disappearance of Dan "D.B." Cooper is one of the great unsolved mysteries of the 20th century. It happened on Thanksgiving Eve at the Portland International Airport (PIA) when a smartly dressed, middle aged man calling himself Dan Cooper purchased a one-way ticket on flight 305 to the Seattle-Tacoma (Sea-Tac) airport with a $20 bill. Just past four in the afternoon, Cooper passed most of the other 36 passengers and sat in the back of Capt. William Scott's Boeing 727. He had row 18 to himself as the plane was only a quarter full. Once aloft he threatened to blow up the plane and demanded $200,000 and four parachutes. After the plane landed at Seattle-Tacoma Airport and his demands were met, Cooper ordered the 727 to take off and head for Mexico. He jumped from the rear of the plane somewhere over Washington state, taking the cash with him. Despite exhaustive searches, Cooper's body was never found and his whereabouts are unknown. The actual Boeing 727-051 used by Northwest that day was flown for one last time to the "scrap yard" in 1993 where it was destroyed.

Disney, Walt
12174 Euclid Street (south of Chapman Avenue, in the Stanley Ranch Museum) • Anaheim, California • 714-530-8871

From 1923 to 1926, Walt Disney worked within this barn-like structure, creating some of his first animated works. In 1982, the garage was removed from its original location in Los Angeles' Silverlake district and put into storage, eventually making it here to this museum featuring antique buildings.

Dean, James

Here are a few sites related to Dean's last day, along with some other memorable James Dean landmarks.

Birthplace

Corner of 4th Street and McClure Street • Marion, Indiana

At this corner stood the house where James Byron Dean was born at 2:00 A.M. on February 8, 1931. A stone with a plaque and a star in the sidewalk now commemorate the spot where the house, known as "The Seven Gables," once stood. Each September 30, to commemorate the day Dean was killed, the town honors its favorite son with a festival. Note: The nearby Fairmount Historical Museum (203 East Washington Street) holds the James Dean Memorial Gallery where you can see the actual speeding ticket issued to Dean just before his fatal crash, as well as the Lee Rider jeans he wore in *Giant*.

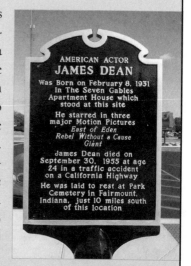

Fairmount Historical Museum

203 East Washington Street • Fairmount, Indiana • 765-948-4555

This local museum also provides the visitor with a chance to experience the life of James Dean traced through hundreds of rare photographs, his motorcycles, bongo drums, movie costumes, and many rare keepsakes donated by family and friends.

Friends Church

124 West First Street • Fairmount, Indiana

On October 8, 1955, James Dean's funeral was held at this church. Hundreds of fans sobbed as they waited outside, and Liz Taylor sent flowers.

Gas Station
14325 Ventura Boulevard • Sherman Oaks, California

Early in the afternoon of September 30, 1955, James Dean stopped here to fill his Porsche with gas one last time before he and his crew hit the freeway and headed north. Photographer Sanford Roth, who was documenting the trip with Dean (and would go on to take the famous accident pictures), shot a memorable photo of the actor right here at the pump, posed near his car after he'd filled it with gas. Today, a Whole Foods Market occupies the site.

Highway 99 North
(Approximately one mile before the Maricopa/Taft exit at pole marker 166) • Near Bakersfield, California

Shortly before his fatal car crash on September 30, 1955, at about 3:30 P.M., James Dean was stopped here for speeding. He was issued a ticket by patrolman Otie V. Hunter, on which he signed his last "autograph." Dean was clocked at what would typically be considered a snail's pace for him—70 mph. This had to be particularly embarrassing for the actor, as he had just finished a commercial for highway safety. Regardless of the ticket, Dean was speeding recklessly along Highway 446 (now renamed Hwy 46), hurtling toward a death that would occur less than three hours later. The telephone pole at the exact site where Dean was stopped is marked with the metal letters D-E-A-N.

The James Dean Gallery
425 North Main Street • Fairmount, Indiana • 765-998-2080

The James Dean Gallery features the world's largest private collection of memorabilia and archives dealing with the short life and career of the bigger-than-life actor. It traces his entire life, from his local accomplishments in sports and drama to his days growing up at Fairmount High School to his acting years in New York and Hollywood. Some of the items on display include clothing worn by Dean in his films, original movie posters, books, magazines, and novelty items from over 20 different countries from around the world. There is also a screening room that shows a 30-minute video of rare television appearances and screen tests.

Kuehl Funeral Home
1703 Spring Street
Paso Robles, California
805-238-4383

After being pronounced dead at the nearby War Memorial Hospital in Paso Robles, Dean's body was taken here. Several days later, his body was driven to Los Angeles in preparation for the trip home to Fairmont, Illinois. The hospital, which no longer exists, had been located at 1732 Spring Street in Paso Robles.

Tip's Restaurant
Castaic Junction • Intersection of I-5 and SR-126
West Newhall, California

Once a thriving intersection, this is where Tip's Restaurant was located in the 1950s, and it was here, on September 30, 1955, that James Dean stopped for a meal (pie and milk) as he continued on his journey the day of his tragic crash. The original Tip's later became J's Coffee Shop—where four CHP officers were gunned down in 1970—and, still later, a Marie Callender Family Restaurant. Today the building is gone.

Villa Capri
6735 Yucca Street
Hollywood, California

This former Rat Pack haunt was also a favorite of James Dean, and it was here that he ate his last supper on the evening of September 29, the night before he was killed. Dean would always come and go through the back door, which is still visible on the left. These days the building houses a radio station, with an original menu from the building's restaurant days hanging on the wall.

The Winslow Farm
County Road 150 East • Fairmount, Indiana

This was the boyhood home of James Dean. While it is not open to the public, photos can be taken from road and driveway.

Double Rainbow
Yosemebear Mountain Farm • Mariposa, California

"Double Rainbow" was a viral video filmed by Paul "Bear" Vasquez. The clip, filmed in his front yard just outside Yosemite National Park, showed his ecstatic reaction to a double rainbow which he described as the "Eye of God." The video proved inspirational around the world, gaining nearly 50 million views on YouTube and making Vasquez a celebrity, with appearances on *Good Morning America* and other national programs.

The amateur video showed the view from Vasquez's property into the skies above the Yosemite Valley. Vasquez's reaction captured his intense emotional excitement; he wept with joy and moaned ecstatically, uttering phrases such as "Double rainbow all the way across the sky," "What does this mean?" and "Too much!" Vasquez posted the video to YouTube on January 8, 2010. On July 3, comedian and late-night talk show host Jimmy Kimmel linked to the video in a post on Twitter, saying that he and a friend had declared it the "funniest video in the world." The video quickly gained over one million views. On July 26, 2010, Bear was interviewed by Kimmel on *Jimmy Kimmel Live!* On the December 16 episode, he was awarded Video of the Year and appeared in a video short created by the show for the event.

On July 5, 2010, the Gregory Brothers auto-tuned the video under the name "Double Rainbow Song." Their video gained over 39 million views and became a viral video in itself, almost surpassing the original in number of views. The song was covered by Amanda Palmer, Jimmy Fallon (as Neil Young), and The Axis of Awesome during a live recording of a charity show in the UK. In 2011, Vasquez appeared in a commercial for Vodafone New Zealand parodying the video. Vasquez died in 2020. His daughter inherited his property, which suffered major damage in a 2022 fire.

Einstein, Albert
Princeton Inn
(now Forbes College)
99 Alexander Street
Princeton, New Jersey

The famous picture of physicist Albert Einstein sticking out his tongue was shot in front of the beautiful Princeton Inn, at one time an expansive, rambling hotel. The legendary thinker was leaving the Inn after celebrating his 72nd birthday on March 14, 1951 (part of the day's celebration also included the first Einstein Awards presentations), and he was asked by photographers to smile for them. Perhaps weary, bemused, or both, he got a bit frisky and thus created one of the most unexpected, most famous images ever captured. The building that once housed the Princeton Inn still stands and is now part of Forbes College. NOTE: Einstein lived nearby at 112 Mercer Street.

E-Mail (First)

BBN Technologies • 10 Moulton Street • Cambridge, Massachusetts
617-873-8000

It is generally believed that the first network "e-mail" was sent by a man named Ray Tomlinson, a principal scientist at BBN, in 1971. At the time, Mr. Tomlinson was working for Boston-based Bolt, Beranek and Newman, which was helping to develop Arpanet, the forerunner of the modern internet.

Tomlinson sent the first message between two machines that were side-by-side in his lab here in Cambridge, then kept sending messages back and forth from one machine to the other until he was comfortable with how the process worked. The first e-mail message he sent outside of the lab was to the rest of his work team. A message announced the existence of network e-mail and explained how to use it, including the use of the @ sign to separate the user's name from the host computer name.

Father's Day

Central United Methodist Church • 301 Fairmont Avenue
Fairmont, West Virginia • 304-366-3351

On December 6, 1907, a West Virginia mine explosion killed more than 360 men, 210 of whom were fathers. A local woman named Mrs. Charles (Grace) Clayton approached her pastor, the Reverend Webb, about a special day to honor fathers. Rev. Webb agreed it would be a good idea. To that end, he held a special mass to honor all fathers here at this church on July 5, 1908, and it is generally considered to be the first formal celebration of Father's Day. Over the years, the holiday continued to gain popularity and was finally officially established by President Nixon in 1972.

The First Glass Door Oven

2701 Spring Grove Avenue
Cincinnati, Ohio

There's a first for everything, even the first full-size glass door oven, which was invented and manufactured by Ernst H. Huenefeld of The Huenefeld Company here at this exact site back in 1909. It featured

specially designed and patented sheet metal frames in the door which allowed for expansion and contraction of the glass. The large window (which was guaranteed against steaming up or breaking from heat), allowed users to view their baking without opening the oven door. Imagine how novel that must have seemed at the time! A standard feature in homes today, the glass door oven was a technological breakthrough in 1909. The red brick building is still there today, along with a plaque.

First Pizzeria in North America
Lombardi's • 53⅓ Spring Street • New York City, New York

The first known pizza shop was the Port 'Alba in Naples, Italy, which opened in 1830 (and is still open today!). But, the first pizzeria in North America was opened in 1905 by Gennaro Lombardi at 53⅓ Spring Street in New York City. Lombardi's is still going strong today, but at a new address: 32 Spring Street in New York's Little Italy. Some more pizza geography: A Neapolitan man named Totonno Pero came to New York from Naples and as a teenager worked for Lombardi. In 1924 he opened Totonno's, a coal-oven pizzeria in Brooklyn, originally located on West 15th Street in Coney Island (now they're on West 16th Street). Today, Totonno's holds the record for the oldest continuous pizzeria in business in the U.S. run by the same family.

First Traffic Light
105th Street and Euclid Avenue • Cleveland, Ohio

Did you know that Cleveland boasted America's first traffic light? It happened on August 5, 1914, when the American Traffic Signal Company installed red and green traffic lights at each corner of the intersection of 105th Street and Euclid Avenue. They were very primitive—in fact, they were "railroad switch stand" types of signals that had to be rotated manually by a policeman 90 degrees to show the indication "STOP" or "GO." The first "actuated" signals to be used (not requiring manpower) were installed on February 22, 1928 at the corner of Falls Road and Belvedere Avenue in Baltimore, Maryland.

Food

Chasen's

9039 Beverly Boulevard (corner of Beverly and Doheny)
Beverly Hills, California

One of the most legendary restaurants (and celebrity hangouts) in Hollywood history, Chasen's closed its doors on April 1, 1995. It had stood for 59 years, and throughout its history, played host to many stars. Frank Sinatra, Greta Garbo, Jack Benny, and Eleanor Roosevelt were all huge fans of Chasen's chili, which was first served here in 1936 when the restaurant was known as vaudevillian Dave Chasen's "Chasen's Southern Pit." (The name became "Chasen's" in 1940.)

Elizabeth Taylor made it even more famous while filming *Cleopatra* in 1962, when she had the chili flown to Rome packed in dry ice. Though the restaurant is closed, the original building still stands, albeit in the form of an upscale market. And today, you can still order up Chasen's famous chili in the market's café, and enjoy it in one of the original Chasen's booths located there. Note: The booth where Ronald Reagan proposed to Nancy is gone, but it was located where the cheese section stands today.

"Cheezeborger, Cheezeborger!"

Billy Goat Tavern • 430 North Michigan Avenue at Lower Level
Chicago, Illinois • 312-222-1525

Famously portrayed on *Saturday Night Live* in the mid-'70s as a burger diner where John Belushi barked in the orders in broken-Greek ("Cheezeborger, no fries—chips!"), this place has long been a local legend, since original owner William Sianis was forbidden by the Chicago Cubs to bring his goat into Wrigley Field during a 1945 World Series game. Sianis' curse that the Cubs would never again win a championship has seemingly held true. A popular newspaper writer hangout, the walls here are plastered with blown-up bylines and numerous articles, and old-time SNL fans still arrive to hear the famous food orders.

Cobb Salad

The Brown Derby
1620–28 North Vine Street
Hollywood, California

One night in 1937, Bob Cobb, then-owner of The Brown Derby, prowled hungrily in his restaurant's kitchen for a snack. Opening the huge refrigerator, he pulled out a head of lettuce, an avocado, some romaine, watercress, tomatoes, some cold chicken breast, a hard-boiled egg, chives, cheese, some old-fashioned French dressing—in short, a little of everything. He started chopping, added some bacon, and bingo—the Cobb salad was born.

It was so good, Sid Grauman (of Grauman's Chinese Theatre), who was with Cobb that midnight, asked the next day for a "Cobb Salad." It was then put on the menu and Cobb's midnight invention became an overnight sensation with Derby customers like movie mogul Jack Warner, who regularly dispatched his chauffeur to pick up a carton of the mouth-watering salad.

The Vine Street landmark restaurant was demolished in 1994, but the famous huge Derby Hat that housed the Wilshire Boulevard location lives on atop a downtown strip mall, across the street from the former Ambassador Hotel site. It's now the Boiling Crab restaurant at 3377 Wilshire Boulevard in Los Angeles.

Egg McMuffin

3940 State Street • Santa Barbara, California • 805-687-6164

Perhaps the biggest innovation in McDonald's history was a product that ushered in the era of fast-food breakfasts. It happened like this: In 1971, a McDonald's restaurant owner/operator named Herb Peterson heard that some other McDonald's proprietors had started serving pancakes and doughnuts during breakfast. Peterson liked the idea of serving breakfast, but thought it needed to be something unique—and something that could be eaten by hand, like all other McDonald's products.

Experimenting with a newfangled version of an "Eggs Benedict Sandwich," Peterson discovered that when he added a piece of cheese the sandwich took on the exact consistency he was looking for. It was food history in the making. Peterson invited the legendary Ray Kroc to try the product and Kroc gave it the thumbs up. So why did the Egg McMuffin take nearly four years to roll out? Because McDonald's wanted to first perfect pancakes and sausage and add scrambled eggs as a third option so as to have an entire breakfast menu as opposed to just one item. A plaque here at this McDonald's identifies it as the home of the Egg McMuffin.

Hamburger

Louis' Lunch • 261–263 Crown Street • New Haven, Connecticut
203-562-5507

One day in the year 1900, a man dashed into a small New Haven luncheonette and asked for a quick meal that he could eat on the run. Louis Lassen, the establishment's owner, hurriedly sandwiched a broiled beef patty between two slices of bread and sent the customer on his way, so the story goes, with America's first hamburger. The tiny eatery that made such a big impact on the eating habits of an entire nation was, of course, Louis' Lunch. Today, Louis' grandson, Ken, carries on the family tradition: hamburgers that have changed little from their historic prototype are still the specialty of the house. Each one is made from beef ground fresh each day, broiled vertically in the original cast iron grill and served between two slices of toast. Cheese, tomato, and onion are the only acceptable garnish—no true connoisseur would consider corrupting the classic taste with mustard or ketchup.

Hot Fudge Sundae

C.C. Brown's Ice Cream Shop • 7007 Hollywood Boulevard
Hollywood, California

Legend has it that it was here that the hot fudge sundae was invented in 1906 by Clarence Clifton (C.C.) Brown. For many years, the most celebrated names in the entertainment business frequented this sweet shop;

in fact, many years ago, on days of big movie premiers, fans used to line up outside Brown's for hours while mega-stars like Joan Crawford signed autographs. The location closed in 1996.

Ice Cream Cone
Forest Park • St. Louis, Missouri

Forest Park, officially opened to the public on June 24, 1876, is one of the largest urban parks in the United States. At 1,370 acres, it is approximately 500 acres larger than Central Park in New York. In 1904, it was the site of The St. Louis World's Fair and drew more than 20 million visitors from around the world.

It was here during the fair that Charles Menches, an unlucky ice cream vendor, ran out of dishes in which to put his ice cream. In the stall next to Menches was Ernest Hamwi, who was selling Syrian pastry. Hamwi offered to help and rolled up some of the pastry so that the vendor could put his ice cream inside, thus creating the ice cream cone.

Kentucky Fried Chicken
Harland Sanders Cafe & Museum • 1441 Gardiner Lane
Louisville, Kentucky • 606-528-2163 • www.kfc.com

This was where the Colonel developed his secret recipe for Kentucky Fried Chicken in the 1940s. You can dine in the restored restaurant, tour the Colonel's kitchen, and see artifacts and memorabilia. The museum features the colonel's office and kitchen where he experimented with pressure frying and created the recipe for his fried chicken with 11 herbs and spices.

Potato Chips
Moon's Lakehouse • 700 Crescent Avenue • Saratoga Lake
Saratoga, New York

In the summer of 1853, George Crum was employed as a chef at Moon's

Lake Lodge, an elegant resort in Saratoga Springs along Saratoga Lake. On the restaurant menu were French-fried potatoes, prepared by Crum in the standard, thick-cut French style that was made popular in France in the 1700s. One guest found chef Crum's French fries too thick and asked if Crum could cut and fry a thinner batch. However, the customer rejected these, too.

Frustrated, Crum decided to deliberately annoy the guest by producing French fries that were extra, extra thin and crisp, and salted to excess. But the plan backfired. The guest loved the crispy, paper-thin potatoes, and other guests began to request Crum's potato chips, which subsequently appeared on the menu as "Saratoga Chips." The potato chip had been born. Moon's Lakehouse located at this upstate New York lake is long gone, and the approximate site where it once sat is now occupied with a lakeside house, owned by a technology company.

Toll House Cookies

The Toll House Inn • Corner of Route 18 and Route 14
Whitman, Massachusetts

The original Toll House for whom the famous cookies are named was built in 1709 on the old Boston to New Bedford road, now called Route 18. Back then, travelers paid tolls at the house for the use of the road, but could also rest there and enjoy a meal while their horses were changed.

In 1930, a couple named Kenneth and Ruth Graves Wakefield purchased the property and opened the Toll House Inn. Ruth, a 1924 graduate of the Framingham State Normal School Department of Household Arts, was in charge of the Inn's kitchen. One day, Ruth wanted to make chocolate cookies but was out of baker's chocolate. Instead, she substituted broken pieces of semi-sweet chocolate made by Andrew Nestlé. Instead of melting into the dough like she thought they would, the morsels remained clumps of melted chocolate, and thus the toll house cookie (also known as the chocolate chip cookie) was born.

Ruth licensed the recipe to chocolate maker Nestlé, who, in 1939, began marketing Toll House Morsels designed for her cookie recipe. The Wakefield's place of business grew into a major restaurant, but Kenneth and Ruth sold the Inn in 1966. It became a nightclub, then a restaurant again, but the building burned down on New Year's Eve in 1984. (Ruth Graves Wakefield passed away in 1977.) Today, a Wendy's sits on the original site, but a classic sign from the old Inn still stands nearby.

Gable, Clark/Carole Lombard

The Oatman Hotel • 181 Main Street • Oatman, Arizona • 928-768-4408

The Oatman Hotel, built in 1902, is the oldest two-story adobe structure in Mojave County and has housed many miners, movie stars, politicians, and assorted scoundrels. The town was used as the location for several movies such as *How The West Was Won*, *Foxfire*, and *Edge of Eternity*. But it was Clark Gable and Carol Lombard's honeymoon on March 18, 1939 that made the place really famous. They had been married earlier that day in Kingman, Arizona and stopped here along old Route 66 on their way back to Hollywood. Gable returned here often to play poker with the local miners and enjoy the solitude of the desert. The hotel has 10 rooms available for a $35 donation for a night's stay—except for the honeymoon suite where the famous couple spent their wedding night. That one costs $55.

Girl Scouts

Andrew Low House
329 Abercorn Street • Savannah, Georgia • 912-233-6854

After her marriage, Juliette Low lived in this 1848 house, and it was here where she actually founded the Girl Scouts. After her husband had died (they were already separated), Low met Sir Robert Baden-Powell in 1911. He was a great war hero and the founder of the Boy Scouts. The two quickly became friends and her admiration for the scouting movement led her to begin working with the Girl Guides, the Boy Scouts' sister organization in Great Britain. With Baden-Powell's help and advice, she then made plans to start a similar association for American girls. In 1912, she returned home to Georgia and formed several troops in Savannah in March of that year.

Juliette Low died on the premises in 1927. This home/museum is operated by the Colonial Dames as the Andrew Low House. The Carriage House that became the first headquarters of Girl Scouting is directly behind the Andrew Low House and works as the council shop for the Girl Scouts Council of Savannah. Tours are offered.

Girl Scout Cookies
1401 Arch Street • Philadelphia, Pennsylvania

A marker here reads: "On November 11, 1932, Girl Scouts baked & sold cookies for the first time in the windows of the Philadelphia Gas & Electric Co. here. This endeavor soon became a Philadelphia tradition. In 1936 the Girl Scouts of the U.S.A. adopted the annual cookie sale as a national program."

The background is as follows: On November 11, 1932, Philadelphia Girl Scouts demonstrated their baking skills in the windows here at the Philadelphia Gas Works headquarters. They were baking cookies for day nurseries as a community service project. As the freshly baked cookies

piled up, people walking by asked if they could buy them. The girls agreed to sell the extras and used the money to support troop activities and camping equipment. The next year, a similar sale was held, attracting the public's interest and the attention of the press.

In 1934, then-Philadelphia based Keebler Baking Company was approached about baking and packaging a vanilla cookie in the shape of the Girl Scout emblem, called the "Trefoil." An agreement was made and the first commercial sale in Philadelphia took place from December 8–15, 1934. Cookies sold for 23 cents per box or six boxes for $1.35. The proceeds benefited Girl Scouts of Greater Philadelphia and individual troop projects.

News soon spread of the Philadelphia Girl Scouts enterprise and the national Girl Scouts office, Girl Scouts of the U.S.A., took notice. In 1936, the cookie idea went national when GSUSA contracted with Keebler as the national supplier for their Trefoil cookie. The first national sale was held October 24–November 7, 1936.

Low, Juliette Gordon

10 East Oglethorpe Avenue • Savannah, Georgia • 912-233-4501

This is the birthplace of Juliette Gordon Low, founder of Girl Scouts of the U.S.A., who was affectionately known by her family and friends as "Daisy." The Girl Scouts organization was born a few blocks away at the Andrew Low House, but this historic home was where the Girl Scouts founder entered the world.

Dating back to 1821, the house is an interesting blend of Regency architecture and Victorian-style additions. The tour includes a memorial to Juliette Gordon Low, a Girl Scouts museum, and a chance for scouts to pop in at the home office, as the national headquarters are housed here.

The birthplace of Juliette Low was purchased by National Girl Scouts in 1953 and was restored to a late-1880's décor. It opened to the public in October 1956, and it was the first Registered National Historic Landmark in Savannah. Girl Scouts and Girl Guides from all over the world come to visit.

Juliette Low was laid to rest in the family plot at Laurel Grove North Cemetery. She was buried in her full Girl Scout uniform, her Silver Fish award (a high honor from the Girl Guides), her special jeweled Thanks Badge and a telegram in her pocket from Sir Baden-Powell: *You are not only the first Girl Scout, you are the best Girl Scout of them all.*

Golf

Birthplace of the PGA
Radisson Martinique on Broadway • 49 W. 32nd Street
New York City, New York

The Radisson Martinique on Broadway opened in 1897 with over 500 guest rooms. At the time, it was known simply as the Hotel Martinique on Broadway. And it was here where the Professional Golfers Association of America (PGA) was formed back in 1916.

The Taplow Club at the Hotel Martinique was the site of a luncheon that year that led to the development of the PGA. The luncheon was hosted by Rodman Wanamaker, a department store owner with a vision of the potential marketing opportunities for a professional golf association. He invited 35 golfers, officials, and other dignitaries, including golf legend Walter Hagen, to New York. The Martinique hosted the group for

lunch on January 17 to discuss the possibility of a golf association. At another meeting at the Martinique on April 10, the PGA was formed. The board of directors for the PGA still occasionally hold meetings there. In 2011, the PGA Gallery at the Martinique opened on the second floor of the hotel. It includes many artifacts and photos including an official plaque that reads: "The Professional Golfers Association of America, founded April 10, 1916 at The Hotel Martinique on Broadway."

Jones, Bobby

Forest Hills Golf Club • 1500 Comfort Road • Augusta, Georgia
706-733-0001

On April 7, 1999, the Georgia Historical Society dedicated a historical marker here in Augusta, Georgia commemorating Bobby Jones and the beginning of the Grand Slam. (The event was held at Augusta State University.) The marker, located at the entrance of the club, reads: "Bobby Jones and the Beginning of the Grand Slam. On the golf links of the Forrest Hills-Ricker Hotel, Bobby Jones won the Southeastern Open of 1930. He went on to victory that year in the British Amateur, British Open, U.S. Open, and U.S. Amateur—golf's Grand Slam and a feat yet unmatched. A lifelong amateur, Jones won four U.S. Opens, five U.S. Amateurs, three British Opens, and one British Amateur, but called his 13-shot victory in the 1930 Southeastern Open, "The best-played tournament I ever turned out in my life." Thirteen of the original Donald Ross-designed holes and the 1926 Golf House survive from Jones era.

Palmer, Arnold

Rancho Park • 10460 West Pico Boulevard • Los Angeles, California
310-838-7373

During the first round of the 1961 Los Angeles Open at Rancho Park, legendary golfer Arnold Palmer went out of bounds five times on the par-five ninth (now the 18th) hole to shoot a 12. A plaque right at the hole commemorates the event.

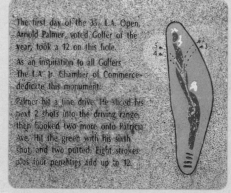

The first day of the 35. L.A. Open, Arnold Palmer, voted Golfer of the year, took a 12 on this hole. As an inspiration to all Golfers The L.A. Jr. Chamber of Commerce dedicate this monument. Palmer hit a line drive. He sliced his next 2 shots into the driving range, then hooked two more onto Patricia Ave. Hit the green with his sixth shot, and two putted. Eight strokes plus four penalties add up to 12.

Sarazen, Gene
940 Wynnewood Road
Pelham Manor, New York
914-738-5074

A plaque here, located to the left of the driveway near the putting green by the 1st hole of the course reads: "Sarazen's Victory in the 1923 PGA Championship at Pelham Country Club. On September 29, 1923 at Pelham Country Club, Gene Sarazen defeated Walter Hagen in the final of the P.G.A. Championship. The 38-hole match is considered the most dramatic match play final in the history of the P.G.A. Championship."

Groundhog Day
Gobblers Knob (one-and-a-half miles from downtown Punxsutawney on Woodland Avenue Extension) • Chamber of Commerce
124 West Mahoning Street • Punxsutawney, Pennsylvania
info@punxsutawney.com • 800-752-PHIL

Groundhog Day, February 2, is a popular tradition in the United States. It is the day that the Groundhog comes out of his hole after a long winter sleep to look for his shadow. If he sees it, he regards it as an omen of six more weeks of bad weather and returns to his hole. This is the charming little town where it all happens, including the momentous ceremony held each year at "Gobblers Knob." (It also inspired the 1993 comedy smash *Groundhog Day* starring Bill Murray and Andie McDowell.) *The Punxsutawney Spirit* newspaper is credited with printing the news of the first observance in 1886 (one year before the first legendary trek to Gobbler's Knob): "Today is groundhog day, and up to the time of going to press the beast has not seen his shadow."

Heaven's Gate
18241 Colina Norte • Rancho Santa Fe, California

On March 26, 1997, 39 rotting corpses were found in a home in this wealthy suburb of San Diego. Wearing purple shrouds, black outfits, and Nike sneakers, the dead were members of the Heaven's Gate cult. Following the preachings of their bizarre leader, Marshall Applewhite, they had believed that a UFO was waiting in the tail of the comet Halle-Bopp to take them to a better place, and so they committed suicide. Before killing themselves, the cult members had their last meal at the Marie Callender's located at 5980 Avenida Encinas in Carlsbad. All 39 members ordered the same thing—turkey pot pie. In June 1999, the house was sold, demolished, and today a new one sits in its place.

Hewlett Packard
367 Addison Avenue
Palo Alto, California

The HP Garage is known as the birthplace of Silicon Valley. It all began here in Palo Alto, California, where Stanford University classmates Bill Hewlett and Dave Packard founded HP in 1939. The company's first product, built in this Palo Alto garage, was an audio oscillator—an electronic test instrument used by sound engineers. The home is now a private residence, and is not open to the public.

Houdini, Harry
Knickerbocker Hotel • 1714 Ivar Avenue (at Hollywood Boulevard)
Hollywood, California

In addition to being a master escape artist, Harry Houdini was known for his crusade to debunk spiritualists, psychics, and others who claimed they could

contact the dead. He even wrote a book on the subject exposing many of their techniques, *A Magician Among the Spirits.* However, as has become legend, just before he died on October 31, 1926, he promised his wife Beatrice that if there were any possible way for him to reach her from the afterlife, he would give her a sign on the anniversary of his death. So, on Halloween night, 1927, Beatrice held a séance at the Knickerbocker Hotel. But the séance did not produce any tangible results (and neither did the yearly Halloween séances she would go on to hold over the following decade). In addition to the Houdini séance, The Knickerbocker is also the place where Marilyn Monroe honeymooned with Joe DiMaggio in January of 1954 and where Elvis Presley stayed in 1956 while shooting *Love Me Tender* (Suite 1016) and it was supposedly part of what inspired him to co-write "Heartbreak Hotel." On March 3, 1966, William Frawley (Fred Mertz on "I Love Lucy") died of a heart attack on the sidewalk in front of the hotel (he had lived there for years). The Knickerbocker is now a senior citizen's home.

"Howl"
1010 Montgomery Street (at Broadway) • San Francisco, California

In 1955, poet Allen Ginsburg lived in a furnished room in this building. Many believe that it was here that he wrote his seminal, run-on classic poem, "Howl" (starting with the ominous phrasing, "I saw the best minds of my generation destroyed by madness . . ."). This became the most famous poem of the Beat movement, and thus helped launch Ginsburg as one of the primary counter-culture spokespeople of his generation (his career was fueled by other works such as "Kaddish" and "America"). Ginsberg died in 1997.

Keller, Helen
Ivy Green • 300 West North Commons • Tuscumbia, Alabama
256-383-4066

Located on a 640-acre tract in historic Tuscumbia, Ivy Green was built in

1820 by David and Mary Fairfax Moore Keller, grandparents of Helen Keller. The old "whistle path" leads the visitor to the outdoor kitchen from the main home. Sprinkled around the estate are the Lion's Club's International Memorial Fountain, the "Clearing" and herb gardens, the Carriage House and Gift Shop. Helen Keller's birthplace cottage

is situated east of the main house and consists of a large room with a lovely bay window and playroom. Originally, the small "annex" was an office for keeping the plantation's books. Later, the cottage would serve as living quarters for Helen and her teacher, Anne Sullivan. The home and museum room are decorated with much of the original furniture of the Keller family.

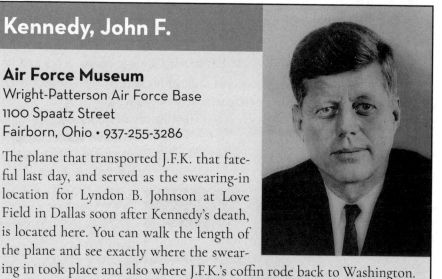

Kennedy, John F.

Air Force Museum
Wright-Patterson Air Force Base
1100 Spaatz Street
Fairborn, Ohio • 937-255-3286

The plane that transported J.F.K. that fateful last day, and served as the swearing-in location for Lyndon B. Johnson at Love Field in Dallas soon after Kennedy's death, is located here. You can walk the length of the plane and see exactly where the swearing in took place and also where J.F.K.'s coffin rode back to Washington.

Interestingly, the Air Force Museum is on the Huffman Prairie where the Wright Brothers did many of their post-Kitty Hawk aviation experiments. As well, some UFO experts say the air force complex is the resting place of the captured Roswell aliens (or at least the controversial debris) recovered in New Mexico in the 1940s.

Birthplace
33 Beals Street
Brookline, Massachusetts • 617-566-7937

This is where John F. Kennedy was born in 1917. Today, this National Historic Site preserves the birthplace and boyhood home of the 35th president of the United States. The modest frame house in suburban Boston was also the first home shared by the president's father and mother, Joseph P. and Rose Fitzgerald Kennedy, and represents the social and political beginnings of one of the world's most prominent families.

Honeymoon
San Ysidro Ranch • 900 San Ysidro Lane • Santa Barbara, California
800-368-6788

This beautiful ranch, built in 1893, is nestled among orange trees and its charming bungalows look out over the rolling Santa Ynez hills. Vivien Leigh and Laurence Olivier were married at San Ysidro, and this is also where John and Jackie Kennedy spent their honeymoon in 1953.

In memory of the romantic and historic honeymoon stay of Jacqueline and J.F.K., the ranch offers the "Kennedy Classic"—a two-night stay in

the Kennedy Cottage, J.F.K.'s favorite dessert delivered to the room, continental breakfast for two, two one-hour Swedish massages in-cottage and a $100 gift certificate for the legendary Stonehouse Restaurant located here.

Hyannis Memorial
Ocean Street • Hyannis, Massachusetts

Overlooking Lewis Bay, a spot J.F.K. used to frequent during his years here, the J.F.K. Memorial attracts some 575,000 visitors from May through October. Money thrown into the memorial's wishing well is used to fund scholarships, sailing lessons for young people, and upkeep of the memorial.

To see the famous Kennedy compound on Irving Avenue in Hyannis, it is best to take one of the several boat tours in the area. Also nearby is the family parish, Saint Francis Xavier Roman Catholic Church, located at 347 South Street. This is where J.F.K. attended Sunday school, and the main alter at the church is dedicated to Lieutenant Joseph P. Kennedy, J.F.K's older brother who was killed during World War II. Lastly, the Hyannis National Guard Armory on South Street is where J.F.K. made his victory speech after the 1960 presidential election.

J.F.K. Residence
3260 N Street • Washington, D.C.

This is one of a series of residences in the Georgetown area of Washington D.C. that J.F.K. occupied briefly in the early 1950s. A magnolia tree that he planted in the backyard remains today.

J.F.K. and Jackie's First Residence
3321 Dent Place • Washington, D.C.

This rented home was the first residence of J.F.K. and his new bride, Jackie; they lived here from 1953–1957. The home is near Georgetown University, where Jackie was taking a course in American government, and Wisconsin Avenue, where Jackie browsed for home furnishings.

Marriage
St. Mary's Church • Corner of Spring Street and Memorial Boulevard
Newport, Rhode Island • 401-847-0475

Established on April 8, 1828, St. Mary's is the oldest Roman Catholic

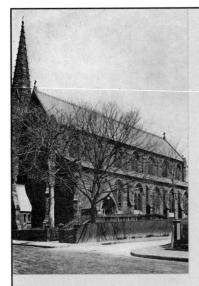

parish in Rhode Island. It was designated a National Historic Shrine on November 24, 1968 and is most famous as the wedding location of Jacqueline Bouvier to John Fitzgerald Kennedy on September 12, 1953. More than 750 guests attended the wedding, which was presided over by Archbishop Richard Cushing. Following the 40-minute ceremony at which a papal blessing was read, the new couple emerged into a throng of 3,000 well-wishers as they made their way by motorcycle escort to Hammersmith Farm, the Auchincloss estate overlooking Narragansett Bay.

Omni Parker House
60 School Street
Boston, Massachusetts

It was in this hotel that J.F.K. announced his 1946 candidacy for a U.S. House seat, thus effectively starting his political career. (One of his bachelor dinners was held here as well.)

Profiles in Courage
Merrywood • Chain Bridge • Road McLean, Virginia

Merrywood, the former home of Jacqueline Kennedy Onassis, is where John Kennedy wrote the book *Profiles in Courage*. He had recently had back surgery after he and Jackie were married, and thus was bed-ridden for eight months. During this period, needing to occupy his time, he wrote the book that became a best-seller and won him a Pulitzer Prize.

Reilly Stadium
1200 East 6th Street • Salem, Ohio

A plaque in one of the urinals here in the men's room commemorates where John F. Kennedy once relieved himself during a 1960 campaign stop.

The Rossmore House
522 North Rossmore Avenue
Los Angeles, California

During the Democratic National Convention in 1960, John F. Kennedy used what is now apartment 301 in this building as his private residence when things got too crazy at the downtown Biltmore Hotel. Back then it was a hotel, The Rossmore House, but today it's an apartment building.

Texas Hotel
815 Main Street • Fort Worth, Texas • 817-870-2100

On Thursday, November 21, 1963, J.F.K. and his wife, Jacqueline, arrived at this hotel (now the Radisson Hotel) where they spent the night on the seventh floor. The next morning, Kennedy gave a brief speech in front of the hotel, then spoke at a breakfast held in his honor inside the hotel, before heading to the airport where Air Force One was waiting to take him to Dallas.

   These were the last public speeches Kennedy gave, as he would be assassinated later that day while en route to a banquet being held at the Dallas Trade Mart. The suite in which he and Jackie Kennedy stayed that November became known as the "Kennedy Suite."

Union Oyster House
41 Union Street • Boston, Massachusetts
617-227-2750

Established in 1826, the historic Union Oyster House is officially America's oldest restaurant.

Located on the Freedom Trail near Faneuil Hall, it was also a favorite spot of J.F.K.'s when he was a bachelor living on nearby Bowdin Street. In fact, he sat, ate, and strategized so much at table number eight that today a plaque there honors the former President.

Winthrop House
Harvard University • Cambridge, Massachusetts

J.F.K. spent his Harvard years in Gore Hall in the Winthrop House. Today, the rooms are called the Kennedy Suite and are used by the John F. Kennedy School of Government to house guest speakers.

Kennedy, Jr., John F.

Cathedral of St. Matthew the Apostle
1725 Rhode Island Avenue NW • Washington, D.C.

It is one of the most memorable images in U.S. history: A three-year old John F. Kennedy, Jr., standing in front of both his mother, Jacqueline, and his uncle Robert, saluting the casket of his assassinated father, President John Kennedy. It took place on November 25, 1963, as the funeral procession passed outside St. Matthews Cathedral in Washington, D.C. Today, where the child stood near the front doors of the cathedral remains virtually unchanged.

Essex County Airport
125 Passaic Avenue • Fairfield, New Jersey • 973-575-0952

This is where John F. Kennedy, Jr.'s single-engine Piper Saratoga II HP took off from on Friday, July 16, at about 8:30 P.M. They departed from Runway 22, and the plane flew about 62 minutes in the air before crashing. They were headed to Massachusetts for the wedding of Rory, one of Bobby and Ethel Kennedy's children. The plan was to drop Lauren off in Martha's Vineyard, and then continue on to Hyannis, where the wedding was to take place on Saturday the 17.

The First African Baptist Church
Cumberland Island (off the coast of Georgia) • Saint Mary's, Georgia
912-882-4335

It was on this remote Georgia Island that John F. Kennedy, Jr. married Carolyn Bessette on September 21, 1996. The small, ultra-secret wedding began just after sunset in a Roman Catholic ceremony at this Baptist church which was built by freed slaves after the Civil War. Cumberland Island National Seashore is north of the city of St. Mary's. National Park Service visitor centers are located at the Sea Camp and Dungeness docks. A National Park Service passenger ferry provides access to the island from St. Mary's.

J.F.K., Jr.'s Apartment
20 North Moore Street
New York, New York

This is the loft in Tri-Beca where the married couple lived and, for weeks after their deaths, it became a shrine where thousands gathered to mourn (and leave flowers).

Killer Bees
Hidalgo, Texas • Chamber of Commerce: 956-843-2734

Killer Bees have been heard of for some time and a lot of hysteria surrounded the arrival of the Killer Bees in the U.S. These bees attack to defend their hives. They have been involved in reported cases which left more than 700 people dead (though none in the U.S.) since their northward migration from Brazil that began in the 1950s. The first of the aggressive insects—called Africanized honeybees—were found in the United States on October 15, 1990 just outside the City of Hidalgo. After that, Hidalgo became the home of "The World's Largest Killer Bee," a statue built 20 feet long and 10 feet high to commemorate the first colony of "Killer Bees" discovered in the city.

Lee, Bruce
4145 Broadway, between 41st and 42nd Streets (part of the Downtown Auto Center—Downtown Toyota to be exact) • Oakland, California

In 1964, legendary martial artist Bruce Lee founded his second school here in Oakland (the first, the Jun Fan Gung Fu Institute, was located in Seattle at 4750 University Way). The notable event that took place here in Oakland is the stuff of Kung Fu legend. Upset that Lee was teaching martial arts to Caucasians, venerable master Wong Jack Man challenged Lee to a fight. According to witnesses, Lee overwhelmed Wong Jack Man in a matter of minutes, but still, Lee was unhappy with his performance. This dissatisfaction pushed him to develop his own style of fighting, which of course made him world famous. Incidentally, Bruce Lee was born nearby at:

Chinese Hospital

845 Jackson Street (between Stockton and Powell Streets)
San Francisco, California • 415-982-2400

A plaque in the lobby identifies the hospital as Bruce Lee's birthplace.

Maltese Falcon Alleyway

450 Sutter Street • San Francisco, California

Literary fans take note. A plaque here reads: "On approximately this spot, Miles Archer, partner of Sam Spade, was done in by Brigid O'Shaughnessy." Of course, Miles Archer, Sam Spade, and Brigid O'Shaughnessy are not historical characters, but the creations of author Dashiell Hammett, and the death of Miles Archer is just a moment in the film *The Maltese Falcon*. Interestingly, this alleyway is only a few blocks away from Hammett's apartment at 891 Post Street, an address which he shared with his fictional character Spade.

McDonald's

1398 NE Street (at 14 Street) • San Bernardino, California • 909-885-6324

Despite several other claims, this is where the hamburger empire truly started in 1940. Brothers Maurice and Richard McDonald (pre-Ray Kroc) opened a restaurant on this site. Though the place served ribs and pork sandwiches, within eight years it reopened as McDonald's Hamburger with the famous paper-wrapped burgers, etc. Eight more outlets would open within the next six years, and that's when Ray Kroc got involved. Although the original is gone (the headquarters of the Juan Pollo chicken restaurant chain sits here now), there is a nice little museum on the site that's free to the public. Crammed with thousands of McDonald's items, it'll make you long for the days when the menu was simpler and more charming.

NOTE: The oldest functioning McDonald's is in Downey, California. It's 44-years-old and is the last one with a red-and-white striped tile exterior. After opening in 1953, it immediately become the standard for the fast food franchises across the country. The building and its 60-foot-high neon sign with "Speedee the Chef" are eligible for listing on the National Register of Historic Places. It's located at 10207 Lakewood Boulevard (at Florence Avenue). The phone number is: 562-622-9248.

The McDonald's Coffee Spill
5001 Gibson Boulevard SE • Albuquerque, New Mexico

In February 1992, 79-year-old Stella Liebeck was in the passenger seat of her grandson's car here when she received a cup of coffee that was served in a Styrofoam cup at the drive-through window. Her grandson pulled the car forward and stopped so Stella could add cream and sugar. Placing the cup between her knees while trying to remove the lid, the hot coffee spilled into her lap. (Her sweatpants absorbed the scalding coffee and then stuck to her skin.)

A vascular surgeon determined that Liebeck suffered "third-degree burns over six percent of her body, including her inner thighs, perineum, buttocks, and genital and groin areas." After eight days in the hospital and undergoing skin grafting, she sought a settlement from McDonald's of $20,000. McDonald's refused though, and so it was off to court they went, where a jury eventually awarded Liebeck $200,000 in compensatory damages (reduced to $160,000 because the jury found Liebeck 20 percent at fault).

In addition, the jury also awarded Liebeck $2.7 million in punitive damages, equaling approximately two days of McDonald's total coffee sales. (The court later reduced the punitive award to $480,000.) In the end, a "secret" settlement was reached, so the final amount may never be known. However, this event changed the way hot beverages (and lawsuits) are served and gave late-night TV gag writers a wealth of material.

Mickey Mouse
2725 Hyperion Avenue (at Griffith Park Boulevard)
Los Angeles, California (Silverlake District)

Though it seems now that Walt Disney's partner Ub Iwerks and not Disney himself actually created and animated Mickey Mouse, this is the spot where it all happened in 1928. Disney had opened his first studio here in 1926, and it was also here in the mid-1930s that Disney created the first feature-length cartoon, *Snow White and the Seven Dwarfs*. In fact, the Tudor-style cottages that inspired the look of the dwarfs' home can still be seen around the corner at 2906-12 Griffith Park Boulevard. Though the current site is occupied by a market, a light pole on the sidewalk in the parking lot holds a sign that marks the site as the approximate entrance to the Disney studio.

Monroe, Marilyn

Los Angeles General Hospital
1200 State Street • Los Angeles, California

Marilyn Monroe (Norma Jeane Baker) was delivered here at 9:30 A.M. on June 1, 1926, to Gladys Baker (it is believed that her father was not present). This hospital is now called the L.A. County USC Medical Center.

Foursquare Gospel Church
4503 West Broadway • Hawthorne, California

Norma Jeane was baptized here, in July 1926, at this church founded by the controversial evangelist Aimee Semple McPherson (who, it is believed, may actually have performed the baptism).

Los Angeles Orphans Home
815 North El Centro Avenue • Los Angeles, California

Norma Jeane Baker was brought here on September 13, 1935, at the age of nine. It was to be her home for about two years. The original building has since been torn down.

First Marriage
432 South Bentley Avenue
West Los Angeles, California

Norma Jeane Baker married Jim Dougherty here at the home of the Howells on June 19, 1942. The Howells were close friends of the Bakers—they had had even thought of adopting Marilyn when she was a young girl. The bride was given away by Ana Lower, and the couple was married by Reverend Benjamin Lingen-Felder. Norma Jean had met her husband the year before, while she was a student at Van Nuys High School.

Honeymoon
4524 Vista Del Monte Street • Sherman Oaks, California

Norma Jeane Baker and Jim Dougherty spent their first night as husband and wife here, at this one-room bungalow, where they had taken a six-month lease. The bungalow was so small that, as soon as the lease was up, they moved into the old Dougherty house at 14747 Archwood Street in Van Nuys, California. They lived there for a year, and then moved into another house in Van Nuys for a short while, and in 1944 ended up living in Hollywood at 5254 Hermitage Avenue. At his point, Jim had shipped out with the Marines, leaving Marilyn on her own.

Radio Plane Corporation
2627 North Hollywood Way • Burbank, California

It was here, at the Radio Plane Company (a munitions outfit), that Norma Jeane Baker was discovered on June 26, 1945, by U.S. Army photographer David Conover. Marilyn was working here (her first job), when Conover spotted her and took photographs of her for an army training magazine. Conover had received the assignment to snap various women on the base from his commanding officer, Ronald Reagan. The photos, featuring the beauty, led everyone who saw them to take notice and, of course, the rest is history. Today this is the site of Bob Hope (formerly Burbank) Airport.

Marilyn Monroe Dyed Here

Frank and Joseph's Salon
6513 Hollywood Boulevard
Hollywood, California

Norma Jeane Baker was offered a
modeling job in the winter of 1945.
The photographer wanted the bru-
nette to become a blonde, and Norma Jeane's agent, Emmeline Snively,
agreed. And so it was here, at Frank and Joseph's Salon, that Norma Jeane
Baker, soon to be Marilyn Monroe, first became a blonde—thus dramat-
ically changing the course of her career and her life. The peroxiding was
done by stylist Sylvia Barnhart, who went on to do Marilyn's hair for
several more years. Today, there is a toy store at this location.

Roosevelt Hotel

7000 Hollywood Boulevard
Los Angeles, California
800-950-7667

It was here, on the diving board of
the famous Roosevelt swimming
pool, that a young Marilyn Monroe posed for her first ad (it was
for suntan lotion).

Mira Loma Hotel

1420 North Indian Canyon Drive • Palm Springs, California
760-320-1178

Today you can stay in the very room that Marilyn loved to stay in from
the late 1940s on. Each room here is cleverly (and elaborately) themed after celebrities, movies, etc., and room 103 (the "Pretty in Pink" suite) was
Marilyn's special hideaway in the desert. The pool-side room is tricked
out with Marilyn images and even has its own 1,000-piece Marilyn Monroe jigsaw puzzle. The hotel is now called Ballentines Hotel.

Franco's Restaurant
10639 Merritt Street • Castroville, California • 831-633-2090

This small, central California town is known as "The Artichoke Center of the World" (and they've got the world's largest artichoke to prove it), and in February of 1948 they became an interesting footnote in the ca-

reer of the budding starlet. Having just changed her name from Norma Jean Baker to Marilyn Monroe, the actress had traveled to nearby Salinas for a jewelry store promotion. A local, enterprising artichoke grower seized the opportunity and had her transported to Castroville for a trumped up "crowning" as that year's Artichoke Queen. The "crowning" ceremony took place at the headquarters of the California Artichoke and Vegetable Growers, then Monroe was shuttled off to the Franco Hotel for a luncheon. Today, the headquarters at the corner of Wood and Del Monte Streets still remains (though it's just a storage building now), and the Franco Hotel is called Franco's Restaurant. Her legacy is intact at the restaurant though, as evidenced by the "Norma Jean's Club" they still run there.

Marilyn Meets Joe
Villa Nova • 9015 Sunset Boulevard • Hollywood, California

It was here (at table 14), in March 1952, that Marilyn Monroe had a blind date with Joe DiMaggio. She arrived two hours late and, though the meal itself was reported to be a bit stiff and awkward, the couple drove around Hollywood that night after dinner and eventually began opening up to each other. They later married in January 1954. The club is now called The Rainbow Bar and Grill.

Hotel Bel-Air
701 Stone Canyon Road (at Bellagio Road) • Bel Air, California
800-648-4097

The posh, mission-style Hotel Bel-Air is located on 11 acres of beautifully groomed grounds, situated high above Beverly Hills. To enter the secluded grounds, you drive through tropical gardens, across a stone bridge, and past a swan-filled lake. Marilyn lived here (in room 133) in 1952. On the evening of her 26th birthday, she celebrated alone in her suite with a steak dinner and a good bottle of champagne. She returned here for several more stays, most notably during the filming of *Some Like It Hot* (staying again in room 133), and in June 1962, when photographer Bert Stern photographed "The Last Sitting" session. The nearly 2,700 photos were taken in room 261 and bungalow 96.

Doheny Apartments
882 North Doheny Drive
Hollywood, California

Marilyn moved into apartment #3 in 1953, and stayed here until she married Joe DiMaggio in January 1954. At the end of 1961, after returning to Los Angeles, she moved back into the same apartment.

Marriage to DiMaggio
San Francisco City Hall • 1 Dr. Carlton B. Goode Place
San Francisco, California

Marilyn Monroe and Joe DiMaggio were married here in a third-floor office on January 14, 1954. There was a slight delay in the ceremony while the clerk located a typewriter for the marriage license, and reporters all but swarmed the building before the couple could escape in Joe's blue Cadillac.

Monroe-DiMaggio Honeymoon
Clifton Motel • 125 Spring Street • Paso Robles, California

After getting married in San Francisco, Marilyn and Joe DiMaggio spent their first night as husband and wife here, in room 15. They were driving down the coast en route to Palm Springs when they arrived in Paso Robles, about 200 miles south of San Francisco (and not far from where James Dean would be killed in little over a year). For years, while this was still a hotel, a plaque outside room 15 read, "Joe and Marilyn Slept Here." It is now the Clifton Apartments.

Monroe-DiMaggio Home
508 North Palm Drive • Beverly Hills, California

This is the house Marilyn and DiMaggio lived in after their wedding in 1954. They rented the house for $700 per month. Together for less than one year (a tumultuous year punctuated with many arguments—and two film shoots for Marilyn), the couple announced their plans for divorce on October 5, 1954. The residence was swarmed with more reporters than ever, and on October 6, Marilyn, dressed all in black, made a dramatic appearance in front of the house to answer several reporter's questions. (Marilyn would soon move to a duplex at the Brandon Hall Apartments at 8336 DeLongpre Avenue in Hollywood.)

The Seven Year Itch
164 East 61st Street • New York City, New York

This is the apartment building that was used for the famous scene in *The Seven Year Itch* in which Marilyn dangles actor Tom Ewell's shoes out of the window. The movie also featured the now-legendary scene where Marilyn's white dress billows up over the subway grating (see below).

The Seven Year Itch

Subway grating • Northwest corner of
52nd Street and Lexington Avenue
New York, New York

It's one of the most enduring, iconic scenes in Hollywood history. More a publicity stunt than a vital scene in Billy Wilder's 1955 comedy *The Seven Year Itch*, the press had lots of advance notice the night this event took place. That's why over 2,000 people crowded the street in front of the old Trans-Lux movie theater (where Monroe and co-star Tom Ewell emerge from in the actual movie) to ogle Marilyn as she posed suggestively over the subway grating in a sheer white dress (close-ups of her legs were later re-shot in Hollywood). Monroe's then-husband Joe DiMaggio was supposedly furious at the stunt; their marriage dissolved soon after. The Tran-Lux theater is no longer there, but the subway grating remains in the identical spot where Monroe posed on it.

Marilyn Monroe Was Here

155 West 23rd Street • New York City, New York

The words "Marilyn Monroe Was Here" were written in the wet cement in front of the hotel in which Marilyn was staying. Her longtime fan and friend, Jimmy Haspiel, scrawled the message in 1954 after meeting up with her, and it can still be seen here today.

Wrong Door Raid

8122 Waring Avenue
Hollywood, California

The infamous "Wrong Door Raid" took place here on November 5, 1954. During this time, ex-baseball star Joe DiMaggio was having

Monroe tailed by a private detective, Barney Ruditsky. On this infamous night, Joe arrived here with Frank Sinatra, Ruditsky, and another detective, Phil Irwin, hoping to catch Marilyn with another man. Mistakenly, they busted into the wrong house—one where a lady named Florenz Kotz lived. (It is believed that Kotz went on to sue the group, and that they eventually settled out of court for $7,500.) Marilyn, who had been staying a door or two away, was alerted by the commotion and slipped away.

Bement Visit
101 East Wing Street • Bement, Illinois

In the summer of 1955, Marilyn paid a brief visit to the small village of Bement as part of their centennial celebration. She spent the day there and hosted part of a function called "Art for the People." Accompanying Monroe was photographer Eve Arnold, who shot one of her famous sessions with Monroe during the trip. The town still recalls the visit fondly. This is the house that Monroe used as her home-base while in Bement.

Grauman's Chinese Theatre
6925 Hollywood Boulevard • Hollywood, California

On June 26, 1956, Marilyn and Jane Russell were invited to put their handprints in the wet cement here, in front of Grauman's Chinese Theatre (now Mann's Chinese Theatre).

Greene Home
595 North Beverly Glen Boulevard • West Los Angeles, California

In 1956, Marilyn returned to California for the filming of the movie *Bus Stop*. She rented this house with her friends Milton and Amy Greene, but ended up staying at an unidentified apartment on Sunset Boulevard because of the late-night parties hosted by the Greenes.

The Walk of Fame
6774 Hollywood Boulevard • Hollywood, California

Marilyn's star is just down the street from Grauman's Chinese Theatre, on the Hollywood "Walk of Fame" along Hollywood Boulevard. It sits on the sidewalk just outside the front door of a McDonald's restaurant. The star was placed here on February 9, 1960.

Marriage to Arthur Miller
Westchester County Court House
111 Grove Street
White Plains, New York

Marilyn married playwright Arthur Miller here on June 29, 1956 (they divorced January 20, 1961). The day was marred by a tragic event when, earlier that day, a journalist for the French magazine *Paris-Match*, sent to cover the event, was killed in an auto accident.

White House Restaurant
17307 Gulf Boulevard • St. Petersburg, Florida

Following Marilyn's discharge from two New York City psychiatric hospitals in March 1961, she and former husband Joe DiMaggio traveled to North Redington Beach. Amid rumors of reconciliation and remarriage, they visited the Tides Resort & Bath Club. Built in 1936, the hotel hosted many celebrities. Marilyn and Joe registered in separate guest rooms in the main building. The couple dined nearby at the elegant White House Restaurant, now called The Wine Cellar. The historic Tides was demolished in 1995, and its 1,500 feet of prime beachfront property was developed into The Tides Luxury Condominiums (located at 16450 Gulf Boulevard, North Redington Beach, Florida).

Affair with J.F.K.
Carlyle Hotel • 35 East 76th Street • New York City, New York
212-744-1600

It has been claimed, with some authority, that this elegant hotel played host to the alleged affair between Marilyn Monroe and John F. Kennedy in the early 1960s. In addition to possibly meeting here, it has been fairly well-documented that the couple did indeed spend a weekend together in Palm Springs on March 25, 1962, at Bing Crosby's estate.

Originally, President Kennedy planned on staying at the residence of Frank Sinatra from March 24–26, but as the weekend approached, Bobby Kennedy (the president's brother and attorney general) became concerned about Sinatra's extensive links to organized crime. He persuaded his brother to cancel the stay with Sinatra and opt for Crosby's place instead. Sinatra was supposedly livid after being informed by Peter Lawford, a Kennedy relative by marriage.

Monroe and J.F.K.'s Love Nest
Pacific Coast Highway • 625 Beach Road • Santa Monica, California

Actor Peter Lawford's beach home is where Marilyn Monroe and President John F. Kennedy allegedly carried on their secret affair in the early 1960s. Essentially a crash pad for all of Lawford's Hollywood pals (including Sinatra and the rest of the Rat Pack), he allowed his President/brother-in-law full use of the place (and Bobby Kennedy, too) whenever he was in town. Monroe called Lawford here that fateful last night just before she committed suicide.

Washoe County Courthouse
5 Virginia Street
Reno, Nevada

Marilyn gets a divorce here (as many others did in real life) in the 1961 film *The Misfits*. The film was directed by John Huston and co-starred Clark Gable and Montgomery Clift.

Madison Square Garden (Former Location)
50th Street and Eighth Avenue • New York, New York

It was Marilyn's final public (and perhaps most famous) appearance. It happened May 19, 1962 at the old Madison Square Garden in New York. The event was a massive birthday celebration for President John F. Kennedy, and emcee Peter Lawford introduced her as "the late Marilyn Monroe." In her now-famous sequined, backless gown, the President's (alleged) girlfriend crooned to him a sultry, coy version of "Happy Birthday." It's become one of the most telling clips of the century, a moment when Monroe, although near the end of her rope, still managed to captivate, tease, and beguile on a level that's still considered jaw-dropping. Kennedy's comment after the rendition? "I can now retire from politics after having 'Happy Birthday' being sung to me in such a sweet and wholesome manner." An office building now occupies the site.

George Barris Photo Sessions
625 Pacific Coast Highway • Santa Monica, California

On June 1, 1962, renowned photographer and journalist George Barris arrived at the set where Marilyn Monroe was making her last film, *Something's Got To Give*. It was Marilyn's 36th birthday, and Barris was assigned by a national magazine to photograph and interview her. For the next six weeks, he photographed Marilyn on the beach at Santa Monica and in a house in the Hollywood Hills (at 1506 Blue Jay Way). They remain some of the most beautiful, emotional images ever captured of Monroe.

Monroe's Suicide
12305 Fifth Helena Drive • Brentwood, California

On the night of August 4, 1962, not long after she'd been fired from the film *Something's Got to Give*, Marilyn Monroe died in this three-bedroom bungalow, which she had purchased with borrowed money early in 1962. Dr. Hyman Engelberg, who gave Monroe 50 Nembutal tranquilizers on the morning of the fourth, was called on the morning of the fifth and pronounced the star dead. Coroner Thomas Noguchi ruled Monroe's death a suicide by intentional drug overdose. Although Monroe had done several photo shoots in the months before her death, she had refused to be photographed inside the Brentwood house, saying, "I don't want everybody to see exactly where I live."

Westwood Cemetery
1218 Glendon Avenue • Westwood, California

Marilyn Monroe rests here at this small cemetery at the corner of Wilshire Boulevard and Glendon Avenue. The chapel is near the southwest corner, and Marilyn's crypt is near the northeast corner. People from all over the world come to visit this site every day, as evidenced by the many lipstick traces at the crypt.

Mother's Day
The International Mother's Day Shrine • Andrews Methodist Episcopal Church • 11 East Main Street • Grafton, West Virginia • 304-265-1589

The Mother's Day Shrine is located in an old church (originally known as the Andrews Methodist Episcopal Church) on Main Street of this once small West Virginia town. It commemorates the first celebration of Mother's Day, which took place here back in May of 1908. The holiday was started by local resident Anna Jarvis, who historians say never enjoyed motherhood herself. President Wilson made it a national holiday in 1914, probably to whip up "Let's defend our mothers from the Hun" sentiments during the pre-World War I build-up.

The "Mothman" Bridge
Spanning the Ohio River between Point Pleasant and Kanauga
Point Pleasant, West Virginia

At approximately 5:04 P.M. on December 15, 1967, the Silver Bridge collapsed and 46 people lost their lives. What made this horrific event even more peculiar were the odd sightings between November 1966 and December 1967 of a creature that became known as "Mothman." Most of the sightings took place in the "TNT Area" near the town of Point Pleasant, and they involved a creature described as resembling a "giant butterfly," a "brown human being" fly, and a "seven foot tall man with big wings folded against its back." The creature also supposedly had huge, glowing red eyes that looked like "automobile reflectors." The TNT Area, which became ground zero for "Mothman" sightings (as the press dubbed him), was a large tract of land with small concrete "igloos" dotting the landscape (originally used during World War II to store ammunition). Interestingly, the sightings ended after the horrible day that the Silver Bridge collapsed. People began to speculate that the Mothman was somehow responsible for the bridge's collapse, due to some cryptic messages it was said to have left behind. Today, a plaque can be found near the entrance of the bridge.

PEZ Visitors Center
35 Prindle Hill Road • Orange, Connecticut

Here you can experience the largest, most comprehensive collection of PEZ memorabilia on public display in the world, including a PEZ motorcycle, the world's largest PEZ dispenser, and viewing windows into the production facility. The visitor's center is an incredible 4,000 square foot PEZ palace where you can literally spend hours perusing. Some background: PEZ was first marketed as a compressed peppermint sweet in Vienna, Austria in 1927 by Eduard Haas III. The name PEZ is an abbreviation of PfeffErminZ (German for peppermint). The original product was a round peppermint lozenge called a PEZ drop. Over time, a new manufacturing process evolved and the hard pressed brick shape known today was created. The factory here at the visitor's center was built in 1973.

Pizza Rat
First Avenue Stop, L Train • East Greenwich Village • New York, New York

In the early hours of September 21, 2015, Matt Little, a comedian who worked at the Upright Citizens Brigade Theatre, was heading home on the subway. There, he witnessed a rat dragging a slice of pizza down the subway stairs. He recorded a video, uploaded it to social media, and within a few hours of the video's posting, #PizzaRat was trending on Twitter. By September 23, the clip had been viewed over five million times. Articles were quickly written by Gawker, BuzzFeed, Gothamist, and others. Pizza Rat costumes, including "sexy" Pizza Rat costumes, were created and worn for Halloween that year. Popular Science identified the rat as a common brown rat, and noted the rarity of humans to be able to get as close to them as Little did while filming the video. The Staten Island Yankees rebranded as the Staten Island Pizza Rats for several games, wearing uniforms and offering merchandise depicting a stylized pizza rat.

The Roswell Incident
The Old J.B. Foster Ranch • Approximately 75 miles northwest of Roswell, New Mexico

DIRECTIONS: From Corona, New Mexico, go east on NM 247. Just past Mile Marker 17, turn right at the Corona Compressor Station sign. The site is about 16 miles southeast of the turnoff. It is on Bureau of Land Management property, which is open to the public, but reaching the site requires passing through private ranch land, which is fenced and gated.

On the night of July 2, 1947 something crashed into the desert outside of

Roswell, New Mexico. Soon after, the military closed off the area. The first announcement made by the military was that a flying saucer had crashed. Quickly after this first announcement the story was changed—what was thought to have been a flying saucer was in reality a weather balloon. Almost 60 years later, people are still asking just what did rancher Mac Brazel and his eight-year-old son, Vernon, find seven or eight miles from the house on the J.B. Foster ranch. Was the large area of bright wreckage (comprised of rubber strips, tinfoil, tough paper, and sticks) the result of a spaceship? Spy balloon? Weather apparatus? We may never know exactly what happened that night, but we do know that no other UFO event has fueled our collective imaginations more than the "Roswell Incident." For more information, you might want to visit (or contact) the interesting International UFO Museum and Research Center at 114 North Main Street, Roswell, New Mexico. Phone number: 505-625-9495.

Site of the First Automobile Crash
W. Carmean Street • Ohio City, Ohio

A small sign here attached to a wooden pole at the side of a main street marks the spot of the world's first car crash. In 1891, inventor James William Lambert had recently built an early single-cylinder gasoline automobile and decided to take it for a ride with his pal James Swoveland. But as the pair drove along the highway, the car hit a tree root and careened off the road and into a hitching post. Fortunately, the two passengers escaped with only minor injuries. Lambert went on to patent over 600 further inventions, most of which were associated with automobiles. The plaque is mounted on a light pole on the north side of OH-709/W. Carmean Street, just west of its intersection with Liberty Street.

Sinatra, Frank

Birthplace
415 Monroe Street • Hoboken, New Jersey

Frank Sinatra was born here on December 12, 1915. The original wooden building burned down in 1967, and a small archway is the only original thing that remains here to-

day. In the sidewalk, near the site, a star-shaped plaque marks the spot. While there are no formal Sinatra memorials in town, other pertinent addresses are 841 Garden Street, where the Sinatra family lived in 1939, and 600 Hudson Street, former site of the Union Club, where Sinatra got his first singing job in 1935.

Cal Neva Lodge
2 Stateline Road • Crystal Bay, Nevada • 800-CAL-NEVA

When Frank Sinatra owned this resort in the 1960s, it became the playground of the stars. Hollywood followers were enamored with Sinatra and the "Rat Pack," an unforgettable fraternity that linked itself with the White House through Peter Lawford, brother-in-law of then president-elect John F. Kennedy. Dean Martin, Sammy Davis Jr., Juliet Prowse, and Marilyn Monroe, among others, "sang for their suppers" in the Celebrity Showroom and the Indian Room, while politicians and Hollywood stars played at the tables and relaxed in the private cottages overlooking Lake Tahoe. Back then, the Cal Neva consisted of 57 chalets, spread around the main lodge-casino complex.

Marilyn Monroe was a frequent guest of the Cal Neva Lodge, and scandal generally surrounded her because of her "alleged" secret rendezvous with John F. Kennedy. Monroe occupied a chalet that had the best view of the lake (Sinatra reserved it for Marilyn to use at any time). Her chalet, near Sinatra's, is still available for guest use.

Sinatra had a tunnel installed leading from his private chalet into the main building. This brick-lined tunnel allowed him to avoid the crowds before and after his performances. The tunnel exists to this day, including a staircase covered by the original patterned casino carpet. Sinatra's chalet, containing the now-sealed tunnel entrance, is still available for guest use. Today, the resort is shuttered, but remains all but intact.

Holmby Hills Rat Pack
232 South Mapleton Drive • Los Angeles, California

This, the former home of Humphrey Bogart and Lauren Bacall, is where Sinatra hung out with the original and infamous Holmby Hills "Rat Pack," back in the 1940s. The group was comprised of Frank Sinatra, Humphrey Bogart, Lauren Bacall, Judy Garland, David Niven, and John Huston.

Mob Photo
Westchester Premier Theater • 555 White Plains Road
Tarrytown, New York

An infamous (and much-publicized) photo of Sinatra and some gangster pals was taken backstage at the Westchester Premier Theater in Tarrytown, New York, on April 11, 1976. According to sources, it was Carlo Gambino's idea to go backstage and pay a visit to the singer after his performance. Also in the shot were Gambino's brother-in-law Paul Castellano (who would later succeed Gambino as head of the family only to be gunned down in a palace coup orchestrated by *his* successor, John Gotti), and west coast boss Jimmy "the Weasel" Fratianno (who would later turn state's witness against his Mafia pals).

When the Nevada Gaming Control Board asked Sinatra about the picture in 1981, he called the photo the work of "this fink, the Weasel" and explained that the men were not invited backstage. The theater, believed to have had mob connections over the years, was torn down in the mid-1980s.

Palm Springs Airport
3400 East Tahquitz Canyon Way • Palm Springs, California
760-318-3800

On January 6, 1977, Sinatra's mother, Dolly, took off in light rain on a Lear jet headed for Las Vegas, Nevada, from this airport. The plane climbed to 9,000 feet, but never changed its runway heading and flew directly into a nearby mountain range at an altitude of 9,700 feet. The 82-year-old Natalie "Dolly" Sinatra and her traveling companion were killed, and crew error was determined as the cause. After the crash, Phyllis McGuire and Johnny Carson were asked to finish Sinatra's Caesars Palace engagement.

Villa Maggio
Carrizo Road • 12 miles south of Palm Desert, up Route 74 to
Pinyon Crest • Pinyon Crest, California

Frank Sinatra built this secret mountain hideaway compound from 1968 to 1969 in order to have a very private place to share with his family and friends. For a while it was Frank's full-time residence. Select Sinatra VIPs were flown into Palm Springs on his private jet, then brought up to the compound by helicopter. Situated on five acres in Pinyon Crest, Villa Maggio (named for his Oscar-winning *From Here to Eternity* character, Maggio) features panoramic views of the entire Coachella Valley.

Spago
1114 Horn Avenue (just above Sunset Boulevard)
West Hollywood, California

Wolfgang Puck's landmark Hollywood restaurant was, for years, the place to be for the world's biggest celebrities. This was especially true on Oscar Night, when super agent "Swifty" Lazar would hold his annual post-Oscar party here, and just about every movie star in town waited for an invitation. Though "Swifty" died in

1994, Spago remained a star magnet on Oscar Night until the time it closed in 2001. Today, the next-generation Spago is located in Beverly Hills, and remains one of the town's most notable restaurants.

The Spruce Goose

The Evergreen Aviation Museum • 3685 NE Three Mile Lane
McMinnville, Oregon • 503-434-4180

In May 1942, Howard Hughes began to build the world's largest airplane, or what he called at the time "an unsinkable liberty ship." The aircraft was designed to carry 700 troops. Initially, it was a joint venture between Hughes and Kaiser shipping, but Kaiser pulled out. Ultimately, Hughes spent $7 million of his own money on the project, while the U.S. Government spent $17 million. Many people said that it would never get off the ground. On November 2, 1947, they were proved wrong. The giant Spruce Goose, whose wing span was 320 feet, lifted off for a one mile flight across the Long Beach Harbor. The plane was never to fly again. For years, the plane could be seen in Long Beach, but in late 1992 and early 1993, it was moved to this spot in Oregon.

Studio 54

254 West 54th Street • New York, New York
212-517-4065

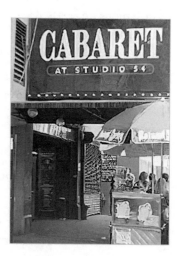

On April 26, 1977 the most well-known Disco of all-time opened up its doors at this site. It quickly became the symbol of the anything-goes, completely hedonistic, late 1970's disco era in New York. Opened by Steve Rubell (who died of hepatitis in 1989) and Ian Schrager (who went on to make a fortune in the hotel business), the club enjoyed huge notoriety for several years until 1979 when an IRS bust put the two away for several years (thus ending the short life of the jet-setters haven.) Today, the space is run by a theater company.

The Tommy Gun
24 E. Third Street • Newport, Kentucky

We've all heard of it. The Clash even did a song by this name. This is where John T. Thompson invented the famed "Tommy gun." Brig. Gen. John T. Thompson, the inventor of the Thompson submachine gun, was born in Newport on December 31, 1860. A West Point graduate of 1882, he was an early advocate of automatic weapons and was awarded the Distinguished Service Medal as Director of Arsenals in World War I. He served for 32 years before retiring. Though some in the time frowned upon the use of automatic weapons, Thompson—according to Explore Kentucky History—wanted "to create an effective rifle that could fire a significant amount of rounds very rapidly." It became a weapon used by many of the organized crime gangs of the day. Thompson died in 1940, feeling sorrow for the notoriety of the Tommy gun as a gangster weapon. Today the same house is a music venue, Thompson House, that celebrates the invention with the Tommy Gun Lounge.

Turquoise McDonald's Sign
2389 W. Highway 89a • Sedona, Arizona

The beautiful city of Sedona, located in the center of Arizona, is famous for its sublime and sacred natural beauty. The red rock landscapes are some of the most famous on earth. Because of the pristine and specific landscape, there are rules in place for buildings in Sedona to make sure that no structure intrudes too much on the surrounding natural scenery. When this McDonald's was built there in 1993, city officials argued that a bright yellow "M" would spoil the aesthetic, claiming that gold would clash with the surrounding red rocks. So, they opted for a more pleasing, soft blue sign—the only one in the world.

Wabash
Chamber of Commerce • 111 South Wabash Street • Wabash, Indiana
260-563-1168

On March 31, 1880, Wabash became the first electrically lighted city in the world. As a test, Wabash had purchased four huge lights from the Brush Electric

Light Company of Cleveland, Ohio. A threshing machine steam engine was used to generate the electricity needed to create the light, and the four lights were mounted atop the still-standing county courthouse. The switch was thrown at 8:00 P.M. as the courthouse clock started ringing. The test was a success—brush electric lights could in fact efficiently light a large outdoor area. One of the original lights is on exhibition in the county courthouse.

Walden Pond

915 Walden Street • Concord, Massachusetts • 978-369-3254

Henry David Thoreau lived at Walden Pond from July 1845 to September 1847. His experience there inspired the book *Walden*, which is generally credited with helping to create awareness and respect for the natural environment. Because of Thoreau's legacy, Walden Pond has been designated a National Historic Landmark and is considered the birthplace of the conservation movement. The Reservation encompasses 333 acres surrounding the pond, which is a 103 foot deep glacial kettle hole pond. There are 2,280 acres of mostly undeveloped woods, called the "Walden Woods," surrounding the pond.

Wright, Frank Lloyd

951 Chicago Avenue • Oak Park, Illinois • 708-848-1976

The famed architect Frank Lloyd Wright added this studio to his home in 1898. The complex served as Wright's primary work center in the years that launched his career, 1889 to 1909. Here, among other things, he developed the Prairie style of architecture. The house is open to the public as a historic museum, and the building has been restored to what it would have been like the last year Wright worked and lived here, 1909.

"War of the Worlds"

CBS Radio (former location) • 485 Madison Avenue • New York, New York

On October 30, 1938 CBS Radio was broadcasting the music of Ramon Raquello and his orchestra live from the Meridian Room at the Park Plaza in New York City. Suddenly, a reporter interrupted: Astronomers had just detected suspicious movement on the surface of Mars. Soon, another interruption: A meteor had landed on a farm near Grovers Mill, New Jersey. A reporter supposedly was on the scene, describing the events; listeners learned that a spaceship bearing a tentacled creature was shooting humans with a deadly laser beam. The broadcast then changed over to full coverage of this ominous event. By the time the night was over, however, most of the audience had learned that the news broadcast was entirely fictitious. It was simply the regular radio show featuring Orson Welles and the Mercury Theatre, and that week, in honor of Halloween, they had decided to stage a highly dramatized and updated version of H.G. Wells' story, "War of the Worlds." Though the popular version holds that the nation was in dire panic from this episode, that's probably more of a hoax than the broadcast itself, which was never intended to fool anyone. At four separate points during the program, it was clearly stated that what people were hearing was a play. The notion that millions of people panicked was the result of an overzealous media fanning the flames of the show in the days following its broadcast.

Wyeth, Andrew

Olson House at the Farnsworth Art Museum • 384 Hathorn Point Road
Cushing, Maine • 207-596-6457

The famous 1948 painting called "Christina's World," artist Andrew Wyeth's signature work of art, was based on an image that was modeled here, at the famous Olson House. Wyeth's depiction of the crippled Christina Olson crawling through a field toward the house she shared with her brother, Alvaro, has become one of only a handful of iconic American paintings, and every year from Memorial Day weekend to October 15, about 8,000 art-loving visitors come here to pay tribute (and some, as seen below, even act as Christina near the house, replicating her pose from the painting). "Christina's World" is now owned by the Museum of Modern Art in New York. Note: The Olson House is located 14.5 miles from the Farnsworth Museum. Admission can be purchased in combination with general museum admission or can be purchased on-site separately.

CHAPTER TWO

BORN IN THE USA

Drive-In Filling Station

Baum and St. Clair Streets • Pittsburgh, Pennsylvania

At this site in December 1913, Gulf Refining Co. opened the first drive-in facility designed and built to provide gasoline, oils, and lubricants to the motoring public (the East Liberty Station). Its success led to construction of thousands of gas stations by different oil companies across the nation. The East Liberty station was the first to offer free road maps produced by Gulf. They also made the employee restroom available to motorists, which greatly contributed to the concept of public restrooms at stations elsewhere. A recently placed marker commemorates the history.

Ice Hockey

Long Pond • Windsor, Nova Scotia

It is believed that this is the birthplace of Canadian hockey. According to scholars, in the early 1800s, King's College School Boys began adapting the Irish field game of Hurley to the ice here on Long Pond. The Long Pond can still be seen on Howard Dill's property just off the campus of what is now King's-Edgehill School.

Food and Drink

Banana Split
805 Ligonier Street • Latrobe, Pennsylvania

In 1904, Dr. David Strickler, a pharmacist at Tassell's Drug Store, invented the banana split here (back then, pharmacists were forever coming up with "sweet" ideas to make people feel better). Strickler's recipe for a banana split starts off with a banana sliced lengthwise, topped with three scoops of ice cream—one vanilla, one chocolate, and one strawberry. Those are topped with pineapple chunks, chocolate sauce, and strawberry sauce. The dessert is finished off with tufts of whipped cream, chopped nuts, and three maraschino cherries. Today, the original building is there but it is unoccupied. How seriously does Latrobe take its sundae history? Put it this way: the town's Elks Club has a banana split on its official pin, and St. Vincent College uses the banana split story in its school recruiting material.

Ben & Jerry's
Southwest corner of St. Paul and College Streets
Burlington, Vermont

In 1963, Bennett Cohen and Jerry Greenfield met in their seventh grade gym class at Merrick Avenue Junior High School in Merrick (Long Island, New York). Both kids were overweight, and both loved ice cream. While going to Calhoun High School in Merrick, Cohen hawked ice cream from a truck. As a student at Oberlin College in Ohio, Greenfield got a job as an ice cream scooper.

After moving to Vermont, the pals decided to embark on their ice cream dreams in May 1978 by opening Ben & Jerry's Homemade here in a renovated gas station. Soon, word of the unique ice cream place with the wildly creative flav ors and community-minded business style spread like crazy. By 1985, Ben & Jerry's annual sales exceeded $9 million and in 1998, they topped over $200 million worldwide. A plaque in the sidewalk marks the spot of the first store, which is now a vacant lot. Note: Nearby, in Waterbury, Vermont, visitors can take a tour of the Ben & Jerry's ice cream factory. Take exit 10 off of I-89 in Waterbury, go north on route 100 towards Stowe. The ice cream factory is about one mile up the road on the left. Phone: 866-BJTOURS.

Big Mac
Uniontown Shopping Center • 942 Morgantown Street
Uniontown, Pennsylvania

The famous Big Mac sandwich was created in 1967 by M. J. "Jim" Delligatti, an early McDonald's owner and operator, at his Uniontown, Fayette County, McDonald's. He developed his brainchild because sales were down and he thought that the way to get things back up were to expand the menu. McDonald's agreed to let him test a large sandwich that featured two patties, which he called the Big Mac. It was a hit, so he introduced them at three of his other McDonald's in Pittsburgh. From there, well, you know what happened.

Boysenberry
Knott's Berry Farm • 8039 Beach Boulevard • Buena Park, California
714-220-5200

Today it's a popular theme park, but Knott's Berry Farm really does have its roots planted in berries, as the name says. In fact, this is where the Boysenberry was born. In 1923, a man named Rudolph Boysen crossed a loganberry with a raspberry near this site, and he called the resulting hybrid the "boysenberry."

Ten years later, in 1933, a Buena Park farmer named Walter Knott started planting boysenberries right here on what he called "Knott's Berry Farm." The depression took hold, and his wife fixed up a roadside stand and began hawking freshly baked pies, plus fresh preserves and delicious home-cooked chicken dinners.

So many people came around to visit the stand (and buy her wares) that Walter thought it would be a good idea to create an old west ghost town so waiting customers would have something to do—and so Knott's Berry Farm was born. Today, Knott's Berry Farm features 165 shows, attractions, and rides.

Cheeseburger I
2776 Speer Boulevard • Denver, Colorado

Smile and say "cheeseburger!" In 1935, Louis Ballas, owner of the Humpty-Dumpty Drive-In in northwest Denver, put a slice of cheese on a hot burger, and the rest is history. The world's first "cheeseburger"—a term patented by Ballas—is honored with a small memorial at 2776 Speer Boulevard, now the parking lot of Key Bank.

Cheeseburger II
Kaelin's Restaurant • 1801 Newburg Road • Louisville, Kentucky
502-451-1801

Carl and Margaret Kaelin *may* have beaten Ballas by one year. Shortly after opening their new restaurant in 1934, Kaelin was cooking a hamburger when he decided to add a slice of American cheese (seems he liked the extra "tang" from the cheese). He christened his new creation the "cheeseburger." A proclamation from the mayor of the city of Louisville designates every October 12 (the date the cheeseburger was invented) as "Kaelin's Cheeseburger Day" here in Louisville.

Cheeseburger III
The Rite Spot • 1500 West Colorado Boulevard • Pasadena, California

Then there are those who believe that Lionel Sternberger first came up with the "cheese hamburger" back in 1926 while working the grill at a place called The Rite Spot (which is no longer there). Sternberger had purchased a roadside burger stand here—the former Hinky Dick—which was located on historic Route 66 just before the entrance to the neighboring town of Eagle Rock.

Coca-Cola
107 Marietta Street • Atlanta, Georgia
Woodruff, Robert Winship
1414 Second Avenue • Columbus, Georgia

On May 8, 1886, druggist Dr. John Stith Pemberton (a former Confederate officer) invented "Coca-Cola" syrup. It was mixed in a 30-gallon brass kettle hung over a backyard fire. After he made a jug of the syrup he took it down to "Jacobs Pharmacy" and talked Willis E. Venabele into mixing it with water and selling it for five cents a glass. It was marketed as a "brain and nerve tonic" in drugstores and sales averaged nine drinks per day.

Pemberton's bookkeeper, Frank M. Robinson, was the person who suggested the name "Coca-Cola," which was chosen because both words actually named two ingredients found in the syrup. He also suggested that the name be written in the Spencerian script, a popular penmanship of that time. It was from his pen that the "Coca-Cola" signature originated. Pemberton liked the easy to remember name, so history was born.

On November 15, 1886, John G. Wilkes (who was drunk) walked into a drugstore complaining of a headache and requested a bottle of "Coca-Cola" syrup. To get instant relief, he asked the "soda jerk" to mix up a glass on the spot. Rather than walk to the other end of the counter in order to mix it with cold tap water, the clerk suggested using soda water. The man remarked that it really tasted great. Soon after, "Coca-Cola" was in fizzy, carbonated form.

The building at 107 Marietta Street where the drink was invented is no longer there. Jacob's Pharmacy, where Coca-Cola formula was dispensed for the first time, was located at the southwest corner of Peachtree and Marietta streets (the site of what is now the Wachovia tower).

Robert Winship Woodruff was born in Columbus, Georgia on December 6, 1889. He was the man who shepherded Coca-Cola into the huge international brand that it is today. At just 33 years old, he took command of The Coca-Cola Company in 1923 and shaped the young soft drink enterprise and its bottler franchise system into a corporate giant with the world's most widely known trademark. A man of enormous stature and personal magnetism, Mr. Woodruff's influence over the affairs of The Coca-Cola Company was absolute until his death in 1985. His birthplace is honored with a historical marker.

Coca-Cola Bottle
Root Glass Company • Corner of Third Street and Voorhees Street
Terre Haute, Indiana

Biedenharn Candy Company Museum
1107 Washington Street • Vicksburg, Mississippi

Terre Haute is the birthplace of the Coca-Cola bottle. The Chapman Root Glass Company invented the "Hobbleskirt," or "contour," bottle specifically for Coca-Cola. They modeled the bottle after a cocoa bean. The bottle was first patented on November 16, 1915, and then renewed on December 25, 1923. The actual shape of the bottle was patented in 1960. A historic marker has been placed at the site of the bottling company. The bottling company is long gone, and a gas station and restaurant now sit at the site. At the Vigo County Historical Society Museum located at 1411 South 6th Street in Terre Haute, visitors can see a huge collection of original Coca-Cola artifacts as well as exclusive products in their gift shop and a rare mold of the original bottle.

The Biedenharn Candy Company Museum is in the restored 19th-century candy store and soda fountain where Joseph Biedenharn first bottled Coca-Cola in 1894. Coca-Cola memorabilia, a bottle collection, and antique bottling equipment are displayed.

Corn Dog
Cozy Dog • 2935 South Sixth Street • Springfield, Illinois • 217-525-1992

The corn dog, named first the "Crusty Cur" and then the "Cozy Dog," was invented by Ed Waldmire Jr., and made popular here at his restaurant. Here's how he once told the story: "In Muskogee, Oklahoma, I saw an unusual sandwich called 'corn-dog.' This sandwich was a wiener baked in cornbread. The corn-dog was very good, but took too long to prepare. The problem was how to cover a hotdog with batter and cook it in a short time. In the fall of 1941, I told this story to a fellow student at Knox College whose father was in the bakery business, and then gave it no further thought.

"Five years later while in the Air Force stationed at Amarillo Airfield, I received a letter from my fellow student, Don Strand. To my surprise he had developed a mix that would stick on a wiener while being french-fried. He wondered if he could send some down that I could try in Amarillo. Having plenty of spare time, I said 'yes.'

Using cocktail forks for sticks, the U.S.O kitchen in which to experiment, we made a very tasty hotdog on a stick, that we called a "crusty cur." They became very popular both at the U.S.O. in town, and at the P.X. on the airfield. My friend continued to send mix and we continued to sell thousands of crusty curs until I was discharged—honorably—in the spring of 1946. We decided to sell them that spring. My wife did not like the name 'crusty curs.' Through trial and error and discarding dozens of names, we finally decided on the name 'Cozy Dogs.'"

Cozy Dogs were officially launched on June 16, 1946 and today at the Cozy Dog Drive-In, you'll still find the delicious, innovative hotdog-on-a-stick at this classic American restaurant.

Dr. Pepper Museum
300 South 5th Street • Waco, Texas • 254-757-1025

Dr Pepper Company is the oldest major manufacturer of soft drink concentrates and syrups in the United States. It was created, manufactured, and sold beginning in 1885 here in the Central Texas town of Waco. Dr Pepper is a "native Texan," originating at Morrison's Old Corner Drug Store (originally located in Waco at the corner of 4th and Austin, it can now be seen here at this museum).

The origin of Dr Pepper is this: Charles Alderton, a young pharmacist working at Morrison's store, is believed to be the inventor of the now-famous drink. Alderton spent most of his time mixing up medicine for the people of Waco, but in his spare time he liked to serve carbonated drinks at the soda fountain. He liked the way the drug store smelled with all of the fruit syrup flavor odors mixing together in the air. He decided to create a drink that tasted like that scent. He kept a journal, and after numerous experiments he finally hit upon a mixture of fruit syrups that he liked.

As to the name, Morrison is credited with naming the drink "Dr. Pepper" (the period was dropped in the 1950s). Unfortunately, the exact origin is unclear, though the museum has collected over a dozen different stories on how the drink became known as "Dr Pepper." The exceptional museum tour includes some interesting smells and flavors in the Old Corner Drug Store, a tour of the bottling room, the chance to crown a soft drink bottle and shoot a "Waco" in the soda fountain, plus a sample-size fountain treat.

French Dip Sandwich
Philippe the Original • 1001 North Alameda Street
Los Angeles, California • 213-628-3781

Philippe the Original is one of the oldest and best-known restaurants in Southern California, if not the world. It was established in 1908 by Philippe Mathieu, the man thought to have created the "French Dip Sandwich." Here's the story: One day in 1918, while making a sandwich, Mathieu inadvertently dropped the sliced French roll into a roasting pan filled with juice still hot from the oven. The patron, a policeman, said he would take the sandwich anyway and returned the next day with some friends asking for more dipped sandwiches. And so the "French Dip Sandwich" was born—so-called because of either Mathieu's French heritage, the French roll the sandwich is made on, or because the officer's name was French. Whatever the  reason, people love this place for all the right reasons—great food, great prices, and great history.

Ice Cream Sundae Birthplace #1
1404 15th Street • Two Rivers, Wisconsin

On July 8, 1881, some claim that the first ice cream sundae was served by accident here at this address in Two Rivers. Druggist Edward Berner, owner of Ed Berner's Ice Cream Parlor, was asked by a man named George Hallauer for some ice cream topped with syrup soda. Realizing how good it tasted, Berner decided to add the dish to his regular menu and charged a nickel, the same price as a serving without syrup. However, the nickel price created too small a profit margin, and so it was decided that the treat would only be served on Sundays to maintain costs.

Sometime later, on a day other than Sunday, a 10-year-old girl insisted on being served a dish of ice cream "with that stuff on top," saying they could "pretend it was Sunday." Not only did she persuade Berner to serve her the special dessert, but, after that, the confection was sold every day in many flavors. It eventually lost its Sunday-only association and came to be called an "Ice Cream Sundae" when a glassware salesman placed an order with his company for the long canoe-shaped dishes in which it was served, and referred to the bowls as "Sundae dishes."

Nearby at the Washington House Hotel Museum in Two Rivers, you'll find a replica of Ed Berner's ice cream parlor. Additionally, the Wisconsin State Historical Society recognizes Two Rivers as the birthplace of the sundae and in 1973 a historical marker was placed in Two Rivers Central Memorial Park to commemorate the event.

Ice Cream Sundae Birthplace #2
216 East State Street • Ithaca, New York

The story here goes that one hot Sunday afternoon in 1891, John M. Scott, the pastor of the Unitarian Church, and one of his faithful parishioners, Chester Platt, retired to the latter's drug store for something cool. Here, Mr. Platt supposedly got two dishes of ice cream from Miss DeForest Christiance, who was tending the soda fountain. He plopped a candied cherry on top of each dish of ice cream and covered the whole thing with cherry syrup, resulting in what many Ithaca folks think was the real first ice cream sundae.

JELL-O Museum
23 East Main Street • LeRoy, New York • 585-768-7433

JELL-O, perhaps America's most famous dessert, was born here in LeRoy, located in upstate New York. In 1845, a man named Peter Cooper patented a product that was "set" with gelatin. But it never caught on with the public. However, in 1897, Pearle Wait, a carpenter here in LeRoy, was concocting a cough remedy and laxative tea in his home. He experimented with gelatin and came up with a fruit-flavored dessert that his wife, May, named Jell-O. He tried to market his product but he lacked the capital and the experience.

In 1899, he sold his formula to a fellow townsman, Frank Woodward, for just $450. Woodward already had some success in manufacturing and selling and was one of the best-known manufacturers of proprietary medicines. At first, sales were so slow that Woodward gave his plant superintendent the chance to buy the JELL-O rights for $35. But before they could complete their deal, sales took off. By 1906, sales reached $1 million.

The marketing was brilliant—they'd send out well-attired salesmen to demonstrate JELL-O and distribute 15 million copies of a JELL-O recipe book containing celebrity favorites and more. In 1923, Woodward's Genesee Pure Food Company was renamed JELL-O Company and later merged with Postum Cereal to become the General Foods Corporation. In 1997, the JELL-O Museum opened its doors in LeRoy. The museum features JELL-O artwork by famous artists such as Max Parrish and Norman Rockwell, and showcases memorabilia from the more than 100 years in the brand's history.

Kellogg Company
235 Porter Street • Battle Creek, Michigan

A plaque here reads: "At the age of fourteen, Will Keith Kellogg (1860–1951) began working as a salesman for his father's broom business. Later he worked with his brother Dr. John Harvey Kellogg, at the Battle Creek Sanitarium. In 1894, John, assisted by Will, developed a successful cereal flake. It was first served to patients at the sanitarium and later sold by the Sanitas Food Company.

"In 1906, W. K. Kellogg launched his own food company to sell Toasted Corn Flakes cereal. The company grew to be the largest manufacturer of ready-to-eat cereals in the world. Kellogg's early personal philanthropies included assistance to rural teachers, to British children orphaned by war, to the blind, and to a number of hospitals and medical programs. In 1930 the W. K. Kellogg Foundation was established to promote the health and well-being of children. Today, it is among the world's largest philanthropic organizations.

"Will manufactured the first boxes of cereal in a three-story building on Bartlett Street at the rate of thirty-three cases per day. In 1907 the original factory building was destroyed by fire, and part of the present structure was erected on this site. Kellogg Company sold more than one million cases of cereal in 1909, and by 1911 the company's advertising budget had reached $1 million. In 1917, production capacity reached nine million boxes per day. In 1980, United States production of Kellogg's ready-to-eat cereals required more than 110,000 bushels of corn, 225,000 pounds of bran, 9,000 bushels of wheat, and 12,000 pounds of wheat germ each day. By its seventy-fifth anniversary in 1981, Kellogg Company had forty-seven plants operating in twenty-one countries."

The site is not open to the public.

Kool-Aid
508 West First Street • Hastings, Nebraska

The town of Hastings, Nebraska is known as the "Birthplace of Kool-Aid" because Nebraska native Edwin Perkins invented the powdered soft drink here in 1927. To honor Kool-Aid on its milestone birthday, the Hastings Museum permanently dedicated a 3,300 square-foot exhibit to portray the Kool-Aid story.

The museum is located at 1330 North Burlington Avenue in Hastings. There, you'll find artifacts including rare early packets, a Kool-Aid cartoon suit worn by its jug mascot, and a large interactive exhibit that tells the story of Kool-Aid and inventor Edwin Perkins. You'll also find a commemorative sign at the site where it was invented.

Lobster Newburgh
Delmonico's • 56 Beaver Street • New York City, New York • 212-509-1144

In 1836, the Delmonico brothers (Giovanni and Pietro) opened this now-famous restaurant in lower Manhattan. Since then, it's not only served some of the city's best meals—it's actually been the birthplace of some of the world's most famous dishes. For instance, in the mid-1800s, shipping magnate Ben Wenberg asked chef Charles Ranhofer to prepare a meal he had discovered in South America—chunks of lobster sautéed in butter and served in a sauce of cream and egg flavored with paprika and sherry. The meal was such a success that it was added to the Delmonico's menu as Lobster Wenberg.

However, some time later, Wenberg consumed too much wine from Delmonico's renowned cellars and got into a fight. He was banned from Delmonico's forever and his name was taken off the menu. But they did not want to lose the dish, so "Wenberg" became "Newburgh"—and that's how Lobster Newburgh began.

In 1876, the Baked Alaska also originated at Delmonico's. It was created in honor of the newly acquired territory of Alaska. George Sala, an

Englishman who visited Delmonico's in the 1880s, said: "The 'Alaska' is a baked ice. . . . The nucleus or core of the entremets is an ice cream. This is surrounded by an envelope of carefully whipped cream, which, just before the dainty dish is served, is popped into the oven, or is brought under the scorching influence of a red hot salamander."

It was later popularized worldwide by Jean Giroix, chef in 1895 at the Hotel de Paris in Monte Carlo. And Eggs Benedict was also created at Delmonico's, back in the 1860s, in response to a complaint that their menu never changed. A couple named Mr. and Mrs. LeGrand Benedict, regulars at the upscale restaurant, asked for something new. To oblige, the chef served up eggs on ham served on a muffin and covered in Hollandaise sauce. They loved it, and so Eggs Benedict was born.

Oreos
Chelsea Market • 88 10th Avenue • New York City, New York
212-247-1423

Today in this funky, cobblestone-floored old building you'll find unbelievably appetizing places such as Manhattan Fruit Exchange, The Lobster Place, the bakery for Sarabeth's Bakery, Fat Witch Brownies, and more (including some of the offices for Major League Baseball). But way back, this was once the headquarters of Nabisco and the actual birthplace of the Oreo cookie. From 1898–1958, Nabisco occupied this building and Oreos were born here in 1912. In fact, some of the original red brick ovens are still visible in the MLB.com offices.

Pepperidge Farm
Sturges Highway at Ridge Common
Fairfield, Connecticut

Margaret Rudkin was a Connecticut housewife and mother of three

young children. In the early 1930s, she discovered that one of her sons had an allergy to commercial breads that contained preservatives and artificial ingredients. So, in 1937, she started baking her own preservative-free bread for her ailing son. Eventually she hit upon a mouth watering whole-wheat loaf that contained only natural ingredients.

Encouraged by her family, Margaret Rudkin began selling her delicious, freshly-baked bread at a local grocery store here in Fairfield (it's called Mercurio's, located at 508 Post Road). The bread caught on with locals and as her business grew, she felt compelled to give her bread business a name. So, she dubbed it in honor of the farm she lived on—Pepperidge Farm (named for the Pepperidge tree located in the front yard). Today, you can still get a glimpse of the original Pepperidge Farm, exactly as it appears on the product packages. A good deal of the property has been sold and subdivided. However, the iconic, vine-covered, stone farmhouse is there, along with the inspirational Pepperidge tree.

Pepsi
256 Middle Street • New Bern, North Carolina • 252-636-5898

This spot was once a pharmacy where pharmacist Caleb Bradham invented "Brad's Drink" in 1898, which he later patented as Pepsi-Cola in 1903. Bradham, like many pharmacists of the day, operated a soda fountain in his drugstore, where he served his customers homemade beverages, the most popular of which was the aforementioned "Brad's Drink." The concoction's recipe included carbonated water, sugar, vanilla, rare oils, pepsin, and cola nuts. (It was later renamed Pepsi after the pepsin and cola nuts used in the recipe.)

Pepsi-Cola went bankrupt in 1923, after Bradham lost his money in the stock market. Then it was bought in 1931 by the Loft Candy Company. Today at the actual place where the drink was invented, there is a recreated soda fountain. Visitors can purchase a wide variety of Pepsi memorabilia inside the store. The birth-place of Pepsi is owned and operated by Pepsi-Cola Bottling Company of New Bern, Inc. It first opened its doors on the 100th Anniversary of Pepsi-Cola.

Reuben Sandwich
Blackstone Hotel • 302 South 36th Street • Omaha, Nebraska

This is the birthplace of the famous Reuben sandwich: the delicious com-bination of rye bread, corned beef, Swiss cheese, and sauerkraut. It was dreamed up at this historic hotel back in 1925 to feed participants in a late-night poker game. Created by a local grocer named Reuben Kulakof-sky (hence the sandwich name), hotel owner Charles Schimmel loved the sandwich so much that he put it on the hotel restaurant menu. Bigger exposure would come later when Fern Snider, a one-time waitress at the Blackstone, entered the Reuben in a national sandwich competition in 1956. The entry won the top prize, and thus vaulted the sandwich into history.

Russell Stover
Highway 24 • 10½ miles south of Alton, Kansas

In 1921 in Omaha, Nebraska, Russell and Clara Stover introduced an ice cream creation called the Eskimo Pie. It was a chocolate-covered ice cream square in a small bag and sales exploded the first year they intro-duced it. At first, it looked as if they'd hit the mother lode, but the patent was too expensive to protect and so they sold their business and moved to Denver where they decided to go into the candy-making business.

From their bungalow home, they started "Mrs. Stover's Bungalow Candies." Clara made the candy and Russell was the salesman. In 1931, they moved their by-now thriving business to Kansas City. Here the cou-ple weathered the Depression and the sugar-short World War II years that followed. But they eventually emerged as a multi-million dollar a year enterprise with world-wide sales. Sixty-six-year-old Russell Stover died May 11, 1954. Clara Stover survived him by 20 years. She carried on the candy business until selling out in 1960. She died on January 9, 1975 at the age of 93. But her candy lives on under the same familiar name. Today, the Russell Stover Birthsite Marker stands next to the field that was the site of the home where Stover was born in 1888.

The Tomato
1792 Graham Road • Reynoldsburg, Ohio

Alexander W. Livingston (1821–1898) was a plant and seed merchant. He became internationally known through his development of the tomato for commercial use. In 1870, after working and experimenting with seeds and plants for several years, he introduced the Paragon Tomato, the first commercial variety grown in these fields. A plaque saluting Reynoldsburg as the birthplace of the tomato and Alexander W. Livingston, the noted horticulturist who developed the domestic strain of the Paragon tomato, can be found in front of the Reynoldsburg Police Station.

Tomato Juice
French Lick Springs Resort and Spa • 8670 West State Road 56
French Lick, Indiana • 800-457-4042

In 1917, the world famous chef Louis Perrin at the French Lick Resort ran out of oranges to serve for breakfast, so he created tomato juice. The renowned hotel has hosted dignitaries like Franklin D. Roosevelt, Lana Turner, Bing Crosby, and Bob Hope.

Kermit the Frog

Leland Chamber of Commerce • Located on the bank of Deer Creek, one and 1/2 miles west of the intersection of Highway 82 and Highway 61. Leland, Mississippi • 888-307-6364

The small town of Leland (12 miles west of Greenville) is where Muppet-creator Jim Henson spent much of his childhood. It is here where Henson met his boyhood friend Kermit Scott, who is believed to have later inspired him to create Kermit the Frog. Today, Leland pays tribute to Hensen (and Kermit) through an exhibit located within their Chamber of Commerce. The exhibit was given by The Jim Henson Company as "a gift to the people of Leland." It features a tableau honoring Kermit the Frog's birth on Deer Creek, photographs from the Henson family album, a video center with many of Jim Henson's early works and a gift shop. A separate room is filled with Muppet memorabilia.

Restaurants

A&W

13 Pine Street • Lodi, California

A&W Restaurants, which claims to be the first U.S. franchise restaurant chain, was founded here in the Northern California town of Lodi. On a sweltering day in June of 1919, an entrepreneur named Roy Allen was passing through town on the day a homecoming parade was taking place to honor World War I veterans. Seizing the opportunity, he mixed up a batch of ice-cold creamy root beer and sold it from a beverage cart to the thirsty locals. Soon, on this spot, he opened his very first root beer stand and the rest is history. After the huge success of this first root beer stand, Roy Allen opened a second stand in the nearby city of Sacramento. In 1922, Allen partnered up with Frank Wright, a worker from the first stand in Lodi. Combining the "A" and "W" initials, the men officially formed what we know today as A&W Restaurants.

Bob's Big Boy

4211 West Riverside Drive
Burbank, California • 818-843-9334

The oldest surviving Bob's Big Boy is located in Southern California. It was designed by Wayne McAllister and built in 1949 (the original Bob's was in Glendale). Today, this structure has been declared a national landmark.

Burger King
3090 Northwest 36th Street
Miami, Florida

In 1954, David Edgerton opened the first Burger King hamburger stand here. Burgers and shakes were 18 cents each. The Whopper, which appeared in 1957, sold for 37 cents.

Dunkin' Donuts
534 Southern Artery • Quincy, Massachusetts • 617-472-9502

Dunkin' Donuts started in 1946 when a man named William Rosenberg founded Industrial Luncheon Services, a company that delivered meals and coffee break snacks to customers on the outskirts of Boston, Massachusetts. The success of Industrial Luncheon Services led Rosenberg to open his first coffee and donut shop, the "Open Kettle." In 1950, the Open Kettle became the first Dunkin' Donuts. Today, with over 6,000 Dunkin' Donut Shops worldwide, the company is the largest chain of coffee, donut, and bagel shops. You'll still find a Dunkin' Donuts on this site.

IHOP
4301 Riverside Drive
Toluca Lake, California

The first International House of Pancakes restaurant opened at this site in 1958 by a man named Al Lapin. The restaurant, whose menu was originally based on pancakes, quickly grew in popularity.

By 1962, there were 50 IHOP locations. Lapin was the one who actually chose the familiar blue roof and A-frame architectural style. Over the years, a number of items have been added to the menu, and today IHOP has a full lunch and dinner menu. (The structure here, though no longer an IHOP, is the original building, so you'll be able to notice the famous, iconic A-frame structure.)

Jack in the Box
6720 El Cajon Boulevard • San Diego, California

In 1951, a businessman named Robert O. Peterson opened the first Jack in the Box restaurant in San Diego on the main east-west thoroughfare leading into city. Equipped with an intercom system and drive-thru window, the tiny restaurant served up hamburgers to passing motorists for just 18 cents, while a large jack-in-the-box clown kept watch from the roof.

Kentucky Fried Chicken
3900 South State Street • Salt Lake City, Utah

This was the site of the world's first Kentucky Fried Chicken restaurant. Known as the original Harman's Kentucky Fried Chicken, it was here in 1952 where Colonel Harland Sanders made the business deal with local Pete Harman that launched the famous fast food. Sanders was visiting from his home in Louisville, Kentucky, fried chicken recipe in hand. Harman ran a hamburger place called the Do Drop Inn. He decided to take a chance on the 65-year-old, down-on-his-luck Sanders. So, on August 4, 1952, the first bucket of chicken was served. (Chicken dinners then cost $3.50 and included 14 pieces of chicken, mashed potatoes, rolls, and gravy. The same meal would cost about $25 today.) Today, KFC, as it is popularly known, is a fast food phenomenon with 12,000 restaurants in 80 countries.

McDonald's
400 North Lee Street • Des Plaines, Illinois • 847-297-5022

The McDonald's #1 Store Museum is a re-creation of the first McDonald's restaurant opened on this site on April 15, 1955 by McDonald's

Corporation founder Ray Kroc. The original red-and-white-tiled restaurant building featuring the Golden Arches underwent several remodels through the years and was finally torn down in 1984. The present facility was built according to the original blueprints with some modifications to accommodate museum visitors and staff. The "Speedee" road sign is original and the customer service and food preparation areas contain original equipment. There are also displays featuring historical photos, early advertising, memorabilia, and a short video presentation. (While this is the first Kroc opened McDonald's, the very first McDonald's was in San Bernardino, as outlined in *James Dean Died Here*.)

Pizza Hut
1845 North Fairmount, Wichita State University • Wichita, Kansas

When the pizza craze started sweeping the nation in the late 1950s, two young college students attending the University of Wichita wanted to capitalize on the trend. Brothers Frank and Don Carney opened the first Pizza Hut restaurant on June 15, 1958. The pair had had been approached by the owner of this small building (then located at the corner of Kellogg and Bluff Streets). She wanted a respectable neighborhood business there and she had read a November 1957 *Saturday Evening Post* article about the pizza craze. The brothers jumped into action.

Interestingly, the building's structure influenced the name of what

would become the famous worldwide pizza chain. The building had a sign that would only accommodate nine characters. The brothers wanted to use "Pizza" in the name, which left room for just three extra letters. A family member of theirs suggested that the building looked like a hut—and so Pizza Hut was born. In the 1980s, the first Pizza Hut building was moved to the Wichita State University campus. It is still used as a meeting place (not to mention a reminder of how far a good idea can go).

Subway
Jewett Street • Bridgeport, Connecticut

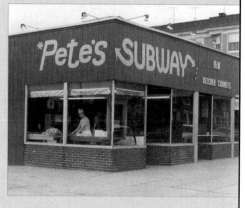

Subway Restaurants was founded in the summer of 1965 in Bridgeport, Connecticut. It was the brainchild of 17-year-old Fred DeLuca and his family friend Dr. Peter Buck, with its purpose being to earn money for Fred's college tuition. With a $1,000 loan from Dr. Buck, Fred opened up the sub shop, then called "Pete's Super Submarines."

In the early days, Fred would personally purchase and deliver all of the produce used by the restaurants from the famous Hunts Point Market in the Bronx. He would remove the passenger and rear seat of his 1965 VW Beetle (his first brand new car) and load it up with crates of fresh vegetables and drive back to Connecticut. When the business started to expand with more locations, he traded in the Beetle for a VW van.

Today, there are more than 20,000 locations in 71 countries, making it the second largest fast food franchise in the world. (NOTE—in 1968 the fifth sandwich shop was opened, and marked the first time the name Subway was used. The oldest continuously operating location is at 1 River Street in Milford, Connecticut.)

Taco Bell
7112 Firestone Boulevard
Downey, California

In 1962, Glen Bell opened the first Taco Bell restaurant here in Downey, California (in 1964 the first Taco Bell franchise was sold). Interestingly, the "Bell" in the name "Taco Bell" is the last name of the founder. Glen Bell would go on to expand Taco Bell worldwide, then sell it for $130 million. The actual building still exists, but has been moved to Taco Bell corporate headquarters in Irvine, California.

Wendy's
257 East Broad Street • Columbus, Ohio • 614-464-4656

On November 15, 1969, the late, great Dave Thomas opened the very first Wendy's restaurant (named for his daughter) and it still stands today. The building was at one time a car dealership. Today, in addition to being a restaurant, it also serves as a living history museum for the popular chain. Its interior features comforting touches like carpeted floors, Tiffany-style lamps, and plenty of foliage. The signature square burgers are made-to-order, and chicken sandwiches are available grilled or fried. Thick fries, meaty chili, and stuffed baked potatoes round out a menu that includes a cool, ultra-thick chocolate Frosty.

Wienerschnitzel
900 West Pacific Coast Highway • Wilmington, California
310-513-8744

In 1961, fast food entrepreneur John Galardi was thinking about how to stand out in the fast food business, which was still in its infancy. Then, the 23-year-old had a brainstorm: Hot dogs! Soon after, the first Der Wienerschnitzel opened here in Wilmington, California. In 1962, a second restaurant was built that featured Der Wienerschnitzel's signature red A-frame roof. The breakthrough design pioneered the drive-thru concept in Southern California. Since then, the company has changed its name to simply "Wienerschnitzel" (it also has over 300 stores in 10 states and Guam). A plaque on the restaurant at this location details its history. Today, Wienerschnitzel is the world's largest hot dog chain, selling more than 75 million hot dogs per year.

Retail

J.C. Penney
722 J.C. Penney Drive • Kemmerer, Wyoming

J.C. Penney (1875–1970) got started in retail when he bought a butcher shop in Longmont, Colorado. In 1898, he went to work for Thomas M. Callahan and William Guy Johnson of Fort Collins, Colorado, who ran a small chain of stores known as "Golden Rule Stores." Penney was assigned to the company's store in Evanston. He was such a huge success that the owners offered him a shot to become a partner in a new Golden Rule store to be opened in Kemmerer. In the early part of 1902, 27-year-old Penney arrived by train here to start the new business. The spread-out mining town had approximately 1,000 residents, a company store that operated on credit and 21 saloons where a good deal of spare cash was spent. The store opened on April 14, 1902, and the first day's receipts totaled an impressive $466.59. The store was open seven days a week, opening on Sundays at 9:00 A.M.

Two breakthrough retail ideas—cash only and do unto others as you would have them do unto you—were the basis for James Cash Penney's new business venture. He named the store the Golden Rule and by 1912, there were 34 Golden Rule stores with sales exceeding $2 million. In 1913, the chain incorporated under the laws of the state of Utah as the J.C. Penney Company, Inc., and the Golden Rule Store name was phased out. By 1928, the J.C. Penney Company had 1,023 stores across the country.

J.C. Penney Museum
312 North Davis Street • Hamilton, Missouri • 816-583-2168

The J.C. Penney birthplace and museum contains items belonging to J.C. Penney and explains his contributions to American retailing. The home was moved to its original farm site and renovated to its 1875–1900 appearance. It's open year round; admission is free to the public.

Target
1515 West County Road B • Roseville, Minnesota • 651-631-0330

On May 1, 1962, the first Target store opened (as part of The Dayton Company) in Roseville, Minnesota, a suburb of St. Paul. It was the first retail store to offer well-known national brands at discounted prices. Today, more than 1,107 Target stores operate in 47 states, including Target Greatland stores and Super Target stores.

Wal-Mart
105 North Main Street • Bentonville, Arkansas • 501-273-1329

This free museum is on the site of Sam Walton's original 5 & 10 cent store in Bentonville, Arkansas (Bentonville is now Wal-Mart world headquarters). The Wal-Mart visitors center traces the origin and growth of Wal-Mart. The center was created as an educational and informative facility for those interested in this American retailing success story.

CHAPTER THREE

HISTORY AND TRAGEDY

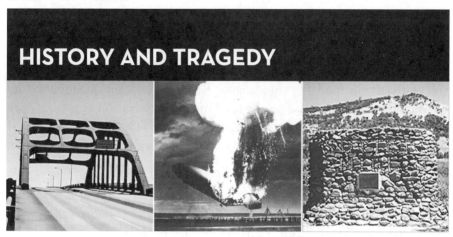

American Flag
Betsy Ross House • 239 Arch Street
Philadelphia, Pennsylvania • 215-686-1252

History says that Betsy Ross made the first American flag after a visit in June 1776 by George Washington, Robert Morris, and her husband's uncle, George Ross. Supposedly, she demonstrated how to cut a 5-pointed star with a single clip of the scissors, if the fabric was folded correctly. However, this story was not told until 1870 by Betsy's grandson, and many scholars believe that while Betsy probably didn't make the first flag, she was indeed a professional flagmaker. Her house, now a museum, remains one of Philadelphia's most visited landmarks.

Birth of the National Park Service
Yosemite National Park • Near Bridal Veil Falls parking area

In the spring of 1903, then-President Theodore Roosevelt embarked on a nine-week cross-country road trip that would bring him to California for the very first time. Part of the reason for his journey was to meet naturalist John Muir and go backcountry camping at Yosemite for three nights with the famed writer and nature lover. Roosevelt wanted no staff or security with him, choosing only to bring along two other men, one to tend to the horses and one to fix the food. For three nights, Roosevelt and Muir communed under the stars. They talked about the need for the preservation of natural open spaces, and the idea inspired what we now know as the National Park Service. A marker can be found near Bridal Veil Falls in the park, marking the spot where the men spent their final night together.

The Boston Massacre
Devonshire and State Street • Boston, Massachusetts

In front of the Old State House, a circle of cobblestones commemorates the Boston Massacre. It was here on March 5, 1770, that a minor dispute between a wigmaker's young apprentice and a British sentry turned into a riot. The relief soldiers that came to the aid of the British were met by an angry crowd of colonists who hurled snowballs, rocks, clubs, and insults. The soldiers fired into the crowd and killed five colonists. Samuel Adams and other patriots called the event a "massacre," thus helping to sow the seeds of resentment towards the British that would culminate in the American Revolution.

Burr, Aaron/Alexander Hamilton
Southern end of Hamilton Park • Boulevard East (atop the Palisades, directly across from Manhattan) • Weehawken, New Jersey

At dawn on the morning of July 11, 1804, political antagonists and personal enemies Alexander Hamilton and Aaron Burr met in this small park on the heights of Weehawken, New Jersey to settle their longstanding differences with a duel. The participants fired their pistols in close succession. Burr's shot met its target immediately, fatally wounding Hamilton and leading to his death the following day. Burr escaped unharmed.

This tragic incident reflected the depth of animosity aroused by the first emergence of the nation's political party system. Both of these men were active leaders in New York. Burr was a Republican, and Hamilton was leader of the opposing Federalist party. They had become political and personal enemies over a variety of run-ins, but it was the 1804 New York Gubernatorial campaign that forced the duel. Hamilton had opposed Burr's closely fought bid for the post and it was on the heels of this narrow defeat that Burr challenged Hamilton to a duel. The actual rock where Hamilton lay after being shot is marked by a plaque at the site.

Chappaquiddick
Dike Bridge • Chappaquiddick Island • Martha's Vineyard, Massachusetts

Shortly before midnight on July 18, 1969, Ted Kennedy was involved in a horrible car accident. He had been driving back from a party on Chappaquiddick, Massachusetts, and had driven off the edge of this bridge. Luckily, he was not severely injured; however, Mary Jo Kopechne, a woman who was in his car, was killed. She was a 29-year-old blond secretary in Washington, D.C., who worked for Senator Robert F. Kennedy and Senator George Smathers. Ted Kennedy's wife was home with their children and had not attended the party.

The accident was not reported until eight hours after the car had sunk to the bottom of the river. On the following Monday, Kennedy was charged for leaving the scene of the accident. Kennedy, who was 37 at the time, said that he was simply in shock, and that was why he had not called the

police. Despite his endless denials, this one incident would continue to haunt Kennedy for the remainder of his political career.

Civil Rights

Bates, Daisy
1207 West 28th Street • Little Rock, Arkansas

The Daisy Bates House, a National Historic Landmark, was the command post for the Central High School desegregation crisis in Little Rock, Arkansas. Mrs. Daisy Lee Gaston Bates and her husband Lucius Christopher (L.C.) Bates, lived here during the crisis in 1957–1958. The house served as a haven for the nine African American students who desegregated the school, and as a place where they could plan the best way to achieve their goals.

The Bates' home became the official pick-up and drop-off site for the Little Rock Nine's trips to and from Central High School each school day, and consequently, a gathering spot for the Nine and members of the press. As such, the house became a frequent target of violence and damage at the hands of segregation's supporters. It is private property and is not open to the public.

Brown, John
1900 4th Corso • Nebraska City, Nebraska
402-873-3115

Abolitionist John Brown hid runaway slaves in the cellar of an old log cabin here on 19th Street in the 1850s. Known as John Brown's Cave, the cellar had a tunnel that led to Table Creek. Brown was later executed for leading the raid on a government armory in Harper's Ferry, West Virginia on October 16, 1859. Today it's part of the Mayhew Cabin & Historical Village

Non-Profit Foundation, which is dedicated to educating the nation's youth in regard to the Underground Railroad. It's open all year for tourists, schools, etc.

Central High School
2125 Daisy L. Gatson Bates Drive • Little Rock, Arkansas • 501-374-1957

In 1957, nine students enrolled here at Central High School. However, when they showed up for classes, they found that the Arkansas National Guard had been sent to prevent them from attending the school. The reason they were singled out was because they were black students who wanted to attend an all-white school. On that morning of September 23, 1957, these nine African American high school students faced an angry mob of over 1,000 whites in front of the school protesting integration. As the students were escorted inside by the Little Rock police, violence escalated and they were removed from the school.

The next day, President Dwight D. Eisenhower ordered 1,200 members of the U.S. Army's 101st Airborne Division from Fort Campbell to escort the nine students into the school. This event, watched by the nation and world, was the site of the first important test for the implementation of the U.S. Supreme Court's historic Brown v. Board of Education of Topeka decision of 1954. Today, this National Historic Site is open to the public as an important museum and Civil Rights landmark.

Coffin, Levi
113 US 27 North • Fountain City, Indiana • 317-847-2432

This was the home of Levi and Catharine Coffin, North Carolina Quakers who opposed slavery. During the 20 years they lived here, the Coffins helped more than two thousand slaves reach safety. Levi Coffin was called the

"President of the Underground Railroad," and to the thousands of escaped slaves, this eight-room Federal style brick home was a safe haven on their journey to Canada. The home is open for tours.

Craft, Juanita
Wheatley Place Historic District • 2618 Warren Avenue • Dallas, Texas

Juanita Craft lived in this house for 50 years, and both Lyndon Johnson and Martin Luther King, Jr., visited her here to discuss the future of the civil rights movement. Craft played a crucial role in integrating two universities and the 1954 Texas State Fair, as well as Dallas theaters, restaurants, and lunch counters.

Craft joined demonstrations against the segregated University of Texas Law School and North Texas State University, each resulting in successful lawsuits in 1950 and 1955. Afterwards, she opened a dropout preparation program in Dallas. Craft also served as a delegate to the White House Conference on Children and Youth, and as a member of the Governor's Human Relations Committee. In 1975, at the age of 73, she was elected to the Dallas City Council, where she spent the next two years working to improve the status of Hispanic and Native Americans. The house is open to the public Monday to Friday, 9:00 A.M. to 5:30 P.M.

Edmund Pettus Bridge
Highway 80 at the intersection of Broad Street and Water Avenue
Selma, Alabama

DIRECTIONS: To get there, take I-65 South toward Mobile and take exit 167 to US 80 West, toward Selma. Follow US 80 West for a little more than 40 miles.

On March 7, 1965, 600 civil rights marchers were attacked by state troopers on the Edmund Pettus Bridge, on what became known as "Bloody Sunday." Two weeks later, there was another march. But by that time, the movement had grown.

The 600 people had swelled to more than 3,000 who began the now-famous four-day march to Montgomery under the leadership of the Reverend Martin Luther King and other black leaders, and under the protection of Army troops. By the time the group reached Montgomery, the marchers numbered more than 25,000. As they progressed, so did the voting rights bill. Powered by public opinion that had been galvanized by "Bloody Sunday," the bill was signed into law on August 6, 1965.

Greyhound Bus Station
210 South Court Street
Montgomery, Alabama

This bus station was the site of a mob riot that greeted Freedom Riders hoping to end discrimination in interstate transportation. It is now a historic landmark.

Liuzzo, Viola
A.M.E. Zion Church • U.S. Highway 80 between Lowndesboro and White Hall, near Wright Chapel • Selma, Alabama

The marker placed on this spot identifies where Mrs. Liuozzo, a Detroit housewife, was shot and killed by four Klansmen when she was driving back to Selma after the successful Selma-to-Montgomery March. Liuzzo, a white woman, was driving with a black man named Leroy Moton. Indicative of how unfair the times were, three of the members of the Ku Klux Klan were acquitted of murder by an Alabama jury, despite the testimony of the fourth man in the car.

However, President Lyndon Johnson instructed his officials to arrange for the men to be charged under an 1870 federal law of conspiring to deprive Viola Liuzzo of her civil rights. And so the men—Collie Wilkins, William Eaton, and Eugene Thomas—were found guilty and sentenced to 10 years in prison.

Malcolm X Home
3448 Pinkney Street • Omaha, Nebraska

On May 19, 1925, Malcolm X (born Malcolm Little) was born in a now-demolished house on this site. As a civil rights leader, he advocated racial separatism over integration and the legitimacy of violence in self-defense. He also championed the beauty and worth of blackness and black Americans' African past. On February 14, 1965, unidentified attackers firebombed Malcolm X's New York house while he and his family were asleep inside. One week later, on February 21, Malcolm X was assassinated by Black Muslim extremists at a rally in New York City's Audubon Ballroom. The home was torn down prior to 1970.

Coconut Grove
200 Stuart Street • Boston, Massachusetts

One of the deadliest fires in the nation's history occurred here in the Bay Village area of Boston. The blaze at the Coconut Grove, a nightclub located where the 57 Restaurant & Bar now stands on Stuart Street, killed 492 people on the night of November 28, 1942. The club was packed with approximately 1,000 occupants, many of whom were people preparing to go overseas on military duty. A lighted match used by an employee who was changing a light bulb has been considered the possible cause for this tragic fire.

Authorities estimated that possibly 300 of those killed could have been saved had the two revolving doors at the main entrance been built to swing outward. The Coconut Grove fire prompted major efforts in the field of fire prevention and control for nightclubs and other related places of public assembly.

The Collinwood School Fire
410 East 152nd Street (at Lucknow Avenue)
Cleveland, Ohio

There's a memorial marker here for the 172 children and two teachers who died in America's deadliest school accident. The Collinwood School fire occurred on March 4, 1908 at the Lakeview Elementary school. The fire began shortly after 9:00 A.M. when an overheated steam pipe came in contact with wooden joists. Tragically, just 194 of 366 students escaped.

Examination of the building along with eyewitness accounts proved that the doors opened outward and that the children's failure to escape resulted from their own panic. The incredibly sad Collinwood School fire caused numerous school inspections across the country along with stricter laws regarding escape plans and routes.

Custer, General George
Little Bighorn • Exit 510 off I-90 • Crow Agency, Montana • 406-638-2621

Little Bighorn Battlefield National Monument near Crow Agency, Montana, commemorates one of America's most significant and famous battles, the Battle of the Little Bighorn. On June 25 and 26, 1876, 400 years of struggle between Euro-Americans and Native Americans culminated on this ground. Like a handful of battles in American history, the defeat of 12 companies of Seventh Cavalry by Lakota (Sioux), Cheyenne, and Arapaho warriors rose beyond its military significance to the level of myth. Thousands of books, magazine articles, performances in film and theater, paintings, and other artistic expressions have memorialized "Custer's Last Stand."

In 1879, the Little Bighorn Battlefield was designated a national cemetery administered by the War Department. In 1881, a memorial was erected on Last Stand Hill, over the mass grave of the Seventh Cavalry soldiers, U.S. Indian Scouts, and other personnel killed in battle.

Declaration of Independence
143 South Third Street • Philadelphia, Pennsylvania • 215-597-8974

National Historical Park, located in downtown (called "Center City"), Philadelphia, is often referred to as the birthplace of our nation. Here, visitors can see the Liberty Bell, an international symbol of freedom, and Independence Hall, a World Heritage Site where both the Declaration of Independence and the U.S. Constitution were created. A section of the park where Benjamin Franklin's home once stood is dedicated to Franklin's life and accomplishments. Spanning approximately 45 acres, the park has about 20 buildings open to the public.

Dinosaur Discovery
Hadrosaurus Park • Maple Avenue • Haddonfield, New Jersey

DIRECTIONS: Haddonfield is located in Camden County, in southern New Jersey, about 10 miles east across the Delaware River from Philadelphia, Pennsylvania. Hadrosaurus Park is located at the end of Maple Avenue off Grove Street in Haddonfield.

In the summer of 1858, Victorian gentleman and fossil hobbyist William Parker Foulke was vacationing here in Haddonfield when he heard that, 20 years earlier, workers had found huge animal bones in a local pit. Foulke spent the next few months directing a crew of hired diggers, and eventually he found the bones of a creature larger than an elephant with the structural features of both a lizard and a bird.

Yes, Foulke had discovered the first nearly-complete skeleton of a dinosaur—an event that would rock the scientific world and forever change our view of natural history. Today, the historic site is marked with a modest commemorative stone and a tiny landscaped park.

Earhart, Amelia
The Harbour Grace Airstrip • Newfoundland, Canada

On May 20, 1932, five years to the day after Charles Lindbergh set off on his legendary flight across the Atlantic, Amelia Earhart took off from the Harbor Grace Airstrip in Newfoundland at 12 minutes after 7:00 P.M. Despite some major technical snafus with her aircraft, she landed at Springfield, six miles from Londonderry, Ireland, on May 21, at 2:30 P.M., becoming the first woman to cross the Atlantic alone. For this epic flight, she was awarded the National Geographic Society Medal by President Herbert Hoover on June 21, 1932.

The Harbour Grace Airstrip was originally built in 1927 to be used for the

journey of William Brock and Edward Schlee, who were attempting an around-the-world flight. From 1927–1936, more than 20 flights, some of them piloted by such famous aviators as Amelia Earhart and Captain Eddie Rickenbacker, took off from Harbour Grace to fly the Atlantic. In 1935, Earhart became the first woman to fly the Pacific Ocean, crossing from Hawaii to California, and later the same year she set a speed record by flying non-stop from Mexico City to New York City in 14 hours, 19 minutes.

But on June 1, 1937, she began a flight around the world, traveling eastward from the Miami Municipal Airport, Florida. Tragically, her plane disappeared on July 2 near Howland Island in the middle of the Pacific Ocean. An extensive search by planes and ships failed to uncover any trace of Earhart, her navigator Fred Noonan, or her Lockheed 10E Electra plane, and her fate remains a mystery.

NOTE: Another interesting Earhart-related landmark is the Amelia Earhart Birthplace Museum: 223 North Terrace Street, Atchison, Kansas. 913-367-4217.

Edison, Thomas

Here are some historic sites related to the great inventor:

Birthplace
9 Edison Drive • Milan, Ohio • 419-499-2135

Thomas Alva Edison, inventor of the phonograph, the incandescent light bulb, and many other devices, was born in Milan, Ohio, in 1847. Here at the Edison Birthplace Museum, you'll find a collection of rare treasures including examples of many of Edison's early inventions, documents, and family mementos. After Edison's death, the opening of his birthplace to the public as a memorial and museum became the private project of his wife, Mina Miller Edison, and their daughter, Mrs. John Eyre Sloane. It opened on the centennial of the inventor's birth in 1947. Today, the Edison Birthplace Association, Inc. maintains this National Historic Site.

Edison Memorial Tower
37 Christie Street • Menlo Park • Edison, New Jersey

The Edison Memorial Tower looms 131 feet and four inches above Menlo Park, New Jersey, and it marks the spot where Thomas Alva Edison conceived the first practical incandescent light bulb. But that wasn't all that happened here. For 10 years, Edison toiled over what would eventually total approximately 400 patented ideas before he moved his "Invention Factory" to West Orange, New Jersey. The Tower, which was erected in 1937, is topped by the world's largest working light bulb. It weighs three tons and is comprised of 153 single pieces of two-inch-thick, amber-tinted Pyrex glass.

Edison National Historic Site
Intersection of Main Street and Lakeside Avenue
West Orange, New Jersey • 201-736-5050

Though he invented the lightbulb some 20 miles away in Menlo Park, this is also an important spot in the course of Thomas Alva Edison's inventive life. For more than 40 years, the laboratory created by Thomas Alva Edison in West Orange, New Jersey, had enormous impact on the lives of millions of people worldwide. Out of the West Orange laboratories came the motion picture camera, vastly improved phonographs, sound recordings, silent and sound movies, and the nickel-iron alkaline electric storage battery.

Central Park
Fourth Street and Park Avenue • Louisville, Kentucky

During the Southern Exposition held here in 1883–1887, the public saw an

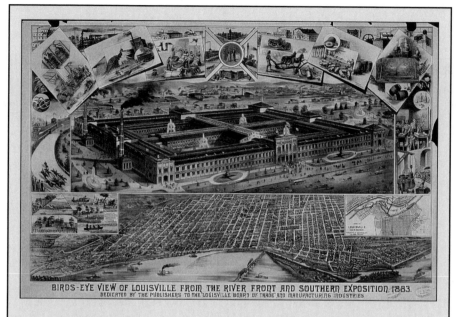

BIRDS-EYE VIEW OF LOUISVILLE FROM THE RIVER FRONT AND SOUTHERN EXPOSITION. 1883.
DEDICATED BY THE PUBLISHERS TO THE LOUISVILLE BOARD OF TRADE AND MANUFACTURING INDUSTRIES

electric light for the very first time, thanks to Thomas Edison, who introduced his incandescent light bulb to huge crowds. The city built an enormous exposition building, thought to be the largest wooden structure in the world at the time: 13 acres under one roof. The building and grounds (Central Park was the midway) were illuminated by over 4,800 incandescent electric lights, the largest concentration anywhere at that time, even more than in New York City. (With Edison's influence, Louisville was one of the earliest electrically lit neighborhoods in the nation.)

Edison House

729-31 East Washington Street • Louisville, Kentucky • 502-585-5247

At age 19, in 1866, Thomas Edison came here to Louisville to work as a telegraph key operator. With his adroit skill at receiving telegraph messages, Thomas Edison easily found a job with the Western Union located on Second and West Main Street—about eight blocks from

the Edison House. There are many artifacts available for viewing at this home, including both cylinder and disc phonographs and Edison Business Phonographs. An Edison Kinetoscope, the first home motion picture projector, is also on display in the museum.

Winter Home
2350 McGregor Boulevard • Fort Myers, Florida • 239-334-7419

This was the winter home of Thomas A. Edison, beautifully situated along the Caloosahatchee River. Thomas Edison first visited Florida in 1885, which is when he purchased this property and built his vacation home. Finished in 1886 and dubbed "Seminole Lodge" by the Edisons, the home was a winter retreat and workplace for the prolific inventor until he died in 1931. (Edison's good friend Henry Ford purchased the neighboring property in 1915.)

The furnishings at Seminole Lodge are those of the Edisons, including brass "electroliers," electric chandeliers manufactured in Edison's own workshop. The house is surrounded by a mature tropical garden that was originally planted as an experimental garden but grew to include thousands of varieties of plants from all over the world. The site also includes Edison's Laboratory, the Edison Museum and the first swimming pool built in Florida. On weekdays, visitors are offered narrated river cruises aboard a replica of Edison's 1903 electric motor launch, The Reliance.

The Edmund Fitzgerald
Whitefish Point, Michigan • 877-SHIPWRECK

When she was first launched, the *Edmund Fitzgerald* was the largest carrier on the Great Lakes, and remained so until 1971. On November 9, 1975, she departed from Superior, Wisconsin (Ford Rouge Dock) with approximately 26,000 tons of ore bound for Detroit. However, the Edmund Fitzgerald was lost with her entire crew of 29 men on Lake Superior on November 10, 1975, 17 miles north-northwest of Whitefish Point, Michigan. Whitefish Point is the site of the Whitefish Point Light Station and the Great Lakes Shipwreck Museum. The tragic loss was behind the well-known Gordon Lightfoot song, "The Wreck of the *Edmund Fitzgerald*."

Facebook
Room H33 • Kirkland House • 95 Dunster Street • Harvard University
Cambridge, Massachusetts

Room H33 is the actual dorm room where, in 2004, the then-19-year-old Mark Zuckerberg and his college roommates/fellow students Eduardo Saverin, Dustin Moskovitz, and Chris Hughes built the Facebook website that would launch social networking and eventually become one of the most valuable and influential companies in the world. It started in 2003 with Facemash, a website developed by Zuckerberg. He wrote the software for Facemash when he was in his second year of college. The website was set up as a type of "hot or not" game for Harvard students by allowing visitors to compare two students' pictures side by side and decide who was more attractive. According to *The Harvard Crimson*, Facemash used photos "compiled from the online facebooks of nine sorority/fraternity houses." Facemash attracted 450 visitors and 22,000 photo views in its first four hours online.

The site was quickly forwarded to several campus group list servers, but was shut down a few days later by the Harvard administration. Zuckerberg faced expulsion and was charged by the administration with breach of security, violating copyrights, and violating individuals' privacy. Ultimately, the charges were dropped. Zuckerberg expanded on this initial project that semester by creating a social study tool ahead of an Art History final exam. He uploaded art images to a website, each of which was featured with a corresponding comments section, then shared the site with his classmates, and people started sharing notes. That collaborative exercise became the nexus to what we today know as Facebook.

Fires

Beverly Hills Supper Club Fire
Located along US 27 south, just south of Moock Road, on the hillside along US 27. (Office buildings and parking lots are in front of the club's old driveway.) • Southgate, Kentucky

On the night of May 28, 1977, a devastating fire swept through the Beverly Hills Supper Club in Southgate, killing 165 people. The club had been built in 1937 atop a hill in Northern Kentucky, just across the Ohio River from Cincinnati, and over the years it hosted some of entertainment's biggest stars. But on this Memorial Day weekend in 1977, with 2,500 people inside, things took a tragic turn.

The first sign that anything was amiss may have come as early as 8:15 P.M., when some complained of unusual heat in one of the reception rooms. It wasn't until 8:50 P.M. that the first smell of smoke appeared and the raging fire was discovered in the reception room. Singer John Davidson was the main act that evening and was just waiting for the comedy act before him in the Cabaret Room to finish up, when Walter Bailey, a young busboy, grabbed the mic and announced there was a "small fire."

At 9:02 P.M., the ferocity of the fire swept down toward the Crystal Room. The fire was so strong at this point that smoke was already pouring out through the ducts, causing intense panic; 1,200 people began scrambling out through three small exits. In the darkness, many encountered locked doors. The official investigations into what caused the fire at the Beverly Hills Supper Club were inconclusive, but the factor most often cited is aluminum wiring. Today, the site is still vacant.

The Great Chicago Fire
558 DeKoven Street (at Jefferson Street—formerly 137 DeKoven Street) • Chicago, Illinois

According to legend, the Great Chicago Fire was started by a cow that belonged to an Irishwoman named Catherine O'Leary. She ran a neighborhood milk business from the barn behind her home, and after carelessly leaving a kerosene lantern in the barn following her evening milking, a cow kicked it over and ignited the hay on the floor. Of course, no proof of this story has ever been offered, but the legend took hold in Chicago and was told around the world.

Regardless of how the fire started though, on Sunday evening, October 8, 1871, Chicago became a city in flames. The blaze burned homes and shops and left 300 people dead and 500,000 people homeless. Firefighters brought the fire under control the next day, but only with the help of a rainstorm. It had been unusually warm and dry that year, and the city's wood buildings burned like matches until finally the rain came down. Today, the site of the fire's origin is ironically occupied by the Chicago Fire Department's Training Academy, and marked with a historic plaque.

Hinckley Fire Museum
106 Old Highway 61 • Hinckley, Minnesota • 320-384-7338

With the coming of the railroad industry, the lumber industry boomed, and for 20 years Hinckley was a growing, prosperous town with a population of 1,500. But on September 1, 1894, everything changed. In just four hours, a raging fire ended up destroying six towns, and over 400 square miles. Located in a restored railroad depot, this museum commemorates the forest fire that destroyed the town in 1894. Photographs, newspaper accounts, and items from the fire are displayed.

The Iroquois Theater Fire
24 West Randolph Street • Chicago, Illinois

On December 30, 1903, a fire broke out in this popular theater during a show by famed comedian Eddie Foy. The tragic fire, believed to have been started by faulty wiring, killed 572 people—another 30 died from injuries. The passageway behind the theater is still referred to as "Death Alley" after the hundreds of bodies placed there during the recovery. It remains the most deadly fire in American theater history. Today the Ford Theater is located here (and the alley still exists behind the building).

The Peshtigo Fire Museum
400 Oconto Avenue • Peshtigo, Wisconsin • 715-582-3244

The Peshtigo fire happened October 8, 1871—the same day as the Great Chicago Fire. Though the Peshtigo fire had many more casualties than the Chicago fire (800 people perished in Peshtigo), and also did much more damage to the town, it's barely a footnote to this nation's history. The fire started easily because it had been a very dry summer with very little rain. Several small fires sprang up that, when combined, formed a monstrous fire that was out of control before anybody could stop its destruction. The Peshtigo Fire Museum is in the first church that was built after the fire.

The Station Nightclub Fire
2-11 Cowesett Avenue • West Warwick, Rhode Island

The Station Nightclub fire on February 20, 2003, was the fourth-deadliest nightclub fire in U.S. history, killing 100 people and injuring nearly 200.

Ninety-six perished on the night of the fire, and four died later from their injuries at local hospitals. It was the deadliest fire in the United States since the 1977 Southgate, Kentucky Beverly Hills Supper Club fire that claimed 165 lives.

The Station was a nightclub in West Warwick, Kent County, Rhode Island. The fire started when pyrotechnics set off by Great White, the rock band playing that night, lit flammable soundproofing foam behind the stage. The flames were first thought to be part of the act; only as the fire reached the ceiling and smoke began to billow did people realize it was uncontrolled. The ensuing stampede in the inferno led to the numerous deaths among the patrons, who numbered somewhat more than 300, the official capacity.

Today, the site at 2–11 Cowesett Avenue has been stripped of the club's debris. The foundation has been filled and the fence surrounding the site has been taken down. A ring of wooden crosses now circle what was the club's perimeter. Balloons, pictures, poems, and candles sit at the bases of the crosses.

Sunshine Mine Fire
Four miles east of Kellogg at Big Creek (Exit 54) • Near Kellogg, Idaho

The 1972 Sunshine Mine fire was the worst mining disaster in recent history, killing 91 miners. This monument near the site, a 12-foot-tall sculpture of a miner with his drill raised, is surrounded by plaques listing the names of the dead. A quirky local landmark nearby is the Miner's Hat. This building, constructed in the shape of a miner's hat, was at one time a tavern. Today, it is the Miner's Hat Realty.

Triangle Shirtwaist Fire
23–29 Washington Place
New York City, New York

The is the site of the worst factory fire in the history of New York City. It occurred on March 25, 1911, in the Asch building at the northwest corner of Washington and

Greene Streets, where the Triangle Shirtwaist Company occupied the top three of 10 floors. Five hundred women were employed there, mostly Jewish immigrants between the ages of 13 and 23. To keep the women at their sewing machines, the proprietors had locked the doors leading to the exits.

The fire began shortly after 4:30 P.M. in the cutting room on the eighth floor, and fed by thousands of pounds of fabric it spread rapidly. Panicked workers rushed to the stairs, the freight elevator, and the fire escape. Most on the eighth and tenth floors escaped; dozens on the ninth floor died, unable to force open the locked door to the exit. The rear fire escape collapsed, killing many and eliminating an escape route for others still trapped. Some tried to slide down elevator cables but lost their grip; many more, their dresses on fire, jumped to their death from open windows.

Pump Engine Company 20 and Ladder Company 20 arrived quickly, but were hindered by the bodies of victims who had jumped. The ladders of the fire department extended only to the sixth floor, and life nets broke when workers jumped in groups of three and four. Additional companies were summoned by four more alarms transmitted in rapid succession. The Triangle Shirtwaist Factory Building, a National Historic Landmark, is now used as classrooms and offices by New York University and is not open to the public.

Winecoff Hotel Fire
Corner of Peachtree and Ellis Streets • Atlanta, Georgia

The Winecoff Hotel fire, a fire that killed 119 of the 280 people who were staying in the hotel at the time, is still listed as the deadliest hotel fire in North America. The fire occurred at approximately 3:00 A.M. on December 7, 1946.

At 15 stories, the Winecoff was Atlanta's tallest hotel. It was advertised as a "fireproof" hotel, and was constructed of brick with a central spiral staircase and an elevator that was under the control of an operator. The remains of the Winecoff Hotel are located on the corner of Peachtree Street and Ellis Street in the heart of downtown Atlanta. A marker stands as a reminder of the devastating fire.

Freedom Summer Memorial
Miami University's western campus, next to Kumler Chapel • Miami, Ohio

This outdoor amphitheater was built in 1999 to memorialize three men who, tragically, were killed after volunteering here to help African Americans register to vote during the "Freedom Summer" of 1964. That summer, more than 800 volunteers, most of them college students, gathered at the Western College for Women (now the western campus of Miami University) to prepare for African American voter registration in the South. Three of the volunteers—James Chaney of Mississippi and Andrew Goodman and Michael Schwerner of New York—disappeared on June 21, 1964 in rural Mississippi just days after leaving here. Their bodies were discovered 44 days later, buried in a Mississippi dam. Ku Klux Klan members were later convicted on federal conspiracy charges.

Gay Rights Movement
The Stonewall Bar and Club • 53 Christopher Street
New York, New York

This is generally considered to be the birthplace of the gay liberation movement because of what happened the night of June 27, 1969. A police inspector and seven officers from the Public Morals Section of the First Division of the New York City Police Department arrived after midnight to look for violations of the alcohol control laws. After checking identifications, they tossed the patrons out while others lingered outside to watch. They were soon joined by passers-by.

The arrival of the police wagons altered the atmosphere of the crowd from passivity to defiance. The first vehicle left without incident, apart from shouts from the crowd. The next individual to emerge from the bar was a woman in male clothing who put up a struggle, which caused the bystanders to take action. The crowd erupted and began throwing cobblestones and bottles. Some officers took refuge in the bar while others turned a fire hose on the crowd. Police reinforcements arrived and soon the streets were cleared. The news spread throughout the day, and the following two nights saw further violent confrontations between the police and the gay community. These incidents became known in history as The Stonewall Rebellion, and it sparked a new, highly visible, mass phase of political organization for gay rights.

Golden Spike National Historic Site
32 miles west of Brigham City on State Routes 13 and 83
Promontory Point, Utah • 435-471-2209

Completion of the world's first transcontinental railroad was celebrated here where the Central Pacific and Union Pacific Railroads met on May 10, 1869. Golden Spike was designated as a national historic site in nonfederal ownership on April 2, 1957, and authorized for federal ownership and administration by an act of Congress on July 30, 1965.

The Gold Rush
Marshall Gold Discovery State Historic Park • 310 Back Street
Coloma, California • 530-622-3470

James W. Marshall discovered gold in 1848 on the South Fork of the American River in the valley the Nisenan Indians knew as "Cullumah." This event led to the greatest mass movement of people in the Western Hemisphere and was the spark that ignited the spectacular growth of the American west during the ensuing decades.

The gold discovery site, located in the still visible tailrace of Sutter's sawmill in present day Coloma, California, is one of the most significant historic sites in the nation. The park has a museum, with exhibits that tell the story of the Gold Rush, a replica of the sawmill, and a number of historic buildings. Visitors also have the opportunity to try panning for gold in the American River or enjoy a picnic under the trees. The monument and statue placed above Marshall's gravesite (who died in 1885) is California's first historic landmark.

Harding, Warren
Palace Hotel • 2 New Montgomery Street • San Francisco, California
415-512-1111

Warren G. Harding, the 29th President of the United States, died at the Palace Hotel in San Francisco on August 23, 1923 under circumstances that began as mysterious and were then varnished by rumor in the aftermath of scandals and salacious revelations that surfaced following the president's demise. The ailing president arrived in San Francisco and was taken to the Palace Hotel where he died either of anxiety, a stroke, a heart attack, food poisoning, or from deliberate poisoning by First Lady Florence, fed up with her husband's philandering.

The legend continues that Mrs. Harding's psychic had, on the eve of his nomination, predicted the president would die in office. The fact that Mrs. Harding refused to allow an autopsy of the president contributed to suspicion of her guilt; the official cause of President Harding's death is listed as a stroke. This exquisite hotel makes no special recognition of Harding's death.

The *Hindenburg* Crash
Naval Air Engineering Station • Highway 547 • Lakehurst, New Jersey
732-323-2620

At 7:25 P.M. on May 6, 1937, the German airship *Hindenburg* was coming in for a landing at the naval air station at Lakehurst, after its flight across the Atlantic from Germany. On board were 61 crew and 36 passengers. Hundreds of people were at this site to watch the beautiful ship land on this early summer evening. A radio announcer, Herb Morrison from WLS Chicago, was de-

scribing how gorgeous the ship looked against the night sky. But we all know what happened as it approached the mooring post. Flames appeared near the stern. Within just a few seconds, the craft exploded in a fireball. Falling tail first, it crashed a mere 32 seconds after the flame was first spotted.

Morrison's audio document of the tragedy ("It's burst into flames. . . . Get out of the way, please, oh my, this is terrible, oh my, get out of the way,

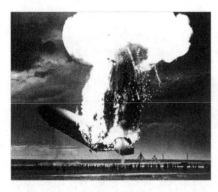

please . . . Oh, the humanity and all the passengers!") has since become one of history's most famous recordings. Thirty-six people died in the crash, and while several theories abound as to what happened that night to the Hindenburg, many experts believe that an electrical storm that night sparked the explosion when it came in contact with the highly flammable hydrogen gas. On May 6 of each year, at 7:25 P.M., a memorial service for those who lost their lives in the *Hindenburg* and all other airship accidents is held on the site.

Jones, Casey

Casey Jones State Park • 10901 Vaughn Road #1 • Vaughn, Mississippi
662-673-9864

On the early morning of April 30, 1900, rushing down the tracks to make up lost time on a run of the "Cannonball Express," engineer Casey Jones approached the station at Vaughan. Three trains were arranging to let the Cannonball pass when an airhose burst on one of the trains, leaving four cars on the mainline. Oblivious to the mishap, Casey careened through the darkness when, without warning, the lights on the stranded caboose became visible. Casey ordered Sim Webb, his fireman, to jump as he tried desperately to slow his train. At 3:52 A.M., the trains collided and Casey Jones became a legend. A marker identifies the site of the wreck at Vaughan. The town also houses a Casey Jones Museum, in operation since 1979, in an old depot. (Ask for details about how to locate the exact site of the crash within the park—it's 1/2 to 3/4 of a mile north of the current site of the museum.)

Kansas City Hyatt Regency Walkway Collapse

2345 McGee Street • Kansas City, Missouri • 816-421-1234

At 7:05 P.M. on July 17, 1981, two 120-foot-long walkways tore loose from their suspension rods, dumping 65 tons of concrete, metal, glass, and dance spectators onto hundreds of people below. That tragic night, 111 persons died, including 18 pairs of husbands and wives. Of the 200 injured, three died weeks or months later, pushing the death toll to 114.

Twenty years later, the Hyatt skywalk tragedy remains the nation's worst structural failure disaster. It triggered multimillion-dollar lawsuits, and focused attention on the importance of treating the psychological scars of rescue workers. Closed during repairs, the Hyatt reopened 75 days later–but without skywalks and without a plaque or other memorial marking what had happened (to date, there is still no memorial or marker).

King, Jr., Martin Luther

Blumstein's Department Store
230 West 125th Street • Harlem, New York

In 1958, Martin Luther King, Jr. was still basking in the success of his 13-month Montgomery bus boycott. His first book was about to be released and the decision was made to bring King to New York for a book tour. During a book signing here at this former department store in Harlem, King was stabbed by a deranged black woman named Izola Ware Curry. He was rushed to Harlem Hospital where a team of doctors successfully removed a seven-inch letter opener from his chest. The building that once held this popular department store still exists.

Dexter Avenue Baptist Church
454 Dexter Avenue • Montgomery, Alabama • 334-263-3970

While serving his first pastoral assignment, Dr. Martin Luther King, Jr., began his Civil Rights leadership at this Montgomery, Alabama church. A mural depicts Dr. King's journey from Montgomery to Memphis. This church was also the backbone of the 1955–1956 Montgomery bus boycott—the first locally initiated mass protest against racial discrimination and a model for other grass-roots demonstrations.

The boycott proved how members of a black community could unite in resistance to segregation, and it heralded a new era of "direct action." The event also propelled Martin Luther King, Jr. into the national spotlight. Today, the church is a National Historic Landmark and individual tours of the church are available Monday through Thursday.

Ebenezer Baptist Church

407 Auburn Avenue NE • Atlanta, Georgia • 404-688-7263

In, 1931, Martin Luther King, Sr. took over as pastor at this church and served until he retired in 1975. Five-year-old Martin Jr. and his sister, Christine, formally joined the church in 1934 at a revival led by a visiting evangelist. In fact, the young King preached his first sermon here at age 17 and joined his father as co-pastor from 1960 to 1968.

Ebenezer was also the scene of tragic events. Crowds gathered here in April 1968 to view Martin Luther King, Jr.'s body as it lay in state. Six years later, in 1974, Dr. King's mother was fatally shot by an assassin as she was playing the church organ. Today, the church is part of The Martin Luther King, Jr. National Historic Site.

Joseph T. Smitherman Historic Building

109 Union Street • Selma, Alabama • 334-874-2174

On January 18, 1965, Martin Luther King successfully registered to vote at the Hotel Albert in Selma and was assaulted by James George Robinson of Birmingham. Today, the hotel is gone but columns from it remain here in a park alongside the Joseph T. Smitherman Historic Building. This small structure, with four paintings by Selma native Kirk Miller which depict the history of the city, is a popular museum dedicated to Alabama heritage.

Mason Temple

938 Mason Street • Memphis, Tennessee • 901-578-3800

Martin Luther King, Jr. delivered his prophetic "Mountaintop" speech in this church in Memphis, Tennessee, on the eve of his assassination—April 3, 1968. Mason Temple served as a focal point of civil rights activities in Memphis during the 1950s and 1960s. Mason Temple was built between 1940 and 1945 as the administrative and spiritual center of the Church of God in Christ, the second-largest black denomination.

The temple is the centerpiece of a group of six buildings that form the church's world headquarters. A vast concrete building designed with simplified Art Moderne styling and detail and capable of seating 7,500 people on two levels, the temple was constructed for regular services as well as to house the annual national convention of church representatives.

Selma City Hall
1300 Alabama Avenue • Selma, Alabama

This building was at one time used as the city and county jail, and it is where Dr. King and other protesters were imprisoned in 1965. It is now the Cecil C. Jackson, Jr. Public Safety Building.

The Steps at the Lincoln Memorial
Washington, D.C.

"I have a dream that one day this nation will rise up and live out the true meaning of its creed: 'We hold these truths to be self-evident: that all men are created equal.'" Dr. Martin Luther King, Jr. delivered his most famous speech on August 28, 1963 from the steps of the Lincoln Memorial in Washington, D.C. He spoke to an audience of about 250,000 people who were protesting against discrimination. The speech was also broadcast to millions on television and radio, and printed in many newspapers. Since 1963, King's speech has since become one of the most famous public addresses of 20th-century America.

Legionnaire's Disease

Park Hyatt Hotel at the Bellevue • Broad and Walnut Street
Philadelphia, Pennsylvania • 215-893-1234

When 200 members of a war veteran's club called the American Legion became seriously ill during a conference at the Park Hyatt Hotel in 1976, doctors were mystified. What was causing the pneumonia-like disease with its
symptoms of fever, chills, aches and pains, cough, diarrhea, and abdominal
pain? By the time the problem was traced to germs breeding in the hotel's air
conditioning system, 34 men were dead and newspaper headlines were talking
about a "new" disease—Legionnaire's Disease named after the club members
who became ill. Because of the size and severity of the outbreak, federal, state,
and local health authorities launched what was at the time the largest cooper-
ative investigation in history to determine the cause of the outbreak.

Lindbergh, Charles

The Mall at the Source • 1504 Old Country Road • Westbury, New York
516-228-0303

There is some question, even controversy, regarding the exact take-off point
of Lindbergh's historic 33 hour, 30 minute nonstop flight to Le Bourget, Paris.
There's a stone monument outside Fortunoff's (in The Mall at the Source) in
Westbury that supposedly marks the spot. But there's also a metal plaque un-
derneath an escalator at nearby Roosevelt Field Mall claiming that as the point
of departure. However, the truth of the matter is that on May 20, 1927, Charles
Lindbergh actually took off in the Spirit of St. Louis from the area near the
present-day Fortunoff's, where the original Roosevelt Field airstrip used to be,
and where the monument is today. The two malls are close to each other, and
Lindbergh's plane was stored where Roosevelt Field Mall is located today.

Marconi, Guglielmo

Lecount Hollow Road off Route 6 (now part of the Cape Cod National
Seashore) • Wellfleet, Massachusetts • 508-255-3421

On January 19, 1901, the "Father of Radio," Guglielmo Marconi, erected his
first ever American wireless radio station on this Cape Cod beach. Following
World War I, the station was dismantled and the towers taken down in 1920.
While the station is no longer there, the Wellfleet Historical Society placed
a bronze plaque near the original site commemorating the station in 1953. It

reads: "Site of the first United States transatlantic wireless telegraph station, built in 1901–1902, Marconi Wireless Telegraph Company of America, predecessor of RCA, transmitted January 19, 1903. The first U.S. transatlantic wireless telegram addressed to Edward VII King of England. By Theodore Roosevelt, president of the United States."

In 1974, an exhibit shelter was built to house a scale model of the wireless station and a bronze bust of Marconi, along with the commemorative plaque dedicated in 1953. It's located on Main Street in the small town of Wellfleet.

Mars Bluff
Mars Bluff, South Carolina

DIRECTIONS: To get there, follow I-20 east to Florence and then to Mars Bluff. After Francis Marion College, turn right on Mars Bluff Road and proceed about a mile.

On March 11, 1958 a B-47 left Hunter Air Force Base in Georgia for a field maneuver to North Africa. However, it experienced a malfunction of its bomb locking mechanism and inadvertently dropped an atomic bomb on the crossroads named Mars Bluff near Florence, South Carolina. The safety devices prevented a nuclear explosion, but the trigger composed of conventional explosives went off, creating a crater 75 feet across and 35 feet deep, damaging houses as far as a half-mile away, knocking cars out of control on a nearby highway, and vaporizing the nuclear material, dispersing a ring of intense plutonium contamination in the surrounding area. The 35-foot crater where a farmhouse once sat is still there, but it's now covered with a swamp.

The McCarthy Hearings
Senate Caucus Room • Russell Senate Office Building • Located northeast of the Capitol on a site bounded by Constitution Avenue, First Street, Delaware Avenue, and C Street, NE • Washington, D.C.

It was in the Senate Caucus Room of this ornate building where the dramatic exchanges were recorded between Sen. Joseph McCarthy and witnesses during the 36-day Army-McCarthy hearings. McCarthy had made a name for himself with his anti-Communist crusade and his highly publicized accusations

of communist influence in the U.S. government, including the military.

Television was there to broadcast the drama of McCarthy's attacks and his debate with counsel Joseph Welch, and it was this exposure that helped turn the tide of public opinion against him. Soon after, McCarthy was censured by his Senate colleagues. (This is also the room where John F. Kennedy announced his candidacy for president; it was also used for the televised special investigation into the Watergate scandal in the 1970s and, in the 1980s, it was used for the Senate investigation into the Iran-Contra scandal.)

The Mormons

Haun's Mill Massacre Site
North of Kingston, Missouri

DIRECTIONS: Haun's Mill is located less than 15 miles east of Far West. Traveling on US 36, turn south onto Highway 13. Turn left on U Street heading east. Continue east on U Street for about 12 miles until the road becomes a less-traveled gravel road. (When the road bends left to K Street, continue straight on gravel to U Street.) Stay on this gravel road (still U Street) as it curves to the south. Signs have been put up to help you find your way, but unfortunately some have been vandalized. Continue south for about 1 mile before coming to a bridge. Don't cross the bridge. Turn right just before the bridge and follow the winding road for 1/2 mile to its end. You are now in the general area of Haun's Mill.

On October 30, 1838, the Missouri militia attacked a settlement of Latter-day Saints here at Jacob Haun's mill, which is located on Shoal Creek in eastern Caldwell County, Missouri. Because the attack was unprovoked in a time of truce, had no specific authorization, and was made by a vastly superior force with unusual brutality, it has come to be known as "The Haun's Mill Massacre." It was one incident in the conflict between the Missourians and the Latter-day Saints that resulted in the Latter-day Saints' expulsion from the state in 1839.

Hill Cumorah

On New York Route 21 • About 4 miles
south of Palmyra, New York

Hill Cumorah figures prominently in events that led to the organization of The Church of Jesus Christ of Latter-day Saints. According to the Church, in 421 A.D., Moroni, the last survivor of a great civilization that had inhabited the Americas since about 600 B.C., buried in this hill a set of gold plates on which was recorded the history of his people. In 1827, Moroni returned as an angel and delivered the plates to Joseph Smith, supposedly here at this site, who then translated them and published them as the *Book of Mormon: Another Testament of Jesus Christ*.

Through paintings, exhibits, and video presentations, the significance of the hill is explained in the visitor center located there. Free guided tours are conducted daily and each summer the Hill Cumorah is the site of a spectacular outdoors religious pageant. The free production, "America's Witness for Christ," features a cast of over 600 and attracts audiences of up to 100,000 each year.

Mountain Meadows Massacre

Mountain Meadows, Utah • (Located in the southwest corner of
Utah, about 35 miles southwest of Cedar City via the old pioneer
road, 54 miles via the current paved highway and 32 miles northwest
of St. George, Utah)

On September 11, 1857, a wagon train laden with gold was attacked while passing through Utah. Approximately 140 people were slaughtered; only 17 children under the age of eight were spared. This incident, which took place in an open field called Mountain Meadows, has ever since been the focus of an important historical debate—were official Mormon dignitaries responsible for the massacre?

The Mountain Meadows Massacre was first blamed on American Indians, but many historians now believe early settlers of the Church of

Jesus Christ of Latter-day Saints carried out the murders. (One of them, John D. Lee, was executed 20 years later for the event.) A monument to the victims is located on Dan Sill Hill, overlooking the valley where the tragedy took place.

Smith, Joseph
307 Walnut Street • Carthage, Illinois • 217-357-2989

The old jail in the town of Carthage, Illinois was the site of the killing of Mormon founder Joseph Smith and his brother Hyrum Smith by a mob of approximately 150 men. The two brothers had been arrested for instigating a riot; to bring calm, Illinois Governor Thomas Ford assured their protection if they would turn themselves in for trial.

The men complied, but on June 27, 1844, the Smiths, who were being held on the jail's second floor along with John Taylor and Dr. Willard Richards, saw a large group of threatening, armed men rush toward the jail. The anti-Mormon mob broke in and shot and killed Hyrum first. Joseph leaped from the window and was shot twice in the back and twice in the chest as he fell from the second story. John Taylor was shot four times but survived, and Willard Richards escaped unharmed. The jail, which was constructed from 1839-40, became a private home until 1903 when The Church of Jesus Christ of Latter-day Saints bought it. They restored the building in 1938 and today it is open for tours.

National Anthem

Fort McHenry National Monument and Historic Shrine
2600 E. Fort Avenue • Baltimore, Maryland • 410-962-429

This late 18th century star-shaped fort is world famous as the birthplace of the United States' national anthem. It was during a British attack on September 13–14, 1814, that a 35-year-old poet-lawyer, Francis Scott Key, was inspired to write "The Star-Spangled Banner." Key was born on August 1, 1779. By 1805, Key had established a law practice in Georgetown, Maryland, and, by 1814, had appeared many times before the U.S. Supreme Court.

In August 1814, Key's friend Dr. William Beanes was taken prisoner by the British army soon after its departure from Washington. Key left for Baltimore to obtain the services of Colonel John Skinner, the government's prisoner of war exchange agent. Together they sailed down the bay on a truce ship and met the British fleet. Key successfully negotiated the doctor's release, but was detained with Skinner and Beanes by the British until after the attack on Baltimore. Key's vessel was eight miles below the fort during the bombardment, under the watchful care of a British warship. It was from this site that he witnessed the British attack on Fort McHenry, after which he wrote the words to "The Star-Spangled Banner."

9/11

On September 11, 2001, 19 terrorists hijacked four airplanes as part of an attack on the Pentagon in Washington, D.C., and the World Trade Center Towers in New York City. Three of the planes were flown into the buildings, resulting in the deaths of over 3,000 individuals, the complete destruction of the Trade Center Towers, and extensive damage to the Pentagon. The fourth plane crashed in Southwestern Pennsylvania, killing all 44 people on board.

The primary crash sites at the former site of the World Trade Center and the Pentagon are well known and a matter of distinct public record. However, there are other lesser-known, but still notable sites related to that terrible day.

Mohammed Atta and Abdul Aziz Al-Omari

Various Sites

Two of the terrorist hijackers, Mohammed Atta and Abdul Aziz Al-Omari, operated mysteriously in Maine on September 10 (the day before the attacks) and on the morning of September 11, 2001. The following is a detailed account of their movements:

Monday, September 10, 2001

- At 5:43 P.M., terrorists Mohammed Atta and Abdul Aziz Al-Omari checked into the Comfort Inn, located at 90 Maine Mall Road, South Portland, Maine.
- Sometime between 8:00 P.M. and 9:00 P.M., two Middle Eastern males were seen at Pizza Hut, 415 Maine Mall Road, South Portland, Maine, for approximately 15 minutes. It is believed the two were Atta and Al-Omari.
- At exactly 8:31 P.M., Atta and Al-Omari were both photographed by a Key Bank drive-up ATM located at 445 Gorham Road, South Portland, Maine. They were driving a 2001 blue Nissan Altima rental car bearing Massachusetts license plate 3335VI.
- At 8:41 P.M., Atta and Al-Omari were photographed by a Fast Green ATM located in the parking lot of Uno's restaurant, 280 Maine Mall Road, South Portland, Maine.
- At 9:15 P.M., Atta and Al-Omari were at Jetport Gas Station, 446 Western Avenue, South Portland, Maine.
- At 9:22 P.M., Atta was seen at Wal-Mart, 451 Payne Road, Scarborough, Maine, for approximately 20 minutes.

Tuesday, September 11, 2001

- At 5:33 A.M., Atta and Al-Omari checked out of the Comfort Inn.
- At 5:40 A.M., the 2001 blue Nissan Altima rental car, bearing Massachusetts license plate 3335VI, entered Portland International Jetport Airport parking lot. It was parked on the first floor directly across from the airport entrance.
- At 5:43 A.M., Atta and Al-Omari both checked in at the U.S. Airways counter.
- At 5:45 A.M., Atta and Al-Omari passed through airport security.
- At 6:00 A.M., Atta and Al-Omari departed on Colgan Air en route to

Boston, Massachusetts, where the attacks would soon commence.

Flight 93 National Memorial
6424 Lincoln Hwy • Stoystown, Pennsylvania

The Flight 93 National Memorial is a memorial built to commemorate the crash of United Airlines Flight 93, which was one of four aircraft hijacked during the September 11 attacks in 2001. The memorial is located in Stonycreek Township in Somerset County, Pennsylvania, and is 78 miles southeast of Pittsburgh and 226 miles west of Philadelphia.

The national memorial was created to honor the passengers and crew of Flight 93, who stopped the terrorists from reaching their target by fighting the hijackers. A temporary memorial to the 40 victims was established soon after the crash. The first phase of the permanent memorial was completed, opened, and dedicated on September 10, 2011. The design for the memorial is a modified version of the entry Crescent of Embrace by Paul and Milena Murdoch. A concrete and glass visitor center opened on September 10, 2015, situated on a hill overlooking the crash site and the white marble Wall of Names. An observation platform at the visitor center and the white marble wall are both aligned beneath the path of Flight 93.

Huffman Aviation International
400 East Airport Avenue • Venice, Florida

Mohammed Atta and Marwan Alshehhi, two of the suicide hijackers, learned to fly the planes that they would ultimately crash into the Twin Towers at this flight school. It is no longer in business.

President Bush
Emma E. Booker Elementary School • Sarasota, Florida

According to most reliable reports, President George W. Bush was informed of the first plane's hit into the World Trade Center while in his motorcade, on Highway 301, just north of Main Street in Sarasota, Florida. He was en route to an appearance at a local school, where he was to spend some time reading with grade school kids. Within minutes of entering the school, Andrew Card, Bush's chief of staff, told President

Bush that a second passenger plane had hit the South Tower of the World Trade center.

Bush left soon after making a statement about the tragedy-in-progress and was then flown on Air Force One to Barksdale Air Force base near Shreveport, Louisiana, where he landed at about 11:45 A.M. From there, President Bush was shuttled to Offutt Air Force Base in Nebraska, home of the Strategic Air Command. There, the president established a telephone link to key security advisers.

Osama bin Laden
Gramercy Towers • 1177 California Street • San Francisco, California

According to the *San Francisco Examiner*, 9/11 terrorist mastermind Osama bin Laden lived here at the Gramercy Towers, 1177 California Street on Nob Hill, in the 1970s. Little is known about his stay in the Bay Area.

Nuclear Reaction
Joseph Regenstein Library • University of Chicago • 1100 East 57th Street
Chicago, Illinois

The Joseph Regenstein Library stands on the site of the original Stagg Field, the University's athletic field from 1892 to 1967. It was here on December 2, 1942 that Enrico Fermi supervised the design and assembly of an "atomic pile," a code word for a device that in peace time would be known as a "nuclear reactor." The bronze memorial "Nuclear Energy" by famed sculptor Henry Moore is situated on the west edge of the 12-acre site of the library, marking the exact spot where Fermi and other scientists achieved man's first controlled, self-sustaining, nuclear chain reaction.

Oklahoma City Bombing
Alfred P. Murrah Federal Building (former site)
Northwest Fifth and Harvey • Oklahoma City, Oklahoma

On April 19, 1995, around 9:03 A.M., just after parents had dropped their

children off at day care at the Murrah Federal Building in downtown Oklahoma City, a massive bomb
inside a rental truck exploded, blowing half of the
nine-story building into oblivion. A stunned nation
watched as the bodies of men, women, and children
were pulled from the rubble for nearly two weeks.
When the smoke cleared, 168 people were dead in
the (then) worst terrorist attack on U.S. soil.

Just 90 minutes after the explosion, an Oklahoma Highway Patrol officer pulled over 27-year-old
Timothy McVeigh for driving without a license plate. Ultimately, McVeigh
was found guilty of the crime and was put to death by lethal injection at 7:14
A.M. on Monday, June 11, 2001. Today, the area is marked by a poignant memorial and monument and recently, a museum dedicated to preserving the
memory of the victims and the scope of the loss was opened right next to it.

Parks, Rosa
251 Montgomery Street • Montgomery, Alabama • 334-241-8661

On December 1, 1955, 43-year-old Rosa
Parks boarded a Montgomery, Alabama
city bus after finishing work as a tailor's assistant at the Montgomery Fair department
store. As black patrons were then required
to do, she paid her fare at the front and then
re-boarded in the rear of the bus. As the bus
became full, the driver soon ordered Parks
to give up her seat to a white man who had
boarded. Parks refused several times, which
prompted the driver to call the police, who then arrested Parks.

This event sparked the bus boycott in Montgomery, which eventually
led to the desegregation of buses throughout the United States. In addition,
Parks became a recognized figure in the Civil Rights Movement. At the arrest site today, where there used to be just a plaque, there is now the Rosa
Parks Library and Museum, built for the woman who was arrested for her
courageous stand against bigoted behavior. It's part of the revitalization of
downtown Montgomery, and even includes a replica of a bus similar to the
one Rosa Parks was sitting on that historic day.

Plymouth Rock

Water Street
Plymouth, Massachusetts
508-866-2580

The smallest park in the Massachusetts state forest and park system, Pilgrim Memorial is also the most heavily visited. Nearly one million people a year come from all over the world to visit the town where in 1620 Europeans first made a home in New England. They also, of course, come here to see Plymouth Rock where, tradition tells us, the passengers on the Mayflower first set foot in the New World. This small boulder has become synonymous with the faith, courage and persistence embodied by the men and women who founded the first New England colony. Near the rock, a replica of the Mayflower is anchored at a park that also provides scenic views of Plymouth Harbor.

Pony Express

Pony Express Museum • 914 Penn Street • St. Joseph, Missouri
816-279-5059 • www.ponyexpress.org

The purpose of the Pony Express was simple: to provide the fastest mail delivery between St. Joseph, Missouri, and Sacramento, California. The service was active from April 3, 1860 to late October 1861. The Pony Express ran day and night, and 183 men are known to have ridden for the organization during its 18-month existence. As far as what it took to be a rider, here's how one recruitment ad read: "Wanted. Young, skinny, wiry fellows. Not over 18. Must be expert riders. Willing to risk death daily. Orphans preferred."

While most riders were around 20 years old, the youngest was 11, and the oldest was in his mid-40s. Riders were paid $100 per month, and a relay system ensured that each rider got a fresh horse every 10

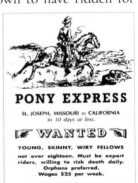

PONY EXPRESS
St. JOSEPH, MISSOURI to CALIFORNIA
in 10 days or less.

☞ WANTED ☜

YOUNG, SKINNY, WIRY FELLOWS
not over eighteen. Must be expert
riders, willing to risk death daily.
Orphans preferred.
Wages $25 per week.

APPLY, **PONY EXPRESS STABLES**
St. JOSEPH, MISSOURI

to 15 miles. Four hundred horses were purchased to stock the Pony Express route—thoroughbreds, mustangs, pintos, and morgans were often used across about 165 stations. The total trail length was almost 2,000 miles, and ran from St. Joseph, Missouri to Sacramento, California, through the present-day states of Kansas, Nebraska, Colorado, Wyoming, Utah, Nevada, and California.

The Revolutionary War

The Midnight Ride of Paul Revere
Hancock-Clarke House • 36 Hancock Street • Lexington, Massachusetts
781-861-0928

This is the home to which Paul Revere rode on his famous "midnight ride" to warn John Hancock and Samuel Adams, "The British are coming!" On the evening of April 18, 1775, John Hancock and Samuel Adams, prominent leaders in the colonial cause, were guests at this residence. Fearing that they might be captured by the British, Dr. Joseph Warren of Boston sent William Dawes and Paul Revere to Lexington with news of the advancing British troops. Arriving separately, they stopped to warn Hancock and Adams, then set off for Concord. Today, few remember Dawes, but Paul Revere's midnight ride has been immortalized by Longfellow.

The Old North Church
193 Salem Street • Boston, Massachusetts
617-523-6676

"One if by land . . . two if by sea." The enduring fame of the Old North Church was inspired by a fleeting moment on the night of April 18, 1775. Robert Newman, the church sexton, hung two lanterns in its steeple to warn that the British troops were arriving "by sea," thereby sending Paul Revere on his famous "midnight ride" to Lexington and Concord to warn Samuel Adams and John Hancock that the British were approaching. Revere's dash on horseback, immortalized by Henry Wadsworth Longfellow's "Paul Revere's Ride," brought out the militia and the shot heard round the world was fired on Lexington Green the following day.

North Bridge
174 Liberty Street • Concord, Massachusetts • 978-369-6993

The Old North Bridge in Concord, Massachusetts, was the site of the first battle between British government soldiers and British colonial rebels, who later became independent Americans. Fought on April 19, 1775, the battle began when government troops, attempting to confiscate weapons from the colonists, found themselves opposed by a determined militia of local farmers. Militia Captain John Parker gave his troops the famous order, "Stand your ground. Don't fire until fired upon. But if they mean to have a war, let it begin here." The "shot heard around the world," as Ralph Waldo Emerson called it in his "Concord Hymn," rang out from this bridge and the American Revolution had begun.

Roosevelt, Theodore
28 East 20th Street • New York City, New York

Theodore Roosevelt, the 26th President of the United States, was born here in 1858 on the site where this Greek Revival house (a replica of the original) now stands. He lived here until 1872 when his family relocated to Europe. The original house was demolished in 1916, but was then rebuilt to its original specifications in 1923. The five-story brick building includes a parlor, library, nursery, dining room, and master bedroom featuring satin with rosewood trim decor. Now a public museum, it is full of period furniture and Roosevelt memorabilia.

Roosevelt, Theodore

Inaugural Site • 641 Delaware Avenue • Buffalo, New York • 716-884-0095

While vacationing in the Adirondack Mountains of New York, Vice President Theodore Roosevelt learned the news that President William McKinley was not expected to survive bullet wounds incurred days earlier during an assassination attempt in Buffalo, New York. When Roosevelt completed the grueling 15-hour journey to Buffalo, President McKinley had indeed died. Deeply saddened over McKinley's tragic death, Roosevelt arrived at the home of his friend Ansley Wilcox. Here, in the library of this stately Greek Revival house, Roosevelt took the oath and became the 26th President of the United States.

Interestingly, in his haste to make it to Buffalo, Roosevelt had not packed any formal clothes. Consequently, he was forced to borrow a long frock coat, trousers, waistcoat, four-in-hand tie, and patent leather shoes. It was a tragic day, but a profound one as well: Roosevelt's 1901 inauguration marked a turning point in the role of the presidency, launching a dramatic change in national policy and propelling the United States into the realm of world affairs. This turning point was the birth of the modern presidency. The house where the inauguration took place has been restored and is open to the public as the Theodore Roosevelt Inaugural National Historic Site.

Scopes Trial

The Scopes Trial Museum and Rhea County Courthouse • 1475 Market Street
Dayton, Tennessee • 423-775-7801

In 1925, John Thomas Scopes, a biology teacher in Dayton, Tennessee, was arrested for the teaching of evolution in schools. The ACLU defended him and America's most famous criminal lawyer, Clarence Darrow, was then enlisted (pro bono) to help Scopes. The prosecution was led by Attorney General A. T. Stewart, and the former presidential candidate William Jennings Bryan. What would eventually become known as the

"Monkey Trial" started on July 11, 1925, and was the first trial in American history to be broadcast via radio to the nation. After Judge John T. Raulston refused to allow scientists to testify about the truth of evolution, Clarence Darrow called William Jennings Bryan to the witness stand and successfully exposed the flaws in Bryan's arguments during the cross-examination. The jury, however, found John Thomas Scopes guilty and the judge fined him $100. This verdict was eventually reversed on appeal as a result of a technicality.

Telephone
The Verizon building • Post Office Square • 185 Franklin Street
Boston, Massachusetts

On March 10, 1876, Alexander Graham Bell transmitted actual speech for the first time in history. Sitting in one room, he spoke into the phone to his assistant Mr. Watson in another room, uttering the now famous words: "Mr. Watson, come here. I need you." This room where Alexander Graham Bell invented the telephone is just off the lobby of the Verizon Building. Originally on Court Street, the attic was disassembled when its building was torn down in 1959 and reassembled here.

Tesla, Nikola
New Yorker Hotel • 481 8th Avenue • New York City, New York
212-971-0101

Nikola Tesla, the brilliant, Serbian-American inventor, electrical engineer, and scientist died here. After his graduation from the University of Prague in 1880, Tesla worked as a telephone engineer in Budapest, Hungary. By 1882, he had devised an AC power system to replace the weak direct-current (DC) generators and motors then in use.

He came to the United States in 1884 and began working for Thomas Edison. However, Edison advocated use of the inferior DC power transmission system, which caused friction between he and Tesla. By 1886, Tesla was out on the street. In 1887, Tesla had enough money from backers to build a laboratory of his own in New York City, so he created one.

In 1888, his discovery that a magnetic field could be made to rotate if two coils at right angles are supplied with AC current (90 ohm) out of phase made possible the invention of the AC induction motor. Tesla would later invent a high-frequency transformer called the Tesla Coil, which made AC power transmission practical. From 1891–1893, Tesla lectured before huge audiences of scientists all over the world. George Westinghouse purchased the patents to Tesla's induction motor and made it the basis of the Westinghouse power system, which still underlies the modern electrical power industry today.

Tesla died alone of heart failure here in this hotel, in room 3327, some time between the evening of January 5 and the morning of January 8, 1943. Despite selling his AC electricity patents, he was essentially destitute and died with significant debts. At the time of his death, Tesla had been working on some form of teleforce weapon, or death ray, the secrets of which he had offered to the United States War Department on the morning of January 5. The papers are still considered to be top secret.

Immediately after Tesla's death became known, the FBI instructed the Office of Alien Property to take possession of his papers and property, despite his U.S. citizenship. All of his personal effects were seized on the advice of presidential advisors. FBI head J. Edgar Hoover declared the case "most secret," because of the nature of Tesla's inventions and patents.

The Thunderstorm Project
Lytle Creek Greenway near Wilmington College
740 Davids Drive • Wilmington, Ohio

Blame it on the weather! During World War II, the U.S. Air Force was not only susceptible to enemy fire, it was also threatened by many thunderstorms. In 1945, Congress began studying this phenomena. The Thunderstorm Project was an undertaking of the U.S. Weather Bureau, Army, Air Force, Navy, and the National Advisory Committee for Aeronautics (predecessor of NASA). Partly because the area received so many thunderstorms, Clinton, Brown, and Highland Counties in Ohio were chosen as sites where flights were monitored during inclement weather. Scientists used tools such as radar to better understand the structure of thunderstorms. Theories they implemented still help us understand weather today. A marker commemorates these important studies.

US Airways Flight 1549
Hudson River/Midtown Manhattan • New York, New York

I'm sure everybody remembers the images of this remarkable event. On January 15, 2009, US Airways Flight 1549, an Airbus A320 on a flight from New York City's LaGuardia Airport to Charlotte, North Carolina, struck a flock of birds shortly after takeoff, losing all engine power. Unable to reach any airport for an emergency landing due to their low altitude, pilots Chesley "Sully" Sullenberger and Jeffrey Skiles glided the plane to a ditch in the Hudson River off Midtown Manhattan. All 155 people on board were rescued by nearby boats, with only a few serious injuries. Today, the actual plane is a part of a museum in Charlotte.

Washington, George
Washington Crossing, Pennsylvania • 215-493-4076

DIRECTIONS: The park is located at Washington Crossing on PA Route 32 just a few miles north of I-95, and seven miles south of New Hope, Pennsylvania. The 500 acres of Washington Crossing Historic Park are divided into two areas. The Thompson's Mill section is 1.5 miles southeast of New Hope on Route 32. The McConkey's Ferry section, 5 miles farther south, is the location of the park's Visitor Center.

On December 25, 1776, Washington's 2,400 troops gathered at McConkey Ferry, now called Washington Crossing. As night fell, the long boat crossing began. As dawn broke, the troops surprised the Hessian mercenaries, who quickly surrendered. Washington Crossing Historic Park was founded in 1917 to preserve this site from which the Continental Army crossed the Delaware.

A stone plaque signifies the place where George Washington crossed the river. Nearby is a statue of Washington and his men in their boat. The monument reads: "Near this spot, Washington crossed the Delaware on Christmas night 1776, the eve of the Battle of Trenton. Erected 1895, Bucks County Historical Society."

World War II

Japanese Internment Camp

Manzanar National Historic Site
Independence, California
760-878-2932

DIRECTIONS: Just off of U.S. Highway 395, 12 miles north of Lone Pine, California, and 5 miles south of Independence, California.

The American internment of Japanese during World War II is one of the black eyes of American history. On February 19, 1942, President Roosevelt signed Executive Order 9066, which called for the forcible internment of 120,000 Japanese-Americans. The Manzanar War Relocation Center was one of 10 camps at which Japanese-American citizens and resident Japanese aliens were interned during the war. Located at the foot of the imposing Sierra Nevada in eastern California's Owens Valley, Manzanar has been identified as the best preserved of these camps (though remnants of others still survive).

The U.S. Mainland is Attacked by the Japanese

Ellwood Oil Field (Access not available)
Goleta, California (12 miles northwest of Santa Barbara)

December 7, 1941, is a "date that will live in infamy," but few people will remember February 23, 1942, the date the Japanese attacked the U.S. mainland. A Japanese submarine fired 25 shells at an oil refinery at the edge of Ellwood Oil Field, 12 miles northwest of Santa Barbara. One shell actually hit on the rigging, causing minor damage. (President Roosevelt was giving a fireside chat at the time of the attack.)

On its face, the shelling of Ellwood beach February 23, 1942, was not a major event of the war. It injured no one and did a mere $500 damage to a shed and catwalk belonging to the Barnsdall-Rio Grande Oil Co. Yet, for a country still recovering from the brutal Pearl Harbor attack just two months before, the five-inch shells were enough to scare many into the belief that Japan could wage war on mainland American soil. After all, this was the first enemy attack on U.S. shores since the War of 1812. The attack also quickened the rounding up of Japanese-Americans in internment camps for the remainder of the war, a move Franklin D. Roosevelt had authorized just four days earlier.

The Japanese Bomb Oregon
North Bank Chetco River Road and Highway 101 • Mt. Emily
Brookings, Oregon

In the uninhabited mountains east of Brookings, Oregon, you can hike a trail and see where a Japanese bomb landed on September 9, 1942 during World War II. The idea had been conceived by the Japanese imperial general staff, still smarting from General Jimmy Doolittle's Tokyo raid. To retaliate, the Japanese hatched a plan to set the Oregon forests afire; they expected that the flames would spread to the cities and panic the entire West Coast. However, three of the bombs were duds; the fourth started a small blaze that was quickly spotted and doused by forest rangers.

There's an Oregon State Historic Marker where North Bank Chetco River Road meets Highway 101 (and directions there about how to reach the exact bombing site up the mountain, where a plaque sits at the site where one of the bombs hit). Interestingly, the pilot of the Japanese bomber, Nobuo Fujita, was invited to Brookings 20 years after the war as a sign of peace, and 30 years later he returned again to plant a commemorative redwood at the bombsite. When he died in 1997, he had just been named an honorary citizen of Brookings by the city council.

Atomic Bomb Test Site
Trinity Site • 110 miles south of Albuquerque between the Oscura mountains on the east and the San Mateo mountains on the west, about 60 miles northwest of Alamogordo, New Mexico.
800-826-0294 • www.wsmr.army.mil

Trinity Site is where the first atomic bomb was tested at 5:29:45 A.M. on July 16, 1945. It is estimated that 100–250 tons of sand vaporized by the blast went up in the cloud following the explosion. The 19-kiloton explosion not only led to a quick end to the war in the Pacific but also ushered the world into the atomic age. A triangular-shaped monument at Trinity Site on White Sands Missile Range marks ground zero.

The 51,500-acre area was declared a national historic landmark in 1975. The landmark includes base camp, where the scientists and support group lived; ground zero, where the bomb was placed for the explosion; and the McDonald ranch house, where the plutonium core to the bomb was assembled. Visitors to a Trinity Site Open House see ground zero and the McDonald ranch house. In addition, one of the old instrumentation bunkers is visible beside the road just west of ground zero. Note: The site is only open to the public twice a year—on the first Saturday in April and the first Saturday in October.

The *Enola Gay*

Tinian Airport on Tinian Island • Part of the Northern Mariana Island chain in the western North Pacific)

Tinian (a U.S. territory) lies north of Guam on the eastern edge of the Philippine Sea, and was one of the primary staging areas for U.S. Pacific air operations during World War II. (Tinian Island airport is toward the southeast side of the island.)

Though little remains of what was once one of the world's busiest airports, a visitor to Tinian's North Field can pause at one of modern history's most somber locations. It is the site where the atomic bombs nicknamed *Fat Man* and *Little Boy* underwent final assembly and were then loaded onto the B-29 bombers—including the *Enola Gay*—that carried them to Hiroshima and Nagasaki.

Though the bomb pits are now home to plumeria and coconut trees, a plaque on one of the pits reads: "Atomic Bomb Loading Pit." The bomber, piloted by Colonel Paul W. Tibbets, Jr., was loaded late in the afternoon of August 5, 1945, and at 2:45 A.M. the following morning it took off on its mission.

Wreck of Old '97

Memorial is located west of Danville on Riverside Drive (U.S. 58) between Locust Lane and North Main Street at the train crash site. • Danville, Virginia

On September 27, 1903, the mail-and-express train No. 97 vaulted off the Stillhouse Trestle in Danville, Virginia, killing 11 people aboard and inspiring "The Ballad of the Wreck of the Old 97," one of the most famous country songs of all time. The song, whose authorship became a source of controversy and led to an extended legal battle, became the first single in U.S. history to sell one million copies after it was recorded by light-opera singer Vernon Dalhart.

Wright Brothers

Wright Brothers National Memorial • National Park Service
1401 National Park Drive • Manteo, North Carolina • 252-441-7430

The first successful sustained powered flights in a heavier-than-air machine were made here by Wilbur and Orville Wright on December 17, 1903. A 60-foot granite monument dedicated in 1932 is perched atop 90-foot tall Kill Devil Hill commemorating the achievement of these two visionaries from Dayton, Ohio. Also placed in this park is "The First Flight Lift-off Commemoration Boulder." The granite marker was placed at the approximate site of the revolutionary 1903 liftoff and the text reads: "The first successful flight of an airplane was made from this spot by Orville Wright December 17, 1903 in a machine designed and

built by Wilbur and Orville Wright. This tablet was erected by the National Aeronautic Association of the U.S.A. December 17, 1928 to commemorate the 25th anniversary of this event."

Yeager, Chuck

Edwards Air Force Base • Located on the western edge of the Mojave Desert, about 90 miles north of Los Angeles. • 661-277-351

DIRECTIONS: From Los Angeles, take the Rosamond exit off the Antelope Valley Freeway (State Highway 14) and travel east on Rosamond Boulevard into the base. Edwards can also be reached via Highway 58 near North Edwards and via 120th Street from Lancaster.

In 1947, flight instructor and test pilot Chuck Yeager was chosen from several volunteers to test-fly the secret, experimental X-1 aircraft, built by the Bell Aircraft Company. The Bell X-1 was designed to test human pilots and fixed wing aircraft against the severe stresses of flight close to the speed of sound, and to see if a straight-wing plane could fly faster than the speed of sound (approximately 760 mph, in air at sea level). No one knew if a pilot could safely control a plane under the effects of the shock waves produced as the plane's speed neared Mach 1.

On October 14, 1947, after taking off from Muroc air Base (now called Edwards), Yeager rode the X-1, attached to the belly of a B-29 bomber, to an altitude of 25,000 feet. After releasing from the B-29, he rocketed to an altitude of 40,000 feet. He became the first person to break the sound barrier, safely taking the X-1 to a speed of 662 mph.

CHAPTER FOUR

CRIME, MURDER, AND ASSASSINATION

Aurora Movie Theater Shooting
14300 East Alameda Avenue • Aurora, Colorado

On July 20, 2012, a mass shooting took place at a movie theater in Aurora, a Denver suburb, resulting in the deaths of 12 people, the youngest of which was a six-year-old girl. At least 70 others were injured. The tragedy took place shortly after the start of a crowded midnight showing of *The Dark Knight Rises*, which opened across the United States that day. It was the deadliest mass shooting in Colorado since the 1999 Columbine shooting, in which 12 high school students and a teacher were murdered. The horror began when 24-year-old James Holmes entered Theater 9 at the Century 16 multiplex through a parking lot exit door and threw gas canisters into the theater. He was dressed in a gas mask and black combat gear, leading some audience members to initially think he was performing a stunt for the film—a Batman sequel eagerly anticipated by fans. Instead, Holmes opened fire at the audience, shooting people at random. Police quickly arrived on the scene, and Holmes was apprehended behind the movie theater; he put up no resistance.

Not long after, law enforcement agents evacuated buildings near Holmes' Aurora apartment after he told them he had booby-trapped his home with explosive devices. When Holmes made his first appearance in court on July 23, his hair was dyed neon orange and he seemed dazed and devoid of emotion. Holmes, who has offered no motive for the shooting spree, eventually was charged with 166 counts of murder, attempted murder, and weapons charges. In May 2013, he pleaded not guilty by reason of insanity. In a 2015 trial, Holmes was sentenced to 12 consecutive life sentences without parole.

Bakley, Bonny Lee
Vitello's Italian Restaurant • 4349 Tujunga Avenue • Studio City, California

This is where actor Robert Blake ate with his soon-to-be-widow Bonny Bakley on Friday, May 4, 2001. It was a favorite haunt of Blake's, the actor who played TV cop "Baretta" back in the 1970s. (According to the restaurant's owner, he ate here twice a week, and even had an item on the menu named after him, "Fusilli a la Robert Blake.")

At about 9:40 P.M., someone shot Blake's wife, while she sat in their black sports car. It was parked on Woodbridge Street, a block and a half away from the restaurant. According to Blake, he had briefly returned to Vitello's to retrieve a gun he had left behind, and when he returned to the car, he found Bonny Lee dying from a gunshot to her head. He ran to a nearby house (of director Sean Stanek) for help and the police were called. At the time of this writing, Blake is being held in prison without bail on charges of committing the murder.

Berkowitz, David/Son of Sam
42 Pine Street (originally 35 Pine Street) • Yonkers, New York

The summer of 1977 was a terrifying one for New Yorkers, thanks to David Berkowitz (a.k.a. the "Son of Sam"). Berkowitz, a chubby, bookish loner, prowled the streets of New York looking for attractive young women to kill with his .44-caliber pistol. The first shooting occurred in early 1976. By the next summer, the city would literally be paralyzed with fear and the night streets would be empty. Police unleashed the largest manhunt in city history to try and stop the killer (whose nickname came from one of the taunting notes he began sending local reporters).

Finally, on August 10, 1977 residents got the news they were waiting to hear. "Police have captured a man whom they believe to be the Son of Sam." David Berkowitz, a then-24-year-old Yonkers postal worker, confessed to a year-long rampage of eight shooting attacks in Queens, the Bronx, and Brooklyn after being arrested in front of this nondescript apartment building. The attacks left a toll of six young people dead and seven others wounded. A trial was avoided as Berkowitz pleaded guilty and he was sentenced to life.

"Black Dahlia"

3925 South Norton Avenue (just south of 39th Street)
South Central Los Angeles, California

The once undeveloped area where the horribly mutilated body of "The Black Dahlia" (aspiring 22-year-old actress Elizabeth Short) was found cut in half on January 15, 1947 is now a residential neighborhood. For a long time the most infamous murder case in the history of Hollywood, the body was found two blocks east of where the Baldwin Hills-Crenshaw Plaza mall is today. The grisly murder inspired the James Elroy best-seller, *The Black Dahlia*, and several movies, most notably 1981's *True Confessions*.

Bobbit, John Wayne and Lorena

Maplewood Drive off Centreville Road (Route 28) • (The apartment complex across from the street from the Maplewood Plaza shopping center) • Manassas, Virginia

John Wayne Bobbit made national headlines when his wife, Lorena, maimed him on grounds of cheating, abuse, forcing her to get an abortion, and other despicable acts. (His organ was recovered from the scene and re-attached.) He later appeared in an adult film of his own life in order to help pay his medical (a nine-hour operation) and legal bills. In two separate trials, Lorena was found innocent by reason of insanity, while John Wayne was acquitted of sexually assaulting his wife.

Bonnie and Clyde Death Site

Route 154, just south of Gibsland, Louisiana

DIRECTIONS: From Shreveport, take the I-20 about 45 miles to the Gibsland/Athens exit, which puts you on Route 154. The marker is about eight miles after you pass the small town of Gibsland.

On Wednesday, May 23, 1934, six officers acting on a tip laid in wait for outlaw Clyde Barrow and his companion in crime, Bonnie Parker. Bonnie and Clyde were accused of killing 12 innocent people, and the entire country had

been searching for them. As they approached the ambush spot, the police shouted a warning. The outlaws drew their guns, but in moments they were riddled with over 50 bullets.

Many believe that had they not been glamorized by the 1967 film *Bonnie and Clyde*, they would have remained what they were—obscure, petty, cold-blooded killers. A stone marker sits at the exact spot where it happened. On the weekend closest to May 23, the town of Gibsland stages a Bonnie and Clyde Festival (318-843-6141). Incidentally, the 1934 Ford in which Bonnie and Clyde were killed is on display in Primm, Nevada at Whiskey Pete's Casino. In 1997, Whiskey Pete's paid $85,000 for the light blue, bullet-ridden, bloodstained shirt that Barrow was wearing when he was killed. The shirt is also on display in the casino.

Borden, Lizzie

92 Second Street • Fall River, Massachusetts • 508-675-7333

Lizzie Borden took an axe
and gave her Mother 40 whacks.
When she saw what she had done
She gave her Father forty-one.

On the morning of August 4, 1892, Lizzie Borden murdered her stepmother with an axe in the Borden's family house. Abby Borden's body was found in the guest room between the bed and bureau. Soon after, Lizzie axed her father, Andrew Borden, to death.

While there is little doubt that Lizzie committed the crime, she was acquitted at trial due to a lack of evidence. Although ostracized by the community, Lizzie lived in the house until she died on June 1, 1927. After her death, the house remained a private residence for several decades before being converted into a bed and breakfast. Guests are allowed to view the murder scene and can sleep in Lizzie and her sister Emma's bedrooms, Abby and Andrew's bedrooms, or the guest room where Abby was killed.

Boston Marathon Bombings
Boylston Street • Boston, Massachusetts

On April 15, 2013 at 2:49 P.M., the first of two bombs was detonated at 671 Boylston Street near the finish line of the Boston Marathon. A second bomb was detonated 13 seconds later, 180 yards away at 755 Boylston Street. It was later determined that the explosions were caused by homemade improvised explosive devices (IEDs) hidden in backpacks and placed on the ground level in these viewing areas just seconds before they were detonated. The explosions took the lives of three individuals and injured 264 spectators—many critically, with 16 survivors suffering traumatic amputations. Following the explosions on Boylston Street, emergency responders and numerous spectators and bystanders quickly responded to the critically injured, triaging their injuries and facilitating their transport to area hospitals. The hospitals that received patients rendered life-saving medical care; as a result, every patient that was transported to a hospital from the scene survived.

Three days later, the FBI released images of the suspected bombers, identified as Dzhokhar Tsarnaev and Tamerlan Tsarnaev, two brothers from Chechnya. Soon after the images were released, the Tsarnaev brothers reportedly killed an MIT police officer and stole an SUV.

The brothers then got into a gunfight with police in Watertown, Massachusetts. Dzhokhar was injured and had run over Tamerlan, who had been shot and killed by police. Dzhokhar escaped from the police and a massive manhunt took place on April 19 in Watertown. He was soon discovered hiding in a boat in a backyard by a resident and after a brief standoff with police, he was arrested and taken to a hospital. Dzhokhar was charged on April 22 and pleaded not guilty. It is believed that the Tsarnaev brothers acted on their own radical Islamic beliefs and were not affiliated with other terror groups.

Boston Strangler
79 Gainsborough Street, Back Bay • Boston, Massachusetts

On October 27, 1964, a man entered a young woman's home at this address, posing as a detective. He tied the woman to her bed, sexually assaulted her, and then suddenly left, saying "I'm sorry" as he went. The woman's description

to the police led to his identification as Albert DeSalvo. After his photo was published, many other women came forward to identify him as their attacker, too.

At this point, DeSalvo was not a suspect in the string of strangling crimes that had taken place over the previous two years. But several months later, while being held on a separate rape charge, DeSalvo confessed in great detail to his activities as the Boston Strangler. However, there was no evidence to substantiate his confession, so he stood trial for a series of earlier, unrelated crimes of robbery and sexual offenses. He was sent to prison for life in 1967, only to be murdered six years later while in his cell.

Brinks Heist
165 Prince Street • Boston, Massachusetts

Shortly before 7:30 P.M. on the evening of January 17, 1950, a group of armed, masked men emerged from the Brink's offices in Boston, Massachusetts, dragging bags containing $1,218,211.29 in cash and $1,557,183.83 in checks, money orders, and other securities. These men had just committed the "crime of the century." As the robbers sped from the scene, a Brink's employee telephoned the Boston Police Department. Minutes later, police arrived at the Brink's building, and Special Agents of the FBI quickly joined in the investigation.

It was the biggest cash haul in history, and it would take six years and the combined investigative efforts of the Boston police and the FBI (not to mention the help of local police departments across the country) to solve the case. At the time, the Brink's offices were located in the North Terminal Garage Building in the North End of Boston—the building still stands today.

Bundy, Ted
Chi Omega Sorority House • 661 West Jefferson Street
Tallahassee, Florida

Though there were many ghoulish scenes in Ted Bundy's history, this was the final eruption—the end of Bundy's infamous six-state murder spree. He had escaped from a Colorado jail, headed to Florida, and in January 1978, broke into Chi Omega and killed four young women while they slept. A month later, he killed a 12-year old girl after taking her from outside her school in Lake City, Florida. Finally, on February 15, 1978, Bundy was arrested in Pensacola, Florida, thus ending his career as a killer. Eleven years later, he was executed by the State of Florida in the electric chair.

Capone, Al

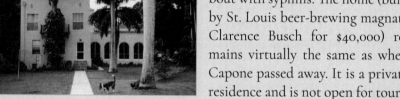

Death Site

C93 Palm Avenue • Palm Island, Florida

Gangster Al Capone died here on January 25, 1947, in his mansion in Biscayne Bay, near Miami. The notorious Capone ultimately expired from both the physical and

mental damage caused by a long bout with syphilis. The home (built by St. Louis beer-brewing magnate Clarence Busch for $40,000) remains virtually the same as when Capone passed away. It is a private residence and is not open for tours.

Hideout

12101 West County Road CC • Couderay, Wisconsin • 715-945-2746

This lakefront retreat was gangster Al Capone's hideout. Built in the 1920s by Capone for $250,000, the house was vacant until 1959 when it was made into a restaurant and museum. The home has bulletproof walls (18-inch thick fieldstone), a secret bunkhouse for the gang, a blockhouse with jail cells, and a guard tower that was manned by armed guards with machine guns.

The 90-acre lake was supposedly used by airplanes to smuggle in liquor during Prohibition, and a dock on the lake let the gang roll barrels of booze into trucks. Today it's called The Hideout, and it's a fun historical restaurant, bar, and museum that lets you experience a real gangster hideout firsthand.

Headquarters
4823 Cermak Road • Cicero, Illinois

Early in 1924, legendary gangster Al Capone made his headquarters here in a hotel called the Hawthorne Inn. At this site on the afternoon of September 20, 1926, 11 automobiles filled with Hymie Weiss gangsters drove slowly past the Inn and poured more than 1,000 bullets into the building, from machine guns, pistols, and shotguns. Capone was having lunch in a restaurant next door, and thus escaped injury.

Later, the Inn was renamed the Towne Hotel, and remained a meeting place of the Chicago Syndicate through the 1960s. On February 17, 1970, a fire which started in the kitchen destroyed the hotel. Other Capone headquarters included the Four Deuces at 2222 South Wabash, the Metropole Hotel at 2300 South Michigan Avenue, and the Lexington Hotel at 2135 South Michigan Avenue, all located in Chicago.

Pony Inn
5613 West Roosevelt Road • Cicero, Illinois

On April 27, 1926, state attorneys William McSwiggen, Thomas Duffy, Myles O'Donnell, and Jim Doherty pulled up in front of the Pony Inn, once located at this site. At the same time, gangster Al Capone's Cadillac approached as McSwiggen and his friends stepped out of their car. Slowly driving by, Capone opened fire with a machine gun, killing Duffy, Doherty and McSwiggen.

Cassidy, Butch

First Bank Robbery
San Miguel National Bank • 129–131 West Colorado Avenue
Telluride, Colorado

On June 24, 1889, Butch Cassidy kicked off his notorious life of crime by robbing the San Miguel National Bank, then located here on a portion of Main Street. (The old bank burned and was replaced by the Maher Building in 1892; the Maher still stands today.) Cassidy had been riding with the McCarty gang, known as the Wild Bunch.

After a few days of drinking and playing cards, they robbed the San Miguel National Bank of about $24,000. Cassidy was almost apprehended at what is now Society Drive, but he managed to escape. It was a valiant attempt, but Butch wrenched the man's prized pearl-handled gun from his hand and bolted out of town with the money, never to be seen in town again.

Hole-in-the-Wall
Kaycee, Wyoming

DIRECTIONS: To access the area, take Interstate 25 south from Kaycee to the TTT Road exit. At TTT Road exit, drive south about 14 miles to Willow Creek Road (County Road 111). Take this road west for about 18 miles to a primitive two-track road that bears north. This is County Road 105. As you travel along County Road 105 there are a number of livestock gates that must be opened and closed.

The Hole-in-the-Wall is approximately 40 miles southwest of Kaycee, Wyoming. It's a colorful and scenic red sandstone escarpment that is rich in legend of outlaw activity in the late 1800s, most notably Butch Cassidy and the Wild Bunch Gang. The "hole" is a gap in the Red Wall that, legend has it, was used secretly by outlaws to move horses and cattle from the area. The area is primitive in nature, with no services.

Montpelier Bank Building (Former Site)
833 Washington Street • Montpelier, Idaho
800-448-2327 (Visitors Bureau)

This building housed the original "Bank of Montpelier" and is the site of a famous Butch Cassidy bank robbery. On August 13, 1896, Butch, Elza Lay, and Bob Meeks arrived at the bank just before closing time, and tied up their horses at the hitching rack across the street. Cassidy and Lay left Meeks to watch, they entered the bank, and forced the employees up against the wall. Lay kept guns on the bank staff while Cassidy quickly scooped money into a gunny sack.

Cassidy left the bank first with the money. He walked nonchalantly across the street, got on his horse, and rode slowly away. Meeks moved across the street with the remaining horses and left Lay's horse standing in front of the bank as he rode away. Finally, Lay left the bank in haste. Cassidy was never brought to trial. Today, the site is occupied by the Mountain Litho printing company, run by a nice man named Kent Bunn. He knows all the history of the place if you have any more questions.

Robbers' Roost
Outlaw Trail San Rafael • Swell, Utah

DIRECTIONS: Travel 3.2 miles north on State Route 158 (Deer Creek Road) from State Route 157 (Kyle Canyon Road). On the right is a parking area and the trailhead is on the left.

This was a popular outlaw hideout for over 30 years. Robbers' Roost is located along the Outlaw Trail, the infamous route in southeastern Utah where many notorious bandits hid out while on the run from the law. Fresh horses were reserved here and there was a large weapons cache.

Butch Cassidy considered it an ideal hideout due to the many lookout points on all sides of the canyons.

Butch Cassidy's original corral remains in Robbers' Roost, in addition to a stone chimney, caves, and several carvings. Due to the difficult terrain, a maze of canyons, and extreme heat the Roost was never successfully penetrated by authorities (but it is a popular hiking spot).

Castellano, Paul
Sparks Steakhouse • 210 East 46th Street • New York, New York
212-687-4855

On February 25, 1985, Paul Castellano was arrested along with several other crime family bosses in what became known as the "Commission Case." Evidently, Castellano planned to rat on the Gambino family, which prompted John Gotti to seek his murder. Using an insider close to Castellano, Gotti arranged for Castellano to meet someone on December 16 at Sparks Steak House in Manhattan. After a meeting with his lawyer, Castellano drove to Sparks where he was gunned down by Gotti's killers. Watching the killing with Gotti from a nearby car was Gambino lieutenant Salvatore "Sammy the Bull" Gravano, who ironically would later rat on Gotti and scores of other mobsters.

Charleston Shooting
110 Calhoun Street • Charleston, South Carolina

A mass shooting occurred in Charleston, South Carolina on June 17, 2015, in which nine African Americans were killed by a white supremacist during a Bible study at the historic Emanuel African Methodist Episcopal Church. Among those people who were killed were pastors Daniel Simmons and Sharonda Singleton, along with state senator Clementa C. Pinckney. This church is one of the oldest black churches in the United States, and it has long been a center for organizing events that are related to civil rights. The morning after the attack, police arrested Dylann Roof in Shelby, North Carolina; the

21-year-old had attended the Bible study before he committed the shooting. He was found to have targeted members of this church because of its history and status. Roof was found competent to stand trial in federal court. In December 2016, Roof was convicted of 33 federal hate crime and murder charges. On January 10, 2017, he was sentenced to death for those crimes. Roof was separately charged with nine counts of murder in the South Carolina state courts. In April 2017, Roof pleaded guilty to all nine state charges to avoid receiving a second death sentence, and as a result, he was sentenced to life imprisonment without the possibility of parole. He will receive automatic appeals of his death sentence, but he may eventually be executed by the federal justice system. The shooting triggered debates about the modern display of the Confederate flag and other commemorations of the Confederacy. Following these murders, the South Carolina General Assembly voted to remove the flag from State Capitol grounds.

Cosby, Ennis
405 Freeway (north) • Skirball Center off ramp (near Mulholland Drive)
Bel Air, California

Ennis Cosby, son of entertainer Bill Cosby, was heading north in his car at about 1:45 A.M. on January 16, 1997. After getting a flat tire, he pulled the car off onto the exit leading to Mulholland Drive (in the Sepulveda Pass). As he changed the tire on the west shoulder of the road, a man emerged from the shadows and shot him to death. Eighteen-year-old Mikail "Michael" Markhasev, from nearby Orange County, was arrested for the crime, tried, found guilty, and sentenced to life in prison. (Ironically, this was almost the exact same location where Frank Sinatra, Jr. was released by kidnappers in 1963 after he had supposedly been abducted.)

Dahmer, Jeffrey
Oxford Apartments • Apartment 213 • 924 North 25th Street
Milwaukee, Wisconsin

One of the most infamous serial murderers of all-time is Jeffrey Lionel Dahmer. On July 22, 1991, two Milwaukee police officers observed a distraught, hand-cuffed man running down the street. He said his name was Tracy Edwards and he was escaping from the apartment of Jeffrey L. Dahmer, a person who, for the last five hours, had terrorized and threatened to kill Edwards and eat his heart out. He led the cops there, and they were stunned at what they found: human remains, including skulls, in the freezer and parts of bodies, along with photographs of dead men who had either been mutilated or completely dismembered.

In February of 1992, Dahmer was sentenced to 15 life terms in prison for his crimes. He was murdered in prison by a fellow inmate on November 28, 1994.

Dillinger, John

Biograph Theater • 2433 North Lincoln Avenue • Chicago, Illinois

On the evening of July 22, 1934, John Dillinger stepped out of this downtown Chicago theater where he and two girlfriends had watched a film called *Manhattan Melodrama* starring Clark Gable. As soon as they reached the sidewalk, Melvin Purvis of the FBI stepped forward and identified himself. He ordered Dillinger to surrender, but no dice. Dillinger turned to run, but several shots rang out and Dillinger went down, his left eye shredded by one of the bullets fired by the other agents. Public Enemy Number One, the most prolific bank robber in modern American history, was dead.

Evers, Medgar

2332 Margaret West Alexander Drive • Jackson, Mississippi • 601-981-2965

Medgar Evers is known for his endless contributions to the black civil rights movement. When he was in his late twenties, he was accepted into the NAACP and became a full time chapter organizer. In his early thirties, Medgar was named state field secretary for the NAACP. On the night of June 12, 1963 while getting out of his car in front of this house, Medgar was shot in the back by Byron de la Beckwith. He died 50 minutes later at a local hospital.

Evers' murder prompted President John F. Kennedy to push for a civil rights bill that would ban segregation. This, in turn, spurred Martin Luther King, Jr. and 250,000 people to march to Washington D.C., where King gave his famous "I Have a Dream" speech. Although Evers died at the young age of 37, he was one of the most renowned civil rights activists in U.S. history. Evers' house, now a museum, was used in the movie *Ghosts of Mississippi*, and many of the current furnishings were put in place during the filming.

Fisher, Amy
Biltmore Shores • One Adam Road West • Long Island, New York

The is the house where 16-year-old Amy Fisher (dubbed the "Long Island Lolita" by New York media), knocked on the door and shot Mary Jo Buttafuoco in the face when she answered it. Incredibly, Mary Jo survived the May 19, 1992 attack. Fisher had allegedly been having an affair with Mary Jo's garage mechanic husband, the infamous Joey Buttafuoco. Fisher served seven years and has since made amends with Mary Jo.

Fleiss, Heidi
1270 Tower Grove Road • Beverly Hills, California

This is the house in which Heidi Fleiss ran a multi-million dollar brothel which was frequented by the rich and famous. Heidi's story was told in the film *Madam of Beverly Hills*. Eventually, she spent two years in a California jail for tax evasion, money laundering, and pandering.

Floyd, George
The intersection of 38th Street and Chicago Avenue
Minneapolis, Minnesota

George Perry Floyd Jr. (an African American) was murdered by a police officer in Minneapolis, Minnesota on May 25, 2020. It happened during an arrest after a store clerk suspected Floyd may have used a counterfeit $20 bill. Derek Chauvin, one of four police officers who arrived on the scene, knelt on Floyd's neck and back for nine minutes and 29 seconds, causing Floyd's heart and lungs to stop. After his murder, protests against police brutality, especially toward black people, quickly spread across the United States and globally.

His dying words, "I can't breathe," became a rallying cry. Today, a gathering place for people to pay their respects and remember Floyd has been created at the site of his death in South Minneapolis. The area is filled with ways to memorialize the life of George Floyd and other victims of police brutality.

Floyd, Pretty Boy
Sprucevale Road between Beaver Creek State Park and Clarkson
Near East Liverpool, Ohio

The gangster Charles Arthur "Pretty Boy" Floyd was killed here on the farm of Mrs. Ellen Conkle. On October 19, 1934, Floyd had been spotted after robbing the Tiltonsville Peoples Bank with two other men. Police and FBI were put on alert throughout Ohio for the suspects. The following day a shootout between the criminals and the Wellsville, Ohio police ended in the capture of Richetti, Floyd's partner, but Floyd escaped.

On October 22, 1934, things would finally come to a fatal end for Pretty Boy Floyd. He entered the Conkle's house by posing as a lost hunter and asked for a ride to the bus. Ellen Conkle fed him (a meal for which Floyd paid one dollar), then sent her brother to drive him to the bus station. As they got into the car, two police cars sped by, and Floyd jumped from the car to hide behind a corncrib. Police spotted and recognized Floyd, who decided to flee. Ignoring the cop's demand to stop, he was shot in the arm. Continuing to run, he was shot again, only this time he fell to the ground. He dropped his gun, grabbed his right forearm where he had been hit, and died several moments later under an apple tree. (His body was taken to the Sturgis Funeral Home in East Liverpool.) A plaque placed by the East Liverpool Historical Society marks the exact spot where Floyd was shot.

Ford, President Gerald
Pathway that runs diagonally from 12th Street and L Street to the State Capitol Building (the event happened about 10 yards from the sidewalk, near a magnolia tree) • Sacramento, California

Gerald Ford may have been setting the country back on course after the Watergate scandal, but that didn't stop two different women from taking potshots at him. On September 5, 1975, Charles Manson follower Lynette "Squeaky" Fromme waited for President Ford here outside a Sacramento, California hotel. As he reached to shake her hand, she pulled out a Colt .45. Fromme pulled the trigger, but the loaded gun didn't fire. (Seems she had neglected to put a round in one of the chambers.) Secret Servicemen took her down before she could attempt to fire another shot, and today, Fromme is serving a life sentence in prison.

Ford, President Gerald

Westin St. Francis Hotel • 335 Powell Street, Union Square
San Francisco, California • 800-228-3000

On September 22, barely two weeks after Squeaky Fromme's attempt on President Ford's life, 45-year-old Sara Jane Moore yanked a pistol from her purse and fired on Ford from a distance of about 30 feet as he made his way toward the St. Francis hotel's Post Street exit after having lunch at the hotel (Moore was across the street from the exit, nearby where the Disney store is located today). The disturbed ex-housewife and newly-christened radical missed, in part due to a bystander who jostled her arm. President Ford was unharmed, and Moore was sentenced to life in prison.

Gacy, John Wayne

8213 West Summerdale Avenue • Des Plaines, Illinois

This is the infamous house where, in late 1978, investigators questioning John Wayne Gacy, Jr. about the disappearance of Robert Piest discovered the crawl space that would eventually prove to be where the serial killer had buried some 29 bodies. Gacy was put to death for the grisly murders on May 9, 1994.

Gallo, Joey

Umberto's Clam House (former site)
129 Mulberry Street, corner of Hester
New York, New York

This was the site of Little Italy's most famous mob hit. At 5:00 A.M. on April 7, 1972, three gunmen smashed through the restaurant's side door, shooting Joey Gallo, a maverick mob leader. Gallo, hit three times, staggered outside and collapsed in the middle of Hester Street. As the famous local saying goes, "He ordered clams, but he got slugs."

Garfield, President James

Union Station (former site) • (Present-day site of The National Gallery of Art) • Located on the National Mall between Third and Ninth Streets at Constitution Avenue NW • Washington, D.C. • 202-737-4215

Less than four months after his inauguration, President Garfield arrived at the Union Station in Washington, D.C. on July 2, 1881 to catch a train for a summer's retreat on the New Jersey seashore. As Garfield made his way through the station, Charles Guiteau, angry because he did not get a government job that he thought he deserved, rushed Garfield and fired two shots into him. One grazed Garfield's arm; the other lodged in his abdomen. Exclaiming, "My God, what is this?" the president collapsed to the floor remaining fully conscious, but in a great deal of pain. The wound eventually spread into peritonitis, and President Garfield died September 19, 1881.

Gein, Eddie

Near Plainfield, Wisconsin

On November 17, 1957, police in Plainfield, Wisconsin arrived at the run-down farmhouse of one Eddie Gein, a suspect in the robbery of a local hardware store and subsequent disappearance of the owner, Bernice Worden. (Gein had been the last customer at the hardware store and had been witnessed lingering around the premises.)

Police found the desolate Gein farmhouse a gross tangle of cluttered chaos, with junk and old rotting food all over the place. But the worst was yet to come. The local sheriff, Arthur Schley, felt something brush against his jacket as he inspected the kitchen. To his shock, he then came face to face with a large, dangling carcass hanging upside down from the ceiling beams. The carcass (which turned out to be Bernice Worden) had been decapitated, slit open, and gutted. Upon further inspection, the shocked deputies soon discovered that they were standing amidst a human corpse warehouse. The funny-looking bowl was the top of a human skull. The lampshades and waste-basket were made from human skin. And there was more: An armchair made of human skin, a human head, four noses, and a heart.

This bizarre scenario soon inspired Author Robert Bloch to write a story about Norman Bates, which became the central theme of Albert Hitchcock's classic thriller *Psycho*. In 1974, Tobe Hooper's horror flick *The Texas Chainsaw Massacre* was also loosely based on the Gein story. Years later, Gein was the inspiration for the serial killer Buffalo Bill in *The Silence of the Lambs*. (Like Eddie, Buffalo Bill treasured women's skin and wore it like clothing in an insane transvestite ritual.)

Gein eventually confessed to killing two women, who, he said, resembled his mother. (Police suspect he killed many more given the physical evidence.) Despite the evidence, he insisted he had not committed necrophilia or canni-balism, but merely decorated himself and his house with female body parts. Although police could only link him to the murders of the two women, he was suspected of having killed five other people, including his brother and two other men who had worked on the farm. Eddie Gein was found insane and committed to Central State Hospital at Waupon. In 1978, he was moved to the Mendota Mental Health Institute where he remained until his death in 1984; he was 77 years old. Today, there is nothing left of the farmhouse.

Giffords, Gabby
7110 N. Oracle • Tucson, Arizona

U.S. Representative Gabby Giffords and 18 others were shot on January 8, 2011 during a constituent meeting held in a supermarket parking lot in Casas Adobes, Arizona, in the Tucson metropolitan area. Six people were killed, in-cluding federal District Court Chief Judge John Roll; Gabe Zimmerman, one of Giffords' staffers; and a nine-year-old girl, Christina-Taylor Green. Giffords was holding the meeting, called "Congress on Your Corner," in the parking lot of a Safeway store when Jared Lee Loughner drew a pistol and shot her in the head before proceeding to fire on other people. Investigators soon discovered evidence at Loughner's home indicating he had targeted the congresswoman in an assassination plot, and that he had a history of posting anti-government rants on the internet. Today Giffords remains an activist, though partially paralyzed from the brutal attack.

Gotti, John

247 Mulberry Street (just below Prince Street)
New York, New York

Until recently, this was the site of the Ravenite Social Club, a longtime Mafia hangout. Most notoriously, John Gotti, "the Dapper Don," was arrested here on December 12, 1990, and charged with racketeering and murder. Even though the Ravenite's facade had been bricked up to evade FBI surveillance, the Feds managed to bug the building and record enough evidence to prosecute Gotti. Over time, many of the incriminating audio and video-tapes were made public. The ground floor's brick facade was recently replaced with a shiny glass storefront, and a boutique has opened.

Hearst, Patty

Kidnap Site

2603 Benvenue Avenue, #4 (at Parker Street) • Berkeley, California

This is where 19-year-old heiress (and grand-daughter of publishing baron William Randolph Hearst) Patty Hearst was abducted in February 1974 by a band of counter-culture revolutionaries called "The Symbionese Liberation Army." The gang beat up Hearst's boyfriend, Steven Weed, as they dragged her away. Soon, the world would learn that Hearst had joined forces with the group, which would result in one of the most captivating, bizarre stories of the century.

S.L.A. Bank Robbery

Hibernia Bank
Sunset District Office
1450 Noriega Street
San Francisco, California

Remember the crude video images of a machine gun-toting Patty Hearst moving through a bank? This is where it happened on April 15, 1974. Just days earlier, Hearst had announced her allegiance to the Symbionese Liberation Army, and that she would fight under the name "Tania." Once the Hibernia Bank, today it's a Hollywood Video store.

Mel's Sporting Goods (Former Site)

11425 S. Crenshaw Boulevard • Inglewood, California

Patty Hearst was also captured here on videotape brandishing a rifle as her S.L.A. comrades robbed the place. Though the store is gone, supposedly a bullet hole is still visible in a light pole outside the store.

S.L.A. Death Site

1466 E. 54th Street (near Compton Avenue) • Los Angeles, California

This is where six S.L.A. members (without Patty Hearst) were killed

on May 17, 1974, in a fire resulting from a police siege which burned their South Los Angeles hideout (a one-story, stucco house) to the ground. Today, it's a vacant lot, and burn marks from the fire are still visible on the trees in front of where the house once stood.

Patty Hearst Capture Site
625 Morse Street (between Guttenberg and Lowell)
San Francisco, California

Hearst's saga came to an end here, a year and a half after being kidnapped. During trial, she claimed to have been brainwashed by her abductors, and though she was found guilty by a jury, she later had her sentence commuted by President Jimmy Carter.

Hickock, "Wild Bill"
Old Style Saloon No. 10 • 657 Main Street • Deadwood, South Dakota
800-952-9398

After his law enforcement career ended, James Butler "Wild Bill" Hickock toured with Buffalo Bill Cody's Wild West Show, then retired to Deadwood for a life of drinking and gambling. That life ended August 2, 1876, when he was shot in the back of the head by a disgruntled laborer, Jack McCall, who had lost a few dollars to Hickock in a poker game. At the time, Hickock held aces and eights (two pairs). Ever since, that's been known as the "dead man's hand." Today, you can see re-enactments staged at this popular tourist attraction, and even see the Hickock "death chair."

Hoffa, Jimmy
Machus Red Fox Restaurant (former site) • 6676 Telegraph Road
Bloomfield Hills, Michigan

Paroled from federal prison three and a half years earlier, former Teamsters President Jimmy Hoffa had announced his plans in 1975 to again seek the union leadership. On July 30, Hoffa left home for an afternoon meeting. He told people the participants would include Anthony Giacalone, reputed by federal authorities to be a captain of organized crime in Detroit.

Hoffa was seen waiting outside in the parking lot of the Machus Red Fox restaurant in Bloomfield Township, and it is known that he made at least two calls from a pay phone outside the hardware store behind the restaurant. But 27 years after James Riddle Hoffa set off for lunch, his remains have not been found and no one has been arrested for his murder. (Though many wild rumors persist as to where his remains might be found.)

James, Jesse

Nimrod Long and Company
296 South Main Street • Russellville, Kentucky

On the afternoon of March 20, 1868, the James Gang, comprised of outlaw Jesse James, his brother Frank James, and four others, robbed Nimrod Long and Company, a local bank. The actual robbery scene is now a private home; the bank (now called The Old Southern Bank) moved down the street to Sixth and Main Streets and today features a lobby mural depicting the legendary heist.

James, Jesse (and the "James Gang")
Between Adair and Anita, along county road G30 (1½ miles west of Adair) • Adair, Iowa

On July 21, 1873, Jesse James and his notorious gang committed what is considered to be the first train robbery in the west. Word had come down to the outlaws that the Rock Island and Pacific train was loaded up with a huge shipment of gold. The gang, thinking this might be the haul of their lives, anticipated a find of more than $100,000 worth of gold. Much to their surprise, the robbery yielded "only" about $2,000 in notes. It seems their timing had been just a bit off. The real haul of valuable gold sped by some 12 hours later.

Today, a locomotive wheel bears a plaque with the inscription: "Site of the first train robbery in the west, committed by the notorious Jesse James and his gang of outlaws July 21, 1873." It was erected by the Rock Island Railroad in 1954.

First National Bank
Scriver Building • 408 Division Street • Northfield, Minnesota
507-645-9268

Today this building houses the Northfield Historical Museum, but back on September 7, 1876, this was where the townspeople of Northfield rose up against the notorious James Gang when they attempted to rob the First National Bank.

James and his gang didn't realize how well-armed and well-prepared the people of Northfield were to do battle, but after killing the bank's cashier, they were engaged in seven minutes of bloody, dramatic gunfire with the townsfolk. The famous band of outlaws saw two of their own killed and several others hunted down over the course of the next 10 days. Only Jesse and Frank James escaped by heading to South Dakota. Thus, the humiliated gang made away with nothing that day, and was disbanded forever.

The James Farm
21216 James Farm Road • Kearney, Missouri • 816-628-6065

Outlaw Jesse James was shot and killed in this house on April 3, 1882, by Bob Ford, a member of the James gang. Ford killed James to collect a $10,000 reward offered by Governor Tom Crittenden. At the time, the 34-year-old Jesse James was living with his wife and two children under the assumed name of Tom Howard. Jesse was shot from behind while he stood on a chair to straighten a picture in his own home.

Today at the farm, visitors can see artifacts from James' grave including the coffin handles; a small tie pin Jesse James was wearing the day he was killed; a bullet removed from his right lung area; and a casting of his skull, showing the bullet hole behind his right ear. (The famous bullet hole from the fatal shot also remains under Plexiglas in the wall.)

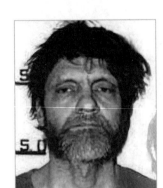

Kaczynski, Ted

Stemple Road • Lincoln, Montana
Lincoln Chamber of Commerce: 406-362-4949

DIRECTIONS TO STEMPLE ROAD: Take the Forest Service Road to Stemple Pass, about 3 miles outside Lincoln. Stemple Road is located on Highway 200 in Lincoln. (There is one blinking light in the center of the town—that's the intersection of Stemple Road.)

The Unabomber, Ted Kaczynski, lived just off this mountain pass road until his arrest in 1997. While the actual cabin is kept under wraps at a California Air Force base, you can still see where the cabin used to sit. The former Harvard math teacher turned mad bomber now resides at the "SuperMax" penitentiary in Colorado.

Kennedy, President John F.

Oswald, Lee Harvey

214 W. Neeley Street • Oak Cliff • Dallas, Texas

This is the house where the well-known "backyard photos" of Oswald holding his rifle were taken. This two-story wood frame structure is crumbling, but the back staircase railing, prominent in the background of all of the Oswald photos, is still intact and easily recognizable (though the original staircase is long gone).

Sixth Floor Museum (Book Depository Building)

411 Elm Street • Dallas, Texas • 888-485-4854

It was from here, at the sixth floor window of the Texas School Book Depository (now called the Dallas County Administration Building), that Lee Harvey Oswald (allegedly) took aim and killed President John F. Kennedy on November 22, 1963. Also called the "Sniper's Nest," the window is visible from the street—it's the last window on the far right on the building's sixth floor side facing Dealey Plaza. Inside the fascinating museum that now exists on the sixth floor, boxes of books have been stacked around the window to simulate what it would have looked like in November 1963.

Zapruder, Abraham
The pergola on the north side of Elm, in Dealey Plaza • Dallas, Texas

The pergola gave a good view of the presidential motorcade, and spectator Abraham Zapruder stood on one of its low columns to take the famous home movie of the motorcade.

Parkland Hospital Emergency Room
5201 Harry Hines Boulevard
Dallas, Texas • 214-590-8000

Although newer buildings have gone up around the Emergency Room, its entrance looks exactly as it did in 1963 when Kennedy was taken after being shot.

Boarding House
1026 N. Beckley Avenue • Dallas, Texas

After Kennedy was assassinated, the School Book Depository was sealed off. Since Oswald had already been interrogated, he returned home to this boarding house, went inside, got a pistol, and hid it inside his jacket. He then hopped a 1:00 P.M. bus about 50 yards west of the house, and rode it approximately one mile south to Jefferson Street.

Officer D.J. Tippit
Tenth Street and Patton Avenue • Dallas, Texas

The houses once standing on the corner have been demolished, but this is where Oswald allegedly shot Officer D.J. Tippit after being stopped. It is believed Tippit stopped him after getting a description

of J.F.K.'s assassin. He then headed off to a shoe store.

The Hardy Shoe Store
213 West Jefferson Avenue • Dallas, Texas

After the shooting at Tenth and Patton, Oswald supposedly ducked into this shoe store. He was spotted by shoe salesman Johnny Brewer, who then followed Oswald to the Texas Theater and alerted the ticket taker to call the police. (The shoe store is now a bridal shop.)

The Texas Theater
231 West Jefferson Avenue • Dallas, Texas

The police rushed into this theater, took the stage, and asked Johnny Brewer to identify the man he'd just followed from the shoe store. Oswald was fingered, and though he put up a struggle, he was then taken into custody. Built by billionaire Howard Hughes, the Texas Theater opened in 1931 and began showing the city's first talking pictures. After being closed for seven years, it reopened in 2002.

City Hall
2001 Commerce Street • Dallas, Texas

This is where Jack Ruby shot Oswald as he was being taken away to jail. The basement entrance to the ramp where cop cars were waiting to deliver Oswald to the county jail can still be accessed from inside the building. Take the stairs at the left of the lobby to the basement and go down the hall to the glass doors, the only addition since the murder.

Love Field
8008 Cedar Springs Road • Dallas, Texas • 214-670-6073

Lyndon Johnson was sworn in on Air Force One at Love Field, and a plaque commemorating the ceremony was placed on a granite pillar at the front entrance to the airport, just inside the double doors from the parking lot.

Kennedy, Robert F.
Ambassador Hotel • 3400 Wilshire Boulevard • Los Angeles, California

On June 5, 1968 at 12.15 A.M., Senator Robert F. Kennedy was making his way from the ballroom at the Ambassador Hotel to give a press conference after winning the California Primary. The prearranged route went through a food service pantry. While walking

through this area, a Palestinian Arab, Sirhan Sirhan, stepped forward and fired a .22 revolver at the senator. Although Sirhan was quickly subdued, Kennedy and five others were shot, although only Kennedy was fatally wounded.

Sirhan was arrested at the scene, charged, and convicted of first degree murder. He was to have been executed, but the U.S. Supreme Court voided the constitutionality of the death sentence before the sentence could be carried out. Sirhan has been incarcerated at Corcoran State Prison, California, ever since.

The hotel was torn down in the early 2000s.

King, Jr., Martin Luther
The National Civil Rights Museum (formerly the Lorraine Motel)
450 Mulberry Street • Memphis, Tennessee • 901-521-9699

Dr. Martin Luther King, Jr., leader of the American civil rights movement, was assassinated on April 4, 1968 in Memphis, Tennessee while lending support to a sanitation workers' strike. He was shot by James Earl Ray at approximately 7:05 P.M. Ray's bullet struck King as he was standing on his balcony at the Lorraine Motel; King died approximately one hour later.

Although no television cameras were in the vicinity at the time of the assassination, television coverage of the event quickly followed. From 1968–1982, business at the Lorraine Motel languished, and in 1982 the property was foreclosed. In 1991, the National Civil Rights Museum opened at the site.

King, Rodney
11777 Foothill Boulevard • Lakeview Terrace, California

In 1993, after a high speed chase, an allegedly drunken motorist named Rodney King was beaten by police officers for resisting arrest. The incident was captured on videotape by a nearby resident and beamed worldwide within days. When the officers charged in the crime were acquitted, it set off the infamous 1992 L.A. riots. The actual beating site is a large, dirt lot in this remote part of the San Fernando Valley, directly across from the Mountainback Apartments at 11777 Foothill Boulevard.

Las Vegas Shooting
Mandalay Bay Hotel • 3950 Las Vegas Blvd. South • Las Vegas, Nevada

Stephen Paddock, a 64-year-old man from Mesquite, Nevada, opened fire on the crowd attending the Route 91 Harvest music festival on the Las Vegas Strip on October 1, 2017. He fired more than 1,000 bullets from his 32nd-floor suite in the Mandalay Bay hotel, killing 60 people and wounding at least 413. Astonishingly, the ensuing panic brought the total number of injured to approximately 867. About an hour later, Paddock was found dead in his room from a self-inflicted gunshot wound. The motive for the mass shooting is officially undetermined. The incident is the deadliest mass shooting committed by an individual in United States history. It focused attention on firearms laws in the U.S., particularly concerning bump stocks, which Paddock used to fire shots in rapid succession at a rate similar to that of automatic firearms. Bump stocks were banned by the U.S. Justice Department in December 2018.

Lincoln, Abraham

Ford Theater
511 10th Street NW • Washington, D.C. • 202-347-4833

John Wilkes Booth, a popular actor, ended his full-time stage career in May of 1864. The Maryland native wanted to spend most of his time on his primary interest—supporting the Confederate States of America. Within months, Booth was working actively with Confederate partisans.

A plan to capture President Lincoln and exchange him for Confederate prisoners of war brought Booth into contact with Dr. Samuel Mudd, John Surratt, Mary Surrat (John's mother), Lewis Thorton Powell, David Herold, George Atzerodt, and others. This plan failed when, on the day chosen for the capture, President Lincoln changed his plans and did not travel on the road where conspirators were waiting. This March 17, 1865 kidnapping failure was quickly followed by two major Confederate defeats. Richmond, the capital of the Confederacy, was abandoned to Union troops, and on Palm Sunday, April 9, Robert E. Lee surrendered his army to General Grant. Soon after these defeats, Booth decided to assassinate President Lincoln while Powell was to kill Secretary of State Seward, and Atzerodt was to kill Vice President Andrew Johnson.

On April 14, 1865 (at about 10:15 P.M.), Booth opened the door to the State Box at the Ford Theater where the President and his party were seated. He shot Lincoln once in the back of the head, stabbed Henry Rathbone in a struggle, and then jumped to the stage, 11 feet below. Breaking his leg in the fall, he made his way across the stage, left through the back door, and escaped on his horse.

The Petersen House

516 10th Street NW • Directly across the street from the Ford Theater, part of the Ford's Theatre National Historic Site • Washington, D.C.

After the shooting, Lincoln was taken across the street to the Petersen House. During the night and early morning, a parade of government officials and physicians was allowed to come inside and pay respects to the unconscious president. Despite the best efforts of the physicians involved, the external and internal hemorrhaging continued throughout the night and on the next day, April 15, 1865, at 7:22 A.M., a doctor leaned over the president and felt his final breath. Lincoln was just 56 years old.

Garrett Farm (Former Site)
Bowling Green, Virginia • (The highway marker is on Route 301, near Route 17, adjacent to the properties of the A. P. Hill Army Base)

Most historians agree that Abraham Lincoln's assassin, John Wilkes Booth, was killed in Garrett's barn on April 26, 1865. However, due to the mystery surrounding the autopsy and subsequent burial of Booth, some surmised that Booth didn't really die that night. But today, it seems almost certain that the actor-assassin did in fact die here that night, shot inside the barn while it burned, then pulled out until he died three hours later.

The marker text reads: "John Wilkes Booth . . . The Garrett place is where John Wilkes Booth was allegedly cornered and killed by Union troops on April 26, 1865. Although several groups believe Booth escaped from the Garrett farm, no proof has been uncovered to confirm nor totally rule out the beliefs. The house stood a short distance from this spot."

Lindbergh, Charles, Jr.
Lindbergh Home (now the Albert Ellis Residential Group Center)
188 Lindbergh Road • Hopewell, New Jersey • 609-466-0740

The kidnapping and murder of Charles Lindbergh, Jr., son of aviation pioneer and American hero, Charles Lindbergh (five years after his famous, solo cross-Atlantic flight) remains one of the most notable crimes in this country's history—the true crime of the century.

On the night of March 31, 1932, Charles, Jr.'s nursemaid, Betty Gow, went to check on the electric heater in the baby's room. To her shock, she found the child's crib empty. Turning on the light in his son's room, Lindbergh discovered a small note which was left on the window sill. "Anne," he said, turning to his wife "they have stolen our baby."

Despite other notes left by the kidnapper in the next few months, everything wound up at a dead end. Two months later, the baby's body was found in a shallow grave in the woods about four miles from the Lindbergh home. A trucker who had stopped to relieve himself stumbled upon the decomposed body along with a handmade ladder, chisel, and some ransom notes.

In 1934, German Immigrant Bruno Richard Hauptmann was arrested for the crime (based initially on some of the ransom money that was found in his possession). A year later he was tried, convicted, and executed at the New Jersey State Prison. Today, the house (which is virtually unchanged from the night of the crime) is used by the Albert Elias Residential Community Home, a residential facility designed to serve younger male juvenile offenders. The youths there are also responsible for the historic maintenance of the house that the Lindbergh family deeded to the State of New Jersey.

List, John
431 Hillside Avenue • Westfield, New Jersey

In 1971, bookish, conservative, 35-year-old John List inexplicably slaughtered his mother, wife, and three children in the ballroom of the family mansion. He left behind a note in which he justified the homicides by explaining that, due to his inability to make enough money (he thought he was in danger of losing job), he didn't feel his family would be happy with the turn their lives would soon be taking. So he "put them out of their misery" and then disappeared. It was one of the most ghoulish massacres in American history.

Eighteen years later, the case was still cold. But in 1989, the popular television series *America's Most Wanted* commissioned an age-enhanced bust of List to aid viewers in identifying the confessed murderer. The creation was so accurate that 350 viewers called with tips, one of which led to List's arrest. List remains in prison today, serving five consecutive life sentences.

MacDonald, Jeffrey
544 Castle Drive • Fort Bragg, North Carolina

On the cold, rainy night of February 17, 1970 at Fort Bragg, North Carolina, military policemen responded to a telephone call from Green Beret group surgeon Jeffrey R. MacDonald. Shockingly, the MPs arrived at the apartment to discover the freshly killed bodies of MacDonald's wife, Colette, 26, and their daughters, Kimberly, 5, and Kristen, 2.

MacDonald, who had sustained minor injuries, told the cops that a drug-crazed bunch of hippies committed the murders while chanting, "Acid is groovy. Kill the pigs." Prosecutors were suspicious at once, given that Mac-Donald's injuries were so slight. He was ultimately convicted of the murders in a civilian criminal court and remains in prison, despite numerous appeals that continue to this day.

Malcolm X
Harlem's Audubon Ballroom • 3940 Broadway Avenue
New York, New York

On February 21, 1965, Malcolm X was shot to death as he delivered a speech in Manhattan's Audobon Ballroom. The following March, three men—Talmadge Hayer, Norman Butler, and Thomas Johnson—were convicted of murdering the 39-year-old black leader. Though prosecutors suggested at trial that the slaying was plotted as "an object lesson for Malcolm's followers," no direct evidence linked the Nation of Islam—from which Malcolm had publicly broken—to the killing, though that speculation still thrives.

Manson, Charles and the Manson Family

The Spahn Ranch
23000 Santa Susana Pass Road (former site) • San Fernando Valley, California • (Located along the south side of Santa Susanna Pass Road near the entrance to the Iverson Movie Ranch. The movie/tourist sets burned down in the wildfires of 1970. Since that time, the property has been regraded and subdivided into at least three separate parcels.)

A ranch outside Los Angeles owned by George Spahn, an 81-year-old blind man who had operated it as a nostalgic Western Movie Ranch, became the home for Charles Manson and his followers. Spahn soon became dependent on the girls in Charlie's family to help him with his daily activities, not knowing they were also acting as "ears" for Manson at the same time.

While here, the paranoid Manson developed a theory based on visions and the Beatles' *White Album*. He interpreted the song "Helter Skelter" as an omen telling of an impending race war in which blacks would rise up and kill off all white people, with the exception of him and his "family." Today, nothing original is left on this private property where the Manson Family once lived.

Tate, Sharon

10048 Cielo Drive
(originally 10050 Cielo Drive)
Beverly Hills, California

The beautiful, willowy actress' husband Roman Polanski was not home on August 9, 1969 when Charles Manson's fanatical family members snuck up on Tate (who was eight months pregnant) and her houseguests (including coffee heiress Abigail Folger). The gang brutally butchered everyone in the house; Tate plead in vain for them to spare the life of her unborn child.

A "revenge" crime for Manson's warped view that he'd been deprived of a recording career by the house's former owner (record producer Terry Melcher), this horrendous act changed the city overnight, making celebrities much more paranoid about their own security. The owners of the house tore the original down and built another in its place—and it is impossible to see the house from the gate (the address was changed to discourage trespassers).

LaBianca, Leno and Rosemary

3311 Waverly Drive (at St. George Street) (originally 3301 Waverly)
Los Angeles, California

This was the site of the second Manson Family strike in the summer of 1969. Allegedly, the Manson Family knew someone who used to live near this house, the home where grocery store owner Leno LaBianca lived with

his wife, Rosemary (the Family did not know the LaBiancas). Written in the victim's blood around the house were "Death to Pigs" and of course, the famously misspelled "Healter Skelter." Though the address has been altered, the house where the murders took place remains virtually unchanged.

Barker Ranch

Ballarat, California • (The "ghost" town of Ballarat is located 90 miles north of Barstow and 31 miles north of Trona. Barker Ranch is on Goler Canyon Road, in Death Valley National Park. Four-wheel drive is recommended. For exact directions call 760-786-3200.)

It was here, at Barker Ranch, that the evil mastermind and 24 members of his gang were finally captured in 1969. The local County Sheriff's Department and National Park law enforcement arrested Manson and his group thinking they were responsible for vandalizing a portion of the Death Valley National Park further north. It wasn't until later that they realized they had the infamous mass murder suspect and his faithful cult members in custody.

Corcoran Correctional Facility

4001 King Avenue • Corcoran, California

This is the central California maximum security prison where Charles Manson is serving his life sentences.

Martin, Trayvon
Retreat at Twin Lakes • 1211 Long Oak Way • Sanford, Florida

African American teen Trayvon Martin was walking home from a trip to a convenience store on February 26, 2012 when he was fatally shot by George Zimmerman, a neighborhood watch volunteer patrolling the townhouse community of the Retreat at Twin Lakes. Zimmerman later claimed to have shot the unarmed 17-year-old out of self-defense during a physical altercation. After police initially opted not to arrest Zimmerman, the case sparked protests and ignited national debates about racial profiling and self-defense laws. Zimmerman later was charged with second-degree murder. Following a high-profile trial, he was acquitted of the charges against him. The term "Black Lives Matter" was then used for the first time by organizer Alicia Garza in a July 13, 2013 Facebook post in response to Zimmerman's acquittal. The phrase spread widely and became a rallying cry against racial injustice.

McDonald's Massacre
(now the Southwestern College Education Center)
460 West San Ysidro Boulevard (about a mile north of the Mexican border) • San Ysidro, California

On July 18, 1984, James Huberty declared to his wife that he was going to "hunt humans." Soon, he would slaughter 21 innocent people in one of the worst mass shootings in U.S. history. After a standoff with cops, Hubert was shot and killed by a single bullet. McDonald's tore the restaurant down and donated the land. A local college was built in its place, and today a monument with 21 columns (one for each victim) can be found there.

McKinley, President William
Northwest side of Delaware Park • Buffalo, New York

On September 6, 1901, Leon Czolgosz shot President William McKinley as he greeted citizens in the Temple of Music, a pavilion of the Buffalo, New York, Pan-American Exposition. Eight days later, on September 14, McKinley was dead, and America's most popular president since Lincoln was mourned throughout the world. A bronze tablet marks the spot where the shooting took place.

The Menendez Brothers
722 North Elm Drive • Beverly Hills, California

This is the site of the infamous Menendez murders, committed in August of 1989 by brothers Lyle and Erik Menendez. As their parents, Kitty and Jose Menendez, were watching TV and eating ice cream, the pair blew them apart with multiple shotgun blasts. The juries in the first trials of their cases were deadlocked, but a new jury found them both guilty of first degree murder. The murders were the subject of two 1994 made-for-TV movies: *Menendez: A Killing in Beverly Hills* and *Honor Thy Father and Mother: The True Story of the Menendez Murders.*

Mob Summit
625 McFall Road • Apalachin, New York

The "Apalachin Conference" of 1957 is one of the landmarks of organized crime history. Just 20 days after syndicate boss Albert Anastasia was killed, more than 50 of the top syndicate leaders in the country got together at the country home of Joseph M. Barbara here in upstate Apalachin, New York. When police had learned that Barbara was making hotel reservations for a large number of people in the Apalachin area, they decided to notify two federal agents from the Alcohol and Tobacco Tax Unit and get a closer look.

Four officers drove onto the grounds on November 14, 1957, and as soon as the gangsters spotted the car, they assumed they were in for a mass arrest and fled the house. Some made it to their cars to escape, but others (some of whom were more than 60 years old and dressed in tailored suits), fled through the countryside on foot. Police set up roadblocks and, soon, many were under arrest.

Parkland Shooting
5901 Pine Island Road • Parkland, Florida

On February 14, 2018, 19-year-old Nikolas Cruz opened fire on students and staff at Marjory Stoneman Douglas High School in Parkland, Florida, murdering 17 people and injuring 17 others. Cruz, a former student at the school, fled the scene on foot by blending in with other students and was arrested without incident approximately one hour later in nearby Coral Springs. Police and prosecutors investigated "a pattern of disciplinary issues and unnerving behavior." The killing spree is the deadliest high school shooting in United States history, surpassing the Columbine High School massacre that killed 15 (including the perpetrators) in Colorado in April 1999. The shooting came at a period of heightened public support for gun control that followed mass shootings in Paradise, Nevada, and Sutherland Springs, Texas in October and November 2017. On October 20, 2021, Cruz pleaded guilty to all charges and apologized for his actions. Sentencing was expected in January 2022, but was delayed numerous times, some due to the COVID-19 pandemic. Cruz was sentenced to life imprisonment in November 2022.

Peterson, Laci
523 Covena Avenue • Modesto, California

On Christmas Eve, 2003, Laci Peterson, the pretty 27-year-old wife of Scott Peterson, disappeared from this Modesto home, prompting a nationwide search. When the body of Laci and her unborn child (she was eight months pregnant) were found four months later, Scott was charged with two counts of murder and was subsequently sentenced to death in 2004. In August 2020, the California Supreme Court reversed Peterson's death sentence, and in December 2021, he was re-sentenced to life imprisonment without the possibility of parole.

From the start, public suspicion fell on Laci's husband. Scott Peterson told detectives that he had last seen his wife on December 24 at 9:30 A.M. when he left their home in the La Loma neighborhood of Modesto for a solo fishing trip in Berkeley, about an hour-and-a-half drive away. Laci, he said, had plans to go grocery shopping and then walk their golden retriever in nearby East La Loma Park. But when he returned home that night, she was gone. The facility, Security Public Storage, is located at 1401 Woodland Avenue.

Pulse Nightclub Shooting
912 S. Orange Avenue • Orlando, Florida

Twenty-nine-year-old Omar Mateen killed 49 people and wounded 53 more in a mass shooting at Pulse, a gay nightclub in Orlando, Florida, on June 12, 2016. Orlando police officers shot and killed him after a three-hour standoff. In a 911 call Mateen made shortly after the shooting began, he swore allegiance to the leader of the Islamic State of Iraq and Syria, Abu Bakr al-Baghdadi, and said the U.S. killing of Abu Waheeb in Iraq the previous month "triggered" the shooting. He later told a negotiator he was "out here right now" because of the American-led interventions in Iraq and Syria and that the negotiator should tell the United States to stop the bombing. The incident was deemed a terrorist attack by FBI investigators. Pulse was hosting a "Latin Night" that night, and thus most of the victims were Latino. It was the deadliest incident in the history of violence against LGBT people in the United States, as well as the deadliest terrorist attack in the U.S. since the September 11 attacks in 2001, and was the deadliest mass shooting by a single gunman in U.S. history until the 2017 Las Vegas shooting. Though the club closed, there is still a memorial at the site.

Ramsey, Jon Benet
755 15th Street • Boulder, Colorado

On Christmas Day, 1996, in the upscale Chautauqua section of Boulder, six-year-old beauty queen Jon Benet Ramsey was discovered missing. Soon, after a search of the house, the little girl was found in the basement, murdered. To date, nobody has been arrested for what was one of the most intensely covered crimes in U.S. history.

Reagan, President Ronald
Washington Hilton Hotel
2015 Massachusetts Ave. NW
Washington, D.C. • 866-597-9330

On March 30, 1981, President Reagan was shot outside the Washington Hilton Hotel. Reagan was rushed to George Washington Hospital, a bullet within an inch of his heart. The president showed grace and a quick wit in the face of death, even telling a joke or two within hours of the shooting (when wife Nancy asked what had happened, he simply said, "Honey, I forgot to duck").

Reagan was shot in the chest, but surgeons removed the bullet and he made a full recovery. Three other people, including Reagan's press secretary, James S. Brady, were also shot. John W. Hinckley, Jr., of Evergreen, Colorado, was charged with the shooting. In 1982, a jury declared that Hinckley was insane at the time of the attempted assassination and found him not guilty of the attempted murder charge. A federal judge later ordered that Hinckley be placed in a mental hospital, where he remains today. (Hinckley was obsessed with actress Jodi Foster and claimed that he committed the act to gain attention from her.)

Sandy Hook Elementary School Shooting
12 Dickenson Drive • Newtown, Connecticut

Twenty-year-old Adam Lanza attacked Sandy Hook Elementary School in Newton, Connecticut on December 14, 2012, shooting and killing 26 people. Most of the victims were children. Lanza killed himself before he could be caught. The attack was recorded as the second-deadliest mass shooting committed by a single gunman in American history and opened up many wide-ranging debates and discussions on gun control and mental health.

Scalise, Steve
Eugene Simpson Stadium Park • 426 E. Monroe Avenue
Alexandria, Virginia

During a practice session for the annual Congressional Baseball Game for Charity in Alexandria, Virginia on June 14, 2017, James Hodgkinson conducted a mass shooting in which the victims shot included U.S. House Majority Whip Steve Scalise, U.S. Capitol police officer Crystal Griner, congressional aide Zack Barth, and lobbyist Matt Mika. A 10-minute shootout took place between Hodgkinson and officers from the Capitol and Alexandria police before officers shot Hodgkinson, who died from his wounds later that day at the George Washington University Hospital. Scalise and Mika were taken to nearby hospitals where they underwent surgery. Hodgkinson was a left-wing political activist from Belleville, Illinois, while Scalise was a Republican member of Congress. The Virginia Attorney General concluded Hodgkinson's attack was "an act of terrorism . . . fueled by rage against Republican legislators." Scalise was the first sitting member of Congress to have been shot since Arizona Representative Gabby Giffords was shot in 2011.

Shepard, Matthew
Snowy Mountain View Road • Approximately one mile northeast of
Laramie, Wyoming

Matthew Shepard, a 21-year-old homosexual man, was lured from a college
campus bar shortly after midnight on October 7, 1999 by Aaron McKinney
and Russell Henderson, who tempted Shepard by falsely saying that they were
also gay. He was driven to a remote area near the Sherman Hills neighborhood
east of Laramie, then tied to a split-rail fence and sadistically beaten while he
begged for his life. He was then left for dead in the cold until a cyclist found
him at 6:22 P.M., some 18 hours after the attack. Shepard was so brutalized
that the cyclist at first mistook him for a scarecrow. Unconscious and suffering from hypothermia, Shepard died shortly after.

Russell Henderson pleaded guilty to felony murder with robbery and kidnapping and was given two life sentences without the chance for parole (in
doing so, he avoided any chance of the death penalty). Henderson said he only
witnessed the murder, but did not take part in it. Aaron McKinney was found
guilty and sentenced to two life terms. He was spared from facing the death
penalty because Matthew Shepard's mother, feeling that it would represent
revenge and not justice, asked that it not be imposed.

Sheppard, Marilyn
28944 Lake Road • Bay Village, Ohio

On July 4, 1954, a pregnant Marilyn Sheppard was murdered, beaten to death
in her own suburban bedroom. Soon after, her successful physician husband
Sam Sheppard was arrested and charged with the slaying. Throughout the
trial, he maintained his innocence, claiming he'd tried to fight off a "bushy-
haired stranger," was knocked completely unconscious, and awoke to find his
wife dead. However, Sheppard was convicted and spent 10 years behind bars.
In 1966, he was re-tried and his conviction was overturned, thanks to a young,
upstart lawyer named F. Lee Bailey.

Broken and battered, Sheppard spent his final years alive struggling with
alcohol and even appearing as "Killer Sheppard" in pro wrestling matches.
The Sheppard murder case is believed to have been the inspiration for the
successful 1960's TV series, *The Fugitive*, starring David Janssen. The Sheppard
house where the murder took place has since been razed and a new one has
been built in its place.

Siegel, Bugsy
810 Linden Drive
Beverly Hills, California

This is the home where mob hit-men blew away mobster Bugsy Siegel in 1947 (they drove by and shot him through the front windows while he was sitting in the living room). Siegel had just built the first major hotel in Las Vegas, the Flamingo. His life story was told in the 1991 movie *Bugsy*, starring Warren Beatty.

Simpson, O. J.

Simpson Home
360 North Rockingham Avenue, located north of Sunset Boulevard, at the southeast corner of Rockingham and Ashford • Brentwood, California

This was the site of the $5 million Tudor mansion of O.J. Simpson, where he and Nicole were married, where he was arrested for her murder on June 17, 1994 (following the Bronco freeway chase), and where he lived after being found "not guilty" in the trial. The scene of much of his trial's focus, Simpson's house became a huge tourist attraction in the months following the tragic events. He was forced to sell the home after losing a civil lawsuit. In July of 1998, the new owner of the estate bulldozed the home and all of the other buildings on the property.

Paul Revere Middle School
1450 Allenford Avenue
Santa Monica, California

At 5:00 P.M. on June 12, 1994, just a few hours before the murders, O.J.

Simpson and his wife Nicole attended their daughter's dance recital at this school. (The video of Simpson directly outside the school after the recital was played many times during the trial.)

Mezzaluna Restaurant (Now Peet's Coffee)
11750 San Vicente Boulevard (at Gorham Avenue)
Brentwood, California

After a school recital, Nicole Simpson and her family went to dinner at the nearby Mezzaluna trattoria at around 6:30 P.M., where Ronald Goldman worked as a waiter. Goldman later offered to return a pair of lost prescription glasses to Nicole's house—where they both were murdered. The restaurant closed in mid-1997 and is now a coffeehouse.

Ronald Goldman's Apartment
11663 Gorham Avenue
Brentwood, California

This is the apartment building where victim Ronald Goldman lived. A waiter at Mezzaluna restaurant, Goldman stopped here to change his clothes on that fateful night, on his way from the restaurant to Nicole Simpson's condo.

McDonald's
20712 Santa Monica Boulevard • Santa Monica, California
310-829-3223

This is where O.J. drove with Kato to grab a few burgers just an hour or so before the murders took place. O.J. stopped by Kato's room to borrow some cash, mentioned he was going out to grab a bite, and then Kato asked if he could tag along. This trip resulted in some important observations

for the trial, such as what Simpson was wearing that night, and where his Bronco was originally parked at the house. It also pinned the time of Simpson's last known whereabouts to about 9:40–9:45 P.M. (which is when they returned to the house). (Note: The Burger King where it was wildly rumored that these two stopped to make a drug score is a few blocks east on Santa Monica Boulevard, just east of Bundy Drive on the north side of the street.)

The Murder Scene

Nichole Simpson's Condominium • 875 South Bundy Drive (now changed to 879 South Bundy) • Brentwood, California

At around midnight on June 12, 1994, Nicole Simpson was found murdered outside of this condominium, lying in a pool of blood on the sidewalk (her throat had been slashed). Her acquaintance, Ronald Goldman, had also been savagely stabbed to death. In the years since the murders, the new owners remodeled the outside of the home to discourage rubbernecking. However, it's an easy address to find, the actual site of the murders is still partially visible, and it remains a popular destination.

O'Hare Plaza Hotel

6600 N. Mannheim Road • Rosemont, Illinois • 847-827-5131

This was the Chicago-area hotel where O.J. was staying when he was "notified" of his ex-wife's murder. He had taken the red-eye here the previous evening from Los Angeles, and it was in his room at this hotel that he allegedly cut his hand on a glass upon hearing the news (his alibi for the severe cut on his knuckle).

Smart, Pamela
4E Misty Morning Drive • Derry, New Hampshire

This is the home where 24-year-old Gregory Smart was killed on May 1, 1990. His wife, high school teacher Pamela Smart, was eventually arrested and convicted for plotting the murder, which was acted out by several of Smart's students. One of the students, 15-year-old William Flynn (the shooter), had been having an affair with the teacher, and later confessed that she had coerced him into committing the crime.

Smart was tripped up by her teaching aid, Cecilia Pierce, who divulged to police that she'd heard Smart plotting the murder with Flynn. Smart then even reportedly attempted to have Pierce killed from prison! Flynn is currently serving a 28-year-to-life sentence; Smart is a serving a lifetime sentence without parole. The incident was made into a 1995 movie *To Die For*, starring Nicole Kidman.

Smith, Susan
John D. Long Lake • Union, South Carolina

A permanent memorial marks the spot where two little boys, three-year-old Michael and fourteen-month-old Alexander Smith, were brutally drowned by their mother on October 25, 1994 so that she could eventually run off with her boyfriend. Despite the fraud that she perpetrated in the days after the crime (claiming a black man had hijacked her car), she eventually confessed after the police proved to her that her story was plausible. Incredibly, she was spared the death penalty, and today serves a life sentence without the possibility of parole.

Sowell, Anthony
12205 Imperial Avenue • Cleveland, Ohio

Anthony Sowell, a.k.a "The Cleveland Strangler," killed at least 11 women from 2007–2009. The former Marine's first recorded crime was the attempted rape of a pregnant woman in 1989. The woman survived, and Sowell served 15 years in prison. After getting out, Sowell began murdering women and keeping the bodies in the empty half of his duplex. Eventually, the woman who was living with him smelled the stench of the dead bodies and notified authorities. The women killed were primarily drug users, and they were lured to his house with the promise of crack cocaine. The original home where he committed his crimes was demolished after his 2011 conviction.

Speck, Richard
Jeffrey Manor • 2319 East 100th Street • Chicago, Illinois

On the night of July 13, 1966, 25-year-old career lowlife Richard Speck spent the early portion of the evening at a Chicago-area bar called The Shipyard Inn. At about 10:30 P.M., he departed for a townhouse where a group of nurses lived. He managed to open the screen door, walk upstairs, and began talking to several of the nurses who were home. He told them that he would not hurt them and merely wanted money to go to New Orleans. However, Speck then began tying the nurses up with bedsheet strips that he had torn with his knife. Frightened by Speck's knife and gun, the women put up little resistance.

Though there were only a few nurses home when Speck first arrived, more nurses continued to come home. Horrifically, Speck took each nurse, one by one, into various rooms of the townhouse and killed them (most by strangulation, some by stabbing). Throughout the butchery, a nurse named Corazon Amurao had managed to hide under a bunkbed. When Speck left the townhouse at about 3:30 A.M. after murdering eight nurses, she survived and ultimately identified him.

Speck was captured after a massive manhunt and was tried and convicted in 1967 of the murders and sentenced to die. However, the U.S. Supreme Court abolished the death penalty in 1972, and so Speck was re-sentenced to eight life terms. He died in prison in November of 1991, just short of his 50th birthday.

Spungen, Nancy
Hotel Chelsea • 222 West 23rd Street, Room 100 • New York, New York
212-243-3700

With Nancy Spungen as his manager, ex-Sex Pistol Sid Vicious played a few gigs at Max's in Kansas City and CBGB'S in New York, but the drugs were taking their toll. Sid and Nancy took a room at the Chelsea Hotel in New

York. It was in the bathroom here that Nancy was killed on October 12, 1978; she was found with stab wounds in her abdomen.

Sid Vicious was charged with her death, but three people were seen leaving the room in the early hours of October 12 and $14,000 was missing. Sid was imprisoned at Riker's Island, but was bailed out for $50,000 (paid for by Malcolm McClaren, manager of the Sex Pistols). He was released on February 1, 1979, and died at his new girlfriend's apartment during a party celebrating his release. His mom had given him $100 to score some heroin to celebrate and it killed him.

The Hotel Chelsea, of course, is famous for many other things, as well. A true Bohemian landmark, it's been called home by writers, musicians, and other artists for decades, including Janis Joplin, Thomas Wolfe, Bob Dylan, Edie Sedgewick, Jimi Hendrix, Arthur Miller, Mark Twain, Dylan Thomas, and many others.

St. Valentine's Day Massacre
2122 North Clark Street • Chicago, Illinois

On February 14, 1929, in the S-M-C Cartage Company warehouse, seven pals of gangster "Bugs" Moran waited to meet with their boss. But Bugs was running late, and arrived just in time to see a cop car pull up and five men get out. Moran took cover and watched as the five men (presumably cops) entered the warehouse. Gun fire rang out from the building. The five cops ran out, dove into the car, and sped off into the snowy Chicago night.

Witnesses soon discovered that the seven gangsters had been lined up against the rear wall of the warehouse and riddled with machine gun fire. Moran, who by now knew he was the target of the hit, was heard to say, "Only Capone kills guys like that!" Bingo. Capone had set the whole thing up, with his men arriving in a stolen police car and wearing fake uniforms.

It was the most notorious gangland shooting in United States history. The warehouse was demolished in 1967, and today the site is a fenced-off courtyard with five trees, adjacent to a nursing home. The tree in the middle is approximately where the wall that the seven men were lined up against stood.

Virginia Tech Shooting
720 Washington St. SW • West Ambler Johnston Hall • Blacksburg, Virginia

The Virginia Tech shooting was a catastrophic shooting "spree" that occurred on April 16, 2007, comprising of two attacks on the campus of the Virginia Polytechnic Institute and State University in Blacksburg, Virginia. Seung-Hui Cho, an undergraduate student at the university and a U.S. resident who was from South Korea, killed 32 people and wounded 17 others with two semi-automatic pistols. Six others were injured jumping out of windows to escape Cho. The first shooting occurred at West Ambler Johnston Hall, a dormitory, where two people were killed; the main attack was a school shooting at Norris Hall, a classroom building, where Cho chained the main entrance doors shut and fired into four classrooms and a stairwell, killing 30 more people. As police stormed Norris Hall, Cho fatally shot himself in the head. It was the deadliest modern U.S. mass shooting until it was surpassed nine years later by the Pulse Nightclub shooting in Orlando, Florida, and later a shooting in Las Vegas. It remains the deadliest school shooting in the U.S.

Wallace, George
Laurel Shopping Center • Baltimore-Washington Boulevard (US-1)
Laurel, Maryland • 301-490-3315

In 1972, George Wallace entered the Democratic presidential primaries, but his campaign ended abruptly on May 15, 1972, when an assassination attempt by Arthur H. Bremer critically wounded him and left him paralyzed below the waist in the parking lot of this suburban mall. However, he was overwhelmingly reelected governor in 1974, and made another unsuccessful bid for the Democratic nomination in 1976.

In 1982, Wallace renounced his segregationist views and was again elected governor, but this time with support from black voters. He retired at the end of that term and died in Montgomery on September 13, 1998. Today, Arthur Herman Bremer is incarcerated at the Maryland Correctional Institution, where he is due to be released in 2025.

"Watergate" Hotel
The Premiere Hotel, Room 723 • 2601 Virginia Avenue NW
Washington, DC • 800-965-6869

On June 17, 1972, a member of the Watergate burglary party stayed in Room

723 to spy on the break-in proceedings happening across the street at the Democratic National Headquarters, then housed in the Watergate Office Building. (That address is 2600 Virginia Avenue NW.) Then, he got to see his five other partners get busted as they fiddled with the taping equipment they'd planted back in May. Today, Room 723 is loaded with memorabilia from the event—just ask for The Watergate Room.

Watts Family Murders
2825 Saratoga Trail • Frederick, Colorado

Simply one of the worst crimes of the century, the Watts family murders occurred here at their former family home during the early morning hours of August 13, 2018. Christopher Lee Watts admitted to murdering his pregnant wife Shanann Cathryn Rzucek by strangulation. He also later admitted to murdering their daughters, four-year-old Bella and three-year-old Celeste, by smothering them with a blanket over their heads. On November 6, 2018, Watts pleaded guilty to multiple counts of first-degree murder as part of a plea deal when the death penalty (which was later abolished in Colorado in 2020) was removed from sentencing. He was sentenced to five life sentences without the possibility of parole, three to be served consecutively. On September 30, 2020, Netflix released *American Murder: The Family Next Door*, a documentary about the murders. The documentary, watched by many, features archival footage including home videos, social media posts, text messages, and law enforcement recordings.

Whitman, Charles
University of Texas • Austin, Texas

On the morning of August 1, 1966, Charles Joseph Whitman, student, honorably discharged marine, sharp-shooter, and ex-Eagle Scout, killed his mother in her apartment and his wife at their residence. He then went out and bought a variety of ammunition and a shotgun; at about 11:30 A.M., he ascended 231 feet to the observation deck of the Tower of the University of Texas in Austin, taking with him a footlocker, six guns, knives, food, and water.

He clubbed the receptionist (who later died) on the 28th floor, then killed two persons and wounded two others who were coming up the stairs. At 11:48 A.M., he started shooting people on the ground. During the next 96 minutes he opened fire on people crossing the campus and walking on nearby streets, shooting 45 individuals and killing a total of 14.

While police returned his fire, other law enforcement worked their way into the tower. At 1:24 P.M., police officers Rammer Martinez and Houston McCoy shot and killed Whitman. Though the autopsy on Whitman revealed a brain tumor, doctors have never been able to agree on whether or not it played a part in Whitman's gruesome actions.

Williams, Wayne
Chattahoochee River Bridge • James Jackson Parkway and South Cobb Drive • Atlanta, Georgia

An investigation was opened in July 1979 in regards to a string of 24 black children and teens who had been murdered. Almost two years later, police made their arrest in the case. It was in May of 1981 when police staking out this bridge heard a splash just before dawn. Wayne Williams, a 23-year-old local, was found with a nylon rope, gloves, and a bloodstain in his car. The blood was later matched to one of the victims. Williams was convicted of murdering just two of the victims and is now serving concurrent life sentences for the crimes.

Wonderland Murders
8764 Wonderland Avenue • Los Angeles, California

On the balmy summer night of July 1, 1981, four people were bludgeoned to death in a split-level home on Wonderland Avenue, a cramped street in the steep, wooded section of Hollywood called Laurel Canyon.

It has been widely speculated that the murders were a hit ordered up by underworld figure, Eddie Nash. Nash had been robbed recently and allegedly had a hunch that the heist had been orchestrated by an adult film star, John Holmes, who had fallen on hard times and was struggling to support a $1,500 a day

cocaine habit. To punish Holmes, police and prosecutors theorized that Nash forced him to lead Nash's thugs to the house on Wonderland Avenue where Holme's accomplices were staying. Holmes was then allegedly made to watch as each of the victims were brutally murdered.

However, even though the Wonderland investigation ran 10 years and included three trials, prosecutors were never able to land one conviction. (While Nash evaded those charges, he was indicted in May 2000 on racketeering charges, including the bribery of a juror in his 1990 trial.) Among the detectives on the case was Tom Lange, who later became one of the lead investigators in the O.J. Simpson murder case.

Wuornos, Aileen
The Last Resort Bar • 5812 S. Ridgewood Ave. Port Orange, Florida

This infamous biker bar is where Aileen Wuornos, the serial killer who murdered seven men between 1989 and 1990, was arrested on an outstanding warrant while drinking a beer on January 9, 1991. Wuornos-related memorabilia covers the walls, including photos, newspaper clippings, and hand-painted memorials. Though she claimed she killed the men in self-defense after they attempted to assault her, Wuornos was still convicted of six counts of first-degree murder and executed by lethal injection on October 9, 2002.

The Zodiac Killer
Intersection of Cherry and Washington Streets, northeast corner, just in front of 3898 Washington • San Francisco, California

From 1966 into the 1970s, the self-proclaimed "Zodiac Killer" was to claim responsibility for the deaths of 37 people throughout the Bay Area. He cryptically gave information about these killings through letters and cards he mailed to various newspapers and authorities.

And it was in this exclusive neighborhood on October 11, 1969, that the much-feared "Zodiac" killer came his closest to being caught. After two children witnessed a dead cab driver's wallet being stolen from him, they called the police. The police dispatcher had mistakenly broadcast that a black man had been spotted committing the crime, so when cops stopped a white man just a block from the crime, they believed it when he said he'd just seen a black guy running the other way. When the cops recovered a correct description of the suspect, they then realized that they had let him escape.

Chillingly, several days later the Zodiac Killer sent a letter to the cops detailing their mistake, complete with a swatch of the murder victim's bloody shirt. Though there have been highly suspicious suspects in the case, an arrest has never been made, and the Zodiac Killer file remains open.

CHAPTER FIVE

CELEBRITY DEATHS AND INFAMOUS CELEBRITY EVENTS

Ace, Johnny

City Auditorium (now Jones Hall) • 615 Louisiana Street • Houston, Texas

Johnny Ace was a promising black R&B singer in the early 1950s. During his short career, Ace recorded several other hit "heart ballads" including "Pledging My Love," "Cross My Heart," "The Clock," "Saving My Love For You," and "Please Forgive Me." He accidentally shot and killed himself while playing Russian roulette backstage on Christmas Day 1954. His last words, to Willie Mae "Big Mama" Thornton, were "I'll show you that it won't shoot."

Ace's recordings continued to gain popularity after his death, and he was immortalized in the song "The Late Great Johnny Ace" by Paul Simon. Demolished in the summer of 1963, City Auditorium is now the site of another popular theater, Jones Hall.

Allman, Duane

Bartlett Street and Hillcrest Avenue • Macon, Georgia

It was almost dusk on October 29, 1971 when guitarist Duane Allman, trying to avoid a flatbed truck, crashed his motorcycle and died at this intersection.

Just about a year later, Allman Brothers Band bassist Berry Oakley died in a similar accident just two blocks south of Allman's crash site.

Arbuckle, Roscoe "Fatty"
St. Francis Hotel (12th floor suite, rooms 1219, 1220, and 1221)
335 Powell Street • San Francisco, California • 800-228-3000

On Labor Day, September 5, 1921, silent film star Roscoe "Fatty" Arbuckle's hotel party was crashed by starlet Virginia Rappe. She became violently ill from internal injuries related to bladder dysfunction and Arbuckle assumed she had had too much to drink.

When Rappe died four days later, word was spread that Arbuckle had raped and crushed the woman. The story stuck. Twelve weeks later, Arbuckle was tried by San Francisco District Attorney Matthew Brady. Fueled by inflammatory press coverage, Arbuckle was convicted in the eyes of the public. However, the case was so weak that the charge was reduced from murder to manslaughter. Two more trials followed until Arbuckle was at last acquitted, but regardless, the star's career was ruined.

Belushi, John
Chateau Marmont Hotel • Bungalow #3 • 8221 Sunset Blvd.
Hollywood, California • 800-242-8328

Built in 1929, this hotel has been host to many major stars of Hollywood and visiting celebrities from all over the world. And it was here that comic actor John Belushi died from a drug overdose. The last day of his life, Belushi had stopped at the Guitar Center to pick up a guitar that had been custom-made for Les Paul. After that, he started drinking at a club above the Roxy Theater called "On the Rox." Lastly, he visited the Rainbow Bar & Grill, where he had a bowl of Lentil soup. Then it was back to Bungalow 2 at the Chateau Marmont.

Belushi was with Catherine Smith by now, and he had her inject him with a speedball—a combination of heroin and cocaine. Belushi overdosed, but Smith thought Belushi had just passed out, so she left for a while, only to return to find pandemonium had broken out after Bill Wallace—one of

Belushi's friends—had discovered his body. They tried frantically to resuscitate him, but were unsuccessful. John Belushi was pronounced dead the morning of March 5, 1982.

Catherine Smith was released after questioning, but then gave an interview to the National Enquirer, admitting that she had injected John Belushi with the speedball. She was re-arrested, and later served time in prison for the administration of the speedball.

Bieber, Justin
Pine Tree Drive • Miami Beach, Florida

In January 2014, pop star Justin Bieber faced charges of drunk driving, resisting arrest, and driving without a valid license in Miami Beach. Shortly after 4:00 A.M., Bieber, with model Chantal Jeffries in the passenger seat, raced his exotic Lamborghini northbound along Pine Tree Drive, a four-lane divided road in Miami Beach. Also on the road was a rented red Ferrari 16M Scuderia Spider driven by Bieber's friend Khalil Amir Sharieff. Miami Beach PD officer Steven Cosner reported seeing two black SUVs behind the exotic cars "as if to stop traffic," which "facilitated an open road for the two cars to race." According to the arrest report, Cosner "observed both vehicles start a contest of speed (drag racing) from a start." He estimated that Bieber's Lamborghini and Sharieff's Ferrari reached speeds of double the posted 30 miles per hour limit. The singer took a plea deal months later, where the DUI charge was dropped in exchange for pleading guilty to careless driving and resisting arrest. He was also ordered to pay a fine and attend an anger management course.

Bono, Sonny
Heavenly Ski Resort • Immediately west of the Nevada border, south of Stateline and South Lake Tahoe • 800-2HEAVEN

On January 5, 1998, the 62-year-old congressman and former pop star was killed after skiing into a 40-foot pine tree. Bono, who was on vacation with his wife and two kids, skied off the main trail of the Upper Orion run into the tougher-to-navigate wooded area.

Bowie, David
285 Lafayette Street • New York, New York

Iconic musician David Bowie died here at his 285 Lafayette Street home in New York City on January 10, 2016 after suffering from liver cancer for 18 months. He died two days after the release of his 26th and final studio album, *Blackstar*, which coincided with his 69th birthday. Born in 1947, Bowie is regarded as one of the most influential artists of the 20th century. Bowie was acclaimed by critics and musicians, particularly for his innovative work during the 1970s, including his own albums *The Rise and Fall of Ziggy Stardust and the Spiders from Mars, Aladdin Sane, Diamond Dogs,* and *Young Americans,* among others. He also produced Lou Reed's *Transformer* album and Mott the Hoople's song "All the Young Dudes" (which he also wrote). His career was marked by reinvention and visual presentation, and his music and stagecraft had a significant impact on popular music. During his lifetime, Bowie's record sales, estimated at over 100 million records worldwide, made him one of the best-selling musicians of all time. In the UK, he was awarded 10 platinum, 11 gold, and eight silver album certifications, and released 11 number one albums. In the U.S., he received five platinum and nine gold certifications. He was also a star of many films and starred on Broadway in *The Elephant Man.* Bowie was inducted into the Rock and Roll Hall of Fame in 1996. *Rolling Stone* named him among the greatest artists in history and—after his death—the "greatest rock star ever." In 2022, Bowie was announced as the best-selling vinyl artist of the 21st century.

Bruce, Lenny
8825 Hollywood Boulevard • Hollywood, California

It was in this Hollywood Hills home that renegade comedian Lenny Bruce killed himself from an overdose of heroin in 1966. A brilliant satirist, Bruce called attention to himself due to his use of so-called "dirty words" in his nightclub act. The satire and darkness of Bruce's largely improvised shows redefined (and often overstepped) the taste standards of what was acceptable in the 1950s and 1960s. Portrayed in the 1974 film *Lenny* by Dustin Hoffman, Bruce was only 41 years old at the time of his death.

Bryant, Kobe

4232 Las Virgenes Road • Calabasas, California

NBA shooting guard legend Kobe Bryant spent his entire 20-year career with the Los Angeles Lakers. Widely regarded as one of the greatest basketball players of all time, Bryant won five NBA championships, was an 18-time All-Star, a 15-time member of the All-NBA Team, a 12-time member of the All-Defensive Team, the 2008 NBA Most Valuable Player (MVP), and a two-time NBA Finals MVP. Bryant also led the NBA in scoring twice, and ranks fourth in league all-time regular season and postseason scoring.

At 9:06 A.M. on January 26, 2020, a Sikorsky S-76 helicopter departed from John Wayne Airport in Orange County, California with nine people aboard: Bryant, his 13-year-old daughter Gianna, six family friends, and pilot Ara Zobayan. The group was traveling to Camarillo Airport in Ventura County for a basketball game at Mamba Sports Academy in Thousand Oaks. Due to light rain and fog that morning, the Los Angeles Police Department helicopters and most other air traffic were grounded. The flight tracker showed that Bryant's helicopter circled above the L.A. Zoo due to heavy air traffic in the area. Then at 9:30 A.M., Zobayan contacted the Burbank Airport's control tower, notifying the tower of the situation, and was told he was "flying too low" to be tracked by radar. At that time, the helicopter experienced extreme fog and turned south toward the mountains. At 9:40 A.M., the helicopter climbed rapidly from 1,200 to 2,000 feet (370 to 610 meters), flying at 161 knots (298 kilometers per hour; 185 miles per hour). At 9:45 A.M., the helicopter crashed into the side of a mountain in Calabasas, about 30 miles northwest of downtown Los Angeles, and began burning. Bryant, his daughter, and the other seven occupants were all killed on impact. Initial reports indicated that the helicopter crashed in the hills above Calabasas in heavy fog. Witnesses reported hearing a helicopter struggling before crashing.

Bryant was posthumously voted into the Naismith Memorial Basketball Hall of Fame in 2020 and named to the NBA 75th Anniversary Team in 2021. A bronze statue has been placed at the exact crash site. Created by sculptor Dan Medina, the statue shows Kobe Bryant in his Lakers uniform with his arm around Gianna, who is also wearing a basketball uniform with a basketball in her hand. The base of the statue has the names of all nine crash victims inscribed on a plaque. The shortest path to the site is the Bark Park Trail, which starts at a dog park at 4232 Las Virgenes Road (red dot on the map), south of Highway 101 in Calabasas. A hike of about one mile with 300 feet elevation gain reaches the spot where the helicopter crashed, near the junction with the New Millennium Trail.

Carter, Rubin "Hurricane"
The Lafayette Bar and Grill • East 18th Street at Lafayette Street
Patterson, New Jersey

On June 17, 1966, at 2:30 in the morning, four people were shot in this bar. Two of the victims died instantly, another died a month later, and the fourth survived the gunshot to his eye. While making plans for a second fight for the middleweight championship, Rubin "Hurricane" Carter and a friend, John Artis, were charged with the triple murder.

Though Carter and Artis were both found guilty and sent to jail, there was always much speculation as to the men's guilt. While in prison, Carter developed a relationship with Lesra Martin, a teenager from Brooklyn. Through the help of Lesra's benefactors and a strong legal defense team, a New Jersey judge dismissed Carter's murder conviction, granting him freedom in 1986. Carter's life was documented both in the film *The Hurricane* (1999) starring Denzel Washington and in the dramatic song "Hurricane" by Bob Dylan (1976).

Celebrity Air Disasters

Dubroff, Jessica
Cheyenne Airport • 200 East 8th Avenue • Cheyenne, Wyoming

On April 11, 1996, seven-year-old pilot Jessica Dubroff was killed while attempting to set a record as the youngest to pilot a plane across the United States. The child died when her plane stalled (due to too much weight) and crashed just after takeoff from the Cheyenne, Wyoming airport. Her father and the pilot-in-command were also killed. They had been flying into a thunderstorm at the time of the crash. Eerily, just

that week in a *London Times* interview, Jessica said, "This started off as a father-daughter adventure, and it's gotten wonderfully out of hand . . . I'm going to fly till I die."

Graham, Bill

Highway 37, between Sears Point and Vallejo, California (where Highway 37 passes Napa Creek)

Famed concert promoter Bill Graham was killed here in a helicopter crash on October 25, 1991. Graham, who was 60 at the time, made a name for himself in the 1960s by promoting shows at San Francisco's Fillmore Auditorium and New York City's Fillmore East, and later in the '70s and '80s by promoting "mega-tours" for bands such as The Rolling Stones. Graham (and two others) died when his Bell 206B helicopter hit an electrical transmission tower and crashed during heavy rain and high winds.

Marciano, Rocky

Near Newton, Iowa

On August 31, 1969, 45-year-old former heavyweight champion boxer Rocky Marciano and two others died in the crash of a Cessna 172H airplane near Newton, Iowa. It had been a dark and rainy night and Marciano was just one day short of celebrating his 46th birthday. The pilot, who was not instrument-rated and had minimum night flying experience, took off at night despite warnings of a building storm front. Marciano was hitching a ride home to a planned birthday party.

Martin, Dino

Mount San Gorgonio, California (20 miles east of San Bernardino)

On the afternoon of March 21, 1987, an F-4C Phantom II fighter jet piloted by 35-year-old Dean Paul "Dino" Martin, son of actor/singer Dean Martin, slammed into a solid wall of granite at the 5,500-foot level of the Mount San Gorgonio foothills while on a routine training flight.

Martin, a California Air National Guard captain, was given permission by controllers to perform a "maximum climb" takeoff from March Air Force Base in Riverside County. Nine minutes after takeoff, while flying into clouds, the jet disappeared from radar. His weapons systems operator was also killed in the crash. Previously, Dino Martin's pop group had had one hit, "I'm a Fool," and it was his death that sent his father Dean into a downward spiral of depression from which many say he never recovered.

Reeves, Jim

10 miles south of Nashville in a wooded area just off US 31
Near Nashville, Tennessee

Country-western star Jim Reeves' Beechcraft Debonair crashed here in a wooded area during a heavy rainstorm on July 31, 1964. Reeves, who was piloting the plane, lost reference with the ground and experienced spatial disorientation. It took searchers two days to find the wreckage. (His manager was also killed in the crash.) The 39-year-old singer was coming home to Nashville after a business trip to Batesville, Arkansas. Voted into the Country Music Hall of Fame in 1967, Reeves continued to have hit records posthumously as recently as the 1970s and '80s.

Rockne, Knute

10 miles south of Cottonwood Falls off
Highway K-177 • Near Bazaar, Kansas

Legendary Notre Dame football coach Knute Rockne was one of eight killed on March 31, 1931 when a Trans Continental & Western Airways Fokker F10A plane crashed during a heavy storm near Bazaar, Kansas. (One of the aircraft's wings separated in mid-flight.) The coach was just 43 years old. Today, a marker rests at the crash site in honor of Rockne. To visit the memorial, which sits off the road on private property, contact the Chase County Historical Society at 316-273-8500.

Smith, Samantha

Auburn-Lewiston Municipal Airport • 80 Airport Drive
Auburn, Maine

On August 25, 1985, 13-year-old Samantha Smith, her father, and six others were killed when their Bar Harbor Airlines Beechcraft 99 crashed while trying to land here at Auburn, Maine. (On approach to Auburn, the plane missed the runway by 200 yards and crashed into the nearby woods.) Samantha was the young girl made famous for writing a letter to Soviet leader Yuri Andropov and then getting invited to visit Russia.

Stewart, Payne

Mina, South Dakota • (The crash site is located on a marshy pasture about two miles south of Mina, in Edmunds County, an area about 20 miles west of Aberdeen.)

PGA golfer Payne Stewart, winner of the 1989 PGA Championship and two-time winner of the U.S. Open, died on October 25, 1999 after his Lear jet lost pressure, causing everyone aboard to lose consciousness. He was only 42 years old.

Stewart, the two pilots, sports agents Van Ardan and Robert Fraley (who headed the sports management firm of Leader Enterprises), and golf course designer Bruce Borland were all killed when the private plane ran out of fuel and crashed here in a field outside Mina, after flying uncontrolled for several hours across the United States. Stewart had been on his way from Orlando, Florida to Dallas, Texas, to play in a golf tournament.

Todd, Michael

Zuni Mountains, near Grants, New Mexico

Broadway and Hollywood producer Mike Todd, his biographer Art Cohn, a pilot, and a co-pilot were all killed when Todd's Lockheed Lodestar private plane, "The Lucky Liz" (named after Todd's wife, Elizabeth Taylor) crashed in bad weather in the Zuni Mountains of New Mexico on March 22, 1958.

During their flight, ice had developed on the wings, which created too much weight on the engines and caused the plane to crash. Todd had been on his way from Burbank to New York City to attend a Friars Club award meeting at which he was to receive the Showman of the Year award.

Turner, Curtis

About one mile northeast of Bell Township
Clearfield County, Pennsylvania

On October 4, 1970, 45-year-old NASCAR driver Curtis Turner and 51-year-old professional golfer Clarence King were both killed when Turner's Aero Commander private plane went into a tailspin and crashed into an abandoned strip mine.

Charles, Ray

349 South Linden Drive • Beverly Hills, California

Legendary singer Ray Charles died of complications from liver disease here at his home on June 10, 2004. He was 73 years old. He was born Ray Charles Robinson in Albany, Georgia on September 23, 1930, and grew up in Greenville, Florida. Charles contracted an unknown illness at the age of four that began to affect his eyesight and within three years, he was completely blind. From 1937 to 1945, he attended a Florida school for the deaf and blind where he learned to read braille, repair and listen to radios, and play piano as well as clarinet, saxophone, trumpet, and organ. After his mother died, he left school for Jacksonville at 15 to begin his career as a professional musician.

Cline, Patsy

Mount Carmel Road (2.2 miles west of Camden) • Camden, Tennessee
877-584-8395

Thirty-year-old country singing star Patsy Cline had traveled to Kansas City to do a benefit concert for a popular disk jockey who had died there. Returning to Nashville in a private plane piloted by her manager, Randy Hughes, they encountered bad weather and crashed in a remote, wooded area near Camden, Tennessee on March 5, 1963. Both were killed in the crash, as were country performers Cowboy Copas and Hawkshaw Hawkins. The crash site (about a three mile hike off the main highway, 641 north) is marked with a commemorative plaque honoring the four victims.

Cobain, Kurt

171 Lake Washington Boulevard East • Seattle, Washington

On the morning of April 8, 1994, an electrician arrived at Kurt Cobain's house in Seattle and spotted what he thought was a mannequin lying on the floor of a small cottage/greenhouse above the garage. Upon closer examination, he realized that what he saw was the body of a young male with a shotgun on his chest. The police arrived and a body, dressed in jeans, a shirt, and Converse trainers, was removed for identification. Fingerprints confirmed that it was Kurt Cobain, Nirvana's much tormented frontman.

In 1996, Cobain's former wife Courtney Love announced that she was tearing down the garage/greenhouse where Kurt killed himself to discourage fans who come to visit.

Coleman, Gary

California Uniforms, Inc. • 13248 Hawthorne Boulevard
Hawthorne, California • 310-676-9180

In 1998, actor Gary Coleman (pint-sized "Arnold" on the TV sitcom *Different Strokes*) was involved in an altercation which led to his arrest on misdemeanor assault and battery charges. Coleman had just gotten a job as a security guard at Fox Hills Mall, and came to this shop for a uniform. A woman in the store asked for his autograph and he allegedly punched her. At trial, he testified that he had feared for his safety after the woman (who was taller than he was) started insulting him. However, he ended up pleading "no contest" and was given a suspended sentence of 200 days, fined $200, and ordered to attend anger management classes.

Cooke, Sam

Hacienda Motel
9137 South Figueroa Street
Los Angeles, California

Popular soul singer Sam Cooke ("You Send Me," "Wonderful World," "Another Saturday Night") was shot to death at the site of the former

Hacienda Motel in December of 1964 by a motel manager armed with a .22 pistol. Cooke had taken a young woman to the seedy motel, and after the shooting she claimed that he had tried to rape her. However, evidence suggests that she may have been a prostitute who may have tried to rob Cooke (leading to Cooke's panic and subsequent chase). When Cooke broke down the door of the manager's office, where he mistakenly believed the woman had gone, the shocked manager shot and killed him. The structure remains but is currently closed.

Crane, Bob
Winfield Apartments #132A (now the Winfield Place Condominiums)
7430 East Chaparral Road (1/4 mile east of Scottsdale Road)
Scottsdale, Arizona

On the afternoon of June 29, 1978, actress Victoria Berryl knocked on the door to this apartment. She expected her knock to be answered by former TV star Bob Crane. There was no answer. She pushed open the unlocked door and went inside. There she found his half-naked body lying in bed. His face was so badly beaten that he was unrecognizable from the left side. An electric cord was wrapped around his neck. Crane's pal and partner in sordid behavior, John Carpenter, was eventually charged but found not guilty of the crime in 1994.

Croce, Jim
Natchitoches Regional Airport • 450 Wallenberg Drive
Natchitoches, Louisiana (off Interstate 49)

Known for hits such as "Bad, Bad Leroy Brown," and "Time in a Bottle," singer/songwriter Jim Croce had just finished a show at Prather Coliseum, the basketball arena at Northwestern State University, on the evening of September 20, 1973. Croce's small private plane crashed immediately after takeoff from runway 17, hitting the trees just east of the runway and killing Croce and five members of his entourage.

Originally, Croce was to have spent the night in Natchitoches and fly to

Dallas the next day, but there was a last minute change of plans and Croce ended up leaving immediately after the show. Today, a plaque commemorating Croce's last concert can be found in the Student Union at Northwestern State University.

Culkin, Macaulay
Interstate 44 & Kelley Avenue • Oklahoma City, Oklahoma

On September 14, 2004, actor Macaulay Culkin was pulled over while driving through Oklahoma City and arrested for possession of marijuana and prescription drugs. Culkin was taken to the Oklahoma County jail and was booked on complaints of possession of a controlled dangerous substance without a prescription, possession of marijuana, and a municipal charge of possession of marijuana. His bail was set at $4,000, which he posted two hours later. He received a suspended prison sentence and had to pay a fine.

Dean, James

Death Site
Intersection of Highways 46 and 41, about 26 miles east of Paso Robles
Cholame, California

Cholame may just be a speck on the map between Bakersfield and Paso Robles, California, but it is an important speck. After all, it's where 24-year-old actor James Dean was killed on September 30, 1955. To be more precise, it's at the remote junction of Highways 41 and 46 that Dean's Porsche Spyder 550 was struck by a black and white 1954 Ford Tudor, driven by a 22-year-old man named Donald Turnupseed.

The roads have been significantly revamped since the accident, but you can still get a sense of what happened if you visit the area. Dean, who was traveling to Salinas for an October 1 rally, was headed west on 46 (then called "466"). The approach to the intersection is a fairly steep hill, and accounts vary as to how fast Dean was going. Turnupseed was approaching the intersection from the opposite direction, which is flat. At the "Y" intersection of the two roads, Turnupseed veered left onto Highway 41, and never saw Dean coming toward him.

Police surmised that the combination of the color of Dean's car and the twilight dusk camouflaged the Porsche. Turnupseed's Ford slammed into Dean's Porsche, almost head-on. Dean's crumpled car was thrown into a ditch against a nearby fence, which is where Dean died. Dean's passenger Rolf Wutherich ended up with a smashed jaw, broken leg, and multiple contusions. Turnupseed walked away from the accident with a gashed forehead and a few bruises. No charges were filed against the young man.

James Dean's Home
14611 Sutton Street • Sherman Oaks, California

This was the last place that James Dean lived, and where he left from the morning of September 30, 1955. The house has since undergone much remodeling.

Competition Motors (Now Called Vine Auto Body Shop)
1219 Vine Street • Hollywood, California

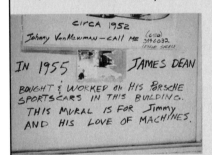

At about 8:00 A.M. the morning of the accident, James Dean came here to get some final tunings made to his new race car. He watched over the mechanics until about 10:00 A.M., at which point he left for the Farmer's Market to have breakfast before hitting the road to Salinas. Today, a church occupies the site.

Farmer's Market
6333 West 3rd Street (at Fairfax Avenue) • Los Angeles, California
323-933-9211

James Dean had his last breakfast—a donut at the Old Ranch Market within the Farmer's Market (L.A.'s oldest outdoor market)—before hitting the road toward Salinas, where he would be killed several hours later.

Blackwell's Corner
Highways 46 and 33
Lost Hills, California • 805-797-2145

This was the last stop made by James Dean and his crew at about 5:00 P.M. on the day he was killed. A gas station/grocery store, Dean parked here for about 15 minutes to grab an apple and a Coke before driving into the Polonio Pass. Though it's been rebuilt, Blackwell's Corner still enjoys its reputation as "James Dean's Last Stop," and the nice folks working inside seem more than happy to provide details of the event.

The Jack Ranch Café
About 100 yards east of the intersection of Highways 46 and 41
Cholame, California • 805-238-5652

This unpretentious roadside diner serves as an unofficial museum to the crash that killed James Dean. Inside you'll find articles, books, and souvenirs related to the event. Outside is a memorial to the crash. Erected in 1977 by a Japanese businessman and huge Dean fan, the metal statue supposedly reflects the exact site where the crash occurred, some 900 yards away.

DeLorean, John
Sheraton Hotel at LAX Airport
9750 Airport Boulevard • Room 501
Los Angeles, California

On October 19, 1979, carmaker John DeLorean was arrested by FBI agents for possession of a suitcase full of cocaine, which he had hoped to sell to raise money for his struggling company. DeLorean had been filmed and recorded at meetings in Washington D.C.'s L'Enfant Plaza Hotel as well as L.A.'s Bel Air Sands, but it was the tape from the meeting in the Sheraton Plaza that made the event famous (the camera had been placed in a gutted-out television).

DeLorean was taken into custody, but ironically, he had just missed a call from a banker who wanted to offer a legitimate $200 million loan that would have saved his company. DeLorean was acquitted in 1984.

Denver, John

Located east of Point Pinos at the northern tip of Monterey Peninsula, between Asilomar Avenue and Acropolis Street, off Ocean View Boulevard in the Pacific Ocean. • Monterey, California

The folk rock troubadour had moved to the Carmel area not long before October 12, 1997, the day he crashed his small, "experimental" craft into the sea. Planning a trip down south, he was actually giving the second-hand plane a test run when the accident occurred. The experts suspect that Denver accidentally adjusted a rudder which caused a nosedive that he was too low to correct. Many of Denver's fans gather nearby to honor the anniversary each year, and also to help clean up the beach in honor of the ecology-minded troubadour.

Dogg, Snoop Doggy

Woodbine Park (on Motor Avenue at National Boulevard) • Palms district West Los Angeles, California

In 1993, rap singer Snoop Doggy Dogg was arrested for murder. Allegedly, on August 25, 1993, he drove a black Jeep Cherokee during a drive-by shooting at this park. Philip Woldemariam, an alleged gang member, was shot and killed. Dogg claimed self-defense, and was eventually acquitted of the murder charges. The jury deadlocked on lesser charges, which were later dropped.

Downey, Jr., Robert

29169 Heathercliff Road • Malibu, California

The 31-year-old actor was busted in Malibu on July 16, 1997 for wandering into his neighbor's house and passing out on their bed. The neighbor, Lisa Curtis, returned home, found a strange man asleep in her house, and called the police, who arrested him for trespassing and being under the influence of drugs.

Dunne, Dominique
8723 Rangely Avenue • West Hollywood, California

This was the home of 22-year-old actress Dominique Dunne, who played the older sister, "Dana," in the *Poltergeist* movies. Dunne had recently ended her relationship with her boyfriend, John Sweeney—a chef at the popular restaurant Ma Maison—causing him to become abusive. On October 30, 1982, Sweeney arrived at her home and strangled Dunne in the driveway. She died several days later at Cedars-Sinai Hospital.

Her father, author Dominick Dunne, later became an outspoken commentator during the O.J. Simpson trial. Incidentally, Sweeney only spent two and a half years in jail (three years and eight months including the time he spent in detention pending trial), most of it at the medium-security state prison in Susanville, California. Today, after changing his name, it is believed he is a chef in the Seattle area.

Frey, Glen
Columbia University Irving Medical Center • 622 W. 168th St.
New York, New York

The legendary co-founder of the band the Eagles, Glen Frey, died at this New York City hospital on January 18, 2016 from complications of rheumatoid arthritis, acute ulcerative colitis, and pneumonia. Frey, born in 1948, was the co-lead singer and front man for the Eagles, along with drummer/singer Don Henley, with whom he wrote most of the Eagles' material. Frey sang lead vocals on songs such as "Take It Easy," "Peaceful Easy Feeling," "Tequila Sunrise," "Already Gone," "James Dean," "Lyin' Eyes," "New Kid in Town," and "Heartache Tonight." A life-sized statue of Frey was unveiled at the Standin' on the Corner Park in Winslow, Arizona on September 24, 2016, to honor his songwriting contributions to "Take It Easy," made famous by the Eagles as their first single in 1972. As well, the road that runs next to the middle school he attended in Royal Oak, Michigan now bears his name.

Fuller, Bobby
1776 North Sycamore Avenue
Hollywood, California

This was the apartment of Bobby Fuller, the singer who (as lead singer of The Bobby Fuller Four) recorded the hit song "I Fought the Law (and the Law Won)." On July 18, 1966, just five months after that song hit the Top 10, Fuller died from carbon monoxide poisoning in his car while parked just outside of this building. Police labeled the 22-year-old's death a suicide.

Gabor, Zsa Zsa
8551 Olympic Boulevard (at Le Doux Road, in a parking spot on
northwest corner, just west of La Cienega Boulevard)
Los Angeles, California

In June 1989, Gabor was pulled over for speeding by a Beverly Hills cop. However, she sped away and was pulled over again at this site, three blocks from the initial incident. When the cop began writing her a ticket, she slapped him, and eventually did jail time for the assault. (Not to mention also generating hundreds of both sarcastic headlines and late-night television jokes.)

Garcia, Jerry
Serenity Knolls • 145 Tamal Road • Forest Knolls, California • 415-488-0400

On Monday, August 7, 1995, Jerry Garcia, lead guitarist and vocalist with the Grateful Dead, drove up this road in West Marin and checked himself into this substance treatment center after telling friends and bandmates that he was going to Hawaii. A week earlier, he had checked out of the Betty Ford

Treatment Center after staying two weeks of a proposed month-long stay.

When a counselor at the facility made a routine bed check at 4:23 A.M. on Wednesday, August 9, they discovered he had died in his sleep. Paramedics were called but were unable to revive him. Jerome John "Jerry" Garcia was pronounced dead, just eight days after his 53rd birthday.

Gaye, Marvin
2101 South Gramercy Place • Los Angeles, California

This is the family home where legendary Motown singer Marvin Gaye was shot to death by his minister father, Marvin Gaye, Sr., during an argument at their home in April 1984. The father pleaded guilty to voluntary manslaughter, but received only five years' probation.

Gaye's career had recently turned around but the resurgence brought with it an increased reliance on cocaine. He returned to the U.S. and moved in with his parents in an attempt to re-gain control of his life. But the return only exacerbated his troubles; he and his father quarreled bitterly and constantly, and Gaye threatened suicide on a number of occasions. Finally, on the afternoon of April 1, 1984—one day before his 45th birthday—Gaye was shot after a final argument and died on the lawn in front of the house after staggering outside.

Grant, Hugh
PICK UP SITE: Northeast corner of Sunset Boulevard and Courtney Avenue • ARREST SITE: Three blocks away at the intersection of Curson and Hawthorn Avenues Hollywood, California

On June 27, 1995, pretty boy English actor Hugh Grant picked up hooker Divine Brown here on Sunset Boulevard. Busted in the act just a few blocks away, Grant ultimately received probation and paid a small fine. Rather than harm his career, if anything, the incident seemed to bolster it.

Harrison, George
3738 Laurel Canyon Boulevard (?) • Studio City, California

Beatle legend George Harrison passed away from cancer on November 29, 2001 at the age of 58. As to the exact location where he succumbed, it remains a bit of a mystery. According to most press reports and obituaries, the ex-Beatle passed away in the L.A. home of a friend (identified by many as security consultant Gavin de Becker). The death certificate listed "place of death" as a residence at 1971 Coldwater Canyon in Beverly Hills, 90210, but that address does not exist. He *may* have actually died in Studio City, at 3738 Laurel Canyon Boulevard, a place which de Becker did in fact manage. Harrison, the youngest Beatle, though considered to be the "quiet" member of the band, influenced them profoundly. His use of sitar on the 1965 track "Norwegian Wood (This Bird Has Flown)" introduced the instrument to Western popular culture. As well, his backwards guitar solo on "I'm Only Sleeping," became a defining feature of psych-rock. Harrison's first solo album, *All Things Must Pass*, was a huge success and Harrison also organized the Concert for Bangladesh, a charity event now recognized as the first celebrity benefit concert. The concert drew over 40,000 people to Madison Square Garden and the resulting live album won the Grammy for Album of the Year.

Hartman, Phil
5065 Encino Avenue (at the NW corner of Embassy) • Encino, California

This is the house where, on May 28, 1998, the comic-actor was executed in his sleep by his wife, Brynn. She committed suicide soon after as police approached the house and the couple's children were taken outside. Hartman, a star on *Saturday Night Live*, had recently landed a featured role on the TV sitcom *NewsRadio*. He was just 49 years old.

Herman, Pee Wee
South Trail Theater (former site) • 6727 S Tamiami Trail • Sarasota, Florida
941-924-6969

While visiting his parents in Sarasota, Florida, Pee Wee Herman (Paul

Reubens) decided to go catch a movie. And it was on that date, July 26, 1991, that Herman was arrested by police for exposing himself in an X-rated movie theater. Pee Wee dolls were recalled from toy stores and CBS dropped plans to broadcast the remaining five *Pee Wee's Playhouse* episodes.

Soon after, Herman, the butt of 10,000 wisecracks—got a rousing ovation that September when he walked onstage at the *MTV Video Music Awards* and casually inquired, "Heard any good jokes lately?" Today, the adult theater has been replaced by a restaurant.

Hoffman, Philip Seymour
1 Sheridan Square • New York, New York

Philip Seymour Hoffman, one of the most acclaimed actors of his generation, died of an accidental drug overdose at age 46 here at his home on February 2, 2014. He had appeared in more than 50 movies, including *Capote*, *Doubt*, and *The Hunger Games* series, and earned a reputation for playing difficult or quirky characters. Hoffman also was an accomplished stage actor and director. He won an Academy Award in the Best Actor category for his portrayal of author Truman Capote in *Capote* (2005), and received Oscar nominations for Best Supporting Actor for his role as a CIA agent in *Charlie Wilson's War* (2007) and for his performance as a priest in *Doubt* (2008). Hoffman had struggled with drug addiction in his early 20s but was sober for many years before relapsing in 2012. His autopsy revealed that he died from acute mixed drug intoxication.

Holly, Buddy
Off State Road 20, north of Clear Lake, Iowa

DIRECTIONS: Take Interstate 35 (the main road) to Clear Lake. From I-35, take Highway 18 west into town. Turn onto a road marked S28 going north from 18 (there's a gas station on the northeast corner of the intersection). Drive 5 1/2 miles on S28 and turn right onto 310th Street. Turn immediately onto Gull Avenue, a gravel road. Drive north on Gull one half mile and stop at 315th Street. Park. Walk to the west past the sign marking 315th Street into the cornfield. Walk west on the north side of the wire fence for half a mile. Four oak trees (one for each victim) mark the exact site of the crash (where a memorial sits).

"The Winter Dance Party Tour" was planned to cover 24 cities in a short three week time frame, and Buddy Holly would be the biggest headliner. Waylon Jennings, a friend from Lubbock, Texas, and Tommy Allsup would go as back-up musicians. Ritchie Valens (probably the hottest of the artists at the time), The Big Bopper, and Dion and the Belmonts rounded out the list of performers. It was the dead of winter and the tour bus had heating problems when they arrived at the Surf Ballroom in Clear Lake, Iowa on February 3, 1959.

They were cold and tired. So harsh was the situation, that Buddy had decided to charter a plane for himself and his guys.

Dwyer Flying Service was called and charged $36 per person for a single engine Beechcraft Bonanza. At the last minute, Waylon Jennings gave his seat up to the Big Bopper, who was ill and had a hard time fitting comfortably into the bus. When Buddy learned Jennings wasn't going to fly, he said, "Well, I hope your old bus freezes up." Jennings said, "Well, I hope your plane crashes." Allsup flipped Valens for the remaining seat and Valens won.

The plane took off just after 1:00 A.M. from Clear Lake and never got far from the airport before it crashed, killing all onboard. At the next tour stop in Moorhead, Minnesota, the rest of the performers looked for local talent to fill in, deciding the show must go on. They found a 15-year-old singer named Bobby Vee, which was the start of his career.

Houston, Whitney
Room 434 • Beverly Hilton Hotel • 9876 Wilshire Blvd.
Los Angeles, California

Grammy-winning legend Whitney Houston died in Room 434 at the famed Beverly Hilton Hotel on February 11, 2012. The 49-year-old singer was one of the biggest selling performers in the 1980s and '90s on the strength of such hits as "Greatest Love of All," "Saving All My Love for You," "How Will I Know," and "I Wanna Dance with Somebody (Who Loves Me)."

Hughes, John
60 West 55th Street • New York, New York

On the morning of August 6, 2009, acclaimed film director John Hughes (*Sixteen Candles, Breakfast Club*) was taking a walk near his hotel on West 55th Street in Manhattan when he suffered a massive heart attack. He was rushed to Roosevelt Hospital, where he was pronounced dead. He was 59 years old. Witnesses reported that Hughes crossed south, stumbled to the water valves jutting from the wall at 60 West 55th Street, sat there, and attempted to catch his breath. At 8:55 A.M., 911 operators received a call from one of the witnesses, who summoned medics to the building. Hughes was unconscious when they arrived 15 minutes later.

Jackson, Janet
NRG Stadium • NRG Pkwy • Houston, Texas

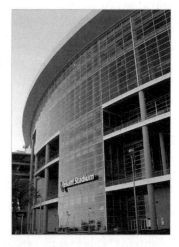

A "wardrobe malfunction" is a clothing failure that accidentally or intentionally exposes a person's intimate parts. Singer Justin Timberlake first used the term when apologizing for the Super Bowl XXXVIII halftime show controversy during the 2004 Grammy Awards. The phrase "wardrobe malfunction" was in turn used by the media to refer to the incident and became a well-known phrase in pop culture. The incident involved a "nip slip" during a dance routine when one of Jackson's breasts, adorned with a nipple shield, was exposed by Justin Timberlake to the viewing public for approximately half a second. The incident, sometimes referred to as "Nipplegate" or "Janetgate," led to an immediate crackdown and widespread debate on perceived indecency in broadcasting.

Jackson, Michael

Ronald Reagan UCLA Medical Center • 757 Westwood Plaza
Westwood, California

The King of Pop died at the age of 50 on June 25, 2009. The cause was believed to be of acute propofol and benzodiazepine intoxication, and it happened at his home on North Carolwood Drive in the Holmby Hills neighborhood of Los Angeles. His physician, Conrad Murray, testified that he discovered Jackson in his room not breathing and with a weak pulse. He then administered cardiopulmonary resuscitation which failed to revive the singer, and then Jackson was rushed to the medical center where he ultimately died. Jackson, arguably the most famous and successful entertainer of his generation, began with his brothers in the Jackson 5 and eventually released some of the most successful solo albums in history, including *Off the Wall*, which sold some 7 million copies worldwide, and *Thriller*, which went on to sell 50 million copies around the globe, making it the best-selling studio album of all time.

James, Rick

Oakwood Toluca Hills apartment complex • 3600 Barham Boulevard
Toluca Lake, California

Rick James began his major label musical career as a songwriter and producer for Motown in the late 1960s. A decade later he began recording as a solo artist for Motown's subsidiary Gordy and had the breakthrough Top 15 pop hit "You and I" in 1978. Three years later he established himself as arguably the top funk artist with the massive hit album *Street Songs*, which featured the definitive "Super Freak." Rick James earned great notoriety for his wild lifestyle. He ended up in courts and tabloids due to drug use and sexual exploits. Rick James was reportedly working on a new album when he died from heart disease on August 6, 2004, at age 56. James, whose given name was James Johnson Jr., was found dead in his Oakwood Toluca Hills apartment by his personal assistant.

Jay-Z

Standard Hotel • 848 Washington Street • New York, New York

Following a museum gala after party at the Standard Hotel in May 2014, surveillance footage obtained by the website TMZ showed rapper/mogul Jay-Z getting into a physical altercation with his wife Beyoncé's sister, Solange. The video showed Solange yelling, hitting, and kicking Jay-Z as a bodyguard tried to restrain the *A Seat at the Table* singer. Beyoncé stepped in to try to break up the two, but Solange continued to attack her brother-in-law. Rumors of what caused the melee ran rampant soon after the release of the footage. Back then, it was reported that Solange had also gotten into a verbal argument with designer Rachel Roy, with a source reporting that Jay-Z had said something that caused her to snap.

Jones, Anissa
2312 Littler Lane • Oceanside, California

Anissa Jones, "Buffy" from the 1966–1971 TV series *Family Affair*, died at this house from a drug overdose on August 28, 1976. Autopsy reports indicated Jones died from "self-administered overdose of barbiturate, phencyclidine, cocaine, and methaqualone poisoning." The death was ruled an accident. After *Family Affair* ended, Jones appeared in occasional guest shots, but eventually drugs took over her life. At 18 years old, she received a $75,000 trust fund and used it to buy a car, get an apartment, and purchase incredible amounts of drugs. She died five and a half months later.

Joplin, Janis
Landmark Hotel (now the Highland Gardens Hotel) • Room 105
7047 Franklin Avenue • Hollywood, California

This is where Janis Joplin accidentally overdosed on October 4, 1970. She died in her room at the Landmark Hotel in Los Angeles, having scored a particularly pure batch of heroin. Her sad, lonely death followed that of Jimi Hendrix, who'd died just two weeks earlier. (Jim Morrison would die within a year.) Janis was cremated and her ashes were scattered along the Marin County coastline of California. The album she was recording at the time, *Pearl*, was released after her death. Although Janis Joplin's career lasted only a few years, she has been hailed as the greatest white female blues singer who ever lived.

Kelly, R.
219 N Justine Street • Chicago, Illinois

This is the studio/warehouse once run by singer R. Kelly that featured in the popular and shocking docuseries *Surviving R. Kelly,* which detailed Kelly's decades of abuse against underage women. Kelly's three-decade career included over 75 million records sold worldwide, making him the most commercially successful  male R&B artist of the 1990s and one of the world's best-selling music artists. The Recording Academy awarded him three Grammys for "I Believe I Can Fly," and nominated him twice for collaborations with Michael Jackson. Starting in the 1990s, Kelly faced accusations of using his fame to lure young fans, including minors, into inappropriate sexual relationships. He stood trial in Chicago for child pornography, winning acquittal. Kelly evaded further legal challenges until the 2019 docuseries provoked backlash. RCA Records terminated his recording contract and law enforcement in New York, Chicago, and Minneapolis built new criminal cases against him. A 2021 trial in Brooklyn federal court convicted Kelly for violations of the Mann Act and racketeering, resulting in a 30-year prison sentence.

Kerrigan, Nancy
Cobo Arena • 600 Civic Center Dr. • Detroit, Michigan • 313-983-6616

Minutes after practicing in Detroit's Cobo Arena for the National Figure Skating Championships and a berth on the U.S. Olympic team going to Lillehammer, skater Nancy Kerrigan was whacked across the right knee with a pipe-like piece of metal. "Why? Why? Why?," she sobbed.

Why? Because Jeff Gillooly, husband of Kerrigan's competitor Tonya Harding, had hired an attacker to put her out of competition. Though Harding won that championship, she bombed in the Olympics and was then implicated in the crime with her husband and his accomplices. Gillooly went to jail, but Harding did not serve any time. They are no longer married.

Kovacs, Ernie
Intersection of Beverly Glen and Santa Monica Boulevards
Westwood, California

On the night of Saturday, January 13, 1962, legendary TV comedian Ernie

Kovacs was driving home from a Christening party for the son of Milton Berle. Driving home on his usual route, south on Beverly Glen, Kovacs supposedly reached for one of his trademark, foot-long Havana cigar specials. Attempting to light it, legend has it he lost control of his car and smashed broadside into a utility pole, which is no longer there.

Ledger, Heath
419–421 Broome Street • New York, New York

On January 22, 2008, the body of then-28-year-old actor Heath Ledger was found by his masseuse and housekeeper on the floor of his rented apartment in the SoHo neighborhood of New York City. Well-known for his portrayal of the Joker in *The Dark Knight* (which won him a posthumous Academy Award for Best Supporting Actor in 2008), he was also nominated for playing the closeted gay cowboy Ennis Del Mar in director Ang Lee's acclaimed *Brokeback Mountain* (2005). Ledger was a former child actor from Australia who first became known to American audiences in the 1999 teen comedy *10 Things I Hate About You*.

Lennon, John
The Dakota Apartments • One West 72nd Street • New York, New York

John Lennon was killed by Mark David Chapman on December 8, 1980, as he returned to his New York apartment from a recording session. At almost

11:00 P.M. that night, Lennon's limo pulled up outside the Dakota and doorman Jose Perdomo left his post to open the car doors for Lennon and his wife, Yoko Ono. Yoko got out first, followed closely by her husband. As Yoko passed him, Chapman said "Hello." As Lennon passed, Chapman pulled a snub-nosed .38

revolver from his pocket, dropped into combat stance, and said, "Mr. Lennon?" As Lennon turned, Chapman fired five shots, four of which hit Lennon.

Mortally wounded, Lennon staggered up the steps into the Dakota's front lobby and collapsed; he died later that evening at Roosevelt Hospital, after losing 80 percent of his blood. After shooting Lennon, Chapman took *The Catcher in the Rye* out of his pocket and tried to read it as he paced the sidewalk and waited for the police to come get him.

Though Chapman's lawyer initially entered a plea of insanity, Chapman later changed the plea to guilty. He was sentenced to 20 years to life in prison, a sentence which he is serving in New York's Attica prison. Chapman was denied parole at his first parole hearing in October of 2000.

Linkletter, Diane
Shoreham Towers • 8787 Shoreham Drive
West Hollywood, California

On October 5, 1969, television star Art Linkletter's daughter, Diane, jumped to her death from her sixth floor apartment while high on LSD. Linkletter, a known drug user, had phoned her brother Robert, threatening suicide. He calmed her and promised to get there as soon as possible, but after hanging up the phone, she screamed and jumped from her kitchen window, killing herself.

Lombard, Carol
Mount Potosi (near the Red Rock Ranch State Park) • Approximately
30 miles southwest of Las Vegas, on the eastern slope of Death Valley
702-363-1922

On January 16, 1942, actress Carole Lombard, her mother, her press agent, and 19 other people were killed when their DC-3 airplane crashed near Las Vegas, Nevada. They were returning from a war-bond promotion tour, and her death was the first war-related female casualty that the U.S. suffered during World War II.

Supposedly, the plane veered off-course because the captain was in the back chatting with Lombard, leaving the less experienced first officer flying solo. The plane clipped a rocky ledge on Mt. Potosi, flipped, and exploded. At the foot of the mountain, Lombard's husband, Clark Gable, waited with the rescue squad of ambulances and motor cars that had marshaled in the faint hope that some of those on the plane had survived. Tragically, all aboard had been killed. The Red Rock Ranch, where her plane crashed, was owned by Chet Lauck and Norris Goff, who played "Lum and Abner" on radio. It is now a state park.

Lovato, Demi
8000 Laurel View Drive • Los Angeles, California

After appearing on the children's television series *Barney & Friends* from 2002–2004, Demi Lovato rose to prominence for playing Mitchie Torres in the musical television film *Camp Rock* and its sequel *Camp Rock 2: The Final Jam*. The first film's soundtrack contained "This Is Me," Lovato's debut single and duet with Joe Jonas, which peaked at number nine on the U.S. Billboard Hot 100. After a history of struggling with substance abuse, Lovato overdosed on a near-lethal mix of the opioid drugs heroin and fentanyl here at her home on July 24, 2018. According to reports, the night of the overdose, Lovato called her drug dealer after friends left her home. Her dealer came over and, according to Demi's friend Sirah Mitchell, gave her heroin "laced with fentanyl." She survived, and according to reports, is now sober.

Lynyrd Skynyrd
Off Highway 568, near Gillsburg, Mississippi

Near dusk on October 20, 1977, while flying from Greenville to Baton Rouge, the plane carrying southern rock legends Lynyrd Skynyrd crashed, killing singer/songwriter Ronnie Van Zant, guitarist Steve Gaines, backup singer Cassie Gaines (Steve's sister) and road manager Dean Kilpatrick. Pilot Walter Wiley McCreary and co-pilot William John Gray, both of Dallas, also died.

The aircraft had become low on fuel and both engines quit before the twin engine Convair 240 (built in 1947) could reach McComb Airport, so a forced landing was made in a wooded area. The swamp where the plane crashed is eight miles from McComb Airport. In all, 20 other members of the band and road crew were injured, many critically. The actual crash site is a good distance from the nearest road, so a track had to be cut from the thick forest. Today, the track has grown over, so the site is nearly impossible to reach.

Madonna

6432 Mulholland Highway (at Canyon Lake Drive, just below the
Hollywood sign) • Hollywood Hills, California

This is Madonna's former estate, the "Castillo del Lago," where on May 29,
1995, a stalker scaled the wall and was shot three times in a struggle with one
of the Material Girls' armed guards. The stalker was later convicted and sentenced to a lengthy prison term. Earlier, another stalker had been arrested at
the same Madonna estate and sentenced to a year in jail. Both men claimed
to be Madonna's husband. Back in the 1930s, long before Madonna lived here,
this gaudy terra cotta and yellow-striped palace was a casino run by mobster
Bugsy Siegel.

Mansfield, Jayne

Slidell, Louisiana

DIRECTIONS: Drive from Biloxi toward New Orleans along old Highway 90. The
site is just before the Rigolets Bridge, near a restaurant called the White Kitchen.

Like all the bleach-blonde sex goddesses, Jayne Mansfield's career was wan-
ing in the wake of Marilyn Monroe's death when she met her own untimely
end at the age of 33. In Slidell, Louisiana, at about 2:00 A.M. the morning of
June 29, 1967, a 1966 Buick Electra carrying Mansfield and six other passengers—including Mansfield's three children and dog—plowed into the back of
a tractor-trailer, obscured by haze released by a mosquito fogger. While the
children survived, Mansfield, her lawyer and boyfriend Sam Brody, driver
Ronnie Harrison, and the dog did not.

Michael, George

Will Rogers Memorial Park • 9650 Sunset Boulevard (just across from
the Beverly Hills Hotel) • Beverly Hills, California

On April 8, 1998, pop star George Michael decided to enter the men's room
at this well-mannered park and engage
in what police described as a "lewd act."
(The park was under fairly regular surveillance after cops realized that it had
become a "hot zone.") Michael was alone
in the restroom at the time—which is

located near the northwest corner of the park. Michael was arrested, found guilty of the charge, and eventually sentenced to perform community service.

Miller, Mac
11659 West Valley Crest Drive • Studio City, California

Malcolm James McCormick, a.k.a "Mac Miller," was an American rapper and record producer. Starting out in Pittsburgh's hip hop scene, Miller signed a record deal with independent label Rostrum Records at age 18 and released his breakthrough mixtapes *K.I.D.S.* (2010) and *Best Day Ever* (2011). Miller's debut studio album, *Blue Slide Park* (2011), became the first independently distributed debut album to top the U.S. Billboard 200 since 1995. In 2013, he founded the record label imprint REMember Music. Miller struggled with addiction and substance abuse, which was often referenced in his lyrics. On September 7, 2018, he died from an accidental drug overdose of cocaine, fentanyl, and alcohol at his Studio City home, at just 26 years old. Miller was posthumously nominated for a Grammy for Best Rap Album for his 2018 album *Swimming*.

Mineo, Sal
8563 Holloway Drive (just off the Sunset Strip)
West Hollywood, California

This is the two-story apartment complex where actor Sal Mineo (*Rebel Without a Cause*) was stabbed to death by a robber in the carport behind his apartment building, in February of 1976. The 30-year-old actor had been in the stages of trying to shed his teen-idol image, and so he'd recently turned to directing. On this night, returning from rehearsal of the play *P.S. Your Cat Is Dead*, a neighbor heard him screaming out for help, but he got there too late—Mineo was already dead. Nothing was stolen, and a white male with long hair had been seen running from the scene.

Mineo's killer, Lionel Ray Williams, was eventually caught, convicted, and sentenced to life in prison in 1979, for what was believed to have been a random act of murder. (Williams was found-out when, while a prison inmate in Michigan, he began bragging to fellow inmates that he had killed a star.)

Mix, Tom
Florence, Arizona

DIRECTIONS: From Phoenix, take U.S. 60 east to Florence Junction. Follow Arizona 79, the Pinal Pioneer Parkway, south. You'll pass through Florence then continue south about 20 miles toward Oracle Junction. The Tom Mix Memorial is near mile 116, the marker at Tom Mix Wash.

A black iron silhouette of a riderless bronco stands at the spot in the road where Tom drove to his death on October 12, 1940. Tom Mix died after ignoring warnings about a gully bridge that was out due to road work. The gully into which his 1937 Cadillac plunged has been renamed Tom Mix Wash.

Mix was the highest paid actor in the 1920s and easily the most famous cowboy actor of his era. By the mid-1930s though, he had made his last picture, and by 1940 Mix's popularity had waned.

He had come to Phoenix for a promotional visit at a downtown moviehouse. After making his appearance at the RKO Theatre, he made the rounds of a few downtown bars. By nightfall he was drunk, and decided to drive toward Tucson on the Florence Highway in his new Cadillac roadster. Mix took one of the curves at 80 miles per hour, his Caddie left the road and plowed into a clump of mesquite; he died instantly. His body was taken to Los Angeles for a burial service at which thousands of fans turned out.

Neil, Vince
The Esplanade at Sapphire Street • Redondo Beach, California

Mötley Crüe frontman Vince Neil had been living it up at his Redondo Beach home for three days when he decided to make a run to a local liquor store for more booze. Nicholas "Razzle" Dingley (a member of the Finnish punk band Hanoi Rocks), went along for the ride. Coming home from the booze run, Neil, driving with a personal blood alcohol level almost twice the legal limit, swerved sharply to avoid a parked fire truck. His red 1972 Ford Pantera then smashed into a white Volkswagen, killing "Razzle" Dingley. Neil escaped with minor injuries, but the man in the Volkswagen was left with brain damage and paralysis. Though Neil was arrested for vehicular manslaughter, amazingly, he got off with just a 30-day jail sentence.

Nelson, Rick
Near FM Road 990, outside DeKalb, Texas

DIRECTIONS: Take Highway 82 east of out DeKalb and cross the train tracks to FM Road 1840. FM Road 990 will come up in about half a mile, make a right onto it. From there, the crash site is about 400 yards west of 990 a half mile from the intersection of 1840 and 990.

Rick Nelson was the all-American kid on *The Adventures of Ozzy and Harriet* and had several major hits in the late 1950s and early 1960s, such as "Hello Mary Lou," "It's Late," "Poor Little Fool," and "Travelin' Man." In 1972, he hit the Top 20 with "Garden Party."

While on tour on December 31, 1985, Rick Nelson's plane went down due to a fire started in a faulty heating unit. The rumors of a fire caused by freebasing coke were entirely incorrect, yet still persist. The fire began in the rear of the plane and the fumes quickly spread throughout the plane, causing the crash. Rick Nelson was only 45 years old. The pilot and co-pilot survived, but Nelson, his fiancée, and five other people perished when the DC-3 hit the ground.

Nicholson, Jack

The corner of Riverside Drive and Moorpark Street (near the Lakeside Golf Course) • Studio City, California

On February 8, 1994, Jack Nicholson allegedly hopped from his car here and attacked motorist Robert Blank's Mercedes-Benz with a golf club. It seems Blank had cut him off in traffic. He smashed the windshield and dented the roof with his golf club, and then drove away. Though Nicholson was charged with misdemeanor assault and vandalism, Blank also sued him, eventually settling out of court.

Notorious B.I.G.

6060 Wilshire Boulevard • Los Angeles, California

It was here outside the Petersen Automotive Museum, the site of a *Soul Train* awards party on March 9, 1997, where rapper (real name Christopher Wallace, also known as Big E. Smalls) was gunned down and killed by a drive-by shooter shortly after midnight while sitting inside his Chevrolet Suburban. It has been reported recently that Smalls may have supplied the gun which killed rival rapper Tupac Shakur in Las Vegas the year before he himself was murdered (as well as possibly putting a $1 million bounty on Shakur's head). However, the Smalls family disputes the charges leveled by *Los Angeles Times* Pulitzer Prize-winning journalist, Chuck Phillips.

Parker, Charlie

Stanhope Hotel • 995 Fifth Avenue • New York, New York • 212-774-1234

On the night of March 12, 1955, legendary sax player Charlie Parker died of pneumonia here at this luxury hotel while visiting his friend, the "jazz baroness" Nica de Koenigswarter. Though he was only 34 years old, the coroner estimated Parker's age to be 64 due to the wear and tear on his drug-and-alcohol ravaged body. Parker was a revolutionary giant among jazz musicians of the time, but it would take the general population years to discover his musical genius.

Parsons, Gram

Joshua Tree Inn • 61259 Palms Highway • Joshua Tree, California
760-366-1188

Room 8 is the destination for many music aficionados from the world over. While registered in this room on September 18, 1973, musician Gram Parsons (a veteran of the Byrds and the Flying Burrito Brothers), died at the age of 26 after too much tequila and morphine. Parsons had just finished his "Fallen Angels" tour featuring his duet partner, Emmylou Harris.

On the peach-colored wall of the room hangs the same mirror and picture that hung in the room back in 1973. Also, a journal is kept on a bedside table for the scores of fans who come to pay homage. Yvo Kwee, the owner, says that the mirror sometimes rattles inexplicably around 4:00 A.M. and the backdoor sometimes opens itself.

A few miles from the Inn is one of the most bizarre landmarks in rock and roll. It seems that after Parsons died, his road manager and pal Phil Kaufman and an accomplice hijacked Parsons' body from LAX where it was on its way to New Orleans. The two drove back out to Joshua Tree National Park, up to a landmark called Cap Rock (where, it has been reported, Parsons used to get high with his musical soulmate Keith Richards and look for UFOs) and lit Parsons' body on fire, as per an earlier agreement he had made with Parsons.

Kaufman and his accomplice were eventually charged with misdemeanor theft for stealing the coffin and fined just over $1,000. Though he never achieved great commercial success, Gram Parsons still has a small but intense following. Some of these fans laid a plaque at Cap Rock, featuring the words "Safe at Home" (the name of one Parsons' songs). Today the plaque has been moved to just outside of room 8. The site continues to draw people from all over the world. The road leading to the West entrance of Joshua Tree State Park is located just down the street from the Joshua Street Inn. The number at the park is 760-367-5500, and Cap Rock is located about 10 miles in from the park's West entrance.

Prince
Paisley Park estate • 7801 Audubon Rd. • Chanhassen, Minnesota

The revolutionary musician Prince (Prince Rogers Nelson) was found dead at his Paisley Park estate on April 21, 2016. He was only 57 years old. An autopsy later revealed that he had died from an accidental overdose of fentanyl, a powerful opioid. He was scheduled to meet with addiction medicine specialist Howard Kornfield on April 22, but the Carver County Sheriff's Office got an emergency call informing him about an unidentified person being unconscious at Paisley Park. Widely regarded as one of the greatest musicians of his generation, Prince was known for his flamboyant, androgynous persona and extraordinary vocal range. Prince produced his albums himself, pioneering the Minneapolis sound. His music incorporated a wide variety of styles, includ-

ing funk, R&B, rock, new wave, soul, synth-pop, pop, jazz, and hip hop. He often played most or all instruments on his recordings. He also wrote songs for many other successful artists including the Bangles and Sinead O'Connor. Today, fascinating tours and more are offered at Paisley Park, Prince's home and studio.

Prinze, Freddie
Beverly Hills Plaza Hotel • 10300 Wilshire Boulevard
Los Angeles, California • 310-275-5575

The son of a Puerto Rican mother and a Hungarian father, Freddie Prinze was

a 20-year-old stand-up comedian when he landed a starring role on the sitcom *Chico and the Man.* It debuted in 1974 and was a huge ratings success. By 1977, Prinze was one of the biggest stars on TV. At the height of his popularity, despondent over personal problems and apparently under the influence of drugs, he shot himself in the head and died several hours later at the nearby UCLA Medical Center.

This is the location where he killed himself, though hotel employees are tight-lipped about the room in which it happened. However, on his death certificate, "#216" is noted as the address of the incident.

Phoenix, River
The Viper Room
8852 Sunset Boulevard
West Hollywood, California

This is the Johnny Depp-owned club where 23-year-old actor River Phoenix (*Stand By Me*) died of an overdose of heroin and cocaine. He collapsed on the sidewalk outside of this club on Halloween night of 1993. He was pronounced dead at Cedars-Sinai hospital, located nearby at 8700 Beverly Boulevard.

Polanski, Roman
12850 Mulholland Drive • Hollywood Hills, California

It was here in actor Jack Nicholson's house where director Roman Polanski (*Chinatown* and *Rosemary's Baby*) allegedly had sex with a 13-year-old girl. The scandalous event resulted in Polanski's 1977 trial, conviction, and self-exile in Europe.

Pryor, Richard
17267 Parthenia Street (west of Hayvenhurst) • Northridge, California

This is the house where, back in the 1980s, comedian Richard Pryor accidentally set himself on fire while free-basing cocaine, then ran through the streets
looking for help. "One thing I learned," said Pryor, "was that you can run really fast when you're on fire!" Pryor used the incident as a springboard to review
his life in the 1986 movie, *Jo Jo Dancer, Your Life is Calling.*

Pusser, Buford

North side of Highway 64 near Lawton, Tennessee (about halfway
between the towns of Adamsville and Selmer) • Adamsville, Tennessee
731-632-1401 (City of Adamsville information)

Revered in his home state as a
mythical figure, Buford Pusser
was the target of assassination
attempts, one of which killed
his wife and left him physically
scarred, his jaw shot off and replaced by wire and plastic. Pusser
left the Sheriff's department in
1970 and three movies would be
made about his life: *Walking Tall,*

Walking Tall II, and *Walking Tall: The Final Chapter.* On the night of August 21,
1974, the 36-year-old Pusser was killed in a one vehicle car crash on Highway
64 between Selmer and Adamsville, Tennessee. There's an interesting museum dedicated to Buford Pusser at 342 Pusser Street, Adamsville, Tennessee
(731-632-4080).

Rather, Dan

1075 Park Avenue • New York, New York

One night in 1986, CBS anchorman Dan Rather was walking on Park Avenue when he was supposedly accosted by two men. According to his report,
the men repeatedly asked him, "Kenneth, what's the frequency?" Rather, not
knowing what to say, was beaten up for his lack of response. He managed to
escape their grasp and headed into the lobby of this building as the men ran
away.

When the story broke the next day, it seemed so strange and incomplete,
that some began to question the legitimacy of it. But the incident became

memorable to the point that the band REM even released a hit song called "What's the Frequency Kenneth?"—forever memorializing the event. Some years after it happened, an incarcerated man supposedly confessed to the attack, claiming insanity at the time.

Redding, Otis

Lake Monona (The memorial is located in the William T. Evjue Rooftop Garden, part of the Monona Terrace.) • Madison, Wisconsin

This was where the plane carrying soul singer Otis Redding and his backup band the Bar-Kays crashed on the afternoon of December 10, 1967. They were traveling from Cleveland to do two shows in Madison that evening when the plane went down on approach to Madison Airport. No cause was ever uncovered, though witnesses heard the engine sputtering.

A memorial to Redding was erected on the western shore of Lake Monona that consists of three benches and a plaque in Law Park on John Nolan Drive. Supposedly, if you sit on the middle bench and face east, you're facing the part of the lake where the plane went down.

Reeves, George

1579 Benedict Canyon Drive • Beverly Hills, California

This is where actor George Reeves, TV's *Superman*, was found dead of a gunshot wound on June 16, 1959. The incident was immediately controversial in that his relatives believed he was murdered, thereby disputing the official ruling of suicide. Interestingly (and somewhat morbidly), he was buried in the same suit that he wore on the show while playing "Clark Kent."

Rhoads, Randy
Flying Baron Estates • Leesburg, Florida

On March 18, 1982, the Ozzy Osbourne band played what would be their last show with Randy Rhoads at the Civic Coliseum in Knoxville, Tennessee. On the way to Orlando they were to pass by the Flying Baron Estates, home of tour bus driver Andrew C. Aycock. They stopped there to get some spare parts for the bus, and the next morning Aycock took out a red and white 1955 Beechcraft Bonanza F-35 that was parked at the estate and started giving rides. With Randy Rhoads and a woman named Rachel Youngblood on board, the plane "buzzed" the band's tour bus several times. Then, the plane's left wing struck the left side of the band's tour bus and hit a nearby pine tree, killing all on board.

Rogers, Will
13 miles south of Barrow, Alaska

Humorist and American icon Will Rogers was killed with his good friend, flying ace Wiley Post, on August 15, 1935. Post's Lockheed Orion-Explorer crashed at Point Barrow, Alaska in fog due to engine failure, and both men were killed on impact. A Will Rogers and Wiley Post Monument was placed across from the Wiley Post-Will Rogers Memorial Airport. However, the exact crash site is marked 13 miles down the coast at a spot that is only reachable by boat or by taking a four-wheeler across the tundra. Each year around the anniversary of the crash, Barrow holds a 13 mile run in honor of the two men.

Schaeffer, Rebecca
120 North Sweetzer Avenue • Los Angeles, California

On the morning of July 18, 1989, this up-and-coming actress who starred in the sitcom *My Sister Sam* was shot and killed by Robert Bardo, a deranged fan who had become obsessed with her. This is the tragic event that made the term "stalker" a part of our everyday vernacular. Bardo, who was captured soon after and prosecuted by a pre-O.J. Simpson trial Marcia Clark, is now serving a life sentence without parole.

Rebecca Schaeffer's murder helped prompt then-California Governor George Deukmejian to sign a law prohibiting the DMV from releasing addresses (it also pushed the Los Angeles Police Department to create the first Threat Management Team). The law was the first of its kind and later helped to convict Jonathan Norman, who was sentenced to 25 years in prison for attempting to carry out threats against director Steven Spielberg.

Selena

Days Inn • 901 Navigation Boulevard • Corpus Christi, Texas • 866-231-9330

On March 31, 1995, the popular Tejano singing star Selena (Selena Quintanilla-Perez) was shot and killed by Yolanda Saldivar, 34, the former president of the Selena fan club. After holding police at bay for nine hours, she finally gave up and admitted that she had shot her longtime friend. Selena was just 23 years old.

According to testimony from the trial, Selena was meeting with Saldivar to discuss allegations that Saldivar had embezzled money from her when the shooting occurred. The defense argued that Saldivar had accidentally fired the shot that killed Selena, while the prosecution maintained that the shooting was deliberate. Saldivar was eventually found guilty and sentenced to life in prison. If you're interested in searching for Room 158, where the murder occurred, forget it—the hotel renumbered the entire floor.

Shannon, Del

15519 Saddleback Road • Canyon Country, California

This the home where singer Del Shannon committed suicide. Shannon's first big hit was "Runaway" in 1964. It charted at number one for four straight weeks. He had other hits such as "Keep Searchin' (We'll Follow the Sun)" and "Hats Off to Larry," but nothing matched the success of "Runaway." On February 8, 1990, Shannon shot himself in the head with a .22 caliber rifle. He had apparently been suffering from depression.

Shakur, Tupac

On Flamingo Road, just east of Las Vegas Boulevard, near the
intersection of Koval Lane • Las Vegas, Nevada

Though the popular gangsta rap star Tupac Shakur had made headlines over a
series of run-ins with the law, none got more attention than the gangland-style
hit that ended up taking his life on September 13, 1996. After leaving the Ty-
son/Seldon fight at the MGM Grand Hotel in Las Vegas (he was videotaped
getting into an altercation on the way out), the BMW Shakur was riding in
with record executive Suge Knight was stopped on Flamingo Road near the
Strip. Based on eyewitness accounts, two men jumped out of a Cadillac and
blasted 13 rounds into the BMW, hitting Shakur four times (Knight suffered a
minor head wound). Shakur died several days later as a result of the wounds
suffered in the ambush.

Smith, Anna Nicole

Seminole Hard Rock Hotel & Casino • Hollywood, Florida

Buxom blonde plus-size model and actress Anna Nicole Smith was found
dead in Room 607 of this hotel on February 8, 2007 after accidentally over-
dosing on at least nine prescription drugs. She was 39 years old. Smith had
endured a miserable last several days with a stomach flu, a 105-degree fever,
and numerous infections.

Smith, Elliot

1857 1/2 Lemoyne Street • Los Angeles, California

On the night of October 21, 2003, sing-
er/songwriter Elliot Smith allegedly
committed suicide here in a small Echo
Park bungalow where he lived with his
girlfriend, Jennifer Chiba. She stated
that after an argument, she locked herself in the bathroom and then heard
Smith scream. She unlocked the door to
see him standing with his back to her.

When he turned around, she then saw a knife sticking out of his chest. Smith
was rushed to a nearby hospital, where emergency surgery to repair the two
stab wounds to his heart couldn't save his life.

Smollett, Jussie
East Lower North Water Street • Chicago, Illinois

On January 29, 2019, actor Jussie Smollett called the Chicago Police Department and reported a hate crime that, as it turned out, he had staged earlier that morning. He planned the hate crime with two Nigerian brothers, Abimbola and Olabinjo Osundairo, who had worked as extras on the set of the television drama *Empire*, in which Smollett was a cast member. During the attack, which took place in Chicago's Streeterville neighborhood, the disguised brothers shouted racial and homophobic slurs while one poured bleach on Smollett and the other placed a noose around his neck. In addition to falsely reporting that he had been attacked by two unknown individuals, Smollett described one of them as a white male. He also told police the men shouted "MAGA country" during the attack, a reference to the Trumpian political slogan "Make America Great Again." The brothers later testified that Smollett staged the attack near a surveillance camera so that video of it could be publicized. Smollett was found guilty later of staging the event.

Spears, Britney
Tognozzi's Salon • 18360 Ventura Boulevard • Tarzana, California

It was the buzz cut heard 'round the world. When Britney Spears and her bodyguards showed up at the door at Esther Tognozzi's salon in February 2007, the hairstylist had no idea what was happening. Spears sat down at one of the stations and asked Tognozzi to shave off her recently brunette-colored locks. Tognozzi resisted, but when Spears grabbed a sideburn trimmer and started shaving her head herself, Tognozzi watched and then cleaned up the close shave when Spears was done. Spears' bizarre new look was the latest turn in her well-chronicled struggles since splitting the year before with husband Kevin Federline, the father of her two sons. After one of her bodyguards paid $50 cash for the $45 haircut, Spears got two new tattoos as a walk-in client at Body and Soul in Sherman Oaks. (Today, the salon is called Esther's Haircutting Studio.)

Stratton, Dorothy
10881 Clarkson Road • West Los Angeles, California

This was the end of the line for Playmate and actress Dorothy Stratton. "Discovered" in Canada by her hustler boyfriend Paul Snider, Stratton was

Playmate of the Month in August 1979, and soon after the pair married. But the obsessed, megalomaniac Snider soon made her life tortuous. She eventually left him for film director Peter Bogdonavich, which drove Snider nuts. (He had hired a private detective to follow her around and report on her activities.)

One evening, Snider convinced her to come to their apartment, where he tied her up and put a shotgun to her head, pulling the trigger. He then turned the gun on himself. In the 1983 film about her life *Star 80*, the murder scene was filmed in the actual apartment where she died.

Swift, Taylor
Radio City Music Hall • 1260 Sixth Avenue • New York, New York

The 2009 MTV Video Music Awards, which honored the best music videos from the previous year between June 2008 to June 2009, were presented on September 13, 2009. The ceremony was hosted by Russell Brand. The event was marred when Kanye West interrupted Taylor Swift's acceptance of the award for Best Female Video in order to proclaim that despite Swift's victory, Beyoncé still had "one of the best videos of all time" (in reference to Beyoncé's "Single Ladies"). When Beyoncé was eventually awarded Video of the Year, she invited Swift back to the stage to finish her acceptance speech. The incident was highly publicized after the ceremony, with *Rolling Stone* naming it the "wildest" moment in the history of the Video Music Awards in 2013.

Switzer, Carl
10400 Columbus Avenue
Mission Hills, California

He was cute, freckle-faced "Alfalfa" on *The Little Rascals* (And *Our Gang* comedies) in the 1930s and early '40s. But like many child actors, after Carl Switzer outgrew his cuteness, the roles stopped coming (though he did have a small part in *It's A Wonderful Life*). As he got older, he took jobs primarily as a hunting and fishing guide, but his life ended at this house on January 21, 1959 at the age of just 31.

Switzer was shot and killed by Moses Stiltz here at the home of Rita Corrigan (wife of stuntman "Crash" Corrigan). The two were arguing over money when Stiltz shot Switzer in a back bedroom. The shooting was ruled as a justifiable homicide and Stiltz never served any time for the shooting.

Thunders, Johnny
St. Peter's Guest House • Room 37 • 1005 St. Peter Street
New Orleans, Louisiana • 504-524-9232

Though over the years there were always many rumors that he had died, this was actually the last stand for the heroin-addled guitar slinger, Johnny Thunders. He died here on April 23, 1991. The former New York Doll had thought about moving to New Orleans, finding some new musicians, and maybe starting a new band, but he never got the chance to complete his plan. Thunders checked into Room 37 of the St. Peter Guest House in the late hours of April 23, and the following morning he was dead. Apparently, he had scored heroin upon arriving and dealt himself a lethal shot and died overnight.

Todd, Thelma
17531 Posetano Road • Pacific Palisades, California

The sexy young actress Thelma Todd had made a name for herself by vamping it up in comedies with the Marx Brothers (*Horse Feathers*, *Monkey Business*), Laurel & Hardy, and Buster Keaton. She also ran a popular beachside restaurant, "Thelma Todd's Sidewalk Cafe,"

located in this building just north of Sunset Boulevard.

Her death remains mysterious. In 1935 at the age of 30, Todd's lifeless body was found in her car—parked in the garage just above her café—and police ruled it an accidental suicide. But many, due to the large amount of blood that was found, suspected something more sinister; perhaps an organized crime hit. Nobody was ever arrested for the crime, and Todd's life story was told in the 1991 TV movie *White Hot: The Mysterious Murder of Thelma Todd*, with Loni Anderson playing the lead.

Vaughan, Stevie Ray
Alpine Valley Resort • East Troy, Wisconsin (85 miles northwest of Chicago) • 1-800-227-9395

Guitar hero Stevie Ray Vaughan was killed in a post-gig helicopter crash in East Troy, Wisconsin, on August 27, 1990. He was 35. Vaughn and three members of Eric Clapton's entourage perished when their helicopter crashed into a ski slope about a mile from the Alpine Valley Music theater, where they'd just finished playing a concert.

Versace, Gianni
1116 Ocean Drive • South Beach • Miami, Florida

Cunanan, Andrew
5701 Collins Avenue • Miami Beach, Florida

At 8:45 A.M. on July 15, 1997, world famous designer Gianni Versace was returning home from a short walk to the nearby News Café, where he purchased magazines. He was wearing shorts with $1,200 in the pocket, sandals, and a dark colored shirt. He walked up the steps to the front gate, put the key in and was about to turn it, when Andrew Cunanan approached him. Versace was shot twice—once, point blank in the center of his face, the other in his neck. He fell to the steps, and landed on his right side.

On July 25, 1997, two weeks after gunning down Versace, murderer Andrew Cunanan killed himself on a houseboat about 40 blocks away from where he had shot the designer. Cunanan, who had left a trail of dead across a number of states, shot himself in the mouth with the same pistol he had used on all of his other victims. For two months before killing Versace, he'd holed up at the somewhat seedy Normandy Plaza Hotel (rooms 205 and 322) located at 6979 Collins Avenue in Miami Beach.

Von Bulow, Claus
Clarendon Court • Bellevue Avenue at Rovensky Avenue, across from Rovensky Park • Newport, Rhode Island

In 1979, Claus Von Bulow was convicted of trying to murder his wealthy wife Sunny at this opulent Newport mansion by injecting her with insulin (allegedly, so he could make off with her money.) In 1982, however, he was acquitted after a successful appeal. Sunny remained comatose at New York City's Columbia-Presbyterian Hospital until her death in 2008.

Walker, Paul
28385 Constellation Rd. • Valencia, California

At around 3:30 P.M. on November 30, 2013, actor Paul Walker (of *The Fast and the Furious* franchise) and his friend Roger Rodas were driving along this street in a 2005 Porsche Carrera GT when the vehicle spun out of control. The car struck a lamp post and two trees before bursting into flames. Both of the men suffered serious traumatic injuries and were burnt beyond recognition. According to the Los Angeles County coroner's office, Paul Walker died because of the combined effects of the impact and the resulting fire. Investigators determined that Rodas was driving nearly twice the speed limit at the time. Furthermore, the vehicle was fitted with two nine-year-old tires.

Warhol, Andy
The Factory (former site) • 33 Union Square West • New York, New York

Valerie Solanas walked into the Factory, Andy Warhol's studio, on June 3, 1968, pulled out a gun that was given to her by a guy she met in a copy shop, and fired on America's most famous artist. Warhol would eventually recover from the injuries. Solanas, a radical feminist and sometime acquaintance of Warhol, was sentenced to three years in jail for assault; she later spent time in various mental hospitals.

Williams, Robin

95 St. Thomas Cay
Paradise Cay, California

Actor/comedian Robin Williams was found dead in his home in Paradise Cay, California on August 11, 2014. The actor was discovered with a belt around his neck, and investigators later found cuts on his left wrist. Tragically, it was soon confirmed that Williams died by suicide. He was 63 years old. A talented comedian and Academy Award-winning actor, Williams was highly respected among his peers and cherished by his millions of fans. But despite his happy-go-lucky persona, Williams struggled with alcoholism and drug addiction early on in his career. And later on in his life, he would grapple with mental health issues and physical ailments.

Wilson, Dennis

Basin C at dock 1100 • Maruesas Way • Marina del Rey, California

This is where Beach Boys' drummer Dennis Wilson died at the age 39 in a drowning accident off of a friend's boat. With his brothers and Mike Love, Dennis helped the Beach Boys turn out such hits as "California Girls," "Fun, Fun, Fun," and "Wouldn't It Be Nice." Apparently, on December 28, 1983, Wilson had too much to drink, decided to go swimming, and subsequently drowned.

Wood, Natalie

Two Harbors • Catalina Island (26 miles off the coast of California)

Around Thanksgiving 1981, Natalie Wood, her husband Robert Wagner, and a friend—actor Christopher Walken—sailed their yacht to Catalina's main harbor, Avalon. They spent the night there and then set off for the more remote seaport area known as Two Harbors, on the island's north side. The group had a few drinks at a little place called Doug's Harbor Reef Saloon, and then headed back to their boat.

Based on the skipper's account, tensions later arose with Wagner after Wood flirted with Walken. Wood went to her cabin alone, and then about an hour later was discovered missing. Searchers soon found her dead in the water, about a mile east of Two Harbors, off Blue Cavern Point.

CHAPTER SIX

LET'S GO TO THE MOVIES

The African Queen

Holiday Inn Key Largo and Marina • 99701 Overseas Highway
Key Largo, Florida • 305-451-2121

Though the boat in the 1951 classic John Huston film starring Humphrey Bogart and Katherine Hepburn appeared to be blown apart in Kabalego Falls, Uganda (where the film was shot), it actually still exists here in Florida. Since the early 1980s, it has lived on as a tourist treat at this hotel.

The Alamo

FM 674 (7 miles north of Bracketville)
Bracketville, Texas • 830-563-2580

Made for almost $8 million in 1960, John's Wayne's epic *The Alamo* was, at the time, the costliest movie ever made. It became too expensive to shoot at its original Mexico location, so John

Wayne leased 400 acres on a ranch at this site, located about 100 miles west of San Antonio. The full-size movie set was built here and remains open today as not just a tourist attraction, but also a location for many other movies.

American Beauty

SPACEY/BURHAM HOME: 11388 Homesdale Street • Brentwood, California
COLONEL'S HOME: 330 South Windsor Boulevard • Hancock Park
(Los Angeles), California

These two homes were used in the filming of the 1999 Oscar winner *American Beauty*. Interestingly, both the exteriors of the Spacey/Burnham home and the Colonel's home next door were movie sets. But for the interiors, the producers used these two actual homes. Incidentally, the fast food drive-through where Lester catches his wife cheating with "The King" is actually a Carl's Jr. restaurant located at 20105 Saticoy Street, Canoga Park, California.

American Graffiti

Petaluma, California • Petaluma Visitors Program: 1-877-273-8258

The movie was inspired by the small town of Modesto, where filmmaker George Lucas grew up. But this is where it was primarily shot. You can take a walking tour of the town's many movie sites, with a guide from the tourist information office at 799 Baywood Street. A few points along the way:
• The main drag used in the movie is Petaluma Boulevard North, between D Street and Washington Street.
• Richard Dreyfuss gets drafted into the Pharaohs gang in front of the Old Opera House, 149 Kentucky Street.
• The used car lot where Dreyfuss is made to chain the axle of the police car is still a vacant lot. It's located along the McNear Building, 15–23 Petaluma Boulevard North.

Animal House

The University of Oregon at Eugene
Agate and Thirteenth Avenue • Eugene, Oregon • 541-346-1000

Because of Universal Pictures' tight budget for 1978's *Animal House*, director John Landis had to find a real college campus for the filming. Fortunately for the filmmaker, the University of Oregon agreed to lend their campus to the production, and the rest is frat house history.

The entire movie ended up being filmed in Oregon, and many of the movie's most famous locations remain today, with the unfortunate exception of the actual "Animal House." The building used for shooting the Delta House's exterior scenes was located at 751 East 11th Street, across from the small Northwest Christian College. Back then, it was a halfway house for criminals. In 1986, the building was torn down (Delta House Bricks were sold as souvenirs for $5 each). It is now an empty lot.

But, you can still find the following locations:
- The Sigma Nu fraternity, at 763 E 11th Avenue, was used for the Delta House interiors and for the Tri Pi sorority exteriors, where Belushi peeped in the sorority windows.
- The Kappa Sigma fraternity, at 1090 Alder Street, is where the Toga Party was shot.
- The Phi Kappa Psi house, at 729 E 11th Avenue, was both the interior and exterior of the uptight Omega House.
- The dining area in the Erb Memorial Union (EMU), was where the infamous Belushi "zit" scene and ensuing food fight were staged.
- The school office building where the horse drops dead is Johnson Hall, the university's administration building. All of the scenes in Dean Wormer's office were actually filmed in the offices of the university president.
- Remember when Pinto and Clorette made out in the middle of the football field? That was shot in Autzen Stadium.
- Located about 15 miles southeast of Eugene, the Dexter Lake Club is the roadside club where the boys go out and "surprise" Otis Day and the Knights. It is located at 39128 Dexter Road in Dexter, Oregon.

Annie Hall
8301 Sunset Boulevard • West Hollywood, California

This 1977 film is considered by many to be Woody Allen's best (it won the Oscar that year for Best Picture), and although it was filmed primarily in New York, one of the most popular scenes was filmed at an existing landmark in West Hollywood, California. It's the scene near the film's end at the health food restaurant where Woody's character Alvy Singer (with Diane Keaton) orders alfalfa sprouts and mashed yeast before being arrested in the parking lot for bad driving. Back then it was The Source, a popular health food restaurant. As of this writing, the structure remains but it is boarded up.

Bad News Bears
10500 Mason Avenue
Chatsworth, California

The original *Bad News Bears* (1976) was filmed throughout Chatsworth, Reseda, and Tarzana, but the baseball field scenes were shot at Mason Park in Chatsworth. The field was created for the film and left for the community to use once production wrapped up. It is still used today for Little League.

The Bagdad Café
46548 National Trails Hwy • Newberry Springs, California • 760-257-3101

Located off old Route 66 east of Barstow on Highway 40, this is the oddly charming roadside café from the 1988 film starring Marianne Sagebrecht and Jack Palance. It was called The Sidewinder Café in the film, today it's been re-named in honor of the movie that made it famous.

Big Fish
Spectre, Alabama

Tim Burton's fantastical *Big Fish* takes place in the fictional town of Spectre, Alabama, along the banks of the Alabama River. The entire "town" was built for the purpose of filming in, and was actually located within Millbrook, Alabama at Jackson Lake Island. While the once idyllic town is currently in various states of decay, the now private property remains open for tourists to explore. For just a small bridge toll, guests can lose themselves among the rundown streets and last surviving buildings.

The Birds
The Potter Schoolhouse
17110 Bodega Lane
Bodega Bay, California

The center of the attacks in Hitchcock's 1963 classic was this small town located 50 miles north of San Francisco. Several miles inland is the town of Bodega, and the Schoolhouse where Suzanne Pleshette teaches (and the birds gather outside) still stands (though it's a private home).

The Blair Witch Project
Seneca Creek State Park • 25 miles west of Burkittsville, Maryland
Patapsco Valley State Park • 8020 Baltimore National Pike
Ellicott City, Maryland • 410-461-5005

Seneca Creek State Park was actually the "Black Hills Forest" featured in this surprise low-budget smash from 1999. The rest of the film was made throughout Burkittsville, Maryland and the 200-year old Griggs House that was featured in the movie still stands in Patapsco State Park, western Baltimore County.

Breakfast at Tiffany's
727 Fifth Avenue (at 57th Street)
New York, New York

This is where Holly Golightly (Audrey Hepburn) spent her mornings eating breakfast to the strains of "Moon River." It is not uncommon to find people posing for photos outside of the store, in the exact spot near the window into which Hepburn used to gaze. Perhaps the most popular jewelry store in the world, it remains virtually unchanged from the day they shot the scene in 1961.

The Breakfast Club
9511 Harrison Street • Des Plaines, Illinois

This 1980s teen angst classic was actually filmed at Illinois State Police Station (formerly, Maine North High School), located in Des Plaines, Illinois. The library where the majority of the film is set was built from scratch in the building's former gymnasium. The high school had been closed for two years before the filming of the movie, and was used by the park district before the Illinois State Police bought it and turned it into a Police Station.

The Bridges of Madison County
Winterset, Iowa

Madison County is a real place in Iowa (it's where John Wayne was born), and it's where the famous bridges are located. Specifically, they're in a place called Winterset (the place Meryl Streep visits to buy her new Frock), which is about 30 miles southwest of Des Moines on I-169.

Of the original 19 bridges that were built and named after the closest resident, only six remain. In the movie you can see the Roseman Bridge, which was built in 1883, and the longest of the bridges, the Holliwell Bridge.

The farmhouse where Streep lived (at one time an abandoned ruin) is still maintained as a tourist attraction and it's open from May to October. For brochures, maps of the county with bridge locations, other historical information, and movie sites, contact the Madison County Chamber of Commerce toll-free at (800) 298-6119.

Caddyshack

Rolling Hills Golf and Tennis Club • 3501 West Rolling Hills Circle
South West 36th Street • Davie, Florida • 407-834-6818

Located about 10 miles from Fort Lauderdale, this is the country club where most of the 1980 comedy took place. The poolside scenes however were shot at the Boca Raton Hotel and Country Club, located at 501 East Camino Real in Boca Raton, just north of Fort Lauderdale.

Carrie

Hermosa Beach Community Center • 710 Pier Avenue (at Pacific Coast Highway) • Hermosa Beach, California • 310-318-0280

The 1976 thriller *Carrie* had its memorable prom scene shot in this gym. The Brian DePalma classic (co-starring John Travolta and Amy Irving) became famous primarily for the scene in which the aforementioned actors rigged a bucket of pig's blood to fall on the head of Sissy Spacek (whose portrayal of Carrie White got her nominated for the Best Actress Oscar that year). The gym is located in the back of the building and looks much the same today as it did in the movie.

Casablanca

Van Nuys Airport
6590 Hayvenhurst Avenue
Van Nuys, California
(Exact hanger location,
16217 Lindbergh Street)

It's one of the most famous scenes

in movie history, and though there is some dispute among purists, this is generally believed to be the spot where it took place. The year was 1942 and the scene is Humphrey Bogart's poignant farewell to Ingrid Bergman at the end of *Casablanca*. Today it's called Van Nuys Airport, but back then it was Los Angeles Metropolitan Airport and it was used regularly for Hollywood productions.

While the bulk of *Casablanca* was filmed on a Warner Bros. backlot, a pair of key scenes was shot at this location. One was the arrival of Captain Strasser (played by Conrad Veidt), the other, the tearful finale where Bogart tells Bergman one last time, "Here's looking at you, kid." Keep in mind, it's tricky to find. The hangar where the scene was filmed is no longer part of the airport complex and it's exact location is on the south side of Waterman Drive, west of Woodley Avenue, on a small street called Lindbergh.

Chaplin, Charlie

Alexandria Hotel
501 South Spring Street
Los Angeles, California

Opened in 1906, for years the Alexandria Hotel was a magnet for celebrities and other notable guests. During its heyday, Winston Churchill, Enrico Caruso, King Edward VIII, and American presidents such as Taft, Wilson, and Roosevelt all stayed here. Charlie Chaplin lived here on and off in his early years in Los Angeles.

It was here, in 1919, that D.W. Griffith, Charlie Chaplin, Mary Pickford, and Douglas Fairbanks made movie history by announcing the formation of their independent company, United Artists. The once grand hotel is today a low-rent flophouse.

Chaplin Studios
1416 North La Brea Avenue • Hollywood, California • 323-802-1500

Hollywood consisted mainly of orange groves when film legend Chaplin

built his own movie studio in 1917. For 20 years, Chaplin shot all of his classic silent films here including *The Gold Rush* (1925), *City Lights* (1931), *Modern Times* (1936), and *The Great Dictator* (1939). He once left his footprints in some wet cement outside of the studio's Sound Stage 3, supposedly giving Sid Graumann the idea to immortalize actors by having them leave their handprints in the forecourt of his famed Chinese Theatre.

Chaplin left the studio in 1953, at which time CBS filmed several well-known TV series there, including *The Adventures of Superman*, *The Red Skelton Show*, and *Perry Mason*. Until 1999, it was the headquarters of A&M Records, and today it's the home of Jim Henson Productions. In honor of the studio's history, they've erected a statue of Kermit, dressed like Chaplin's "Little Tramp" character, above the main studio gate. Though no tours are given, a plaque near the entrance notes that the studio has been designated as Historic Monument #58.

City Lights
Wilshire Boulevard and Commonwealth Avenue
Los Angeles, California

Arguably Chaplin's greatest love story of all time, 1931's *City Lights* is the tale of Chaplin's heart-rending relationship with a blind flower girl. Shot at many locations throughout the Los Angeles area, this stretch of Wilshire Boulevard (at Commonwealth) is famous as the place where Chaplin walks arm in arm with the blind girl. Virtually unchanged today, the stroll took place alongside the Town House Hotel.

Former Mack Sennet Studios
1712 Glendale Boulevard
Los Angeles, California

Today it's a self-storage facility, but in 1912 the same building was a soundstage called

"Keystone," named by Mack Sennet and the place where he created and filmed his famous "Keystone Kops" comedies. It's also where Charlie Chaplin supposedly first donned a hat, picked up a cane and created his "Little Tramp" character. Interestingly, some of the old wooden lighting grids are still visible against the ceiling inside the building.

The Kid
24 Olvera Street • Los Angeles, California

Who can forget Chaplin's 1921 tearjerker about the Tramp and the Kid, played by Jackie Coogan (who would one day gain more fame as Uncle Fester on *The Addams Family* TV show). The Kid, who is abandoned by his rich mother, inadvertently ends up in the care of Chaplin's sweet Tramp character, who becomes a father figure to the child.

This is the exact spot where they arrive and Chaplin reclaims the Kid near the film's dramatic climax, when Chaplin chases down the authorities who have taken the child away from him. Back then it was just an anonymous side street with an alley in downtown Los Angeles. Today, it's the tourist mecca known as Olvera Street, a celebration of Los Angeles' rich Mexican heritage, a place where shoppers can enjoy authentic Mexican restaurants and shops.

The Gold Rush
Truckee Hotel • 10007 Bridge Street • Truckee, California
800-659-6921

For more than 125 years, this classic mountain-town hotel (located about 90 miles east of Sacramento) has served travelers. One important traveler in particular was Charlie Chaplin, who in 1925 stayed here at length while filming his classic *The Gold Rush* throughout the area. The historic hotel is still going strong; it's a charming retreat that's a throwback to the days when one of the film's greatest film legends called this his part-time home.

A Christmas Story
3159 W 11th St • Cleveland, Ohio

The quirky, charming 1983 holiday movie starring Peter Billingsley (in search of a Red Rider air powered BB gun) and Darren McGavin, though set in Indiana, was actually shot on this "Anywhere, U.S.A"-looking street in Cleveland. The house today is a museum dedicated to the film.

Clerks
Quick Stop Groceries • 58 Leonard Avenue
Leonardo, New Jersey

Director Kevin Smith actually worked in the convenience store where this 1994 indie hit was filmed. At 60 Leonard Avenue (next door) is RST Video, the store next to the market in the movie.

Culver Studios
9336 Washington Boulevard • Culver City, California • 310-202-1234

Located in Culver City, the exterior of Culver Studios became famous in its own right after being featured in the opening credits of many of David O. Selznick International's productions, such as *Gone With the Wind*. The colonial mansion (easily visible from Washington Boulevard) is an exact copy of George Washington's Mount Vernon. The 1939 epic was shot on Stages 11 and 12 in 1939; the exteriors of Tara, Twelve Oaks, and the city of Atlanta were created on the back lot, and were then set on fire when it came time to film the burning of Atlanta sequence.

Dazed and Confused
Bedichek Middle School
6800 Bill Hughes Road
Austin, Texas

Richard Linklater's 1993 nostalgic

homage to high school life in the mid-1970s was centered here at this real high school in Austin, the director's hometown. The movie featured early performances by (among others) Matthew McConaughey (his first movie), Parker Posie, and Ben Affleck.

Dead Poets Society

St. Andrews School • Noxontown Pond Road
Middletown, Delaware

This school stood in as Welton Academy in the 1989 teacher-tearjerker starring Robin Williams. It's a private school that sits on 2,000 acres.

Deliverance

Chattooga River (sections III and IV) • Rabun County • Northeastern corner of Georgia (on the border of North Carolina and South Carolina)
Rabun County Chamber of Commerce (706-782-4812)

It's hard to define exact sites in this 1972 backwater horror show that starred Jon Voight, Burt Reynolds, and Ned Beatty. The area is simply too broad. However, the river that the men canoe down is the Chattooga River, which runs along the border of South Carolina. The waterfall is Tallulah Falls. Interestingly, this film was shot in sequence and the dialogue was looped—recorded without sync sound and dubbed in later by the actors. After the movie came out, tourists came to the area in droves, thus fueling a white water rafting craze.

Die Hard

FOX Plaza • 2121 Avenue of the Stars
Century City, California

The 34-story "Nakatomi tower" that Bruce Willis saves from a bunch of terrorists in the 1988 thriller *Die Hard* is actually part of the Century City complex. Considered one of the greatest action movies of the late 1980s, *Die Hard* (directed by John McTiernan) created a new standard for action films.

Double Indemnity
6301 Quebec Street • Hollywood, California

Generally considered to be one of the greatest films of all-time, *Double Indemnity* is certainly one of the greatest film noir achievements. Directed by Billy Wilder, this shady 1944 classic tells of an illicit affair between an insurance agent (Fred MacMurray) and the wife of an oilman (Barbara Stanwyck). They then hatch a plan to fraudulently sell her husband an accidental death insurance policy so that they can kill him and collect the insurance money, and the rest is movie-making history.

The house where Stanwyck lived (a centerpiece of the film) sits high up in the Hollywood Hills. It's tough to find, but well worth the effort in that it looks almost identical to how it appeared in 1944.

Duel
Route 14 near the Angeles National Forest
North of Los Angeles, California

This was Steven Spielberg's incredible debut. Made in an astonishing two weeks, this tense battle between an anonymous, taunting truck driver and a dweeby salesman (Dennis Weaver) remains an efficient thriller. Though most of the "duel" takes place on Route 14, the gas station/launderette is in a town called Acton just south of Route 14. The film's finale, where Weaver finally defeats the truck in a blaze of glory, is at Soledad Canyon, off Route 14 toward Raveena.

Dumb and Dumber
Main Street • Breckinridge, Colorado

In the 1994 comedy classic *Dumb and Dumber* featuring Jim Carrey and Jeff Daniels, the two goofball pals take a riotous cross-country adventure. Much of the film was shot in Colorado, and one of the main locations was of the famed ski resort, Aspen. However, filming for the shots of Harry and Lloyd walking through Aspen took place in nearby Breckenridge, on Main Street. (This picturesque ski town is at a higher altitude than Aspen, so had the covering of snow needed for filming.)

Easy Rider
Bryan's Gallery • 121 Kit Carson Road • Taos, New Mexico • 800-833-7631

This is the jail cell where Dennis Hopper and Peter Fonda meet up with Jack Nicholson in the counter-culture 1969 road picture, *Easy Rider*. Though the exterior of the jail is in Las Vegas (at 157 Bridge Street), the interior still exists in Taos, New Mexico. Today, it's an art gallery located in the town square. A plaque describes the building's history.

E.T.
7121 Lonzo Street • Tujunga, California

This is the house used as Elliot's home in Steven Spielberg's classic 1982 film, *E.T.* Situated in the hills of the Tujunga Valley, northeast of the San Fernando Valley, it's located at the end of a cul de sac and can be easily recognized by the familiar mountain peak behind it.

The Exorcist
3600 Prospect Avenue • 36th Street NW
Georgetown, Washington D.C.

Though the window of Reagan's room was just a façade built for the movie, the rest of the house looks pretty much as it did in the 1973 horror film based on the book by William Peter Blithe. The interiors of the movie were shot in New York City at Ceco Studios, but you can see the set of stairs that Father Karras gets tossed down. They're on the side of the house leading from Prospect Avenue to M Street.

Fast Times at Ridgemont High
CANOGA PARK HIGH SCHOOL: 6850 Topanga Canyon Boulevard (at Vanowen Street) • Canoga Park, California
VAN NUYS HIGH SCHOOL: 6535 Cedros Avenue • Van Nuys, California

This 1982 comedy featured Sean Penn as the quintessential stoner/surfer Jeff Spicoli, and was written by Cameron Crowe (*Vanilla Sky, Almost Famous, Jerry Maguire*). The movie was actually shot at two high school campuses in the San Fernando Valley (Marilyn Monroe once attended Van Nuys High School). The mall featured in the film was known as the Sherman Oaks Galleria, located at 15303 Ventura Boulevard, Sherman Oaks, CA. It has since been turned into an office/shopping complex.

Ferris Bueller's Day Off
4160 Country Club Drive • Long Beach, California

In the 1987 smash comedy *Ferris Bueller's Day Off*, this is the Buellers main home. It's featured at many times throughout the film, from the very first shot to the very end. It's right here where Ferris plays sick to get a day off school, where the school principal ends up in a confrontation with Ferris' sister (after coming over to try and bust Ferris), and where Ferris races back in the end. Interestingly, the rest of the movie was shot in Chicago.

Field of Dreams
28963 Lansing Road • Dyersville, Iowa • 888-875-8404

"If you build it, they will come," the voice in the movie promised. The off-screen narration may have been referring to baseball legends, but today it's tourists who flock to play on the very site where Kevin Costner's 1989 movie was filmed. You can run the bases, play catch, bat—even just sit in the bleachers and dream of simpler days. The house is also open to visitors. And of course, so is the cornfield.

Forrest Gump
Chippewa Square • Intersection of Bull and McDonough Streets • Savannah, Georgia

This lovely southern city has many squares, but this is the one made famous by the musing Tom Hanks character in the 1994 film that earned him his second Best Actor Oscar. The bench was placed there especially for the movie, and though it's since been removed, there's another one nearby where you can sit and talk to strangers.

The French Connection
Brooklyn, New York

Amazingly, one of the most famous chase scenes in movie history was shot at full speed and with real pedestrians and real traffic (in addition, there were five staged stunts as part of the chase). The incredible chases from the 1971 film were shot over the course of five weeks beneath the Bensonhurst Elevated Railway. The 26-block path of Brooklyn's Stillwell Line is as follows: It starts at the Bay 50th Street Station along Stillwell Avenue, into 86th Street and finally right into New Utrecht Street (ending at 62nd Street Station).

Friday the 13th
Camp No Be Bo Sco • 11 Sand Pond Road (on Lake Cedar)
Just south of Blairstown on Route 818, northwest New Jersey

This was the site of the infamous Camp Crystal Lake, where Jason made his first appearance in the campy 1980 slasher film. Camp No Be Bo Sco is actually a Boy Scout camp from the 1920s.

The Fugitive
Smoky Mountain Railroad • Dillsboro, North Carolina

One of the first scenes in *The Fugitive* sees Dr. Richard Kimble (Harrison Ford) as he escapes from a prison transport bus that collides with a freight train. The scene took an estimated $1.5 million to film, and was done in a single take. Luckily, the crew got the shot. But what about all that debris? Turns out, it was cheaper to leave the wreckage behind than attempt to clean it up. You can still see the remnants from the iconic collision scene near Smoky Mountain Railroad.

Ghostbusters
14 North Moor Street • New York, New York

Though the interiors were shot on the West Coast, this was the actual headquarters featured in the popular 1984 film, *Ghostbusters*. Sigourney Weaver's apartment building can be found at 55 Central Park West at 65th Street (overlooking the park). A few of the upper stories were added in via special effects.

The Godfather
You could probably write an entire book based on *Godfather* shooting locations, but here are sites from some of the more well-known scenes in this 1972 film masterpiece.
1. The place where most of the film's interiors were shot was called Filmways Studios. Originally located at 246 East 127th Street in East Harlem, the studio has since closed and on the site is a supermarket.
2. The wedding scene at the Corleone compound is on Staten Island (a borough of New York) in the upscale area of Emerson Hill. The address is 120 Longfellow Road.
3. The Corleone family compound is right next door at 110 Longfellow.
4. Sonny beat the daylights out of his brother-in-law Carlo at 118th Street and Pleasant Avenue in East Harlem.
5. Later, Sonny gets obliterated in a flurry of gunfire at a tollbooth that was constructed at an old airfield (Floyd Bennet Field) southeast of Brooklyn at the end of Flatbush Avenue.
6. Moe Green is shot through the eye in the steamroom of the McBurney

YMCA at 215 West 23rd Street.

7. Barzini is taken down on the front steps of the New York County Courthouse, 60 Centre Street in Lower Manhattan.

8. The Christening where Michael becomes a godfather took place inside Old St. Patrick's Church at 264 Mulberry Street in Little Italy (between East Prince and Houston Streets).

Gone With the Wind
Bidwell Park • Manzanita Avenue • Chico, California

DIRECTIONS: From Chico, California, take West Sacramento Avenue 5 miles until it intersects with River Road. Big Chico Creek (the area of much of the filming) is to the left.

Dozens of movies have been filmed here over the years, including the scene in *Gone With the Wind* where Gerald O'Hara (Thomas Mitchell) makes his first horseback ride. The park, which features towering oaks and many creeks, was also popularized in the original *Adventures of Robin Hood* starring Errol Flynn in 1937.

Goodfellas
Copacabana • 10 East 60th Street • New York City, New York

Martin Scorsese's gritty, graphic gangster film, 1990's *Goodfellas* was shot almost entirely on the streets of New York, like several other Scorsese classics. The film incorporated a lengthy tracking shot that purists drooled over for its timing and ingenuity. The scene was shot at the old (now closed) Copacabana nightclub and the entrance today looks exactly as it did in the film.

Good Will Hunting
Woody's L Street Tavern
658 East 8th Street #A South
Boston, Massachusetts • 617-268-4335

This is the unpretentious, local Irish bar made internationally famous after appearing in the Oscar-winning movie *Good Will Hunting*, which filmed several scenes here. The movie's stars, Matt Damon and Ben Affleck, are from nearby Cambridge, and they, along with co-star Robin Williams, all hung out here quite a bit during the filming. A sign on the wall outside the pub denotes its place in movie history.

The Graduate

THE AMBASSADOR HOTEL: 3400 Wilshire Boulevard Los Angeles, California • UNITED METHODIST CHURCH OF LAVERNE: 3205 D Street • LaVerne, California (just east of Los Angeles)

Though it's been closed for more than 10 years, this landmark hotel is steeped in history. Used for dozens of motion pictures, this once elegant hotel is the place where Benjamin (Dustin Hoffman) conducts his affair with Mrs. Robinson (Anne Bancroft). The church at the end of the movie where Benjamin disrupts Elaine's wedding—though supposedly in Santa Barbara—is actually the United Methodist Church of LaVerne.

Grease

Venice High School • 13000 Venice Boulevard • Venice, California

This was "Rydell High" from the 1978 blockbuster starring John Travolta and Olivia Newton John. It was used for exterior shots because it looked like a typical school from the '50s. The bleachers where Travolta and his crew sang "Summer Nights" are still standing behind the school, as are the lunch tables where Olivia Newton John and her girlfriends sang their parts in the song. Naturally, the track where Travolta ran is just in front of the bleachers.

The Hal Roach Studios (Former Site)

8822 Washington Boulevard (intersection of National Boulevard, near the train tracks) • Culver City, California

The Hal Roach Studios were, for over 30 years, famous as the place that produced everything from *Our Gang* and *The Little Rascals* to Laurel and Hardy classics. Roach sold the studio in 1955 to his son, Hal Roach, Jr., who eventually declared bankruptcy, and in 1963 the property was sold and the studio knocked down for good.

A historic plaque sits right near where Mr. Roach's office once resided. A trip back through the car dealership on the site reveals virtually nothing of what was once there, except for the abandoned train tracks near the entrance. Another plaque rests in a small park near where the studio entrance would have been.

Halloween
1530 Orange Grove Avenue
Los Angeles, California

This is where Jamie Lee Curtis made her movie debut in the creepy 1978 classic directed by John Carpenter. Set in the midwestern town of Haddonfield, Illinois, the film was actually shot on this tree-lined, midwestern-looking street in Hollywood, just north of Sunset Boulevard. Most of the action in the movie took place in this house where Curtis was babysitting. The house where her best friend was murdered while babysitting is just down the street at 1537 Orange Grove Avenue.

Heaven Can Wait
Filoli Mansion • Woodside, California
(off Highway 280 between
San Francisco and San Jose)
650-364-8300

This was the mansion Warren Beatty lived in after assuming the body of a rich industrialist in his 1978 remake of *Here Comes*

Mr. Jordan. The manor was also seen in the opening credits of TV's *Dynasty.* The house and gardens are open to the public from February to October.

High Noon
Main Street • Columbia, California (just off highway 49, north of Sonora)
Chamber of Commerce: 209-536-1672

Gary Cooper won a Best Actor Oscar and *High Noon* won three more awards in what is considered to be the best Western ever produced. In the 1952 film, the townspeople of "Hadleyville," New Mexico completely turn their backs on the quiet sheriff as he faces the bad guys.

Several spots along Main Street were used, including the McConnell house (where Grace Kelly lived) and the exterior of the City Hotel and Saloon, a great place to visit for a taste of California history (209-532-1479). Many other films have been shot in this remarkably well-preserved gold rush town.

Several miles southeast of Columbia off Route 108 is Tuolumne City, where you'll find St Joseph's Catholic Church. This was the town church in Hadleyville where Gary Cooper went to plead for help from the town's residents. It is located on Gardner Avenue at Tuolumne Road.

Home Alone
671 Lincoln Avenue • Winnetka, Illinois

This was the MacAllister home where Macaulay Culkin outsmarted a pair of bumbling burglars in 1990's *Home Alone.* Not far from the home is the mall where he met Santa Claus—Winnetka Village Hall, 501 Green Bay Road.

Hoosiers
355 N Washington Street • Knightstown, Indiana

The movie *Hoosiers* recounted the thrilling 1954 Boy's State Basketball Championship between powerhouse Muncie Central and tiny Milan High School.

The smallest team in history to win the state title, Milan was victorious with a heart-stopping last second shot by Bobby Plump.

The Knightstown Hoosier Gym where the team (the fictitious Hickory High) played its home games in the movie is located in the quaint town of Knightsbridge. Today, after-school programs allow youths to play basketball in the gym, and church basketball leagues use it as well.

The bigger, more modern gym where Gene Hackman and the Hickory High players actually go to the state playoffs in the movie is the Hinckle Fieldhouse, located at Butler University, Indianapolis.

The Hunger Games
Swan House • 130 W Paces Ferry Rd. NW • Atlanta, Georgia

The Edward Inman "Swan" House is an Atlanta mansion designed by Philip T. Shutze and built in 1928 for Edward and Emily Inman. The house is currently part of the Atlanta History Center, and it has been featured in *The Hunger Games: Catching Fire* and *The Hunger Games: Mockingjay, Part 2*. The mansion was chosen for its classical style and antique details, as the directors wanted a location which "looked like it had been there forever." The Swan House is listed on the National Register for Historic Places and is open for public tours.

In Cold Blood
600 Oak Avenue • Holcomb, Kansas

The famous 1967 film based on the Truman Capote true crime novel was actually shot in the infamous farmhouse where the gruesome 1959 murders were committed by Perry Smith and Dick Hickcock. (The trial in the movie was even shot in the actual courthouse were both men were tried—it's the Finney County Courthouse in Garden City, Kansas.)

On November 15, 1959, the murderers broke into the Clutter family home thinking they had a safe full of money. Upon learning that they did not have any such riches, they proceeded to kill (in cold blood) Herbert Clutter, his wife Helen, and their two teenage children, Nancy and Kenyon. The men were captured, convicted, and hanged at the Kansas State Prison at Lansing on April 14, 1965.

Iron Man 2
Randy's Donuts • 805 West Manchester Boulevard • Inglewood, California

In one scene of the 2010 smash sequel *Iron Man 2*, Iron Man, clad in shades, enjoys a box of the popular donuts while relaxing in the restaurant's giant donut signage. The Randy's Donuts sign is one of the most iconic photo ops in Los Angeles and the site of many movies, commercials, and TV shows.

Into the Wild
Alaska Museum of the North • Fairbanks, Alaska

The film (and book that inspired) *Into the Wild* tells the true and harrowing story of Christopher McCandless, a young hiker who embarked on an ill-advised hike across the U.S. and sadly wound up dead in his campervan in the wilds of northern Alaska in 1996. The infamous "Bus 142" became a tourist attraction in its own right, with many having attempted the challenging three-day hike to get there. In fact, the bus is so dangerous to get to that two hikers died and at least 15 had to be rescued while attempting to reach it. In 2020, the Alaska Army National Guard stepped in and helicopter-lifted the bus away from the site and today, visitors can see it at an outdoor exhibit at this museum.

Invasion of the Body Snatchers
Sierra Madre, California (just east of Pasadena)

The location of the 1956 sci-fi classic is virtually unchanged since the time the film was shot. Originally, director Don Siegel wanted to shoot where the movie's fictional town of "Santa Mira" was supposedly based—Mill Valley, just north of San Francisco.

However, they stayed in the L.A. area in this little town near Pasadena. It's the meeting place where residents (turned aliens) met to distribute the "pods" from trucks. It's also where stars Kevin McCarthy and Dana Wynter attempt to escape the town, but blow their own cover by displaying emotion (they yell when a dog is almost struck by a truck).

It's a Wonderful Life
Beverly Hills High School • 241 South Moreno Drive
Beverly Hills, California

During the courtship scene between Jimmy Stewart and Donna Reed in this 1946 holiday classic, the two young stars are dancing in the Bedford Hills High School gymnasium. A button is pushed (by Carl "Alfalfa" Switzer from *The Little Rascals*) which results in the dance floor opening, thus causing everyone to fall into the swimming pool that is located under the gymnasium floor. The "Swim/Gym" is still functioning at Beverly Hills High. It's just south of the main school building, next to the school's sports field.

Jaws
Martha's Vineyard, Massachusetts

Steven Spielberg's 1975 classic was set on fictitious "Amity Island" but it was really Martha's Vineyard, the trendy retreat off the coast of Massachusetts. There are several easily identifiable locations that would be of interest to fans of the movie.

1. Joseph A. Sylvia State Beach is where swimmers go crazy after the attack on the young boy. Next to it is the American Legion Memorial Bridge where we see the shark swim safely back to sea.
2. At the intersection of Water and Main Streets in Edgartown is the town center where Chief Brody collects materials for the beach closure signs they suddenly need.
3. Quint's workshop was located in Menemsha, a fishing port at the southwest tip of the island. It's exact location was the inlet between the General Store and the Galley Restaurant. It's now an empty lot.

The Jazz Singer
KTLA Studios • 5858 Sunset Boulevard (between Bronson and Van Ness)
Hollywood, California

This 1927 film location is notable because it was the first movie ever to be produced with sound. At the time, this wonderfully ornate building was the Warner Bros. lot (they moved to Burbank in 1929), and today it houses the studios of KTLA Channel 5.

La La Land
Intersection of 110 and 105 Freeways • Los Angeles, California

The popular 2016 movie opens with a song and dance number in a traffic jam on a freeway ramp. The scene was filmed on the eastbound 105 freeway transition to the 110 freeway. You can't stop there to take a photo, but if you take the Metro Green Line to the Harbor Freeway Metro Station or park near 11500 S Figueroa and walk or take the elevator up to the platform, you can get a similar view over the freeway.

The Lasky Barn/DeMille Studio Barn
2100 North Highland Boulevard • Hollywood, California • 323-874-2276

This structure was rented by Cecil B. DeMille as the studio in which he made the first feature-length motion picture in Hollywood, *The Squaw Man*, in 1913. It was originally located at the corner of Selma Avenue and Vine Street, and in 1927 was transferred to Paramount Studios.

The museum is now located on Highland Avenue across from the Hollywood Bowl entrance. It was named a state historical monument in 1956. Though a small structure, the museum houses the largest public display of early Hollywood photographs and memorabilia and makes for a fascinating visit.

The Last Picture Show
Royal Picture House • 115 East Main Street • Archer City, Texas
940-574-2489

Peter Bogdanovich's 1971 paean to small town life (based on a Larry McMurty novel) remains one of the most poignant films of its era. One of the centerpieces of the film was the Royal Picture House movie theater, which still stands.

Melody Ranch
24715 Oak Creek Avenue • Newhall, California • 661-255-4910

Originally Monogram Studios (opened in 1915), this ranch in the hills north of Los Angeles is where hundreds of classic Westerns were filmed, including 35 John Wayne films (part of *High Noon* was also shot here). If you are a fan of singing cowboy Gene Autry, then the name "Melody Ranch" will raise fond memories of Gene and Smiley singing songs around the campfire. Gene's radio show was named *Melody Ranch*, and most of Gene Autry's western adventures were shot here.

The Music Box
927 Vendome Street
Los Angeles, California

Located in the Silverlake district just south of Sunset Boulevard, this is the legendary staircase where Laurel and Hardy struggled to haul a piano in their classic, Academy Award-winning 1932 comedy *The Music Box*. On one of the steps near the bottom, you'll spot a memorial plaque in the sidewalk bearing images of the boys. In the movie, there is a house they make it to at the top of the stairs—that was shot on a set. Here, you'll find a road, not a house, at the top.

National Lampoon's Vacation
Six Flags Magic Mountain
26101 Magic Mountain Parkway
Valencia, California • 661-255-4100

Remember the amusement park where Chevy Chase and his long-suffering family wind up after their eventful trip from the mid-west? The park that was closed, the one that John Candy was forced to open for the family, is actually Six Flags Magic Mountain in Valencia, California.

Napoleon Dynamite

The deadpan 2004 indie smash hit was filmed almost entirely in the town of Preston, Idaho, the hometown of the film's director, Jared Hess. Today, essentially all of the locations still exist and the town even offers a map to make it easier to find the filming locations.

Deseret Industries Thrift Shop
36 South State Street • Preston, Idaho

The store where Napoleon buys his famous suit is also the store where most of the film's wardrobe came from.

Napoleon Dynamite's House
1447 East 800 North Road
Preston, Idaho

Both the exterior and the interior home scenes were filmed in this house (where Napoleon lived with his grandma and his brother, Kip).

Napoleon Dynamite's Tetherball Court

525 South 4th East • Preston, Idaho

The famed tetherball court that closes out the movie's final scene is located at a local school.

Pedro's House

59 South 2nd East • Preston, Idaho

This is where Napoleon iconically tries to jump on Pedro's Sledgehammer bike.

Pop'n Pin Lanes

411 South Hwy 91 • Preston, Idaho

This is the bowling alley where Kip and Rico plan their sure-fire business venture.

Preston High School

151 East 200 South • Preston, Idaho

The actual local high school was used extensively throughout the film.

Summer Wheatley's House

3384 South Parkinson Road • Preston, Idaho

This is where Pedro leaves a homemade cake for the girl of his dreams.

Trisha's House

253 South 2600 East • Preston, Idaho

This location appears when Napoleon delivers a portrait to Trisha, in an attempt to try and tempt her to go to prom with him.

Nightmare on Elm Street
1428 Genesee Avenue • Hollywood, California

This is where Freddie Krueger terrorized Nancy Thompson in her dreams. The two-story home featured in this 1984 horror classic is located on a pleasant, tree-lined, residential street just two blocks east of Orange Grove Avenue—the street featured in the original *Halloween* movie. The neighborhood has a quaint, small-town feel, which is why it's used for so many motion picture productions.

Night of the Living Dead
Evans City Cemetery • Evans City, Pennsylvania

DIRECTIONS: On Franklin Road, 1/4 mile up the hill from the intersection with Route 68 (at the railroad crossing).

George Romero's creepy 1968 horror flick set the standard for other low budget horror movies, and the grim, grainy look of this film is still haunting today. Romero is from Pittsburgh originally, and so (like John Waters to follow) he kept his productions close to home. The cemetery from *Night* is in Evans City, just to the north of Pittsburgh, and the since-demolished farmhouse was located on banks of the Monongahela River.

North by Northwest
Wasco, California (about 25 miles northwest of Bakersfield on Highway 46)

One of Alfred Hitchcock's most famous scenes took place in this stylish 1959 thriller. Remember when Cary Grant is attacked by a crop dusting plane in the middle of a desolate Indiana farmland? The scene actually took place in Central California in a small town called Wasco ("The Rose Capital of the Nation"). As Robert Coe explains (he's the man who actually piloted the

cropduster which chased Cary Grant!), the exact field is about three miles north of town on Corchoran Road.

Ocean's 8
The Metropolitan Museum of Art • 1000 Fifth Avenue
New York, New York

The 2018 film *Ocean's 8* was both a continuation of and a spin-off from Steven Soderbergh's *Ocean's* trilogy and featured an ensemble cast including Sandra Bullock, Cate Blanchett, Anne Hathaway, Mindy Kaling, Sarah Paulson, Awkwafina, Rihanna, and Helena Bonham Carter. The film followed a group of women led by Debbie Ocean, the sister of Danny Ocean, who plan a sophisticated heist at the annual Met Gala at the Metropolitan Museum of Art in New York City.

An Officer and a Gentleman
Tides Inn • 1807 Water Street • Port Townsend, Washington • 360-385-0595

This was the place where Richard Gere and Debra Winger spent their romantic night together, in Room 10 to be exact. Naturally, it's called the "Officer and a Gentleman" room. The Tides Inn is reachable from Seattle by ferry across the Puget Sound, and the area also features some other recognizable locations from the movie.

One Flew Over the Cuckoo's Nest
Oregon State Mental Hospital • Between 24th and 25th Streets
Salem, Oregon (about 50 miles south of Portland)

The 1975 film starring Jack Nicholson and Louise Fletcher (who both won Oscars for their roles as R.P. McMurphy and Nurse Fletcher, respectively), was shot almost entirely on location at the Oregon State Mental Hospital in Salem. Dean Brooks, the hospital's actual superintendent, played the film's psychiatrist. It was named one of the 20 greatest films by the American Film Institute, and remains only one of three films to sweep the top five categories at the Oscars (the other two are *It Happened One Night* and *The Silence of the Lambs*.)

The Oregon Film Trail

This is such a wonderful story. As the organizers tell it: "Through a unique partnership between Oregon Film, the Oregon Made Creative Foundation, and in collaboration with Travel Oregon, Oregon Coast Visitors Association, the Astoria-Warrenton Area Chamber of Commerce, Willamette Valley Visitors Association, and many other community partners, a new statewide network of trail markers are being placed in many iconic filming locations across Oregon. Stitching together these locations, communities, and films has created a framework, both virtual and real, where we can retell stories, and celebrate Oregon's contribution to filmmaking since 1904. This collection of trail markers aims to strengthen the correlation between the film/TV industries, economic development, tourism, and local interest alike."

Imagine if every city did this! In December 2018 and January 2019, the first group of informative markers were placed in various spots around Astoria to mark and celebrate the productions of *Short Circuit*, *Kindergarten Cop*, and *The Goonies*. As the Oregon Film Trail detail on their website, "One sign, in particular, is positioned at the East End Mooring Basin near the Astoria Riverfront Trail to give an alternative view of the 'Goonies

House' in an effort to eliminate trespassing on the hill of the privately owned residence. While the sign signifies a location for that viewpoint, the sign copy shares information about the nearby Astor Elementary School which was featured in *Kindergarten Cop*. The lesser-known Alameda Park offers a great viewpoint of the Astoria-Megler Bridge and it is the topic of the *Short Circuit* sign located there. The sign for *The Goonies* is located by the Oregon Film Museum and speaks to it and the Flavel House's roles in that film."

Learn more here: www.historicoregonfilmtrail.com

Here are just a few more of the markers that have been placed (thank you to Oregon Film for this information):

Brownsville

"In May 2019, three more signs were placed in Brownsville to recognize the filming of Rob Reiner's film adaptation of Stephen King's novella *Stand By Me*. Through a partnership with the Lane County History Museum, The City of Brownsville, The Brownsville Chamber of Commerce, and Lane County Parks, the signs were unveiled at the Museum, City Hall, and Pioneer Park—the latter of which was the filming location of the infamous blueberry pie eating contest where more than 100 local residents took part as extras. The City Hall sign also occupies a space just yards from the spot where Verne found a penny in the road at the end of the film—a cinematic event commemorated by a penny permanently embedded in the roadway."

Cottage Grove

"Cottage Grove has five Oregon Film Trail markers in and around this picturesque city. Buster Keaton's *The General*, *Stand By Me*, *Lost In The Stars*, and *Animal House* were all filmed here. These signs are a collaborative partnership between the Oregon Film Office (partnered with the Oregon Made Creative Foundation), the City of Cottage Grove, and the Cottage Grove Historical Society and have been funded in part by a grant from Travel Oregon. Additional logistical help came from Travel Lane County and the BLM."

Depoe Bay

"A new Oregon Film Trail sign was installed in December 2019 in Depoe Bay harbor. The sign honors the town harbor's starring role as a location in *One Flew Over The Cuckoo's Nest*. The Oregon Coast Visitor's Association, Depoe Bay Chamber of Commerce, and Travel Oregon partnered to bring this newest sign on the Oregon Film Trail in the World's Smallest Harbor—between Dock 1 and 2. This sign was made possible, in part, by a grant from Travel Oregon and the Oregon Coast Visitor's Association."

Portland Train Station

"Noah Dille, a local welder and fabricator with a background in the motion picture industry, presented his winning design bid for a *Portlandia*-themed bike rack that now sits outside the Portland train station in commemoration of the city's involvement in the series that shot for eight seasons. Additionally, a commemorative plaque hangs outside the Mayor's office inside City Hall. The plaque and bike rack were specifically commissioned by the Oregon Governor's Office of Film & Television and the Portland Film Office, with support from the Oregon Media Production Association (OMPA), as a gift to Portland City Hall to celebrate *Portlandia*'s contributions to the city."

Silver Falls State Park

"Installed in August 2020 at the Howard Creek Trailhead parking lot near the campground utilizing a grant from the Willamette Valley Visitors Association, this sign marks filming locations related to the popular romantic vampire fantasy feature film, *Twilight*, that was based on Stephenie Meyer's novel of the same name. The film was directed by Catherine Hardwicke, starred Kristen Stewart and Robert Pattinson, and was the first film in this popular saga series. Other films have used Silver Falls State Park as a filming location, such as the William Friedkin thriller *The Hunted*, the horror movie *Just Before Dawn*, and the opening scenes from Warner Bros. animated feature *Yogi Bear*."

St. Helens

"St. Helens is no stranger to film productions, and two standouts were *Twilight* and *Halloweentown*. *Twilight*, the romantic fantasy film based on Stephenie Meyer's novel, was directed by Catherine Hardwicke and starred Kristen Stewart and Robert Pattinson. *Twilight* filmed many scenes here, such as the restaurant where Edward tells Bella he can read minds, the bookstore, Bella's house, the dress shop, and the alley where Edward saved Bella. In the Riverfront District of St. Helens, the Disney family classic *Halloweentown* was filmed. This film starred Debbie Reynolds as the witch 'Aggie' and every year during the month of October, the Plaza Square comes alive with the 'giant pumpkin' and the Spirit of Halloweentown festival."

Warrenton

"In July 2019, in partnership with the Astoria-Warrenton Chamber of Commerce, the City of Warrenton, and the Oregon Coast Visitor's Association, a sign was placed at Hammond Marina next to the breakwater where the Orca Willy jumped to freedom."

Pink Flamingoes
894 Tyson Street (at Reed) • Baltimore, Maryland

This 1972 John Waters cult classic was shot (like most of Waters' productions) throughout his hometown of Baltimore. ("Trashtown, U.S.A." he's called it.) In *Pink Flamingoes*, the family's trailer was located on the grounds of an abandoned commune (it's since been carted away). But the scene that made this effort famous was the one in which Divine actually eats dog poop at the end of the movie. Still perhaps the most shocking act ever released in a commercial film, it happened right here on Tyson Street, just off Reed. At the time, the location was the home of Pat Moran, Waters' casting director. (The dog was hers, too.)

Planet of the Apes
Westward Beach • Westward Beach Road (between Zuma Beach and Point Dume) • Malibu, California

Many locations all over California and Arizona were used in this 1969 classic, but this is the one that people seem to remember best: The spot at the end of the 1969 film where Charlton Heston realizes that he's been on earth all along, where the crumbled remains of the Statue of Liberty sit near the surf. Of course, the statue was not really there—it was painted in as a special effect once the film was shot. However, the cove is open to the public and is one of the area's prettiest stretches of beaches.

The Player
Rialto Theater • 1023 South Fair Oaks Avenue • South Pasadena, California

The is the theater to where the movie mogul (Tim Robbins) is lured in Robert Altman's 1992 satire of Hollywood. A writer is sending him death threats, and when he ultimately meets the writer at the Rialto, Robbins ends up killing him in a nearby parking lot.

Poltergiest

4267 Roxbury Street (north of Walnut, between Rachel Avenue and Tapo Street) • Simi Valley, California

This is the house where the Freelings lived in the 1982 Steven Spielberg film, *Poltergeist*. (No, the house is not actually built upon an old burial ground.) The ordinary, suburban neighborhood served as the backdrop for the modern day ghost story about a tract home that suddenly becomes a gateway for enraged ghosts.

Pretty Woman

738 North Las Palmas Avenue • Hollywood, California

Considered to be the movie that made Julia Roberts a bonafide star, this "fairy tale" (directed by Garry Marshall) about the prince who rescues the streetwalker turned into one of the biggest blockbusters of all time. The building from the movie's final scene where Richard Gere "rescues" Julia Roberts from the fire escape is a little hotel just north of Hollywood Boulevard, ½ block off Hollywood Boulevard. Other locations from the movie include:

1. Regent Beverly Wilshire Hotel, 9500 Wilshire Boulevard (310-275-5200)
2. Boulemiche Boutique, 9501 Santa Monica Boulevard (310-273-9653)—Where Roberts is snubbed by the staff.

Psycho

100 Universal City Plaza • Universal City, California • 800-777-1000

Most of the 1960 Hitchcock suspense classic, *Psycho*, was filmed on the Universal lot. The famous shower scene took place on Stage 18-A, and the iconic house still stands, changing very little since the film was made. Likewise, the car dealership where Janet Leigh swaps cars was shot on location just north of Universal Studios at 4270 Lankershim Boulevard and—surprise—after all these years it's still a car dealership.

Pulp Fiction
Hawthorne Grill • 13763 Hawthorne Boulevard (at 137th Place, southwest corner) • Hawthorne, California

This is the coffee shop where John Travolta sat with Samuel L. Jackson discussing heady matters when Amanda Plummer and Tim Roth pulled their guns. The place was torn down in 1999 (after 40 years in business) and is currently a vacant lot. The spot where Travolta and Jackson are eating Kahuna Burgers in their car before committing their hit on the guys who crossed Marsellus is on Van Ness Avenue, immediately north of Hollywood Boulevard, in Hollywood.

Purple Rain
First Avenue • 701 1st Avenue North • Minneapolis, Minnesota
612-338-8388

Originally called "The Depot," this club opened in 1970, and in 1982 it became First Avenue. A former Greyhound bus station, this club was the central location in Prince's 1984 film, *Purple Rain*. It's still a thriving musical center, and in its history has hosted everyone from Frank Zappa to REM.

Raging Bull
Carmine Street Recreation Center • 1 Clarkson Street (at Seventh Avenue South) • New York, New York • 212-242-5228

This 1980 Martin Scorsese classic won the Oscar for Best Picture. The tough, gritty depiction of Jake LaMotta's life includes several recognizable places where movie fans can go and re-live some of the magic from this film, widely considered to be one of the best pictures ever made.

The public pool where Robert DeNiro first comes upon Cathy Moriarty is the Carmine Street Public Pool located in Greenwich Village. Long shots and crowd scenes at the boxing matches were filmed at the Olympic Auditorium (1801 South Grand Avenue, Los Angeles, California—also see *Rocky*). The actual fight sequences were shot on a studio stage.

Raiders of the Lost Ark

Conservancy of Music • University of the Pacific • 3601 Pacific Avenue Stockton, California • 209-946-2415

Of course, much of Spielberg's 1981 gem was shot all over the world—Kauai, France, England, Tunisia, etc. However, this is the location of the classroom where Harrison Ford teaches archaeology.

Rebel Without a Cause

Griffith Park Observatory • 2800 East Observatory Road Los Angeles, California

This Los Angeles Planetarium was the scene of the famous shootout at the end of this film, arguably Dean's most famous cinematic moment. In fact, the movie scene became so famous that it firmly established the observatory as a well-known tourist landmark.

Return of the Jedi

The Moon of Endor • Jedediah Smith Redwood State Park 4241 Kings Valley Road • Crescent City, California

The towering redwood trees of Northern California (some up to 300 feet tall) served as the Moon of Endor in George Lucas' third *Star Wars* installment, *Return of the Jedi*. These were some of the first scenes from the series filmed in this country. Additionally, the Tatooine scenes (including the battle at Jabba's Sail Barge above the Sarlacc Pit) were shot near Yuma in the Arizona Desert in Buttercup Valley.

Rocky

The 1976 film Rocky featured several places in Los Angeles and Philadelphia that have become recognizable locations to millions of filmgoers.

Olympic Auditorium
1801 South Grand Avenue (at Olympic Boulevard) • Los Angeles, California

Built originally for the 1932 Olympics, this is where the famous fight scenes with Apollo Creed were shot. (The fight scenes from *Raging Bull* were also shot here.)

Oscar De la Hoya Boxing Youth Center
1114 S. Lorena Street • East Los Angeles, California

This gym was seen in the film's opening amateur fight scene, and featured a religious mural overlooking the ring.

Philadelphia Museum of Art
26th Avenue (at Benjamin Franklin Avenue)
Philadelphia, Pennsylvania

The famous 68-step staircase still attracts people who make the flight and then thrust their arms in victory a la Rocky when they reach the top.

Shamrock Meats, Inc.
3461 East Vernon Avenue (at Alcoa Avenue) • Vernon, California (southeast of downtown Los Angeles)

Of course, this is the place where Rocky trained for the title fight,

punching the hanging sides of beef in the cold, refrigerated air. He was also interviewed here by a news reporter in the movie, in a comic scene that featured his brother-in-law, Paulie (who worked there), trying to poke his head into the shot.

Rosemary's Baby

Dakota Apartments • One West 72nd Street • New York, New York

Roman Polanski's macabre 1968 film took place primarily at this venerable Manhattan landmark apartment building. It's where Mia Farrow and John Cassavetes lived. Many famous people have lived here (it's adjacent to Central Park) and, of course, it's where John Lennon was murdered on December 8, 1980.

Safety Last

550 West 7th Street • Los Angeles, California

Everyone remembers the classic scene where Harold Lloyd hangs from a huge clock, dangling high above Los Angeles. That scene was from the 1923 silent classic called *Safety Last*, and it was filmed at the Brockman Building, located in downtown Los Angeles in the 500 block of 7th Street, between Grand Avenue and Olive Street (a block south of the Biltmore Hotel). While it looked like Lloyd was risking it all, he was actually never in any danger; the scene was shot on a portion of the building that merely allowed a view of the city which gave the illusion of being up high.

The Sandlot

1386 Glenrose Drive • Salt Lake City, Utah

The famed local diamond featured in the 1993 classic *The Sandlot* is located in the Glendale area of Salt Lake City. The privately owned field is unrecognizable as the sacred site where Ham, Squints, Smalls, Yeah Yeah, The Jet, and others enchanted filmgoers with their pure approach to the game. Overgrown and seemingly abandoned, it feels in desperate need of a little baseball TLC.

Saturday Night Fever
Brooklyn, New York

Saturday Night Fever was one of those rare films that actually sparked a pop culture phenomenon. The wave of 1970s disco-influenced culture was in large part due to this film, which featured arguably the most influential soundtrack in history. John Travolta became an icon, as did disco, and there are several key places you can visit that helped define some of the film's most dramatic, entertaining moments.

1. The movie's opening sequence with Travolta swinging the paint can was shot along 86th Street in Brooklyn.

2. The bridge where the gang likes to play daredevil stunts is the Verrazzano Narrows Bridge, where I-278 connects Brooklyn to Manhattan, south of Bay Ridge.

3. The Manero family lived in the house at 221 79th Street, Bay Ridge, Brooklyn.
4. The famous 2001 Odyssey Nightclub where Travolta tore up the pulsating dance floor while wearing the white suit is located in Brooklyn at 802 64th Street at 8th Avenue. It's now Spectrums, a gay dance club: 718-238-8213.
5. The famous dance studio where Travolta and Karen Lynn Gorney practice is the Phillips Dance Studio, 1301 West 7th Avenue, Brooklyn, New York (718-265-2081).

Scarface
728 Ocean Drive • Miami, Florida

Al Pacino's brutal 1983 turn as two-bit thug Tony Montana (as directed by Brian De Palma) was set in Miami and Bolivia (though most of the actual

locations were divided up between Florida and California). Now a hamburger joint, this was the site of the "Sun Ray Apartments," where Montana's brother was cut up by a chainsaw. (The two garish estates in the movie were actually located in the tiny town of Montecito, located just a few miles east of Santa Barbara, California.)

The Shawshank Redemption
Ohio State Reformatory • Mansfield, Ohio • 419-522-2644

This 1880's landmark (closed as a prison in 1990) now offers "ghost tours" of its gothic grounds. It also served as "Shawshank State Prison" in the 1994 Tim Robbins film, *The Shawshank Redemption*. The moving, uplifting film (based on a novella by Stephen King, *Rita Hayworth and the Shawshank Redemption*) is widely held as one of the finest of the 1990s.

The Shining
Timberline Lodge • Route 26
Portland, Oregon (60 miles east)
503-272-3311

This lodge was used for the exterior shots of the Overlook Hotel in the creepy 1980 Kubrick-directed film of the Stephen King novel. However, the movie was shot almost entirely in studios in England.

Silver Linings Playbook
Llanerch Diner • 95 E Township Line Road • Upper Darby, Pennsylvania

This 24-hour diner became well-known for feeding stars Jennifer Lawrence and Bradley Cooper in the 2012 film *Silver Linings Playbook*. You can even sit at the booth where Lawrence's character destroys items on the table in a pivotal moment in the film.

The Social Network
Boston University Wheelock College • 200 The Riverway
Boston, Massachusetts

Yes, Facebook creator Mark Zuckerberg went to Harvard University, but it was actually Wheelock College in Boston that was used as the set location for the 2010 film, *The Social Network*. (Wheelock College merged with Boston University in 2018.) A major critical and commercial success, the film grossed $224 million on a $40 million budget and was widely acclaimed by critics. (Interestingly, Harvard no longer allows filming on campus.)

Some Like It Hot
Hotel del Coronado • 1500 Orange Avenue • San Diego, California
619-435-4131

This 700-room Victorian masterpiece is steeped in history. Built in 1888, it's where Frank L. Baum wrote *The Wizard of Oz* (it's believed that the hotel's ornate appearance actually inspired the description of Oz), and it was also featured as the Miami hotel where Jack Lemmon and Tony Curtis hid out in drag with Marilyn Monroe in the 1959 Billy Wilder comedy classic.

Spiderman
Rockwell/Boeing/NASA Defense plant • Bellflower Boulevard and
Imperial Highway • Downey, California

In the scene where news photographer Peter Parker (Tobey McGuire) is covering a "World Unity Festival" in Times Square when the crowd is attacked by the evil Green Goblin (Willem Dafoe), Spiderman springs into action, and the fight between the superhero and the Green Goblin ensues. Some of the broader establishing shots were actually done in Times Square, but most of the "World Unity Festival" scenes were shot on a huge re-creation of Times Square, constructed at an old defense plant on this historic 160-acre lot.

It was here where the Apollo Command and Service Module was built (for the first mission to the moon in 1969) and also where the original Space Shuttle components were constructed. The now-empty lot is bordered by Bellflower Boulevard on the east, Lakewood Boulevard on the west, Imperial Highway on the south and Stewart and Gray Roads on the north.

Star Trek: Into the Darkness
The Getty Center • 1200 Getty Center Drive • Los Angeles, California

For 2013's *Star Trek: Into Darkness*, the famed Getty Center museum was transformed into "Starfleet Headquarters." Today, visitors can tour the museum for free any day of the week, except for Tuesdays (when it's closed). Opened in 1997, the purpose-built art complex houses Western art from the Middle Ages to the present and receives around 1.3 million visitors a year. It's reached by a three-car, cable-pulled hovertrain funicular from the visitors' parking center at the bottom of the hill.

Sudden Impact
Burger Island • 695 Third Street • San Francisco, California

It was in the fourth "Harry Callahan" film, *Sudden Impact*, that Clint Eastwood's famed vigilante character created his catchphrase, "Go ahead—make my day." Clint confronts the bad guy holding the customers in a restaurant hostage, and when the criminal threatens to kill him, Clint utters his now famous line.

In the mid-'90s, the original restaurant was moved across the street to 701 Third Street, where it operates today. The original structure has been torn down and a McDonald's restaurant is now sitting at the exact site where the scene was shot.

Taxi Driver
226 13th Street • New York, New York

This is the fleabag hotel where Robert DeNiro took Jodie Foster in the disturbing 1976 Martin Scorsese classic. It's also the site where the film's bloodbath finale was filmed. Other New York City locations include the outside of the St. Regis-Sheraton Hotel at 2 East 55th Street (where Cybil Sheppard picks up DeNiro), and Seventh Avenue at 38th Street, where the political rally was shot.

This is Spinal Tap
Raymond Theater • 129 North Raymond Avenue • Pasadena, California

This classic 1921 vaudeville theater (also used in *Pulp Fiction*) is where many of the concert scenes from this 1984 "Rockumentary" were shot by Rob Reiner. (From the Stonehenge production "extravaganza" to the stage pods, one of which trapped bassist Derek Smalls, played by Harry Shearer). From 1979 through 1991, The Raymond Theatre was known as the live music venue Perkins Palace, and many memorable concerts were presented here, from Fleetwood Mac to Van Halen.

Top Gun
Kansas City Barbecue Restaurant • 610 West Market Street
San Diego, California • 619-231-9680

In the blockbuster 1986 film *Top Gun*, this popular eatery was the flyer's hangout where Anthony Edwards banged out "Great Balls of Fire." The movie, starring Tom Cruise, Val Kilmer, and Kelly McGillis, was a major hit due to the blend of the Giorgio Moroder score, the romance, and of course the wild F-15 dogfight sequences.

Towering Inferno
Bank of America World Headquarters
555 California Street (at Kearney)
San Francisco, California

A five-story set was built in Malibu to actually burn down in this 1974 disaster movie, but this location in San Francisco was used for the shots of the entrance to the building. Additionally, the lobby and the glass elevators that were used are located at the Hyatt Regency Hotel at 5 Embarcadero Center, also in San Francisco.

The Twilight Zone
Indian Dunes Park (near Six Flags Magic Mountain Amusement Park)
Valencia, California

DIRECTIONS: Go north of Los Angeles on the 5 freeway, turn left on Highway 126 near Valencia. The site is on the left side, several miles down the road. • The park is no longer there, but this was the site where, at 2:20 A.M. on the morning of July 23, 1982, the final shot of Jon Landis' segment for the movie *The Twilight Zone* was being filmed. The segment, entitled "Time Out," featured veteran actor Vic Morrow and two child actors, Myca Dinh Le and Renee Shin-Yi Chen, ages seven and six, respectively.

As Morrow waded through a knee-deep river with both kids in his arms (amidst a village under military siege), a helicopter was to come towards them. But something went terribly wrong and all three actors were killed by the out-of-control chopper (whose pilot may have been distracted by the many explosions going off). The park, a one-time popular dirt bike riding area, is gone now and the area is inaccessible private property.

Urban Cowboy
Gilley's (former site) • 4500 Spencer Highway • Pasadena, East Texas

John Travolta rode the mechanical bull in 1980 at this site, where the famous country western club Gilley's used to sit. It burned down however, and to date, the lot remains empty.

The Wizard of Oz
Sony Pictures Studios (formerly MGM)
10202 West Washington Boulevard • Culver City, California • 323-520-8687

MGM's classic Culver Studio has since become Sony Pictures Studio where today, shows like *Jeopardy* and *Wheel of Fortune* are filmed. However, the soundstages still exist where many of the scenes from *The Wizard of Oz* were filmed (and much of the history can be experienced during a two-hour walking tour).

The "yellow brick road" itself is

long gone, but you can see where it once existed on Stage 27. The tornado scene was filmed on Stage 14, and the cornfield and apple orchard (where the evil apple trees came to life) were on Stages 15, 25, and 26. Munchkinland was filmed on Stage 27, and the poppy field was shot on stage 29.

When Harry Met Sally

Katz's Deli • 205 East Houston Street (at Ludlow) • East Village
New York, New York • 212-254-2246

Shot in many locales throughout New York and Chicago in 1989, the scene that "made the most noise" was the one where Meg Ryan demonstrated (quite credibly) the ease with which an orgasm can be faked. At the very table where the scene was shot, a plaque reads, "You are sitting at the table where Harry met Sally."

White Heat

Mobil Oil Refinery
198th Street and Figueroa
Torrance, California

"Made it Ma—top of the world!" so screams James Cagney at the end of this classic 1949 gangster movie from atop the burning oil refinery. This demented, blaze of glory finale remains one of the most enduring images in motion picture history.

The Wild One

Johnny's Bar and Grill • 526 San Benito Street (and up and down the street) • Hollister, California • 831-637-3683

During the July 4 weekend of 1947, 4,000 motorcyclists (part of what was called "The Gypsy Tour") converged onto Hollister, a sleepy California town of about 4,500 people. Several small riots and fights broke out among some of the drunken bikers, which spilled out from this bar all along San Benito Street.

Several years later, the 1953 movie *The Wild One*, starring Marlon Brando and Lee Marvin, came out, and it is believed that it was loosely based on the 1947 events. Many feel that the film, a tale of two motorcycle gangs terrorizing small town America, greatly changed American culture with its shocking attack on small-town life and ideals. Thanks in some degree to myths surrounding the movie and the original event, bikers still flock to this small town every July 4.

CHAPTER SEVEN

LET THERE BE MUSIC

Aerosmith

1325 Commonwealth Avenue #2B • Boston, Massachusetts

This building was pictured in the 1991 video for the classic song "Sweet Emotion," and it was here from 1970 to 1972 that the band members of Aerosmith lived, wrote, played, and ate (and maybe even slept a little) until being signed by Columbia Records.

"There were six of us in the group, some of us were living in the kitchen, eating brown rice and Campbell's soup. Those days, you know, when a quart of beer was heaven. It was hard times and it was really good. During lunch

we would set up all our equipment outside of BU [Boston University] in the main square and just start wailing. That's basically how we got billed. We never got much publicity in the magazines and newspapers." (Steven Tyler speaking to *Circus Magazine* in June 1975.)

Album Covers

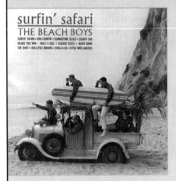

Beach Boys—*Surfin' Safari*
Paradise Cove (just north of Malibu on
Pacific Coast Highway)
Malibu, California

On a chilly morning in 1962, the Beach Boys
posed here on this stretch of California beach
for the cover of their first album. (The site is
open to the public, but there is a charge for
entry.)

Browne, Jackson—*Late for the Sky*
215 South Lucerne Street • Hollywood, California

Jackson Browne's third album, 1974's classic
Late for the Sky, had its title track featured in
Martin Scorsese's film *Taxi Driver*. The album
also boasted other Browne standards "For a
Dancer" and "Farther On." The house fea-
tured on the cover is in the upscale Hancock
Park section of Los Angeles.

Creedence Clearwater Revival— *Willie and the Poor Boys*
3218 Peralta Street • Oakland, California

This is where Creedence shot the cover of their fourth album, 1970's *Willie
and the Poor Boys*. The art direction was an effective representation of the
smash single, "Down on the Corner."

Crosby, Stills and Nash—*Crosby, Stills and Nash*
North of 809 Palm Avenue • West Hollywood, California

The house where famed rock photographer Henry Diltz shot CSN's 1969 debut album cover is long gone from this site. The album featured "Suite: Judy Blue Eyes," "Marrakesh Express," and "Guinnevere" among others. Interestingly, after the album cover was shot, it was pointed out that the singers were posed as Nash, Stills, and Crosby. When they returned to re-shoot, the house had been demolished, so they settled for the photo they had.

The Doors—*Strange Days*
150–158 East 36th Street, between Lexington and Third Avenues
New York City, New York

This dark, 1967 classic featured the bluesy "Love Me Two Times" and the dramatic "People Are Strange." A mysterious, surreal cover, it was photographed in this New York City courtyard known as Sniffen Court. (The original mid-18th century stables in the courtyard were converted to housing in the 1910s.)

Lewis, Huey and the News—*Sports*
2 A.M. Club • 382 Miller Avenue
Mill Valley, California • 415-388-6036

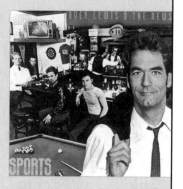

"The Heart of Rock & Roll," "Heart and Soul," "I Want A New Drug"—these were the songs that launched Huey Lewis and the News on a national scale in 1983. The cover of their smash album *Sports* was shot at this popular Mill Valley bar, the 2 A.M. Club

McCartney, Paul—*Run Devil Run*
Miller's Rexall Drugs • 87 Broad Street • Atlanta, Georgia

When Paul McCartney was passing through Atlanta, he saw Miller's Rexall Drugs, and the store inspired the title of his 1999 album. McCartney had been in town with two of his children. (His daughter Heather was unveiling her household creations at a trade show at the Americas Mart Atlanta.) After wandering into this funkier district of town, McCartney saw a bottle of bath salts called "Run Devil Run" in a Rexall shop window.

He thought it was a good title for a song—then it became the name of the album (and inspired the album cover art as well).

Pink Floyd—*Wish You Were Here*
Warner Brothers Studios • 4210 West Olive Avenue
Burbank, California

Considered by many to be the ultimate Pink Floyd effort, 1975's *Wish You Were Here* is a thematic LP dedicated to Pink Floyd's original frontman, Syd Barrett, who'd burned out years before. The famous cover photo was shot on the lot at Warner Brothers Studios in Burbank, with a guy who was actually on fire (not a photo after-effect). Though the studio is private, VIP tours are offered and while on the tour it is possible to view this location.

Ronstadt, Linda—*Livin' in the U.S.A.*
Irv's Burgers • 8289 Santa Monica Boulevard
West Hollywood, California

The inner sleeve of Linda Ronstadt's 1978 smash LP *Livin' in the U.S.A.* featured the singer sitting here at Irv's Burgers.

Spirit—*The Family That Plays Together*
Sunset Highland Motel • 6830 Sunset Boulevard
Hollywood, California

The classic 1968 release from this popular California band featured the FM staple "I Got a Line on You." The cover was shot at the Sunset Highland Motel, just across from Hollywood High School. (On January 2, 1997, Spirit guitarist and bandleader Randy California—born Randy Craig Wolfe—drowned off the coast of Molokai, Hawaii.)

The Sweet—*Desolation Boulevard*
8852 Sunset Boulevard
Hollywood, California

The Sweet shot the cover of this 1975 album near the front of a Los Angeles rock 'n' roll club called The Central. Today it's the site of The Viper Room, where River Phoenix died.

The Youngbloods—*Elephant Mountain*
Elephant Mountain • Marin County, California

Released in April 1969, this was the third Youngbloods LP and their first after the departure of founder Jerry Corbitt. Produced by Charlie Daniels, the album featured an eclectic mix of jazz, blues, country, and rock from the group who sang the smash hit "Get Together." The cover featured the scenic landscape of Northern California's Elephant Mountain.

Alice's Restaurant
Housatonic Church—The Guthrie Center • 4 Van Deusenville Road
Great Barrington, Massachusetts • 413-528-1955

Alice's Restaurant isn't around anymore. But, as the song says, "Alice didn't live in a restaurant. She lived in the church nearby the restaurant. . . ." And the old Trinity Church, where Alice once lived and where the saga began, has become home to The Guthrie Center and The Guthrie Foundation. Arlo Guthrie, working to provide a place to bring together individuals for spiritual service, founded the Guthrie Center, an Interfaith Church, in 1991. So the Trinity Church where the song "The Alice's Restaurant Massacree" began and where the movie *Alice's Restaurant* was filmed, continues to service the local and international community.

Altamont Concert
Altamont Raceway • 17001 Midway Road • Tracy, California • 925-606-0274

It was billed as a West Coast Woodstock—a huge free concert in a windswept racetrack headlined by the Rolling Stones. Instead, the gathering became one of the most violent days in the history of rock 'n' roll. For the final show of their 1969 American tour, the Rolling Stones "hosted" a one-day concert at the Altamont Speedway in Livermore, California. The show took place on December 6, 1969 and was intended as a "thank you" gesture to Stones fans. In addition to the Rolling Stones, the show's lineup included Santana, the Jefferson Airplane, the Flying Burrito Brothers, and Crosby, Stills, Nash and Young. The Grateful Dead never got to play, though they were scheduled to perform.

The haphazardly organized festival was "policed" by the Oakland chapter of the Hell's Angels motorcycle gang, a move that haunts the Stones to this day. The calamitous festival reached its climax during the Stones' set, when 18-year-old Meredith Hunter rushed the stage with a gun and was stabbed to death before the band's eyes. The moment is the ugly centerpiece of the Maysles Brothers' classic 1970 documentary *Gimme Shelter*.

American Bandstand Studio
WFIL • 4548 Market Street (46th and Market) • Philadelphia, Pennsylvania

The old WFIL Studio was the home of the original *Bandstand* and then *American Bandstand* from 1952–1963, arguably the show's most influential years. Built in 1947–48, it is notable as one of the first buildings in the United States designed specifically for television broadcasting, and was placed on the National Register of Historic Places on July 28, 1986. Today, it's an "incubator" building for small businesses.

Avalon Ballroom

Regency II Theater • 1268 Sutter Street (at Van Ness)
San Francisco, California • 415-776-8054

In the 1960s, this is where Janis Joplin debuted with Big Brother and the Holding Company. A legendary concert venue through the 1960s, the Avalon's trademark was the swirly, psychedelic lights that were projected on the backdrop behind the stage. The area that served as the ballroom is on the second floor of this theater and access is not allowed to the public.

Beach Boys' Hamburger Stand

Foster's Freeze • 11969 Hawthorne Boulevard (just north of 120th Street)
Hawthorne, California • 310-644-9653

The Beach Boys grew up in Hawthorne, California, and the "hamburger stand" mentioned in their hit song, "Fun, Fun, Fun," was actually this very Foster's Freeze (which they nicknamed "Frostie's"). It seems that Brian Wilson spotted a friend here driving by in her daddy's T-Bird. This Foster's Freeze is still open for business.

Beach Boys' Home

3701 W 119th Street • Hawthorne, California

The site of the Wilson home, the childhood home of Brian, Dennis, and Carl Wilson (three of the original five Beach Boys), was once located at what would have been this address, which is now near the intersection of West 119th and Kornblum Avenue in Hawthorne. However, it was demolished for the construction of the 105 Freeway in Los Angeles County back in the mid-1980s.

A commemorative landmark plaque and monument was dedicated on May 20, 2005, at the site of the house where the Wilson brothers grew up and The Beach Boys began as a group. Harry Jarnagan, with help from Paula Bondi-Springer, worked with the Hawthorne City Council and the state Historical Resources Commission to install the incredible landmark plaque. The project had the full support of the Wilson family, who were out in full force for the ceremony. (Dennis' eldest

son Scott Wilson provided construction services for the monument.) About 1,000 people attended the event, which was hosted by Fred Vail and included speakers and musical performances. Brian Wilson and members of his current touring band sang "In My Room" and "Surfer Girl." Fellow Beach Boys Alan Jardine and David Marks were also there.

The Beatles

Blue Jay Way
North of Sunset Strip • Hollywood, California

DIRECTIONS: Turn north on Sunset Plaza Drive off Sunset Boulevard. Head north to Rising Glen when Sunset Plaza goes east. Go left on Thrasher, follow it around west, then turn north on Blue Jay Way.

On August 1, 1967, George Harrison was staying at a rented house on this street. He wrote the song "Blue Jay Way" while awaiting the arrival of former Beatles publicity man Derek 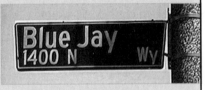 Taylor, who had gotten lost in the fog. Shortly thereafter, the piece was recorded by The Beatles for the Magical Mystery Tour film and soundtrack record. You may have a hard time determining if you are actually on Blue Jay Way, because folks keep stealing the sign.

Candlestick Park
602 Jamestown Avenue • San Francisco, California • 408-562-4949

 On August 31, 1966, The Beatles gave their final American concert at Candlestick Park in San Francisco. The official song list that cold and windy night included: "Rock and Roll Music," "She's a Woman," "If I Needed Someone," "Day Tripper," "Baby's in Black," "I Feel Fine,"

"Yesterday," "I Wanna Be Your Man," "Nowhere Man," "Paperback Writer," and "Long Tall Sally."

Delmonico Hotel
502 Park Avenue • New York, New York • 212-355-2500

This midtown hotel actually hosted two significant Beatle events. The first was in late 1963 when their manager Brian Epstein visited Ed Sullivan (who lived in the hotel) to square away details for The Beatles' first U.S. TV appearance on Sullivan's show in a few months. The next year, on August 28, Bob Dylan paid a visit to the group's hotel room while they were in the middle of their first U.S. tour and introduced them to pot, thus getting them high for the very first time.

The Ed Sullivan Theater
1697 Broadway Avenue • New York, New York

This is where The Beatles made their United States television debut on February 9, 1964, during a musical segment of *The Ed Sullivan Show*. The CBS Television office had more than 50,000 requests for tickets to a studio that held 700. It is estimated that 73,700,000 viewers watched The Beatles' historic debut. Their thirteen-and-a-half minute performance included the songs "All My Loving," "Till There Was You," "She Loves You," "I Saw Her Standing There," and "I Want to Hold Your Hand." Today, of course, this theater is famous as the place where Stephen Colbert now does his show.

Washington Coliseum
3rd and M Streets NE • Washington, D.C.

On February 11, 1964, just two days after their debut on *Ed Sullivan*, the Beatles gave their first concert in the United States at the Washington Coliseum. Today, the building is used as a parking and storage facility for garbage trucks.

John Lennon

Astor Towers Hotel
1340 North Astor Street • Chicago, Illinois

The Beatles' last U.S. tour in 1966 had a different feel than the first tour two years earlier. Much of the mania had died down and on August 11, John Lennon created a PR nightmare during a televised press conference in this hotel. Grilled about an interview he had given a few months earlier on religion (where he had stated that the Beatles were "more popular than Jesus now"), Lennon on this day apologized for his remarks as a means of trying to quell the numerous Beatle record burnings that were taking place throughout the Bible Belt. The hotel has since been converted into an apartment building.

Doug Weston's Troubadour
9081 Santa Monica Boulevard • West Hollywood, California
310-276-1158

This legendary club has seen its share of history. The Troubador is where Elton John performed his first show in the United States on August 25, 1970 (he was introduced by Neil Diamond). Randy Newman started out here. Cheech & Chong were discovered on its stage. And on and on.

But it was also here on March 12, 1974, that a drunken, despondent, Yoko-less John Lennon made infamous headlines when, after he and (also drunk) Harry Nilsson were about to get tossed for heckling the Smothers Brothers, he taped a Kotex to his forehead. When a waitress refused to give him what he thought was proper respect, he snapped, "Don't you know who I am?" "Yeah, you're some asshole with a Kotex on his head," was her response.

Fairmont The Queen Elizabeth
900 Rene Levesque Boulevard West • Montreal, Canada • 514-861-3511

On May 26, 1969, newlyweds John Lennon and Yoko Ono took the corner suite rooms (1738-40-42) at the elegant Queen Elizabeth Hotel to stage their week-long "bed-in for peace." A couple of weeks before that, the couple had bedded down in the Amsterdam Hilton for their first bed-in for peace, as documented in the song, "The Ballad of John and Yoko." On June 1, the lovebirds ordered up some recording equipment, and with comedian Tommy Smothers playing guitar, the song "Give Peace a Chance" was recorded. Joining them in the suite to sing were Dr. Timothy Leary, Montreal rabbi Abraham Feinberg, musicians Derek Taylor and Petula Clark, and members of the Canadian Radha Krishna Temple. The single was released a month later. Today, couples can make their own peace in the same bed as John and Yoko in that very suite. The weekend package includes a souvenir photo of the 1969 event, breakfast for two, a bottle of wine, and a welcome gift.

First New York Apartment
105 Bank Street • New York, New York

John and Yoko first moved to New York City in 1971 and lived in this small West Village apartment. Lennon loved the fact that he could live in relative quiet and anonymity among the busy New Yorkers and soon, he and Yoko relocated to a more grand residence at the Dakota Building, a famous landmark at 72nd Street and Central Park West. Tragically, it was at the Dakota where Lennon was shot to death on December 8, 1980.

Strawberry Fields
Central Park West
New York, New York

Strawberry Fields memorial is the name given to a landscaped section in New York's Central Park that is dedicated to the memory of musician John

Lennon, and named after one of his songs, "Strawberry Fields Forever." It was designed by landscape architect Bruce Kelly, one of the principal members of the Central Park Conservancy's management at the time and the chief landscape architect for the Conservancy's restoration planning team. Yoko Ono, who had underwritten the project, inaugurated it on John Lennon's birthday, October 9, 1985.

The entrance to the memorial is located on Central Park West at 72nd Street, directly across from the Dakota Apartments, where Lennon lived for the latter part of his life. It is not uncommon for the memorial to be covered with flowers, candles in glasses and other belongings left behind by fans of Lennon and The Beatles. On Lennon's birthday and on the anniversary of his death (December 8), people gather to sing songs and pay tribute, staying late into what is often a cold night.

Big Pink
2188 Stoll Road • Saugerties, New York

This is the house where Bob Dylan recovered from his infamous 1966 motorcycle accident and invited The Band to hang out and play with him. In addition to *The Basement Tapes*, the sessions also resulted in The Band's debut album, *Music from Big Pink*. The singles, "The Weight" and "This Wheel's on Fire" became instant classics.

The Blues

Blues Alley
Clarksdale, Mississippi

Blues Alley is the name for Clarksdale's Historic Blues District. It is here that you'll find Clarksdale Station, the newly renovated passenger depot of the old Illinois Central Railroad and, just about a hundred yards away, the Delta Blues Museum.

The station is extremely significant to the history of the blues. After all, this is where many famous blues musicians such as Muddy Waters boarded the train to Chicago, seeking jobs and a potential career in music. The Delta Blues Museum houses a collection of memorabilia from

B.B. King, Sonny Boy Williamson, Bessie Smith, and Muddy Waters, along with many other exhibits. The Delta Blues Museum is located at #1 Blues Alley, Clarksdale, Mississippi (662-627-6820).

Johnson, Robert
109 Young Street • Greenwood, Mississippi

On the night of Saturday, August 13, 1938, blues legend Robert Johnson was playing guitar in a juke joint located on the outskirts of Greenwood, Mississippi—in the back room of a place called the Shaples General Store at Three Forks. (The store, which is gone now, was located where highways 82 and 49E cross today.) Legend says this is when Johnson was poisoned by a jealous husband with either strychnine or lye.

In the middle of the night, Johnson was supposedly taken to a house in nearby Greenwood, where his condition worsened. Three days later, on August 16, he died at the house that stood at this address (a new house now stands in its place). Johnson was buried in the Mt. Zion churchyard before being re-interred in the nearby Mt. Payne graveyard.

Smith, Bessie
G.T. Thomas Hospital (now the Riverside Hotel)
615 Sunflower Avenue • Clarksdale, Mississippi

Bessie Smith, known as the *Empress of the Blues*, died here in 1937 after an infamous auto accident on Highway 61, outside of town. She was in a car driven by her companion (and Lionel Hampton's uncle) Richard Morgan. In the accident, Smith was critically injured. A doctor arrived and ordered that she be taken to a "colored" hospital in Clarksdale, However, she had lost a lot of blood and ended up dying at the hospital—she was just 43 years old.

Around the time of her death, John Hammond wrote in *Down Beat* magazine that she might have died because she was initially refused entrance to a white hospital and her treatment was delayed while she was taken to a black hospital. Although Hammond later recanted his story, playwright Edward Albee went ahead and wrote the play *The Death of Bessie Smith*, which forever branded the story in the public's mind.

Tutwiler Train Station
Tutwiler, Mississippi (about 15 miles down Highway 49 from Clarksdale)

A plaque here and a commemorative mural near the foundation of the

"WHERE THE SOUTHERN CROSSES THE DOG"
This intersection of the Southern R.R. (now the C. & G.) and the Yazoo Miss. Valley (now Ill. Central) inspired countless folksongs, stories & paintings. Crossing dates from 1895.

old train station mark where W. C. Handy made his remarkable blues discovery in 1902 or 1903. Handy wrote later of falling asleep while waiting for a late night train and being awakened by the sound of a lone figure playing a guitar by using the edge of a pocketknife as a slide, and singing about the place "where the Southern crosses the Dog."

Bowie, David

Cleveland Public Hall Convention Center • 500 Lakeside Avenue
Cleveland, Ohio

David Bowie made his American concert debut here in Cleveland on September 22, 1972, when he premiered his outrageously revolutionary *Ziggy Stardust* show with the Spiders from Mars at the Cleveland Music Hall. The orange-haired Bowie, who sailed over to America due to a fear of flying, almost saw the show cancelled by his manager, Tony DeFries, over the size of the piano that was provided in the 3,500-seat hall. However, a new piano was borrowed from the Cleveland Symphony Orchestra and the show went on. (The band Fumbal opened the show.) A post-concert party was held that night at the Hollenden House Hotel, which was located in Cleveland at 610 Superior Avenue. (Bowie would return to play this venue in 1974 during his elaborate *Diamond Dogs* tour.)

The Brill Building

1619 Broadway • New York, New York

"The Brill Building sound" came out of the stretch along Broadway between 49th and 53rd Streets. The building—named after the Brill Brothers whose clothing store was first located in the street level corner and who would later buy it—contained 165 music businesses in 1962, including many of the songwriting teams who would help craft the sounds of the 1960s.

Jerry Leiber and Mike Stoler worked here, writing many of Elvis' hits, plus Phil Spector, Doc Pomus, and Mort Shuman. And of course, the famous Aldon staff hired by Don Kirshner, which included Carole King, Gerry Goffin, Neil Sedaka, Barry Mann, Cynthia Weil, and Howard Greenfield. This was the group who wrote such hits as "The Loco Motion," "One Fine Day," "Up on the Roof," and "Will You Still Love Me Tomorrow?" Though these names have moved on, the building still houses some music companies today.

Brown, James

430 Douglas Road • Beach Island, South Carolina

On July 7, 2000, an electric company repairman showed up here at the residence of the Godfather of Soul, James Brown. Brown allegedly swung a steak knife at the man and called him "you son-of-a-bitch white trash." No charges were filed against Brown, who's had a history of run-ins with the law. (In 1988,

Brown pleaded no contest to PCP possession and guilty to carrying a gun and resisting arrest. He received a two-year suspended sentence and $1,200 fine. Another time, Brown interrupted an insurance seminar at his headquarters in Georgia by waving a rifle and demanding to know who had used his personal bathroom. The subsequent police chase through two states ended with Brown being sentenced to a six-year jail term.) Sadly, Brown passed away in December 2006.

Cal Jam
Ontario Motor Speedway • Ontario Mills Shopping Center (at the intersection of Interstate 10 and Interstate 15, approximately 40 minutes east of Los Angeles) • One Mills Circle • Ontario, California 909-484-8300

```
ONTARIO MOTOR SPEEDWAY
      ONTARIO, CALIF.
A.B.C. ENTERTAINMENT INC.
      BRINGS YOU
033887  "CALIFORNIA JAM"
APR.    SATURDAY 10 A.M. TO 10 P.M.
        GATES OPEN AT 8:00 A.M.
6       GENERAL ADMISSION
        $10.00  ADVANCE
                (INCLUDES PARKING)
1974    COORDINATED BY PACIFIC PRESENTATIONS
        NO REFUND — NO EXCHANGE
```

The "Cal Jam" concerts heralded in a new era of rock festival: organized, detailed, and packaged. Technically, they were slick, and the stage and lighting designs were the prototypes for today's tightly run festivals. They were also filmed for television's *In Concert* series, giving them an even more polished edge.

Cal Jam I took place on April 6, 1974 and featured the Eagles, Deep Purple, Rare Earth, Emerson, Lake & Palmer, and Black Sabbath. Two-hundred thousand fans paid $10 each and so the show grossed $2 million, at that time one of the largest gates in the history of rock and roll.

Aerosmith co-headlined California Jam II on March 18, 1978 in front of 350,000 people. The other performers at that show were Bob Welch, Dave Mason, Santana, Heart, Ted Nugent, Foreigner, Frank Marino & Mahogany Rush, and Rubicon. Aerosmith included a couple of cuts from this show on their *Live Bootleg* LP.

Carpenters
"Close to You" and "Only Just Begun" Apartments • 8356 5th Street Downey, California

Born in New Haven, Connecticut, Karen Carpenter moved with her family to Downey, California in 1963. Karen's older brother, Richard Carpenter, decided to put together an instrumental trio with him on the piano, Karen on the drums, and their friend Wes Jacobs on the bass and tuba. In a battle of the bands at the Hollywood Bowl in 1966, the group won first place and landed a contract with RCA Records. Stardom would soon follow with the smash hit "Close to You," which had been written in 1964, first  turning up on the debut album of Dionne Warwick. It became a number one record for the Carpenters in the summer of 1970, and with their royalties they bought an apartment building and named it "Close to You."

Soon after, they bought the building across the street and named it, "Only Just Begun" after their big hit that was written by Paul Williams (and originally appeared in a bank commercial). Today, the buildings remain as they did back in the '70s: monuments to two locals who made good. More Carpenters in Downey: The Downey Library at 11121 Brookshire Avenue houses The Carpenters Collection. Donated by Richard Carpenter, it comprises CDs, books, songbooks, albums, videocassettes, a fan club newsletter series, and publicity materials. Many of the books, CDs, and videos may be checked out. Other materials are housed in a display case located near the circulation desk.

CBGB-OMFUG
315 Bowery at Bleeker Street • New York, New York • 212-982-4052

It may stand for "Country, Bluegrass, Blues and Other Music for Uplifting Gourmandisers," but it was ground zero for some of the most influential rock and roll ever spawned. From the mid-'70s on this hole-in-the-wall club was home to such bands as Television, Blondie, The Dead Boys, The  Ramones, The Talking Heads, and many other punk legends. Considered the home to NYC's underground rock scene, it's still a vital place to experience music. On many nights in the seventies, it would not be uncommon to find Debbie Harry, Patti Smith, Joey Ramone, Iggy Pop, David Johansen, or any other number of local legends holding court at the bar. Today, the location is a John Varvatos clothing store.

Chess Records
2120 South Michigan Avenue • Chicago, Illinois • 312-808-1286

This is one of the most famous addresses in rock and roll history. After settling at this two-story building in 1957, the Chess Bothers (Polish-Jewish immigrants Leonard and Phil) continued the tradition they had started 10 years ago of recording the jazz players who performed at the brothers' nightclubs. Only now they had a permanent address and a real recording studio, as opposed to the various rented storefront offices they'd been using.

Over the years, many classic records were cut at Chess. Chuck Berry recorded "Johnny B. Goode" there on February 29, 1958, and Bo Diddley, Muddy Waters, Howlin' Wolf, Willie Dixon, Ramsey Lewis, James Moody, and many other blues greats recorded here.

British blues bands like the Rolling Stones and the Yardbirds treated Chess like Mecca—the Stones even cut a song called "2120 Michigan Avenue" in homage. After years of being used as a dance theater, today it's been restored and tours are available.

Clapton, Eric
461 Ocean Boulevard • Highway (A1-A) • Golden Beach (20 miles north of downtown Miami, Florida)

461 Ocean Boulevard was the name of Eric Clapton's 1974 "comeback" album. It's the address of the posh beach house Clapton stayed in while recording the disc nearby, and he liked the place so much, he used it as the name of the album. Though the house is on private property, you can still get a good view of it from the beach.

The Clash
The Palladium • 126 East 14th Street • New York, New York • 212-473-7171

A famous concert venue and then disco in the '80s and '90s, it was here that the famous cover of The Clash's 1980 album *London Calling* was photographed. The picture, which shows bassist Paul Simonon smashing his guitar onstage, is considered to be one of the most definitive in rock and roll.

Costello, Elvis

Holiday Inn City Center • 175 East Town Street • Columbus, Ohio
614-221-3281

Elvis Costello found himself in hot water in 1979 after making racist comments about Ray Charles and James Brown. While on tour promoting his
new *Armed Forces* album, Costello was at this Holiday Inn bar discussing British and American music with Stephen Stills and Bonnie Bramlett, when the
remarks were made. Bramlett responded by punching Costello in the face,
thereby ending the discussion. After much publicity about the incident,
Costello held a press conference and apologized.

Dead Man's Curve

Sunset Boulevard near Whittier Drive • Beverly Hills, California

The story of "Dead Man's Curve," made
famous in the Jan & Dean song, ironically
came true near this site on April 12, 1966,
when singer Jan Berry had a near-fatal car
accident in his Corvette Stingray 427 that
left him permanently disabled. The infamous curve originally mentioned in their
hit song referred to a curve slightly west on
Sunset Boulevard, near Groverton Place, just north of UCLA.

Disco Demolition Night

Comiskey Park • 333 West 35th Street • Chicago, Illinois

Chicago DJ Steve Dahl is credited by many
with single-handedly ending the disco era.
On July 12, 1979, after several smaller an-
ti-disco events, Dahl's "Disco Demolition"
between games of a twi-night doubleheader at old Comiskey park ended up with the
field completely trashed, and the White
Sox forced to forfeit the second game.

The Doors

Alta Cienega Motel

1005 N. La Cienega Avenue
West Hollywood, California
310-652-5797

Jim Morrison kept a room here from 1968–1970, as the sign on Room 32 attests. Inside the tiny space, fans from all over the world have scrawled messages upon the wall. Inside the motel office, an interview with Morrison that was conducted within that very room hangs on the wall.

Cinematique 16

8818 Sunset Boulevard • West Hollywood, California

Today it's the wonderful store Book Soup, but back in the 1960s it was a small movie theater called Cinematique 16, and it was here where Jim Morrison read his poetry during a Norman Mailer Benefit on May 30–31, 1969. He was accompanied by former Doors member Robby Krieger on guitar, and the song "Far Arden Blues" was recorded during this stint and later appeared on the album called *An American Prayer*.

Coconut Grove Exhibition Center

2700 South Bayshore Drive (at Pan American Way)
Coconut Grove, Florida • 305-579-3310

On March 1, 1969, at Miami's Dinner Key Auditorium, Jim Morrison of The Doors was arrested for allegedly exposing his penis during the show. Morrison was officially charged with lewd and lascivious behavior, indecent behavior, open profanity, and public drunkenness. Found guilty in October 1970 of indecent exposure and profanity, his sentence totaled eight months hard labor and a $500 fine. The case was still on appeal when Morrison died in Paris in 1971. The auditorium still stands, but has been enveloped by the Coconut Grove Exhibition Center.

Courson, Pamela
108 N. Sycamore Avenue • Hollywood, California

It was in this house that Jim Morrison's longtime girlfriend Pamela Courson died of a heroin overdose on April 25, 1974. She is laid to rest at: Fairhaven Cemetery • 16572 E. Fairhaven Avenue • Santa Ana, California

The Doors' Office
8512 Santa Monica Boulevard
West Hollywood, California

This building once housed The Doors' office (up on the second floor), and the classic album *L.A. Woman* was recorded in the space they used downstairs. Today, the world-famous "Tail O' the Pup" hotdog stand can be found at the site, and the office building is still part of the restaurant complex.

The Extension
8500 Santa Monica Boulevard • West Hollywood, California

Today it's an Al and Ed's Autosound, but back in the 1960s it was called The Extension and it was a regular hangout for Jim Morrison. This is where he'd often meet with journalists to give interviews and, in fact, the now famous *Rolling Stone* magazine interview with Jerry Hopkins was conducted at this site.

George Washington High School
1005 Mount Vernon Avenue • Alexandria, Virginia

From 1958 until he graduated two-and-a-half years later, this is where Jim Morrison spent some formative high school years. His dad had been transferred to work at the Pentagon and that's what brought the Morrison family out from Alameda, California. (Morrison skipped the graduation ceremonies.)

Gil Turner's Liquor Store
9101 Sunset Boulevard • West Hollywood, California • 310-652-1000

This is sometimes called the "liquor store to the stars" and The Doors would often walk over here from the nearby Whisky in between sets to buy booze (the Whisky did not yet have a liquor license).

Kaleidoscope
8433 Sunset Boulevard • West Hollywood, California

Today it's the world famous Comedy Store, but back in the 1960s, after first starting out as Ciro's restaurant and nightclub, it was known as The Kaleidoscope. Many bands played here during that time, including The Doors, who appeared here April 21–23, 1967.

Morrison Hotel
1246 South Hope Street • Los Angeles, California

The squalid hotel depicted on the cover of The Doors' album *Morrison Hotel* is located in downtown L.A., just two blocks east of the Los Angeles Convention Center. The hotel's owner supposedly chased The Doors away when they came by to shoot the cover for the 1970 LP, but they snuck back and grabbed the shot anyway (the picture was taken by famed photographer, Henry Diltz).

Morrison's Last Residence
8216 1/2 Norton Avenue • West Hollywood, California

This was Jim Morrison's last residence. He lived here in 1970 with Pamela Courson (who was never legally married to the singer). It was here where Chuck Berry came to visit Morrison, who, according to his friends, was surprised and thrilled to be visited by the rock 'n' roll legend.

New Haven Arena
State and Grove Streets • New Haven, Connecticut

There's a parking lot here where the arena used to be, where on December

9, 1967, Doors lead singer Jim Morrison had one of his more memorable run-ins with the law. Morrison had been found entertaining a woman in a shower stall before the show by a cop who, not recognizing the singer, maced him. Later, onstage, Morrison recounted the episode for the crowd during the song "Back Door Man" and was then arrested and charged with "indecent and immoral exhibition."

Olivia's (Former Site)
2615 Main Street • Santa Monica, California

At one time there was a restaurant called Olivia's here and it's the place that inspired Jim Morrison to write the song "Soul Kitchen."

Themis
947 La Cienega Boulevard • West Hollywood, California

This antique store also plays a part in the history of Jim Morrison. It's the former site of Themis, the boutique run by Morrison's girlfriend Pamela Courson. It was basically financed by Morrison and was in business for about three years starting in the late 1960s. Back then, it would not be uncommon to find the singer hanging out here.

Turkey Joint West
116 Santa Monica Boulevard • Santa Monica, California

Rick and the Ravens (Ray Manzarek's band) played at this club as the house band in the mid-1960s and it was here on June 5, 1965, that Jim Morrison made his first public appearance as a singer. Today, it's a popular English pub called Ye Olde King's Head.

Topanga Corral
2034 Topanga Canyon Boulevard • Topanga Canyon, California

There used to be a restaurant here that served as the inspiration for the Doors song "Roadhouse Blues." A fire destroyed it back in the 1960s, and there was a cabin behind the restaurant that Jim Morrison bought for his girlfriend Pamela Courson (in the song he referred to the cabin as a "bungalow").

Dylan, Bob

Birthplace
519 North 3rd Avenue East • Duluth, Minnesota

Dylan was born Robert Allen Zimmerman on May 24, 1941 in Duluth, and spent his first six years in this port city at the end of Lake Superior. The Zimmermans lived on the top floor of this house, which incidentally was auctioned off on eBay in 2001 for $94,600. When Dylan was in kindergarten, his family moved to his mother's hometown of Hibbing, a mining town about 75 miles north of Duluth.

The Bitter End
147 Bleecker Street at La Guardia Place • New York, New York
212-673-7030

When Dylan started hanging out again in Greenwich in the summer of 1975, he made several appearances here with the likes of Patti Smith, Ramblin' Jack Elliot, Bobby Neuwirth, and others before hitting the road with the Rolling Thunder Revue tour. The club is now called The Other End.

Cedar Street Tavern
82 University Place • New York, New York • 212-741-9754

An old-fashioned tavern that was once a popular watering hole of artists

such as Jackson Pollock, Willem de Kooning, and Mark Rothko in the 1950s, by the '60s it had become a favorite Dylan hangout.

Childhood Home
2425 7th Avenue East • Hibbing, Minnesota

For most of Dylan's life in Hibbing, he lived here. He graduated from Hibbing High School in 1959 (the 1959 yearbook is locked in a cabinet at Hibbing Public Library) and moved to Minneapolis to attend the University of Minnesota. In 1960, he dropped out of the university and moved to New York City. His first album, *Bob Dylan*, was released in 1962. That year, he legally changed his name from Robert Allen Zimmerman to Bob Dylan. A collection relating to Dylan's life and accomplishments is located at the Hibbing Public Library at 2020 East 5th Avenue.

The Commons
130 West 3rd Street • New York, New York • 212-533-4790

Dylan played here at The Commons, a sprawling basement club, within a week of his arrival in New York City. It was also here, in 1962, that Dylan started writing a song. After finishing it, he took it over to Folk City and played it for Gil Turner, who thought it was incredible. Gil got up on the stage and played it for the audience, while Dylan stood in the shadows at the bar—which is how the world first heard the Dylan classic, "Blowin' in the Wind."

Denver Home
1736 East 17th Avenue • Denver, Colorado

Bob Dylan lived at this address for a short period in the early 1960s—around the time he was playing regularly at the legendary Satire Lounge located at 1920 East Colfax Avenue. Incidentally, the Satire Lounge was also the starting point for Tommy and Dick Smothers, better known as the Smothers Brothers (they lived in the only apartment above the Satire). Judy Collins also played here many times—she attended East High School just a few blocks away.

Duluth National Guard Armory
Armory Arts & Music Center • 2416 London Road #779
Duluth, Minnesota

At the 1998 Grammy Awards, Bob Dylan spoke about a pivotal moment in his life. "When I was about 16 or 17 years old, I went to see Buddy Holly play at Duluth National Guard Armory," said Dylan, "and I was three seats away from him, and he looked at me, and I don't know how or why, but I know he was with us all the time we were making this record in some kind of way." Dylan witnessed this performance on January 31, 1959. Buddy Holly would die in a plane crash just a few days later.

Forrest Hills Tennis Stadium
1 Tennis Place • Forest Hills, New York

The U.S. Open Tennis Tournament used to be held in this classic, ivy-covered, open-air stadium. They've held big concerts here, too, including The Beatles, Jimi Hendrix, Talking Heads, Hall and Oates, and others. None were bigger, though, than the show held by Bob Dylan in the summer of 1965. It was just a month after Dylan's controversial "electric" set at the Newport Folk Festival and Dylan wasn't ready to stop pushing the envelope. The first set was acoustic, as the folkies liked. But he tore into the second set with an electric band headed by Robbie Robertson and Levon Helm. Much of the crowd booed and pelted the stage with garbage and it remains another defining night in Bob Dylan's illustrious career.

The Freewheelin' Bob Dylan
161 West Fourth Street • New York, New York

Dylan and his girlfriend, Suze Rotolo, first lived here in an apartment between Jones Street and Sixth Avenue. They moved here in December 1961, just after Dylan had finished recording his debut album for Columbia. Outside the apartment, in the middle of West Fourth Street, Dylan and Suze were photographed together in February 1963 for the cover of *The Freewheelin' Bob Dylan* album by Columbia staff photographer Don Hunstein (even though they had been separated for seven months at that point). The shot features Dylan and Suze walking toward West 4th with the camera facing Bleecker Street.

Gaslight Cafe/Kettle of Fish Bar
116 MacDougal Street • New York, New York

One of young Dylan's favorite haunts, the Gaslight was originally a "basket house," where performers were paid the proceeds of a passed-around basket. Opened in 1958 by John Mitchell—legendary pioneer of Greenwich Village coffeehouses—the Gaslight had already become a showcase for beat poets Allen Ginsberg and Gregory Corso. However, it was transformed into a folk club when Sam Hood took it over. It was here that Dylan premiered "Masters of War" and many other of his songs. The Kettle of Fish Bar, located upstairs above the Gaslight, was also a regular drinking hangout for Dylan and other bohemian artists of the day.

Gerde's Folk City
11 West 4th Street • New York, New York

This former folk music landmark is where Bob Dylan played his first professional gig on April 11, 1961, supporting blues legend John Lee Hooker. He played here again on September 26 of that same year, a show that was reviewed by Robert Shelton in the *New York Times*. The rave review

helped set the Dylan legend in full motion. The site is today occupied by the Hebrew Union College.

Greenwich Village Townhouse
94 MacDougal Street • New York, New York

When the Dylan family left Woodstock in 1970, they moved into this tasteful Greenwich Village townhouse. It was here that Dylan found himself constantly (and infamously) harangued by the seemingly obsessed Dylan expert, A.J. Weberman. It was outside this very house that Weberman made off with the Dylan family's garbage for further study of the legend.

Greystone Park Psychiatric Hospital
West Hanover Avenue • Morris Plains, New Jersey • 973-292-4096

When Bob Dylan first came east in February 1961, he headed straight here to visit his hero, the long-ailing Woody Guthrie, famous singer, ballad-maker, and poet. This marked the beginning of a deep friendship between the two singers. Although separated by 30 years and two generations, they were united on many personal and artistic levels. Woody Guthrie was eventually transferred to Brooklyn State Hospital, where he spent the rest of his life. The Greystone Hospital still houses some patients, but many of the buildings are vacant and in need of repair.

Hard Rock Cafe
279 Yonge Street • Toronto, Canada • 416-362-3636

The first plaque marking a rock 'n' roll historic site in Toronto was installed at the Hard Rock Cafe in January 2002. It commemorates the spot where Bob Dylan first rehearsed with Levon and the Hawks. The plaque inscription reads: "An event that *Time* magazine once called 'the most decisive moment in rock history' took place a few steps from where you are now standing. Here in the early morning of Thursday, September 16, 1965, Bob Dylan first heard Levon and the Hawks, a hard-edged Toronto rock group, later to become famous as The Band. After the show, Dylan began rehearsing with The Hawks for what turned out to be his stunning eight-month debut tour on electric instruments."

At the time, this building was famous as the Friar's Tavern. It was one of Toronto's most popular nightclubs and Levon and the Hawks were the city's top band. One of their biggest fans was Mary Martin, a Toronto woman who in 1965 was working in New York City for Albert Grossman, Bob Dylan's manager. Mary watched as Dylan grew fed up playing folk guitar alone in front of silent, reverential crowds. She also witnessed his electric first performance at the Newport Folk Festival.

So Mary Martin decided to play matchmaker. She knew that Dylan needed a fiery band like The Hawks to help him launch his new direction, and that the Hawks needed a star like Dylan to take them beyond the Friar's. On September 15, 1965, Dylan arrived in Toronto. For the next two nights, after hours, he rehearsed with The Hawks on a stage along the north wall—now the window side of the restaurant. One week later, their tour opened in Austin, Texas, unleashing a whole new sound.

Hibbing High School
801 East 21st Street • Hibbing, Minnesota • 218-263-3675

A grand staircase leads to the medieval castle-like framework of the historic school, built in the early 1920s for almost $4 million. Unique hand-molded ceilings in the foyer welcome visitors and accent the breathtaking auditorium designed after the Capitol Theatre in New York City. Cut-glass chandeliers of crystal, imported from Belgium, light the 1,800-velvet-seat grand auditorium. The cost of each chandelier in 1920 was $15,000 and today they are insured for $250,000 each. The auditorium

boasts a magnificent Barton pipe organ, one of only two that still exist in the United States. Containing over 1,900 pipes, the organ can play any orchestra instrument except the violin. Bob Dylan attended this school and played some legendary performances here in 1958 and 1959.

"Like a Rolling Stone"
Columbia Studios • 799 Seventh Avenue • New York City, New York

Bob Dylan's classic "Like a Rolling Stone" was recorded on June 15, 1965, in Studio A at what was then the New York headquarters of Columbia Records. The studio has since been relocated.

Newport Folk Festival
Festival Field • Intersection of Girard Avenue and Admiral Kalbfus Road • Newport, Rhode Island

On July 25, 1965, Bob Dylan (and band) upset the folk music generation by plugging in at the Newport Folk Festival and cranking out "Maggie's Farm," "Like a Rolling Stone," and a few other choice selections. While Dylan's seminal show allegedly generated way more disgust than glee amongst the crowd, it became a turning point in his career (and the course of popular music). In one shining moment, he had fused rock 'n' roll with protest songs. The field where the festival was held in 1965 is now the sight of the Festival Field Apartments.

Rotolos' Apartment
One Sheridan Square • New York, New York

Formerly the location of the legendary club called Cafe Society Downtown, it was above this little theater that the Rotolos lived (mother Mary, a widow, and her two daughters, Carla and Suze). Seventeen-year-old Suze Rotolo had fallen for Dylan after seeing him play at a folk music day at the Riverside Church on July 29, 1961. Dylan crashed at a friend's place here on the fourth floor and soon, he and Suze were lovers. It's believed that after Suze left Dylan in May 1962, the heartache inspired him to compose such classic love songs as "Tomorrow Is a Long Time," and "Don't Think Twice, It's All Right."

Sound 80
2709 East 25th Street • Minneapolis, Minnesota

At this one-time recording studio called Sound 80, Bob Dylan recorded his classic mid-1970s album, *Blood on the Tracks*, which featured both "Tangled Up In Blue" and "Idiot Wind," among others. The popular studio had also been used by Leo Kottke and Cat Stevens; the 1980 dance hit "Funkytown" was also cut here. Today, the building where so much musical history was made is used by Orfield Laboratories for testing products' acoustical properties.

The Ten O'Clock Scholar
416 14th Avenue SE • Minneapolis, Minnesota

Robert Zimmerman entered the arts school of the University of Minnesota, located in Minneapolis, in the fall of 1959. While a student at the university, he performed his first solo shows here at the Ten O'Clock Scholar, a local coffeehouse. In October 1959, Robert Zimmerman went into the coffeehouse to see if he could play there. When asked his name by owner David Lee, he responded "Bob Dylan." He maintained a regular job playing at the Scholar until May 1960. Today, the site is a video store parking lot.

Tinker Street Café
59 Tinker Street • Woodstock, New York

Today it's the Center for Photography at Woodstock, but until recently this was the Tinker Street Café, a popular cafe/hangout in the famously bohemian town. Hendrix, Joplin, Van Morrison, and many others ate and played here over the years, but the building had a famous tenant, too. In a room above the cafe, Bob Dylan wrote songs for *Another Side of Bob Dylan* and *Bringing It All Back Home* while living here in 1964.

Village Gate
158 Bleecker Street • New York, New York

In 1962, in the basement apartment of the renowned Village Gate theater, Dylan wrote the song "A Hard Rain's A-Gonna Fall." (The small apartment was then occupied by Chip Monck, later to become one of the most sought-after lighting directors in rock music.) Today, the Village Gate still presents music and theater; it's now called The Village Theater.

White Horse Tavern
567 Hudson Street (at 11th Street) • New York, New York • 212-243-9260

This 18th-century bar was a popular Dylan haunt back in 1961, where he would come to hear the Clancy Brothers play. It's also famous as the place where the Welsh poet Dylan Thomas ate his last meal before drinking himself to death. His last words were supposedly, "I've had 19 straight whiskies. I believe that's the record." He died later that night. Founded in 1880, the White House Tavern is the second oldest bar in New York City.

The Eagles
Beverly Hills Hotel • 9641 Sunset Boulevard • Beverly Hills, California
310-276-2251

This, one of the most famous hotels in the world, served as the cover for the Eagles' Grammy-winning 1976 masterpiece, *Hotel California*. To get the shot of the "mission bell," a cherry picker was used (making it hard to imagine the angle when you stand in front of the hotel). The inside photo of the band in the hotel "lobby" was actually shot inside the Lido Apartments, located in Hollywood at 6500 Yucca Street.

Fender Guitars
Corner of Santa Fe and Pomona Streets
Fullerton, California

Guitar design-wiz Leo Fender once operated his factory on this site, where he mass-produced his breakthrough creations such as the Fender Broadcaster, the Telecaster and the Fender Precision Bass from 1945–1952. Though he never played guitar himself, Fender was inducted into the Rock and Roll Hall of Fame a few months after his death in 1991. Fender was born right here in Fullerton on August 10, 1909 and has displayed a certain genius for electrical engineering since his youth.

Fillmore East
105 Second Avenue • New York, New York

The Fillmore East, another of promoter Bill Graham's psychedelic concert venues, hosted hundreds of memorable rock and roll events. Jimi Hendrix's Band of Gypsys played here on New Year's Eve, 1969. John Lennon showed up one time to jam with Frank Zappa. The Jeff Beck Group (featuring Rod Stewart) made their American debut here in 1968, on a bill with the Grateful Dead. Today it's a bank.

Fillmore West
San Francisco Honda • 10 South Van Ness Avenue at Market Street
San Francisco, California • 415-441-2000

From 1968 to 1971, the theater at this site (originally called the Carousel Ballroom) hosted everyone from The Who to the Jefferson Airplane to Cream. Famed promoter Bill Graham took it over in 1968, renamed it the "Fillmore West," and thus created one of rock and roll's most legendary venues. Today, it's the second floor of a Honda dealership. Supposedly, there's some graffiti in the rear stairwell that's an actual artifact from the theater.

Fleetwood Mac
Sound City • 15456 Cabrito Road • Van Nuys, California • 818-787-3722

In late 1974 when Mick Fleetwood was looking for a studio to record the next Fleetwood Mac album, he went to Sound City on a recommendation, liked the sound, and hired engineer Keith Olsen to produce and engineer the album. In the process of hearing a demonstration of that studio's sound and Olsen's production work, Fleetwood also stumbled upon two musicians who would soon become members of the band when Bob Welch departed.

Fleetwood came down to hear what the studio sounded like and Olsen put on a song called "Frozen Love" from the Buckingham Nicks album, which had been recorded there. Fleetwood decided to hire Lindsey Buckingham and Stevie Nicks based on the experience, and within two years the "new" Fleetwood Mac had the number one album in the country. (Nirvana also recorded *Nevermind* here, and Dennis Wilson brought a singer named Charles Manson to cut demos here in the late '60s.)

Freed, Alan—"Moondog Rock 'n' Roll Party" Radio Show
WJW (former site) • One Playhouse Square Building
1375 Euclid Avenue • Cleveland, Ohio

Seminal disc-jockey Alan Freed (who popularized the term "rock 'n' roll") began broadcasting his "Moondog Rock 'n' Roll Party" over WJW radio in 1951. The station's 50,000 watt power made the show's influence enormous and helped bring many early rock and roll records to a huge audience. A small plaque near the building's entrance acknowledges the history, even though the radio station is long gone.

Gold Star Recording Studios
6252 Santa Monica Boulevard • Hollywood, California

The reason Brian Wilson of the Beach Boys wanted to record here was because he knew it was where Phil Spector had created his famous "Wall of Sound" approach to recording: the dense, layered, echo-filled sound that surrounded songs like "He's a Rebel," "Be My Baby," "Baby, I Love You," and "You've Lost That Loving Feeling" to name a few. The result was *Pet Sounds*, the dynam-

ic 1967 album that supposedly pushed the Beatles to up the ante with *Sergeant Pepper's Lonely Hearts Club Band*. Small and lacking air conditioning, the main recording studio at Gold Star sat on the southeast corner of Santa Monica and Vine, but was razed in the mid-1980s to make room for the mini-mall that's there now.

The Grateful Dead

The Château
838 Santa Cruz Avenue • Menlo Park, California

Back in the early 1960s, a rambling old house stood here, sort of a hostel for various musicians, artists, and beatniks. Banjo player Jerry Garcia resided here with lyricist Robert Hunter. So, for many fans, this is the group's spiritual birthplace. Once they started up as The Warlocks (they would change their name soon after), they played a local pizza place, Magoo's Pizza Parlor, which had been located at 639 Santa Cruz Avenue in Menlo Park. Today, the site is a furniture store.

Grateful Dead House
710 Ashbury • San Francisco, California

This house was home to Jerry Garcia, Pigpen, manager Rock Scully, and other Dead associates. It was a popular community center until 1967, when the police arrested everyone for a very small amount of marijuana that was found on the premises (Garcia and his girlfriend were out shopping at the time). In March of 1968, the band performed a farewell concert from the back of a flatbed truck with power lines attached to the Straight Theatre. The band then moved to Marin County.

Lesh, Phil
1012 High Street • Palo Alto, California

The Warlocks met here at band member Phil Lesh's house in 1965 and decided a name change was in order. Thumbing through an encyclopedia, they came upon a reference to "the grateful dead" and settled on that as the new group name. Their first gig under that name took place in December 1965.

Magoo's Pizza Parlor
639 Santa Cruz Avenue • Menlo Park, California

When the Grateful Dead first started up as The Warlocks, they'd play a local pizza place, Magoo's Pizza Parlor, which had been located at 639 Santa Cruz Avenue in Menlo Park. Today, the site is a furniture store.

The Onion
9550 Haskell Avenue • Sepulveda, California
818-894-9251

The odd-shaped, onion-dome church can be rented today for many different kinds of events. But, in February 1966, the Grateful Dead played here as part of the infamous Acid Test Series, organized by the LSD-touting group the Merry Pranksters.

Royal Sonesta Hotel
300 Bourbon Street • New Orleans, Louisiana • 504-586-0300

In the legendary Grateful Dead song, "Truckin'," the band sings of being "Busted, down on Bourbon Street." The lyric was based on a real incident that took place in Room 2134 of this Big Easy hotel in January 1970. Though marijuana and hashish were recovered in the room by undercover cops, charges against several band members were eventually dropped.

Soldier Field
425 East McFetridge Drive • Chicago, Illinois

The Grateful Dead played their last shows here in Chicago on July 8–9, 1995. Guitarist Jerry Garcia died later that year from drug complications, thus ending the band's tenure.

A Great Day in Harlem
17 East 126th Street • Harlem, New York

Jean Bach's documentary *A Great Day in Harlem* told the story of a day in 1958 when many of America's greatest jazz artists were gathered at 10:00 A.M.—an ungodly hour for musicians who had played until dawn that very morning—to this stoop for a photograph. Amazingly, many showed up, and the photograph, taken by Art Kane and featuring Dizzie Gillespie, Charles Mingus, Thelonious Monk, Marian McPartland, Art Blakey, Milt Hinton, Count Basie, Sonny Hawkins, Lester Young, and dozens of other old lions and upcoming stars assembled on and around the steps of a nondescript brownstone in Harlem, became famous the world over.

Guns N' Roses
1114 North Clark Street
Hollywood, California

In the early 1980s, this apartment complex was where the band Guns N' Roses lived with their then-manager, Vicky Hamilton. The pad is located right near the famous Whisky nightclub, where the band would often hang out.

Hall and Oates
Adelphia Ballroom • 1400 North 52nd Street • Philadelphia, Pennsylvania

The is where Daryl Hall first met John Oates. It happened in 1967 when both young singers were part of competing doo-wop groups. A gang fight broke out and they made their acquaintance while hiding out in the freight elevator of the theater. (They didn't go on to record together until 1972.)

Hendrix, Jimi

Ashbury Tobacco Center
1524 Haight Street, near Ashbury • San Francisco, California

The Hendrix song "Red House" was supposedly written about this old Victorian mansion, which at the time in the 1960s was painted red. Though he never lived here full-time, Hendrix did spend many nights here as he kept two girlfriends living on the second and third floors.

Café Wha?
115 MacDougal Street
Greenwich Village, New York • 212-254-3630

An early Bob Dylan hangout, this is where Animals bassist Chas Chandler first saw the unknown Jimi Hendrix play in 1966. Under Chandler's guidance, Hendrix soon moved to England, where his career began to crystallize.

Drake Swissotel
440 Park Avenue • New York, New York

In April of 1968, Jimi Hendrix stayed here after being tossed out of the nearby Warwick Hotel. In his room (which cannot be identified at this time—anyone know?) he recorded a batch of songs including "Cherokee" and "Angel Mist." This is also the hotel where Led Zeppelin's gate receipts from their Madison Square Garden concerts were supposedly stolen in 1973, worth upwards of $200,000.

Electric Lady Studios
52 West 8th Street • New York, New York • 212-677-4700

In 1968, Jimi Hendrix was looking to buy a recording studio when he found the Generation Club on West 8th Street in the heart of Greenwich Village. After shelling out the $50,000 asking price, Hendrix turned it into a recording facility, becoming the first major artist to own and operate his own studio. Sadly, Hendrix died within a month after the studio opened.

In June 1997, the original, distinctive, curved brick facade entrance to Electric Lady Studios was demolished (the New York Landmark Society unsuccessfully attempted to halt the renovation of the building, which would have been eligible for landmark status in just three years).

Freedman's Loans
1208 1st Avenue • Seattle, Washington • 206-622-3086

Jimi Hendrix's father, Al, had once bought himself a saxophone from this pawnshop. Thirty years later, he bought his son, Jimi, his first guitar here. It's still in business after all these years.

Garfield High School
400 23rd Avenue • Seattle, Washington

Jimi Hendrix attended high school here before dropping out to join the Army (he was later given an honorary diploma). Other famous attendees of this school were music great Quincy Jones and martial arts legend Bruce Lee. There is a bronze bust of Hendrix located in the library.

Greenwood Memorial Park
4th Street and Monroe Avenue • Renton, Washington

This is the grave of Jimi Hendrix, who overdosed in London on September 18, 1970. Today, it's become a shrine for Hendrix fans all over the world. The graveyard is located in Renton, a suburb of Seattle, which was Jimi's birthplace. The site contains the graves of Hendrix, his half-brother Leon, half-sister Janie, father Al Hendrix, and his wife Ayako. Hendrix's headstone reads: "Forever In Our Hearts—James M. "Jimi" Hendrix—1942–1970."

Holly, Buddy

Childhood Home
1911 6th Street • Lubbock, Texas

This is the house where the Holley family lived at the time their fourth child, Charles Hardin Holley, was born on September 7, 1936. He would one day become "Buddy," and would also drop the "e" from his last name. A vacant lot sits where the house used to stand.

Fair Park Coliseum
Avenue A and 10th Street • Lubbock, Texas

Back in the mid-1950s, Buddy Holly and the Crickets played on the bottom part of tickets at concerts for both Elvis Presley and Bill Haley and the Comets here at this local arena (which still stands today). Holly's influence can still be felt all around his home town, especially at the Buddy Holly Center, located at 1801 Ave. G in Lubbock. One part museum, one part art center, it's a fittingly named place for a favorite local son.

Hutchinson Junior High
3102 Canton Avenue • Lubbock, Texas

Buddy formed a duet here with his friend Bob Montgomery. Calling themselves "The Bob and Buddy Show," they'd regularly entertain at school functions.

KDAV Radio (Now KRFE AM 580)
6602 Martin Luther King Boulevard • Lubbock, Texas • 806-745-1197

Today it's an easy listening station, but back in 1953 Buddy Holly did a weekly radio show here with his partner Bob Montgomery. It's believed by many that KDAV was the first full-time country music station in the United States.

Buddy Holly and Montgomery were initially given a chance to perform on the air during *The Sunday Party*. This later evolved into a regular slot at 2:30 P.M. every Sunday for what by then had become a trio (Holly, Montgomery, and bassist Larry Welborn). The segment was called The Buddy and Bob Show and featured a unique blend of Country and Western and Rhythm and Blues. Tours are offered today, so you can get a chance to see the actual studio where Buddy Holly cut his very first records.

Norman Petty Studios
1313 West Seventh Street • Clovis, New Mexico

The Norman Petty Studios on 7th Street is known worldwide as the place where Buddy Holly recorded the smash hit, "Peggy Sue," as well as 18 other hits in just 15 months. In his studios, Petty mixed songs for other stars, including Roy Orbison. Clovis' own Fireballs also recorded "Sugar Shack," the number one song in 1963, at Norman Petty Studios.

Call the Clovis/Curry County Chamber of Commerce at (575) 763-3435 about information on scheduling a tour.

Jackson, Michael

Garnett Elementary School
2131 Jackson Street • Gary, Indiana

One of Michael Jackson's first big performing moments happened here at the school that all of the Jackson Five attended. In 1963, the five-year-old singer brought the house down with his version of "Climb Every Mountain" from *The Sound of Music*. Michael's first professional debut happened a year later at a club called Mr. Lucky's Lounge, which is still located at 1100 Grant Street in Gary.

Jackson Family Home
641 Hayvenhurst Avenue • Encino, California

In November of 1993, police searched singer Michael Jackson's famous family compound here in the San Fernando Valley, looking for evidence that might support charges of child molestation against Jackson. (The criminal case was eventually dropped for lack of evidence.) Michael Jackson later settled the civil lawsuit out of court with the boy (for a reported $20 million), while insisting that he was innocent of any and all charges. Michael's sister, LaToya Jackson, had earlier alleged that she had been abused as a child by her father at this same Jackson family home, though the rest of the family heatedly denied all of her explosive charges.

Neverland Ranch
Figueroa Mountain Road • Los Olivos, California

DIRECTIONS: Neverland is located on Figueroa Mountain Road, 6 miles north of Los Olivos, California. Los Olivos is in the Santa Ynez Valley, 25 miles north of Santa Barbara.

You can't get beyond the guard at the gate, but within this sprawling complex is where Michael Jackson houses his zoo, amusement park, and theater. It's from here that he broadcast his 1993 speech declaring his innocence when charges of child molestation arose.

Pasadena Civic Auditorium
300 East Green Street • Pasadena, California • 626-449-7360

On March 25, 1983, Michael Jackson, in front of his Motown brethren, slid across the stage and introduced "moonwalking" to the strains of a pre-recorded "Billie Jean" during the Motown 25th anniversary television show. Both the live and television audiences went wild at the sight of Jackson seemingly floating above the floor.

Santa Maria Courthouse
312 East Cook Street • Building E • Santa Maria, California

Singer Michael Jackson was arraigned here in Santa Maria on January 16, 2004, at the court of Santa Maria. He was admonished by the judge for turning up 20 minutes late and entered a plea of "Not Guilty." Hundreds of fans and an international media circus surrounded the event, which became notable for Jackson's bizarre, post-plea circus whereby he jumped on a van in front of the courthouse and began dancing for the throngs of people who showed up (as well as for the ever-present videographer Jackson had hired for the day).

Thriller Video
1345 Carroll Avenue • Glendale, California

In the 1982 music video *Thriller*, Michael Jackson is chased by ghouls through a neighborhood of old Victorian homes, and this is the main house that was used.

Jazz is Born

Congo Square (now called Armstrong Park) • Located off North Rampart Street, near the intersection of St. Philip Street • New Orleans, Louisiana

In the early 1800s, this area was known as Congo Square and was the only legal place where slaves could get together on Sunday afternoons. On those days, they would gather to play drums, gourds, banjo-like instruments, marimbas, and such European instruments as the violin, tambourine, and triangle—creating what many consider to be the origins of American Jazz music. Today, Congo Square has become Armstrong Park, a Jazz Historical Park named for legendary trumpeter Louis Armstrong, who was born in New Orleans in 1900.

Jefferson Airplane

2400 Fulton Street at Willard Street North (facing the northern side of Golden Gate Park) • San Francisco, California

This is where the Jefferson Airplane parked it during their heyday in the late '60s and early '70s. Many of rock's royalty paid a visit to this stately manor for what are considered some of the most legendary parties in rock and roll history.

King, Carole

Tapestry • 8815 Appian Way • Los Angeles, California

This was the house where Carole King lived while recording *Tapestry*, then one of the best-selling albums in history. The famous cover of the album was taken sitting next to one of the windows in this house.

KISS

10 East 23rd Street • New York, New York

Back in the pre-makeup days of 1972, this is where the band KISS (Gene Simmons, Paul Stanley, Ace Frehley, and Peter Criss) got together to start rehearsing, up in a loft on the fourth floor. Today it is the site of Cosmic Comics.

Led Zeppelin

Absinthe Bar
400 Bourbon Street • New Orleans, Louisiana • 504-525-8108

This famous bar, the walls of which are covered with thousands of yellowed business cards and dollar bills, was re-created in a London studio for the cover of the band's last album, 1979's *In Through the Out Door*. The actual bar had long been a  Zeppelin hangout; Jimmie Page even met his wife there, and so the band wanted to pay tribute.

Edgewater Inn
Pier 67 • 2411 Alaskan Way • Seattle, Washington • 1-800-624-0670

Located on the edge of beautiful Puget Sound, this hotel (now called simply The Edgewater) is the site of the infamous 1969 Led Zeppelin "Shark Incident." On July 25, Zeppelin checked into this hotel, which back then was a favorite with musicians because guests could fish from their rooms. (Zeppelin was in town to play at the Seattle Pops Festival scheduled for July 25–27, at Woodenville, Washington.) The band caught some red snapper, and then, though versions vary, partook in some unseemly behavior with a 17-year-old redhead named Jackie in Room 242. (Members of the band Vanilla Fudge were also present.)

Physical Graffiti
96 St. Mark's Place • New York, New York

This old brownstone served as the cover for the band's 1975 album, *Physical Graffiti*. If you compare the building to the album cover, you will notice that the only difference is that the third floor was removed from the final photo. Located

in the lower righthand corner of the building is the "Physical Graffiti" used clothing store (named after the record came out). This is also the building where Keith Richards sat with a bunch of Rastafari waiting for Mick Jagger in the Rolling Stones' 1981 video, "Waiting on a Friend."

Sunset Sound
6650 Sunset Boulevard • Hollywood, California • 323-469-1186

When musician Tutti Camarata opened his studio in 1958, his main client was Walt Disney (and many soundtracks were cut here.) But once the 1960s kicked in, rock and roll took over and this unpretentious little building near the intersection of Cherokee and Sunset became enormously popular for musicians seeking a recording studio.

Led Zeppelin recorded their second and fourth albums here, the latter of which included "Stairway to Heaven." The Doors did the majority of their recording here, and the Rolling Stones cut *Beggars Banquet* here. Other famous recordings include James Taylor's "Fire and Rain," Janis Joplin's "Me and Bobby McGee," Michael Jackson's "Beat It," and hundreds of others.

Little Richard
J & M Studios • 523 Gov. Nichols Street • New Orleans, Louisiana

Legendary recording engineer Cosimo Matassa owned several recording studios around the Big Easy. In the one that was located at this site, Little Richard recorded some of the most influential records in rock and roll history: "Tutti Frutti," Lucille," and "Good Golly Miss Molly." The structure is now a condominium.

Live Aid
JFK Stadium • Broad Street (near Patterson Avenue)
Philadelphia, Pennsylvania

This is where the American portion of the legendary "Live Aid" benefit concerts was held on July 13, 1985 (the London portion took place at Wembley Arena). That day saw the likes of Bob Dylan, Led Zeppelin, Mick Jagger, Neil Young, and many more come together to help raise funds to feed the world's hungry. J.F.K. Stadium, the longtime home of the Army/Navy football game, was torn down in the 1990s.

"Louie, Louie"
Northwest Recorders • 415 SW 13th Street • Portland, Oregon

The Kingsmen had formed in Portland in 1960 and consisted of Lynn Easton on drums, Mike Mitchell on guitar, Don Gallucci on keyboards, Bob Nordby on bass, and guitar player and lead singer Jack Ely. By the time they recorded "Louie, Louie," they ranged in age from 17 to 20. On a Friday night in April, 1963, The Kingsmen performed at an outdoor concert and did a marathon version of the song. The following morning, they went to a small recording studio in Portland called Northwest Recorders to lay down the tracks. Paul Revere & The Raiders recorded the tune in the same studio the same month, but it was The Kingsmen's version that was destined for greatness. The building is no longer used as a studio, but a plaque commemorates its importance.

Lynyrd Skynyrd
Robert E. Lee High School
1200 South McDuff Avenue
Jacksonville, Florida

This was where the unpopular gym teacher Leonard Skinner taught— the hardass eventually made famous when some students changed the name of their band from "My Backyard" to "Lynyrd Skynyrd" in honor of him.

Martin, Dean/Rolling Stones
The Hollywood Palace • 1735 Vine Street • Hollywood, California
213-462-3000

Opened in 1927, the Hollywood Palace is where Groucho Marx filmed his TV quiz series *You Bet Your Life*. It was also the site of the *Merv Griffin Show*, and for a TV variety show called, appropriately enough, *The Hollywood Palace* (hosted by Jimmy Durante) which showcased a weekly cavalcade of superstars. But it was also here that Dean Martin insulted The Rolling Stones on their first American national TV appearance. After the Stones played, a guy in a suit was

shown bouncing on a trampoline. Martin slurred, "This is the father of the Rolling Stones. He's been trying to kill himself ever since."

Max's Kansas City
213 Park Avenue South (between 17th and 18th off Union Square)
New York, New York

"Max's Kansas City was the exact spot where Pop Art and Pop Life came together in the 1960s." So said Andy Warhol, and he should know, because he held court here for many years. From the mid-'60s through the end of the '70s, this is where much of New York City's music and artistic culture developed. The house band for a time was the Velvet Underground, followed by the New York Dolls. Aerosmith was discovered here. Bruce Springsteen opened for Bob Marley here.

"Upstairs" at Max's was the place to be in the glitter-packed early '70s, hanging out with Alice Cooper, Todd Rundgren, Mick Jagger, Iggy Pop, David Bowie, and the rest of the then-avant-garde establishment. Today, sadly it's a gourmet market.

Mayfield, Curtis
Wingate Field • Winthrop Street and Brooklyn Avenue • East Flatbush
Brooklyn, New York

On August 14, 1990, at an outdoor concert at Wingate Field in the East Flatbush section of Brooklyn, legendary soul artist Curtis Mayfield was struck and paralyzed from the neck down by a lighting scaffold that fell during a windstorm. He released a new album in 1996 (*New World Order*) on which he only sang given that he could no longer play guitar. Sadly, he died on December 26, 1999. Mayfield is remembered for such hits as "It's All Right," "People Get Ready," and "Freddie's Dead," to name a few.

Milli Vanilli
Le Mondrian Hotel • 8440 Sunset Boulevard • West Hollywood, California
800-525-8029

This is where one of the lead "singers" for the pop duo Milli Vanilli tried to kill himself in 1991. The dreadlocked pair had won the Grammy Award for Best New Artist of 1989, but the statue was taken away from them after it was discovered that the two singers hadn't sung at all on their debut item: they had only lip-synched the songs.

One member of the duo, Rob Pilatus (from Germany), took an overdose of pills, slashed his wrists, and tried to jump out of the ninth-floor window of this hotel before the police finally stopped him. Five years later, on North Van Ness Street in Hollywood, Pilatus was arrested on charges of attempted burglary and making terrorist threats after he first tried to steal a car and then tried to break into a man's home. His attempt failed when the victim hit Pilatus over the head with a baseball bat. On April 3, 1998, Pilatus was found dead of an apparent overdose in a Frankfurt, Germany hotel room.

Mitchell, Joni
Garden of Allah • Southwest corner of Sunset and Crescent Heights
Hollywood, California

"They paved paradise, and put up a parking lot," sang Joni Mitchell wistfully about the end of the Garden of Allah, Hollywood's famed apartment-hotel that welcomed transient show business guests from 1935–1955. It was actually a collection of private bungalows, frequented by stars such as Errol Flynn,

Clark Gable, Greta Garbo, W.C. Fields, Humphrey Bogart, F. Scott Fitzgerald, the Marx Brothers, and Orson Welles.

Legend has it that Tallulah Bankhead swam naked in the pool here, and Marilyn Monroe was discovered here sipping a Coke next to that same swimming pool. Today, the site contains a modern strip mall. Until recently, the bank at the mall had a model of the hotel complex in a glass case, but the bank changed names and the model is now gone.

Moon, Keith
Stage 43 • CBS Television City • 7800 Beverly Boulevard
Los Angeles, California • 323-575-2458

On September 15, 1967, Keith Moon affixed explosives in his drums for The Who's appearance on the Smothers Brothers Comedy Hour. At the end of their second song (lip-synching to a live version of "My Generation"), Moon ignited his drums, causing a ferocious explosion which is what originally impaired guitarist Pete Townsend's hearing. Game shows use the stage today.

Monterey Pop Festival
Monterey County Fairgrounds • 2004 Fairgrounds Road (off Fremont Street, near Highway 1) • Monterey, California • 831-372-5863

Held in Monterey, California on June 16–18, 1967, the Monterey Pop Festival was the first commercial American rock festival. Dunhill Records executive Lou Adler and John Phillips of the Mamas and the Papas organized the festival around the concept of the successful Monterey Jazz Festival and staged it at that festival's site.

Featuring the first major American appearances of Jimi Hendrix and the Who, it also introduced Janis Joplin to a large audience and featured performances by the Jefferson Airplane, the Grateful Dead, the Byrds, Canned Heat, Buffalo Springfield, Otis Redding, Ravi Shankar, and many others.

Arguably the most famous moment of the festival, (and one of the most memorable in rock and roll history) was when Hendrix lit his guitar on fire before smashing it at the climax of "Wild Thing." The stage where the show took place has hardly changed at all since then. At the exact spot where Hendrix knelt and "sacrificed" his guitar, "Jimi Hendrix 1967" has been scrawled into the wood floor.

Interestingly, it was here that Mickey Dolenz of the Monkees (a huge commercial act at the time) decided to take the generally unknown Hendrix on the road as the Monkees' opening act. Several shows into the tour however, everyone soon realized that Hendrix was not a good fit for the teenybopper audience and he left the tour.

Morrison, Jim
Alta Cienega Motel • 1005 N. La Cienega Avenue
West Hollywood, California • 310-652-5797

Jim Morrison kept a room here from 1968–1970, as the sign on Room 32 attests. Inside the tiny space, fans from all over the world have scrawled messages upon the wall. Inside the motel office, an interview with Morrison that was conducted within that very room hangs on the wall.

Motown
2648 West Grand Boulevard • Detroit, Michigan • 313-875-2264

The Motown sound was born in this old brick house, which is now home to a museum. Marvin Gaye, Smokey Robinson, Diana Ross and the Supremes, Stevie Wonder, the Jackson Five—they all got their starts here under the orchestration of Motown Records Svengali Berry Gordy, Jr. Today, this declared Michigan historic site looks just like it did in the early 1960s. You can see sheet music and the actual music studio equipment they used, including the piano used by all the greats. Photographs and gold records adorn the walls, and original costumes are also on display.

MTV
Unitel Video • 515 West 57th Street • New York, New York

This was where MTV was launched on August 1, 1981. Today, they've moved downtown a bit to 1515 Broadway, where their state-of-the-art, "open-faced" complex is visible from all over Times Square.

New York Dolls
Gem Spa • 131 Second Avenue • New York, New York • 212-995-1866

Open 24 hours every day of the year, the Gem Spa newsstand has been in business for nearly 70 years. In addition to making what many New Yorkers consider to be the world's best egg cream, this is also where the legendary New York Dolls posed for the back cover of their first album in 1973 (the record was produced by Todd Rundgren). David Johansen, Johnny Thunders, and the rest of the Dolls returned for a follow-up shoot in 1977, after the original group had dissolved. The Gem Spa has since closed.

Nirvana

Maria's Hair Design
107 S. M Street • Aberdeen, Washington

Maria's Hair Design is the shop owned by Nirvana bassist Krist Novoselic's mom, and it's where Krist and Kurt Cobain practiced many a night during the early days of Nirvana.

Morrison Riverfront Park
Sargent Boulevard • Aberdeen, Washington

Riverfront Park is the site of the much publicized fan vigil the night of Kurt Cobain's death.

Seafirst Bank Building
Market Street and Broadway • Aberdeen, Washington

On July 23, 1985, Kurt Cobain was arrested for vandalism when he was caught writing "Ain'T goT no how waTchamacalliT" on the alley wall behind this bank (though today it's a Bank of America).

Osbourne, Ozzy

The Alamo
300 Alamo Plaza • San Antonio, Texas • 210-225-1391

We know of Ozzy's exploits of biting the head off of bats and pigeons, but this hallowed American landmark is the scene of another classic Ozzy moment back in the early 1980s. It was here where, after donning one of his wife's dresses, he wandered out in a drunken state and relieved himself in public. (Contrary to myth, not on the actual Alamo wall, but on a monument called the Cenotaph in Alamo Plaza, across the street from the landmark.) Ozzy was arrested and banned from appearing in the city.

Epic Records
Century Park East and Little Santa Monica Boulevard
Los Angeles, California

In May of 1981, a drunk Ozzy Osbourne bit the head off of a live dove during a promotional visit to the Epic Records building. He was promptly banned from ever re-entering the building and proceeded to release an album under the Epic label, *The Blizzard of Oz*, that would become a triple platinum hit.

Veterans Memorial Auditorium
833 5th Avenue • Des Moines, Iowa • 515-242-2946

During the 1981–82 "Blizzard of Oz" tour, rocker Ozzy Osbourne would bite the heads off of rubber bats as part of his show. Fans got into the act, and throughout the course of the tour would throw their own offerings onstage. On January 20, 1982, someone tossed a very real, very stunned bat on to the stage. Oz, thinking it was a rubber prop, chomped the head off it and thus sealed his own legend as a satanic, ritualistic animal killer. He was taken to the hospital right after the show and checked for rabies.

Pandora's Box

Sunset Boulevard and Crescent Heights • Hollywood, California

It was the tearing down of this club in 1966 that helped fuel the Sunset Strip riots. During late 1966, Pandora's Box was a center of controversy. One of the few underage clubs of its day, it became a flashpoint of the era as defiant teenagers got into fights with cops who began handing out curfew violations. These riots are what inspired the Buffalo Springfield song "For What It's Worth." The exact location of the club is the island in the middle of Sunset at Crescent Heights.

Perkins, Carl

Route 13 (between Dover and Woodside, about one mile north of Woodside) • Dover, Delaware

Carl Perkins was traveling on March 2, 1956 from Memphis to appear on Perry Como's TV show in New York when, at about 6:40 A.M. after an all-night drive, the car he and his band were driving struck the rear of a truck heading in the same direction. Perkins was riding the huge success of "Blue Suede Shoes" at the time—it would make it to number two on the charts.

The driver of the truck was killed in the wreck and Perkins' brother Jay died later. His career never recovered from the six months he had to spend in the hospital recuperating, and his legend remains one who might have been.

Presley, Elvis

Baptist Memorial Hospital

899 Madison Avenue • Memphis, Tennessee

Elvis had checked in and out of here for various ailments over the years, but he was pronounced dead here in August 1977. (Lisa Marie Presley was born here in February of 1968.) The hospital was recently torn down.

Best Western Trade Winds Courtyard Inn

2128 Gary Boulevard
Clinton, Oklahoma
580-323-2610

Elvis stayed at this hotel four times back in the 1960s, and today his room (number 215) is maintained as a mini shrine with memorabilia and time-period furnishings. Elvis and his entourage liked it here because it was a convenient stopover when driving from Memphis to Las Vegas.

Birthplace

306 Elvis Presley Drive • Tupelo, Mississippi • 662-841-1245

Elvis Presley was born here in this modest two-story house on January 8, 1935. Now designated a Mississippi historic landmark, the Elvis Presley birthplace has been restored to the period when Elvis lived there. It is located in Elvis Presley Park, which also includes the Elvis Presley Museum, Memorial Chapel, Gift Shop, and a life-size statue of "Elvis at 13." (The Park offers complete recreation facilities for picnics and community events.)

Civic Arena

66 Mario Lemieux Place • Pittsburgh, Pennsylvania

When it first opened in 1961, the Mellon Arena was known as the Civic Arena. (In December of 1999, the resident Pittsburgh Penguins signed an $18 million, 10-year agreement to rename the Civic Arena the Mellon Arena, after the Pittsburgh-based bank.) Over the years The Beatles played here and part of The Doors' *Absolutely Live* was recorded here, but it's also where Elvis played his very last New Year's Eve show in 1976. His dad Vernon and daughter Lisa Marie were watching that night, and it's thought to be one of Presley's most memorable shows in the last year or so of his life.

De Neve Park
Beverly Glen Boulevard (one block north of Sunset Boulevard)
Los Angeles, California

Elvis Presley's Southern California life in the early to mid-1960s was a hectic tangle of recording, movies, and television. To help unwind on the weekends, Elvis and his entourage would organize spirited touch football games in De Neve Park, not far from where he lived in Bel Air. Their favorite opponent was pop singer and television star Ricky Nelson and his band, although other celebrities—including Pat Boone and Max Baer, Jr.—also took part in the games.

Ellis Auditorium
Main Street and Poplar Avenue • Memphis, Tennessee

This was Memphis' most important concert hall during Elvis' teenage years. Here, the Blackwood Brothers Gospel Quartet organized Saturday night gospel music shows or "sings" that Elvis would often attend. Elvis' pals and bandmates James Blackwood and J. D. Sumner remember Elvis being allowed to enter for free, because he could not always afford the 50 cent admission.

Elvis' Marriage to Priscilla
Aladdin Hotel • 3667 South Las Vegas Boulevard • Las Vegas, Nevada
800-851-1703

On May 1, 1967, Elvis Presley (then 32) married Priscilla Anne Beaulieu (then 21) at Milton Prell's Aladdin Hotel. The couple was wed in a quiet ceremony (attended by a few relatives and close friends) in Prell's suite at the Aladdin at 9:00 A.M. Following the ceremony, an elaborate banquet was held just below the hotel's casino. An estimated 100 people attended the reception, including Mr. and Mrs. Milton Prell and State Supreme Court Justice David Zenoff, who had performed the eight-minute ceremony. Guests dined on ham, eggs, Southern fried chicken, oysters Rockefeller, roast suckling pig, poached and candied salmon, lobster, eggs minnette, and champagne.

Elvis Meets the Beatles
565 Perugia Way • Beverly Hills, California

The original house is gone, but this was the site where, on August 27, 1965, Elvis Presley first met the Beatles. The Fab Four were in town to play the Hollywood Bowl, and it has been reported that the meeting was uncomfortable—the Beatles were in awe and fawned a bit; Elvis didn't care for their music.

Elvis and Priscilla Honeymoon
1350 Ladera Circle • Palm Springs, California • 760-322-1192

On September 16, 1966, Elvis leased this estate in Palm Springs, California for one year for $21,000. The futuristic house is famous today as being the place where, on May 1, 1967, Elvis and Priscilla Presley spent their wedding night. Recently restored, the estate is open for tours, not to mention weddings, corporate meetings, and—wouldn't you know—honeymoons.

First Album
Fort Homer W. Hesterly Armory • 510 North Howard Avenue
Tampa, Florida

The cover of the very first Elvis album was shot here during a concert on May 8, 1955 by William S. Randolph. Interestingly, its art direction would later inspire the cover of the Clash album, *London Calling*.

First Guitar
Tupelo Hardware Store • 114 West Main Street • Tupelo, Mississippi

Elvis fans often consider Tupelo Hardware the second most important

x

Presley site in Tupelo, after his birthplace. It was here that Gladys Presley bought her son his very first guitar. The business was founded by George H. Booth in 1926, and is still owned and managed by the family's third generation under the leadership of George H. Booth II.

Fool's Gold Loaf
4490 East Virginia Avenue • Glendale, Colorado

On the night of February 1, 1976, Elvis Presley was at Graceland hosting Captain Jerry Kennedy, a member of the Denver police force, and Ron Pietrafeso, who was in charge of Colorado's Strike Force Against Crime. Talking with the guys, Elvis began to crave a Denver-area specialty he had indulged in before: the Fool's Gold Loaf.

He'd had it just once, when he'd visited a restaurant called the Colorado Gold Mine Company Steakhouse in Glendale, a suburb of Denver. It was named this for its exorbitant price—$49.95—and Elvis wanted one that night. They hopped into the King's stretch Mercedes along with a couple of Elvis' buddies, drove to the Memphis airport, and hopped aboard Elvis' jet, the *Lisa Marie* (named after his daughter). Next stop, Denver's Stapleton Airport!

The Colorado Gold Mine Company Steakhouse frantically prepared their specialty of the house (22 orders of it, in fact) and had it waiting on the tarmac when the *Lisa Marie* landed a couple of hours later. (A case of Perrier and a case of champagne went with the sandwiches, as ordered.) Elvis and crew landed at 1:40 A.M. at Stapleton Airport and taxied to a private hangar. The owner of the restaurant served them personally and for two hours the entourage and Elvis feasted on the Fool's Gold.

And just what exactly is Fool's Gold Loaf? An entire loaf of bread is warmed and then hollowed out. The loaf is then stuffed with peanut butter and jelly. Lastly, a pound of lean bacon fills the belly of the loaf. Served hot, supposedly the serving size was one loaf per person! Today, the restaurant at this site that prepared the Fool's Gold Loaf is gone, replaced by a construction company, but the memory lingers on.

Graceland

3734 Elvis Presley Boulevard • Memphis, Tennessee • 1-800-238-2000

Where the King lived . . . and died. Even though you're not allowed to see the bathroom where it all ended, you can tour the mansion (which even houses the famous pink Cadillac.) Located on 14 acres, it features a pool room, "jungle room," trophy building, and much more. Don't forget to pay respects in the Meditation Garden. (In 1976, it was reported that

Bruce Springsteen was escorted away by Graceland security guards after trying to climb over the main gates and meet Elvis, who was still alive at the time.)

The Haircut

Fort Chaffee • Highway 22 • Several miles east of Fort Smith, Arkansas
479-452-4554

In 1958, Elvis Presley was inducted into the U.S. army. He began his basic training at Fort Chaffee, and this is where he received, on March 25, what may be the most famous haircut in history—referred to as "The haircut that shook the world." In a mere few minutes, the famous, slicked-back coif had given way to a standard-issue Army buzz cut.

Built in 1941, this 72,000-acre military base was the training site for thousands of troops heading overseas during World War II. Today, several memorial plaques honor World War II units formed here. (No longer a working base, the area of the camp that includes the barracks facilities is now part of the 7,000 acres being developed for commercial, residential, and industrial purposes known as Chaffee Crossing.)

The building where he got the haircut (where the barber shop was located), still stands. It is building #803. Just a stone's throw away is building #823, which was

the barracks where Elvis stayed. It is still possible to view the buildings close up, but you should call for an appointment. Fort Chaffee was also used in the movies *Biloxi Blues* and *A Soldier's Story*.

Hampton Coliseum
1000 Coliseum Drive • Hampton, Virginia • 757-838-5650

This famous arena has hosted everyone from the Rolling Stones to Metallica to Elvis Presley. But only Elvis has a special door. Not many know about the "Elvis Door," but it really exists. It was specially cut out of the Coliseum during one of the King's 1970s appearances so Elvis could go directly from his dressing room to his limo. Elvis' third and final visit to the Coliseum occurred on July 31 and August 1, 1976. Also, the documentary *Elvis on Tour* was filmed in the building during his 1972 appearances. Today, Elvis' shows here are commemorated on a bronze plaque located on the south concourse level of the Coliseum.

Humes High School
659 North Manassas Street
Memphis, Tennessee

Elvis graduated from this high school in 1953. Today, there is a mini Elvis museum, and the school auditorium is now dedicated to him.

Kaiser Arena
10 Tenth Street • Oakland, California • 510-238-7765

Elvis Presley's first western swings included a big show in Oakland on June 3, 1956. It took place at the Auditorium Arena (now called the Henry J. Kaiser Arena). Tickets cost just $2.50. When he returned to the arena on October 27, 1957, prices had gone up a bit ($2.75–$3.75). Elvis' last East Bay performance took place at the Oakland (now McAfee) Coliseum on

November 11, 1972, where he performed a memorable greatest hits set for more than 14,000 fans.

Lansky Brothers Clothing Store
126 Beale Street • Memphis, Tennessee

This shop (which closed in 1990) billed itself as "Outfitter to the King" for years, as it was where Elvis bought many on-and offstage outfits. On the building's west wall is a mural dedicated to Memphis history, in which Elvis features prominently.

Libertyland
940 Early Maxwell Boulevard • Memphis, Tennessee

After he became famous, Elvis would sometimes rent out this entire amusement park so he could throw parties and ride the Zippin' Pippin roller coaster. (Back then it was called the Fairgrounds Amusement Park.)

Loew's State Theater
152 South Main Street • Memphis, Tennessee

Elvis worked here as an usher when he was 15, until he was fired for fighting with another usher. Seven years later, when *Jailhouse Rock* premiered here, Elvis came back and posed for pictures while holding his old usher's uniform. The Loew's State Theater had opened in 1925, and closed in 1964. It was demolished in 1971.

Market Square Arena
300 East Market Street • Indianapolis, Indiana

Elvis Presley gave his last concert at Market Square Arena on June 26, 1977. Twenty-five years later, a commemorative plaque was placed here (the marker is in a gravel parking lot where the arena stood before being demolished). A time capsule encased within holds Presley memorabilia, including a scarf of Presley's and a bootlegged recording of one of his last shows. A bronze plaque reading "Ladies and Gentlemen, Elvis has left the building" sits atop a stone column, just as Elvis' show announcer Al Dvorin would say at the end of each of Presley's shows.

Mississippi-Alabama Fairground
Mulberry Alley off West Mains Street • Tupelo, Mississippi

This now rundown fairground is where Elvis Presley made his first public performance on October 3, 1945, after being entered in a talent contest by one of his teachers (the 10-year-old Elvis sang a tune called "Old Shep" and won five dollars). Eleven years later, he played the same spot, only by this time he'd become an international star and was promoting his first film, *The Reno Brothers* (later renamed *Love Me Tender*.)

Radio Recorders
7000 Santa Monica Boulevard
Hollywood, California

Founded in 1933 as a studio called Radio Recorders (now Explosive Records), it was here in the 1950s that Elvis recorded "Jailhouse Rock," "All Shook Up," "Loving You," and "Teddy Bear" (among others). Among the hundreds of other hits recorded here over the years were Sam Cooke's "You Send Me" and Bobby Darin's "Mac the Knife."

RCA Studios
55 East 24th Street • New York, New York

It now houses classrooms, but in 1956 you could find RCA's Studio "A" in this building, and it was here that Elvis Presley cut three of his most timeless singles: "Hound Dog," "Don't Be Cruel," and "Blue Suede Shoes."

Sun Studio
706 Union Avenue • Memphis, Tennessee • 800-441-6249

Opened in 1950 by a local radio station engineer named Sam Phillips, some of the most legendary moments in rock 'n' roll history were captured at this tiny Memphis studio, and many artifacts from over the years remain here today in this living music museum—including Elvis Presley's microphone and Johnny Cash's dollar-strung guitar.

Phillips started Sun Records in 1952; two years later, a nervous local teenager came in to lay down a few vocal tracks. The date was July 5, 1954. "It was just an audition," remembers Scotty Moore, the country guitarist brought in to back up a green Elvis Presley for his Sun Records tryout. Near the end of the day, Presley broke into an obscure blues tune, "That's All Right," and history was made.

Eventually, Phillips sold his discovery's contract to R.C.A. for $40,000, a huge sum at the time. A few years before Elvis, a local DJ named Ike Turner produced a session at Sun with teenager Jackie Brenston. Their 1951 version of "Rocket 88" is considered by many to be the first genuine rock 'n' roll record. And don't forget that Jerry Lee Lewis recorded "Great Balls of Fire" and "Whole Lotta Shakin' Goin' On" at Sun.

The studio was restored with Sam Phillips' help, and in 1987 opened its doors as both a tourist attraction and a working recording studio. Ringo Starr, Def Leppard, John Fogerty, Tom Petty, Paul Simon, Bonnie Raitt, U2, and Matchbox 20 are only some of the recent music greats who have come to record at Sun Studio since it reopened. In the studio's own words: "Today, Sun Studio carries on the Rock N' Roll Revolution begun here in 1950, by providing a place where a kid with a guitar case full of dreams can stand in the footsteps of giants and carve out a legend." Tours are given on a daily basis.

"Riot" House

Hyatt on Sunset • 8401 Sunset Boulevard • West Hollywood, California
323-656-1234

When British bands first invaded this hotel in the 1960s, it was simply known as the Continental Hyatt House. It didn't take long before the place picked up a more appropriate nickname: the "Riot House." Led Zeppelin supposedly had the most fun at the hotel, riding Harleys down the hallways, parading groupies in and out, and tossing TVs out of windows. Room 1015 bares the distinction of being where Rolling Stone Keith Richards mooned the world, and in 1986, Guns and Roses frontman Axl Rose tossed sizzling steaks to fans below, after the fire department showed up to halt his balcony barbecue. Now renovated, the hotel still has a sense of what makes it famous, as evidenced by the poster of a long-haired musician posted at the front desk. It says: "Be kind to this customer. He may just have sold a million records."

Rock 'n' Roll Festivals

Atlantic City Pop Festival

Atlantic City Racetrack • 4501 Black Horse Pike
Mays Landing, New Jersey • 609-641-2190

From August 1–3, 1969, 110,000 people attended this festival at the Atlantic City Racetrack—a sort of tune up for Woodstock. Thirty or so bands played, many of whom then headed up to play Woodstock the next week. The show featured (among others) Joan Baez, Arlo Guthrie, Tim Harden, Richie Havens, Ravi Shankar, Sweetwater, Canned Heat, Creedence Clearwater Revival, The Grateful Dead, The Jefferson Airplane, Mountain, The Who, The Band, Blood Sweat & Tears, Joe Cocker, Crosby Stills & Nash, Santana, Jimi Hendrix, Ten Years After, Johnny Winter, and Sha Na Na.

Atlanta Pop Festival
Atlanta Motor Speedway
1500 Highway 41 • Byron, Georgia

From July 3-5, 1970, here in the tiny central Georgia town of Byron (10 miles south of Macon), smack in the middle of a pecan grove (and on what was then known as the Middle Georgia Raceway) somewhere be-tween 350,000 to 500,000 people witnessed the second annual Atlanta International Pop Festival. Exactly like Woodstock the previous summer (but with more people), the event was promoted as "three days of peace, love, and music." On the bill were Jimi Hendrix, the Allman Brothers, Jethro Tull, B.B. King, Ravi Shankar, 10 Years After, Johnny Winter, John Sebastian, and others. (Tickets for the music festival were $14.)

Devonshire Downs Racetrack
Devonshire Street just west of Zelzah Avenue • Northridge, California

This site, a former racetrack, is probably best known for hosting the famed Newport '69 music festival from June 20-22. Despite the name "Newport," the show (which drew about 150,000 fans) actually took place out in the San Fernando Valley. On the bill were Jethro Tull, Jimi Hendrix, The Animals, Led Zeppelin, Creedence Clearwater Revival, The Chambers Brothers, Johnny Winters, the Young Rascals, Booker T. & MG's, Three Dog Night, The Byrds, The Grassroots, Marvin Gaye, and Mother Earth. The site is now a shopping center.

Festival for Peace
Shea Stadium • 123-01 Roosevelt Avenue • Flushing, New York

The Summer Festival for Peace was held here on August 5, 1970, and the scorching hot weather may have played a part in why the festival drew an undersized crowd. However, those in attendance were treated to per-formances by Jimi Hendrix, Janis Joplin, Poco, Steppenwolf, James Gang, Janis Joplin, The Rascals, Johnny Winter, Ten Wheel Drive, Tom Paxton,

Dionne Warwick, Paul Simon, and several others. An under-publicized, under-documented event, it was one of the more diverse lineups featured during the spate of music festivals held in the wake of Woodstock.

Mount Pocono Festival
Pocono International Speedway • Long Pond, Pennsylvania

Held July 8–9, 1972, over 200,000 fans attended this muddy two-day festival which featured (among others) Emerson, Lake and Palmer, Humble Pie, Three Dog Night, Rod Stewart & The Faces, Mother Night, Cactus, Edgar Winter, The J. Geils Band, and Black Sabbath. The festival was marred on Saturday by a three-hour rain delay.

Newport Pop Festival
Orange County Fairgrounds • 88 Fair Avenue • Costa Mesa, California

On August 4–5, 1968, over 140,000 pre-Woodstock fans gathered here to watch (among others) Tiny Tim, The Jefferson Airplane, Country Joe and the Fish, The Grateful Dead, The Chambers Brothers, Charles Lloyd, James Cotton Blues Band, Quicksilver Messenger Service, The Byrds, Alice Cooper, Steppenwolf, Sonny and Cher, Canned Heat, Electric Flag, Butterfield Blues Band, Eric Burdon and the Animals, Blue Cheer, Iron Butterfly, Illinois Speed Press, and Things To Come. Admission was just $5.50 per day and the festival was produced by "Humble" Harvey Miller, a top Los Angeles disk jockey. The site still hosts the popular Orange County Fair each year.

Texas International Pop Festival
Dallas International Motor Speedway • Lewisville, Texas

This track, which closed down in 1973, was located on Interstate 35 East just north of Dallas. Over Labor Day weekend, 1969, (just two weeks after

Woodstock) 120,000 fans converged on the small town of Lewisville for the Texas Pop Festival. They were treated to performances by a diverse range of artists including B.B. King, Canned Heat, Chicago, Delaney & Bonnie & Friends, Freddie King, Grand Funk Railroad, Herbie Mann, Incredible String Band, James Cotton Blues Band, Janis Joplin, Johnny Winter, Led Zeppelin, The Nazz, The Quarry, Rotary Connection, Sam & Dave, Santana, Shiva's Headband, Sly & the Family Stone, Space Opera, Spirit, Sweetwater, Ten Years After, and Tony Joe White.

Toronto Rock and Roll Revival
Varsity Stadium • 277 Bloor Street West • Toronto, Canada

According to Ringo Starr, it was Lennon's first-ever solo performance—the famed Plastic Ono Band concert here at Toronto's Varsity Stadium on September 13, 1969—that proved to be the end of the Beatles' career. With the exception of the famous rooftop concert at Apple Headquarters, this was Lennon's first live appearance since 1966. After the concert, Lennon returned to London with his mind made up to quit. Starr is quoted as saying "After (John Lennon's) Plastic Ono Band's debut in Toronto we had a meeting in Saville Row where John finally brought it to a head. He said: 'Well, that's it lads, let's end it.'"

The show, billed as The Toronto Rock and Roll Revival, also featured The Doors, Chuck Berry, Little Richard, Bo Diddley, Alice Cooper, and others, and for Lennon, resulted in the album *Live Peace in Toronto* and the single "Cold Turkey." The stadium has since been torn down, but the field remains.

Rolling Stones

Black and Blue
Sanibel Island Beach • Sanibel Island, Florida

In February 1976, the Rolling Stones flew here to be photographed by famed fashion photographer Hiro for their album *Black and Blue*. It was the first release that new member Ron Wood played on officially.

Fordyce, Arkansas

(Near 100 S. Main Street) • Fordyce (population about 5,000) is located at the intersection of two U.S. Highways, 79 and 167, and State Highway 8.

On July 5, 1975, police pulled over a rented Chevy after the car swerved on the roadway. Among the car's occupants were guitarists Keith Richards and Ron Wood of the Rolling Stones. Richards was later charged with reckless driving and possession of a knife and his bodyguard Fred Sessler was charged with possession of a controlled substance. (Richards was released on $160 bail and later paid a fine.) Earlier that day the group had dined at the 4-Dice Restaurant in Fordyce.

Fort Harrison Hotel

210 South Fort Harrison Avenue • Clearwater, Florida

The Rolling Stones played to 3,000 teenagers at Jack Russell Stadium in May, 1965, performing only four songs before the crowd turned rowdy and the police stepped in, ending the show. That night, Keith Richards awoke in his room at the Jack Tar Harrison Hotel (today it's the Fort Harrison) with the opening guitar riff of "Satisfaction" in his head. He grabbed his guitar, got the notes on tape, and went back to sleep. The next day, he woke and worked with Mick Jagger on the rest of the song by the hotel pool. Today, the building is owned by the Church of Scientology.

Gosman's Dock

500 West Lake Drive • Montauk, New York • 631-668-5330

Gosman's Dock was founded in 1943 and has since become a legend out on the eastern tip of Long Island, a true seafood lover's paradise. It's no

wonder Mick Jagger came here to eat back in the summer of 1975 while the Rolling Stones rehearsed for their upcoming "Tour of the Americas" at Andy Warhol's nearby Montauk compound. But Jagger got a little more than he bargained for. On May 17, 1975, upon leaving the restaurant, the head Stone inadvertently put his hand through the plate-glass door, opening a huge gash on his wrist. The wound required 20 stitches but, thankfully, did not end up delaying the June 1 start of the tour.

Harbour Castle Westin
1 Harbour Square • Toronto, Canada • 416-869-1600

On February 27, 1977, Royal Canadian Mounted Police crashed into Suite 2223 in this hotel and found five grams of cocaine, 22 grams of heroin, and Keith Richards, who was promptly arrested. After a six-month court battle, stunningly, Richards got off with a slap on the wrist (the Stones were made to play a charity show in Toronto to benefit the blind). The arrest followed club gigs at the El Mocambo, where the Stones had recorded portions of their 1977 concert album *Love You Live*. The El Mocambo Club is located at 494 Spadina Avenue (416-968-2001).

"Have You Seen Your Mother Baby"
24th Street, between Park Avenue South and Lexington Avenue
New York, New York

In 1966 the Rolling Stones released the hit single, "Have You Seen Your Mother Baby (Standing in the Shadow)." To promote it they created an outrageous photo featuring the band in full drag. It was shot by renowned photographer Jerry Schatzberg at this location, and the preparation for the photo took place at Schatzberg's studio, located at 333 Park Avenue South.

"Memory Motel"
692 Montauk Highway
Montauk (Long Island),
New York • 631-668-2702

The Memory Motel is a small, 13-room motel and bar immortalized by the Rolling Stones in the pretty ballad of the same name (which appeared on the band's 1976 album *Black and Blue*). During the mid-1970s, the Rolling Stones—and in particular Mick Jagger—were regulars out on the remote reaches of Montauk, hanging out with artist Andy Warhol at his nearby compound, among other places.

Jagger supposedly spent time at the motel because it had a pool table and a decent jukebox, and one night while here he reputedly was inspired to write the beautiful song about "Hannah, a honey of a girl," and where they spent "a lonely night at the Memory Motel." (Rumor has it he actually wrote part of the tune at the bar.)

Muscle Shoals Recording Studios
3614 Jackson Highway • Sheffield, Alabama

In the 1970 film *Gimme Shelter*, the Rolling Stones are seen recording "Brown Sugar" and "Wild Horses" in this recording studio. The building was then used to sell used refrigerators and stoves but today, thankfully, it's become a museum dedicated to the great music created within the building.

Press Conference
One Fifth Avenue • New York, New York

On May 1, 1975, there was a press conference scheduled at the restaurant called Feathers of Fifth Avenue to announce the Stones' "Tour of the Americas." Professor Irwin Corey, the famous American comedian, was the M.C. Instead, a flatbed truck with the band on top playing "Brown Sugar" came down Fifth Avenue, stopping in front of the hotel. It was so exciting that everybody ran out into the street to watch. The Stones then carried on down the road, tossing out leaflets with tour dates. When they finished the song, they pulled away in their truck, turned the corner, jumped into limos, and were gone.

RCA Records
6363 Sunset Boulevard • Hollywood, California

From the early 1960s through the early 1990s, some of the most famous records of all time were recorded in this building. Elvis was here in the '70s, The Monkees recorded here, the Jefferson Airplane, etc. But the band that perhaps did the most damage was the Rolling Stones, who recorded (among other songs) "Satisfaction," "Paint it Black," "19th Nervous Breakdown," and "Let's Spend the Night Together" at this location. Today, the building houses the Los Angeles Film School.

Theodore Francis Green State Airport
2000 Post Road • Warwick, Rhode Island • 401-737-4000

On July 19, 1972, Mick Jagger, Keith Richards, and three members of the Rolling Stones entourage were arrested in Warwick, Rhode Island, on charges of assault and obstructing police. The five were involved in a scuffle with a photographer as they made their way through the small airport. They pleaded guilty and were released, but the incident caused a four-hour delay of their concert in Boston that night (which, by many accounts, was one of the greatest shows they've ever played).

"Waiting on a Friend"
132 1st Avenue • New York, New York

At one time this bar was called the St. Marks Bar & Grill, and in the 1981 video for their hit, "Waiting on a Friend," Mick Jagger and Keith Richards met the rest of the Rolling Stones here (after Mick waited for Keith on the stoop of the building seen on the cover of Led Zeppelin's *Physical Graffiti* album). The band was filmed performing in this tiny space for the rest of the day, and for years the bar sold T-shirts commemorating the event.

Saturday Night Fever
Criteria studios • 1755 NE 149th Street • Miami, Florida

This Miami studio has recorded many classic songs, like James Brown's "I Feel Good," Derek & the Dominoes' "Layla," and Brook Benton's "Rainy Night in Georgia." But it was the Bee Gee's *Saturday Night Fever*, also recorded here, that became one of the biggest selling records in history.

The Sex Pistols
Great Southeast Music Hall and Emporium • 3871 Peachtree Road NE
Brookhaven, Georgia

It's no longer there, but this one-time shopping center punk club near Atlanta is where the Sex Pistols played their first American show of their first (and only) American tour on January 5, 1978. It's now the site of the Lindbergh Plaza Shopping Center. The band stayed at the nearby Squire Inn, now called the La Quinta Inn, at 2115 Piedmont.

Simon and Garfunkel
P.S. 164 • 77th Avenue and 137th Street • Forest Hills, New York

When they were both about nine, Paul Simon and Art Garfunkel first met at this public school when they appeared together in a production of *Alice in Wonderland* (Paul was the White Rabbit; Art the Cheshire Cat). In their early teens, they were in a doo-wop group called the Sparks, and they soon became a duo (originally calling themselves "Tom and Jerry"). You know what happened after that.

Soulsville, USA
STAX Records • 870 East McLemore Avenue • Memphis, Tennessee
901-946-2535

Stax Records is critical in American music history as it is one of the most popular soul music record labels ever formed—second only to Motown in sales and influence but first in gritty, raw, stripped-down soul music. In 15 years, Stax placed over 167 hit songs in the Top 100 on the pop charts and an astounding 243 hits in the Top 100 R & B charts.

Stax launched the careers of major pop soul stars Otis Redding, Sam & Dave, Carla & Rufus Thomas, Booker T. & the MGs, and '70s soul superstar Isaac Hayes, and Stax songs have become part of the pop music vernacular. "Green Onions," "Sittin' on the Dock of the Bay," "Soul Man," "I'll Take You There," "Hold On, I'm Comin'," and "Theme from Shaft" are classic radio staples that are instantly recognizable by music fans and casual listeners alike. Though the original building is gone, STAX has been rebuilt on its original site and was re-opened in 2003 as a museum/recording studio.

Springsteen, Bruce

Civic Center
143 West 4th Street • St. Paul, Minnesota • 612-224-7403

Bruce Springsteen kicked off his massive "Born in the U.S.A." tour here at this 18,000-seat arena in June of 1984. However, he returned a month later to shoot his "Dancing in the Dark" video, where he pulled a then-unknown Courteney Cox out of the crowd to dance with him.

"E" Street
Belmar, New Jersey (just south of Asbury Park, along the Jersey Shore)

This is the road that gave Springsteen his band's name. A one-way street running for just a few blocks east of Highway 71 (the main route in and out of town), it's where David Sancious' (an early keyboard player in the E Street Band) mom lived.

First New Jersey Home
87 Randolph Street • Freehold, New Jersey

Today the site is a driveway for the St. Rose of Lima church, but until 1957 it was where Springsteen lived with his grandparents, mom, and dad. In a 1987 song called "Walk Like a Man," Springsteen references the home with the line, "By Our Lady of the Roses, we lived in the shadow of the elms."

Freehold High School
Broadway at Robertsville Road • Freehold, New Jersey

It was while attending high school here in 1965 that Bruce Springsteen formed his first band, The Castilles. He graduated from the school two years later, but missed the graduation ceremony after teachers told him his hair was too long.

The Castilles played their first performance in 1965 at the Woodhaven Swim Club in Woodhaven, New Jersey, earning $35. The group closed the show with Springsteen's arrangement of Glenn Miller's "In the Mood." Today, the swim club has become the local YMCA and it's located at 470 East Freehold Road in Freehold.

Harvard Square Theater
10 Church Street • Cambridge, Massachusetts

In 1974, Boston area rock music critic Jon Landau reviewed a concert at the Harvard Square Theater for *The Real Paper*. In his piece, Landau started by bemoaning the lack of passion and soul in the current music scene, and how he had become bored with something that, at one time, had been so vital and relevant. But then he got to writing about the concert, in which a skinny, scruffy, 20-something beach rat from Asbury Park,

New Jersey gave him reason to believe. Landau's words crackle and resonate even today:

"But tonight there is someone I can write of the way I used to write, without reservations of any kind. Last Thursday, at the Harvard Square Theatre, I saw my rock 'n' roll past flash before my eyes. And I saw something else: I saw rock and roll future and its name is Bruce Springsteen. And on a night when I needed to feel young, he made me feel like I was hearing music for the very first time."

Rolling Stone magazine picked-up Landau's quote of seeing the future of rock and roll and the legend of "The Boss" was born. Landau went on to become Springsteen's manager and co-producer; today, the site is a movie theater.

Stone Pony
913 Ocean Avenue • Asbury Park, New Jersey • 732-502-0600

A rock and roll landmark for years, this is the local Jersey bar where Bruce Springsteen's "Glory Days" video was shot. Back in the early '70s, Springsteen played here frequently, as did Southside Johnny and other locals.

The Student Prince
911 Kingsley Street • Asbury Park, New Jersey

It was at this club in the summer of 1971 that Bruce Springsteen first met the man who become one of the foundations of the E Street Band, and the ultimate onstage foil for Springsteen—sax player Clarence Clemons.

Third New Jersey Home
68 South Street • Freehold, New Jersey

Bruce Springsteen and his family moved here in 1961, and it was on the roof of this home where he'd teach himself to play the guitar on summer nights. Later in the 1960s, Springsteen's parents left for California and left Freehold too.

The Sunset Grill
7439 Sunset Blvd • Hollywood, California

Subject of Don Henley's "Sunset Grill" from his *Building the Perfect Beast* album. When the tune came out, the Sunset Grill's owner, Joe Frolich, had no idea he and his establishment had been immortalized. After customers started telling him that he and his restaurant were being sung about by the ex-Eagle, Joe's wife, Eva, finally recognized Henley at the Grill one day. By that time, tourists had already started gawking and pulling up to take snapshots. Henley was quoted back then as saying the song was an indictment not of Southern California, but of urban sprawl in general and the changing nature of American cityscapes.

"Take It Easy"
The Northwest corner of Kinsley Avenue and Second Street
Winslow, Arizona

Mention the name "Winslow, Arizona" and it's sure to trigger the song lyric, "Well I was standing on a corner in Winslow, Arizona," right? The lyrics from the popular Eagles song "Take It Easy," written by Jackson Browne and Glenn Frey, inspired the city to turn this very corner into a park right on historic Route 66. A bronze sculpture of a young man wearing blue jeans with a guitar in hand sums up the hopes and musical dreams of a generation. It's called "Standin' on the Corner Park." The park features the artwork of muralist John Pugh and sculptor Ron Adamson.

The T.A.M.I. Show
Santa Monica Civic Auditorium • 1855 Main Street
Santa Monica, California • 310-393-9961

Filmed in a single day (October 29, 1964) near the ocean in Santa Monica, this rarely seen 1964 concert film represents one of rock and roll's seminal concert events—one of the first major "package" performances which fused together all of music's most primal forces of the day.

Featuring outstanding performances by James Brown (featuring two go-go dancers named Teri Garr and Toni Basil), Marvin Gaye, Chuck Berry, Lesley Gore, the Beach Boys, the Rolling Stones, the Supremes, Jan and Dean, Gerry and the Pacemakers, Smokey Robinson and the Miracles, Leslie Gore and Billy J. Kramer, and the

Dakotas, the concert was documented by television cameras and kinescoped onto film by director Steve Binder.

The title stood for "Teenage Awards Music International" and the show had a huge influence on how other directors (such as D.A. Pennebaker at Monterey Pop) would soon document rock and roll on film.

US Festival
Glen Helen Regional Park • San Bernardino, California

This was the site for the massive 1982 and 1983 festivals put on by Apple Computer's Steve Wozniak. The shows featured dozens of acts, including U2, the Clash, the Talking Heads, the Grateful Dead, the Police, the B52s, Ozzy Osbourne, Van Halen, the Stray Cats, Stevie Nicks, and David Bowie. The park is located just off I-15 about an hour east of Los Angeles, and is a great place for fishing, camping, hiking, and more.

U2
Corner of 7th Street and Main Street • Los Angeles, California

This is the L.A. rooftop where U2 taped the music video for the song "Where the Streets Have No Name" in 1987. They actually performed on the roof of a row of stores located right at the corner of 7th Street & Main Street, near the Skid Row section of downtown, before the cops broke it up.

Valley Girl
Sherman Oaks Galleria • Ventura and Sepulveda Boulevards (northwest corner) • Sherman Oaks, California

Though it's hard to peg who came up with the actual term "Valley girl," for sure the phrase gained widespread recognition in 1982 with the release of the Frank Zappa novelty hit, "Valley Girl." The minor rap mocked the speech and attitudes of rich teenage girls in Southern California, particularly the San Fernando Valley (where Zappa's daughter Moon Unit used to observe the obnoxious brats). In fact, that's Moon Unit herself duetting with her father on the song. Of course, the Galleria (now an office /shopping complex) was prominently featured in the tune.

Velvet Underground

Café Bizarre
106 West 3rd Street • New York City, New York

This is the famed club where Andy Warhol discovered the Velvet Underground. He took them under his wing and made them "his" group. The Velvets had become a kind of house group until the famed artist plucked them from the obscure layers of the New York underground. Today, the site is occupied by a college dorm.

Electric Circus
23 St. Mark's Place • New York City, New York

The brainchild of William Morris agent Jerry Brandt, this former club played host to many crazy shows from 1967–1970, including those featuring The Exploding Plastic Inevitable, an explosive, shocking light/costume/sound revue featuring the Velvet Underground. Today, it's a rehabilitation center.

Reed-Morrison Loft
450 Grand Street • New York City, New York

Lou Reed and Velvet Underground band mate, the late Sterling Morrison lived in a fifth floor loft here in 1965. One wintry day in 1965, the Velvets were hanging out here when journalist Al Aronowitz popped in to check up on a claim Reed had made about being the fastest guitar player in the world.

Waiting out in Aronowitz's limo was Rolling Stone Brian Jones. Velvet guitarist John Cale rushed out to meet Jones, who was a hero of his. But too late—Jones supposedly had gone off to score acid in this rundown part of Little Italy. (Cale's apartment back then was at 56 Ludlow Street in New York.)

Summit High School
125 Kent Place Boulevard • Summit, New Jersey

On December 11, 1965, The Velvet Underground made their performing debut in this high school auditorium, playing a school dance. It was a triple bill with The Myddle Class as headliners and The Forty Fingers as co-support. This gig was arranged by the legendary journalist Al Aronowitz, who was also The Myddle Class manager. At this legendary show the band opened with "There She Goes Again," then played "Venus In Furs" and ended with their epic, "Heroin."

Watkins Glen
Route 16 and Meade's Hill Road • Watkins Glen, New York

On July 28, 1973, the largest rock and roll concert ever presented was held at the Raceway in Watkins Glen, New York. Over 600,000 people attended the single day affair. It was estimated that 12 hours before the show was scheduled to begin, traffic had been blocked for over 100 miles. And Watkins Glen was simply a presentation of three enduring rock and roll bands—the Grateful Dead, The Band, and the Allman Brothers.

The day before the concert, all three bands played short one to two hour sets for the 150,000 people that had already arrived. Then, on the day of the concert, the Dead played for five hours, The Band for three hours, and the Allman Brothers for four hours. To close the show, everyone got on stage for a 90-minute jam.

Wattstax Concert
Los Angeles Memorial Coliseum • 3911 South Figueroa Street
Los Angeles, California

Wattstax was a memorable August 1972 concert held at the Los Angeles Memorial Coliseum. Its purpose was to benefit the neighborhood of Watts some seven years after the Watts riots, and the concert drew an overwhelmingly African American crowd of 100,000 and turned into a memorable black pride event.

A documentary was filmed of the show and remains one of the great (if rarely-seen concert films). The show (hosted by Richard Pryor) featured R&B legend Rufus Thomas, the Bar-Kays, the Dramatics, the Emotions, Isaac Hayes, Albert King, Little Milton, Mel and Tim, the Staple Singers, Johnny Taylor, Carla Thomas, Kim Weston, and others.

Wilson, Jackie
Latin Casino • 2235 Marlton Pike • Cherry Hill, New Jersey

Specializing in Vegas-style floor shows, this onetime nightclub hosted everyone from Sinatra to Diana Ross. On September 25, 1975, while onstage at the Latin Casino, Jackie Wilson had the heart attack (with brain damage occurring) that eventually led to his death in 1984. The Latin Casino was torn down soon after and it's now the site of a car manufacturer's office building.

The Who
Flint Holiday Inn (now a Days Inn) • 2207 West Bristol Road
Flint, Michigan • 313-239-4681

On August 23, 1967, Who drummer Keith Moon celebrated his 20th birthday. That night, the band had opened for The Herman's Hermits at Atwood Stadium, a Flint high school football field. Afterwards, everyone returned to the hotel to celebrate Moon's birthday and the rest is rock and roll history. Moon emptied fire extinguishers, jumped naked into the motel's pool, threw food all over the place, and finally drove a Lincoln Continental into the same pool.

After spending the night at a dentist (who couldn't repair Moon's newly broken teeth—due to the amount of booze in his system he couldn't administer anesthesia), Moon joined his band in leaving Flint the next day. The tab for the "party" came to almost $40,000. And it's the last time the band was ever allowed to stay at a Holiday Inn.

The Who
Riverfront Coliseum • 100 Broadway • Cincinnati, Ohio

Eleven people tragically died here at a 1979 Who concert during the band's first tour after Keith Moon's death some three months earlier. The fans were trampled in a stampede that developed when they were trying to reach unreserved, "festival" seating. An episode of the TV show *WKRP in Cincinnati* later made the incident a focal point of one of its shows.

Winterland
2000 Post Street (at Steiner) • San Francisco, California

On Thanksgiving Day in 1976 (and all through the night), The Band held its farewell concert at the venue where it had played its first live concert—Winterland in San Francisco. Joining them that night were Joni Mitchell, Bob Dylan, Van Morrison, Neil Young, Eric Clapton, and others. The concert and other festivities were filmed by Martin Scorsese and released a year and a half later as *The Last Waltz*.

There's not a trace of the historic venue that hosted this landmark show, nor the hundreds of others that took place there—including many of the selections used on *Frampton Comes Alive*, recorded on June 13, 1975, and the last performance ever given by the Sex Pistols in 1978. At the Post Street entrance to the apartment complex at the site however, you will find a Winterland Photo exhibit, paying homage to what once happened at the location. Winterland closed on New Year's Eve 1978 with a show starring the New Riders of the Purple Sage, the Blues Brothers, and the Grateful Dead.

Woodstock
Hurd and West Shore Roads, outside Bethel, New York

DIRECTIONS: Drive north on Hurd Road off 17B. To get to 17B, drive west from the New York State Thruway on Highway 17. The turn for 17B comes up just as you pass through Monticello. Once you get into the town of Bethel, look for the Bethel County Store—the Hurd Road turnoff is a quarter-mile past the store (look for a white farmhouse stands on the south side of the road at the intersection). Drive up Hurd Road until you hit West Shore Road and you'll be able to locate the marker.

A concrete marker sits at the spot where the stage stood for the original, legendary Woodstock "Music and Art Fair," three days of peace and love that took place on August 15–17, 1969 at Max Yasgur's farm. This seminal event was documented both on film and record. Woodstock festivals in the 1990s were held in the nearby town of Saugerties on the Winston Farm at the intersection of Routes 212 and 32. Among the performers were: The Band, Creedence Clearwater Revival, Crosby, Stills, & Nash, the Grateful Dead, Jimi Hendrix, Jefferson Airplane, Janis Joplin, Santana, Sly & The Family Stone, the Who, and Neil Young (Young performed a few songs with Crosby, Stills, & Nash and later joined the group).

We Are the World
A&M Studios (now Henson Productions) • 1416 North La Brea Boulevard Hollywood, California

The concept for "We Are the World" came from a group of British artists known as "Band Aid" who had gotten together in late 1984 to record a song called "Do They Know It's Christmas?" Given that song's success, singer Harry Belafonte got together Lionel Ritchie, Michael Jackson, and producer Quincy Jones to come up with an American anthem.

Jackson and Ritchie spent just two hours writing the song, which they wanted to record right after the American Music Awards. Immediately after the award show, 45 artists arrived here to record. The result was 21 lead vocal performances from the likes of Paul Simon, Billy Joel, Tina Turner, Huey Lewis, Bruce Springsteen, Bob Dylan, Daryl Hall, and many more. The song went on to sell 7.5 million copies in the U.S. alone., and raise more than $50 million.

CHAPTER EIGHT

CHANNEL SURFING

Academy Awards

Dorothy Chandler Pavilion • 135 North Grand Avenue
Los Angeles, California • 213-972-7211

"The only laugh that man will ever get in his life is by stripping . . . and showing his shortcomings." So quipped host David Niven at the 46th Oscars on April 2, 1974. The suave host was preparing to introduce Elizabeth Taylor, who would be announcing the Best Picture Winner. All of a sudden, a completely nude man ran out from the wings behind Niven, flashed a peace sign and ran off. "Well, ladies and gentlemen, that was almost bound to happen," Niven explained, referencing the streaking fad that had recently become popular. Then, he tossed out one of the smoothest ad-libs of all-time.

All in the Family

89-70 Cooper Avenue • Queens, New York

The private residence shown as the Bunker's home is actually located at 89-70 Cooper Avenue in the Glendale section of Queens. The Cumberbatches, a black family, later moved into this home on the 1994 CBS spin-off series *704 Hauser Street*. Actor Carroll O'Connor, who played the role of Archie Bunker, supposedly came up with the name of the address for the Bunker household (704 Hauser Street) while commuting to the studio one day. Driving along Hauser Boulevard (just a few blocks east of CBS TV City), O'Connor noticed the name and thought it had the feeling of a Queens neighborhood, where the Bunkers were supposed to live.

The Andy Griffith Show
Franklin Canyon Lake • 2600 Franklin Canyon Drive
Beverly Hills, California

Can you hear the song being whistled? In the opening credits of *The Andy Griffith Show*, Andy Griffith and Ron Howard are seen walking with their fishing gear toward an idyllic lake, located one might imagine near Mount Pilot or Mayberry, North Carolina. However, it's Franklin Canyon Lake in Los Angeles, a beautiful wooded area that was chosen because of its tall pine and redwood trees.

This location was heavily used in the 1960s for such TV shows as *The Andy Griffith Show*, *Combat*, *Star Trek*, and *How the West Was Won*, but was also utilized by film companies: one scene from *On Golden Pond* was shot at a small pond next to the reservoir. There are actually two bodies of water here: a duck pond and the reservoir. The reservoir is where Opie tosses the rock. As well, two album covers were shot here: Simon and Garfunkel's *Sounds of Silence* and the Rolling Stone's *Big Hits (High Tide and Green Grass)*.

The Andy Griffith Show
Mount Airy, North Carolina (35 miles northwest of Winston-Salem)
1-800-576-0231

Located at the foot of the Blue Ridge Mountains in western North Carolina, Mount Airy is where actor Andy Griffith grew up, and it's also the place that inspired the town of Mayberry from Griffith's popular 1960s TV show. Today, fans of *The Andy Griffith Show* can visit Floyd's City Barber Shop, the Old

Mayberry Jail, Snappy Lunch, and even Andy's childhood home in this town that proudly wraps itself in its celebrated legend.

Batman
380 South San Rafael Avenue • Pasadena, California

Wayne Manor was the home of Bruce Wayne, Dick Grayson, Aunt Harriet, and Alfred the butler. Though the famous basement was shot on a set at the studio, the exterior footage was filmed here. The house was also used as a convent in the 1991 movie *Dead Again*. Unfortunately, you cannot see the house from the street.

Batman
Los Angeles, California

DIRECTIONS: About a quarter mile walk from the north end of Bronson Avenue (Canyon Drive) on the southwest side of Griffith Park.

The "Bat Cave" in the *Batman* TV series (and the first two *Batman* movies) is located in Griffith Park. Known as the Bronson Caves, it has been used in numerous science fiction, horror, and western movies.

The Beverly Hillbillies
750 Bel Air Road • Beverly Hills, California

Jed and Granny Clampett were supposed to live at the fictional address of 518 Crestview Drive in Beverly Hills. But in fact, this is the huge mansion built in 1935 by millionaire Lynn Atkinson that was used each week on *The Beverly Hillbillies*. Unfortunately, the home has been remodeled, so you won't probably will not recognize it—if you can even see it over the giant wall that's been erected.

Beverly Hills 90210
Torrance High School • 2200 West Carson Street • Torrance, California

The exterior scenes of this TV show were not shot in Beverly Hills, but at Torrance High in Torrance, a pleasant, middle-class community about 30 minutes from Beverly Hills.

The Brady Bunch
11222 Dilling Street (on the south side of the street)
Studio City, California

Though Mike, Carol, and the kids lived at 4222 Clinton Way on the show, this is the actual house. Sure, some trees have grown over and the owners put up a fence to keep tourists off the property, but other than that, it looks

just as it did in the early 1970s. NOTE: Given how the show's interior was designed to be two levels, the *Brady* producers temporarily installed a fake window on the left side of the roof to make the ranch-style home appear to have second story.

Breaking Bad

The hit series Breaking Bad *was created and produced by Vince Gilligan. Set and filmed in Albuquerque, New Mexico, the story follows Walter White (Bryan Cranston), an underpaid, overqualified, and dispirited high school chemistry teacher who is struggling with a recent diagnosis of stage three lung cancer. White turns to a life of crime and partners with a former student, Jesse Pinkman (Aaron Paul), to produce and distribute crystal meth to secure his family's financial future before he dies, while navigating the dangers of the criminal underworld. The show aired on AMC from January 20, 2008, to September 29, 2013, consisting of five seasons and a total of 62 episodes. Better Call Saul, the popular prequel to* Breaking Bad, *was also created by Gilligan. Throughout New Mexico are many key* Breaking Bad *locations.*

Mister Car Wash

9516 Snow Heights Circle
Albuquerque, New Mexico

Together with Walter White's house, the car wash is perhaps one of the most iconic locations in the series. Whether your ride needs a wash or not, check out the shop inside where you'll discover many gadgets inspired by the series, including the reproduction of the ad distributed on the streets of Albuquerque when Walter "disappeared" mysteriously.

Twister's Burgers and Burritos

4257 Isleta Boulevard • Albuquerque, New Mexico

In the show, it's called Los Pollos Hermanos, but inside this fast food joint made popular by the show you'll find murals and posters that all refer to its famous alter ego.

White's House

3828 Piermont Drive NE • Albuquerque, New Mexico

The true Mecca for *Breaking Bad* fans: Walter and Skyler White's house. This is the reason why hundreds of tourists come to Albuquerque, New Mexico. (Please respect the property owners.)

Charlie's Angels
189 North Robertson Boulevard • Beverly Hills, California

From 1976 to 1981, this was the building used as the exterior of "Townsend Investigations," the agency where the nation's three most gorgeous detectives were employed. Today, the small brick building houses a vacuum cleaner store.

Cheers
Bull & Finch Pub • 84 Beacon Street • 617-227-9605

The place "where everybody knows your name" was based upon this bar/restaurant in Boston's Back Bay. Three producers, Jim Burrows and Glen and Les Charles, were looking to create a new sitcom based on an American neighborhood bar. One of them suggested going to Boston, where sports and politics have always been hot issues in the local watering holes. During their search, the producers dropped into the Bull & Finch. After they took a few hundred pictures and gave them to a set designer, they filmed a pilot and sold the show, which they named *Cheers*, to NBC.

The show premiered on September 30, 1982, and became one of the top-rated programs in TV history. All of the actors have been to the Bull & Finch Pub, either for filming or stopping by informally when they visit Boston. The Pub itself was created in 1969 by a Canadian architect, who built it in England and transported it to Boston, where it was carefully reconstructed piece by piece.

The Cosby Show
10 St. Lukes Street • Greenwich Village, New York

The Cosby Show was a breakthrough for African American families, as it portrayed an upper class Brooklyn family of professionals. The number one show from 1985-1988, in eight years it never dropped below the top 20. During its original run, *The Cosby Show* won numerous honors, including several Emmys, Young Artist Awards, Directors Guild prizes, Viewers for Quality Television Awards, PGA Golden Laurels, and Humanitas Prizes, in addition to multiple Golden Globe Award nominations. This is the house that was used for the exterior of the house on the show.

Curb Your Enthusiasm

The hit Larry David show is now 10 seasons strong and there are many Los Angeles-area locations from Season 10, including:

Larry and Leon at Arcade

Sherman Oaks Castle Park • 4989 Sepulveda Blvd.
Sherman Oaks, California

This popular miniature golf park has been seen in many movies and TV shows, including a number of scenes with Larry and his pal, Leon, whom Larry uses to confront people he's afraid of.

Larry Gets Chinese with Jon Hamm

8597 W. Pico Boulevard • Los Angeles, California

In Season 10, Episode 8, Larry dines at Twin Dragon Chinese Restaurant with Jon Hamm, as Hamm continues shadowing Larry for a new role he is working on that is based on Larry.

Larry's Lawyer's Office—Interior

10877 Wilshire Blvd. • Los Angeles, California

When Larry discovers his lawyer here is not Jewish, he fires him and hires Hiram Katz.

Ted Danson's House

250 S. Burlingame Avenue • Los Angeles, California

Actor Ted Danson, a good friend of Larry David, has appeared in almost every season of *Curb Your Enthusiasm* as himself. Danson's real-life wife Mary Steenburgen has also been in many episodes.

Dallas

Southfork Ranch
Event and Conference Center
3700 Hogge Drive
Parker, Texas • 972-442-7800

Tour guides now squire visitors through the "Ewing" mansion and 41-acre estate, pointing out memorabilia from the show: the gun that shot J.R., Lucy's wedding dress, saddles used by the stars, etc.

Dynasty

1145 Arden Road • Pasadena, California

The exteriors of the Carrington mansion from this catty 1980s TV series were shot at this private Pasadena residence.

Emergency

Station 127 • 2049 East 223rd Street (just east of Wilmington Avenue)
Carson, California

This popular 1970s show featured storylines around the Los Angeles County Fire Department's "Station 51" and its paramedics. This is the actual fire station used in that series, and it has since been named "The Robert A. Cinader Memorial" station in honor of the television producer who created the TV show. A large plaque on the outside wall is dedicated in his name.

Fantasy Island

Los Angeles State and County Arboretum • 301 North Baldwin Avenue
Arcadia, California • 626-821-3222

Over 100 movies and television shows have been filmed at this 127-acre property. One of its most recognizable features is the Queen Anne cottage used

in the opening sequences of *Fantasy Island*.
It's located beside the lagoon in the historical area of the park. Interestingly, the sea-
plane which brought guests to the island
had to be lowered into the water by crane.

Friends

97 Bedford Street (corner of
Bedford & Grove)
Greenwich Village, New York

This is the exterior of the building where the six New Yorkers live in *Friends*,
the hit show created in 1994 by David Crane and Marta Kauffman.

Friends

Warner Bros. Studios • 4210 West Olive Avenue • Burbank, California

At the beginning of each episode of this popular sitcom, the entire cast of the
series is seen dancing and goofing around in a fountain (to the tune of The
Rembrandts' *I'll Be There for You*). Though one might assume the fountain is in
New York where the series is based, it's actually on the lot where the show is
taped at Warner Bros. in Burbank, California. You can see the fountain and
other prominent *Friends*' landmarks on the VIP tour that they offer.

General Hospital

County USC Hospital • 1200 North State Street
East Los Angeles, California

In the long-running soap opera *General Hospital*, fans know that the seventh
floor of "Port Charles Hospital" is where most of the action is centered.
Though those scenes are shot at ABC Television Center Studios in Hollywood, this is the hospital exterior that is used.

Gilligan's Island

Alamitos Bay Marina on Enna Drive • Long Beach, California

This is where the opening shot of *Gilligan's Island* was filmed, as The Minnow
left port for her "three hour tour." Portable palm trees were brought in for the

shoot to simulate Hawaii, and today it is rumored that the original Minnow boat is still docked within this Marina.

Gilligan's Island
Coconut Island • Oahu, Hawaii

This is the island seen at the beginning of the opening sequence of *Gilligan's Island*. Coconut Island, located in Kaneohe Bay on the northeast shore of Oahu, is just 25 acres across. However, far from a remote isle for castaways, it boasts cabins, a beach cabana, a swimming lagoon, and a boathouse. Over the years, the island has hosted luminaries such as Presidents Harry Truman and Lyndon Johnson.

Happy Days
565 North Cahuenga Avenue
Los Angeles, California

The house used as the exterior of the "Cunningham" home in the long running (1974–1984) TV series *Happy Days* is located here on North Cahuenga Avenue.

Hawaii Five-O
Iolani Palace • Corner of South and Richards Streets • Honolulu, Hawaii
808-522-0832

This served as Steve McGarret's (played by Jack Lord) headquarters in the wildly popular island cop show, *Hawaii Five-O*. On the air from 1968 to 1980, it remains the longest running police show in TV history. This grand building was once the palace of King Kalakaua, then a legislature and courts building. Today, it houses a local museum.

I Love Lucy
Hollywood Center Studios • 1040 Las Palmas Avenue
Hollywood, California

Built in 1919 as the Jasper Studio, the current Hollywood Center Studios has witnessed a lot of Hollywood history. Shirley Temple made her film debut here, as did Jean Harlow in the Howard Hughes silent movie, *Hell's Angels*. But it was on Sound Stage 2 in 1951 that Lucille Ball and husband Desi Arnaz shot the pilot (and the next two seasons) of *I Love Lucy*. They insisted on filming the series in front of a live audience with three cameras (a first) and the show stayed in the top 10 for nine seasons.

The Jeffersons
185 East 85th Street
New York, New York

When they "moved on up," this is where George and Weezie landed—"a deluxe apartment in the sky." It was used primarily in the opening credits. *The Jeffersons* was one of television's longest running and most watched sitcoms. Starting as a spin-off from *All in the Family*, *The Jeffersons* debuted in September 1975, and ran in prime time for 10 years.

Kojak
35th Street and 9th Avenue
New York, New York

This was the exterior used as the headquarters for *Kojak*, the popular show about the lollypop-sucking detective. The show ran from 1973-78.

Leave It to Beaver
1727 Buckingham Road • Los Angeles, California

The exterior shots for the Cleaver residence on the popular *Leave it to Beaver*—which ran on television from 1957–1963—were shot at this home on Buckingham Road. An identical copy of the home's stone and wood rambler facade was built on the show's back lot on Colonial Street, located on the Upper Lot at Universal City. The Cleaver's house was also used in the 1956 Universal film *Never Say Goodbye* starring Rock Hudson.

L.A. Law
444 Flower Street • Los Angeles, California

This is the office tower seen on the television show, *L.A. Law*, which ran from 1986–1994. Located in downtown Los Angeles, it's right across the street from the famous Bonaventure Hotel at the southeast corner of 4th & Flower.

Little Towns Made Notable by Big Television Shows

There are many places that have become well-known thanks to being brushed by the magic of television. Oftentimes, these instances can lead to an uptick in tourism and general interests from the locals because hey, all of a sudden, your town is famous. Here are a few of those places.

Deadwood, South Dakota
Known all over the world for its gold rush history, the small town of Deadwood, South Dakota is the setting for HBO's acclaimed American Western series *Deadwood*. While the real-life setting is far from lawless as the show portrays, fans can take advantage of a historic tour, throw back a beer at one of the breweries, and lots more.

Genoa City, Wisconsin
The popular soap opera *The Young and the Restless* put this real-life city on

the map and fans come from all over to tour the area.

Lima, Ohio

The setting of the popular music comedy/drama *Glee* was Lima, Ohio and *Glee* put this city on the map in a big way. According to Cara Stombaugh, Director of Tourism for Lima Allen County Visitors and Convention Bureau, "We had a lot of people stop just because they wanted to buy something that said 'Lima, Ohio' on it."

Litchfield, New York

The smash hit Netflix series *Orange is the New Black* brought all kinds of attention to Litchfield, New York. That's because this was the setting of the fictional prison, however, the upstate New York town doesn't even have a federal penitentiary. That said, it's a pretty place that's perfect for nature lovers, located on the hills overlooking the southern rim of the Mohawk Valley and the eastern rim of the Sauquoit Valley.

Monterey, California

Before HBO's *Big Little Lies* became a hit, Monterey was just a tranquil beachfront town with a great aquarium and a charming, Steinbeck-esque downtown.

Scranton, Pennsylvania

It's hard not to think about the American version of *The Office* when Scranton, Pennsylvania is brought up. Despite the show being filmed in California, residents of the small town still got to enjoy shoutouts to real-life locations including Poor Richard's pub, Farley's restaurant, and Abe's deli.

Snoqualmie, Washington

The 1990 hit show *Twin Peaks* used the pretty Pacific Northwest city of Snoqualmie, Washington throughout most of its run. Fans of the show have come from all over the world to discover the notable spots featured in the murder mystery series, making Snoqualmie famous in its own right.

South Park, Colorado

Comedy Central's animated and outrageous *South Park* was born in 1997 and this city is where show creators Trey Parker and Matt Stone spent time in while growing up in Colorado. The real-life South Park, however, bears very little resemblance to the show. The actual location is a gorgeous, charming Colorado town.

Washington, Connecticut
The popular comedy/drama *Gilmore Girls* took place in fictional Stars Hollow. The small town was actually inspired by a very real place: Washington, Connecticut, a charming New England town known for its picture perfect countryside, beautiful architecture, and active civic and cultural life.

Westport, Connecticut
Back in the 1960s, Samantha Stephens (played by Elizabeth Montgomery) on the show *Bewitched* was the prettiest witch of all. She and her husband, Darren, settled down in Westport, Connecticut, residing at 1164 Morning Glory Circle (an address that does not actually exist).

Wilmington, North Carolina
The fictional town of Capeside, Massachusetts was the setting for the teen drama series *Dawson's Creek*. The show was actually shot much further south in Wilmington, North Carolina, which fans were quick to flock to for a glimpse of the cast filming. Landmarks like Elijah's Restaurant and Black Cat Shoppe remain must-visits for fans of the late '90s show.

The Lone Ranger
Iverson Ranch • Redmesa Drive • Chatsworth, California

DIRECTIONS: Exit the 118 freeway at Topanga Canyon Boulevard and turn left, passing under the freeway. Turn right at Santa Susanna Pass Road. At Redmesa Drive, turn right and head up the hill. Park just before you come to the first condominiums. To your right is the "Lone Ranger Rock."

This huge, craggy stone was familiar to virtually every kid who watched television in the 1950s and 1960s. It's the spot where the Lone Ranger's horse, Silver, reared up in the opening sequence of the show. Today, the area is surrounded by apartments.

The Love Boat
The Pacific Princess Ocean Liner • San Pedro, California

The hit comedy that became a prime-time commercial for the cruise industry was filmed predominantly on the real luxury liner. The original show was shot chiefly aboard the Pacific Princess and the Island Princess. The 1990's version was shot aboard the Sun Princess. These Princess "fun ships" dock regularly at the cruise terminal just beneath the Vincent Thomas Bridge in San Pedro, California. For more information on the status of the ships used for the TV show and how you can book passage on one, contact Princess Cruises at 1-800-PRINCESS.

The Marvelous Mrs. Maisel

The Amazon original series The Marvelous Mrs. Maisel, *which tells the story of a sassy, too-quick-for-words housewife-turned-comedienne, featured many easy-to-see locations and bops around New York City from the Upper West Side to Midtown to the Village in blinding, stylish fashion. For four seasons thus far, the show (featuring Rachel Brosnahan as Miriam "Midge" Maisel) has dazzled viewers and again, it's easy to check out many real-life locations seen in the show. Here are some of my favorites.*

Albanese Meats and Poultry
238 Elizabeth St. • New York, New York

This classic Little Italy butcher shop dates back to the 1950s. Midge and her mother, Rose Weissman, buy their meat here (though the shop is called Lutzi's in the show). *The Godfather Part III* was also shot here.

The Catskills
Scott's Family Resort • Oquaga Lake, New York

When Midge and her family went on vacation in the Catskills for the whole summer, this is where they landed. Unfortunately, this classic "Borscht Belt" resort closed in 2020.

La Bonbonniere

28 8th Avenue • New York, New York

When we are treated to flashbacks of Midge and husband-to-be Joel's dating days, we see them here at an old-school diner called La Bonbonniere. They've been in business since the 1930s.

McSorley's

15 E. 7th St. • New York, New York

In Season 2, Midge and her then-boy-friend Benjamin have a drink in this venerable bar which opened in 1857. However, it's referred to as Cedar Tavern. In reality, McSorley's didn't start admitting women until 1970, roughly 10 years after the scene in *Mrs. Maisel* was set.

The Music Inn

168 W. 4th Street • New York, New York

Midge and her, uh, rough-around-the-edges manager Susie Myerson visit the Music Inn early in Season 1—and Midge's estranged husband, Joel, later hears a bootleg recording of Midge's act here. The vintage shop, opened in 1958, is still there. Some trivia: Bob Dylan lived a couple of doors down, at 161 W. 4th St., during the 1960s.

Old Town Bar

45 E. 18th St. • New York, New York

Midge's hubby Joel frequents this pub that has been in business since 1892. The vintage mahogany furnishings and perfectly preserved tin ceiling give it a unique look, and hence, many other productions take advantage of its authenticity.

Village Vanguard
178 Seventh Ave. South • New York, New York

It's been around since 1935, a Greenwich Village landmark that started as a haunt for poetry readings and folk music before jazz kicked in in the 1950s. In Season 1 we see Mrs. Maisel (Midge) here enjoying comedian Lenny Bruce, who opens for a jazz band.

Washington Square Park
New York, New York

This is where Midge wanders into a protest, winding up in front of a microphone talking about herself. The protest is organized by the activist Jane Jacobs and touches on her ultimately victorious fight against Robert Moses, NYC Parks Commissioner and "master builder," and his plan to pave highways through the park.

The Mary Tyler Moore Show
The Nicollet Mall Pedestrian Shopping Area
Seventh Street and Nicollet Mall • Minneapolis, Minnesota

You can hear Sonny Curtis singing "You're gonna make it after all . . ." and then you picture the image, one of the most enduring in television history: Mary Tyler Moore flinging her tam into the air with that big carefree smile on her face. Today, a bronze statue capturing Moore in mid-toss can be found near the exact site where Mary originally twirled in the opening montage from *The Mary Tyler Moore Show*.

In the opening scenes, Moore is actually *in* the intersection when she tosses her tam. The southwest corner of Seventh Street and Nicollet Mall, a pedestrian walkway, in front of the Marshall Field's department store (known as Dayton's when Moore threw her hat) was chosen for the statue.

The Mary Tyler Moore Show
1204 Kenwood Parkway • Minneapolis, Minnesota

This Victorian house was the exterior of Mary Richard's house (before she moved to the apartment building in Season 5). This was the place that also supposedly housed Phyllis and Rhoda, though from the outside it doesn't seem nearly big enough to be an "apartment" house. Nevertheless, it remains one of TV's most recognizable landmarks.

M*A*S*H
Malibu Creek State Park • 1925 Las Virgenes Road • Calabasas, California
818-880-0367

This is where the opening scenes from the television show *M*A*S*H* were filmed, where the choppers landed at the army hospital and unloaded wounded soldiers, and where base camp was for the duration of filming in the 1970s until the memorable final episode. It was also used in the film, *M*A*S*H*. During that final episode there was a forest fire, and the entire set burnt down, so they simply wrote it into the script.

At one time this was the 20th Century Fox movie ranch. Over the years, many films were shot here, including *Planet of the Apes* and the original *Frankenstein*. But it is because of the 4,077th that many make the 2⅓ mile hike from the parking area at Malibu Creek State Park. It's a beautiful, not-too-grueling hike to the site, where you'll find a couple of gutted vehicles from the show, remnants from the helicopter landing pad, and lots of memories.

Medical Center
UCLA Medical Center (South end of UCLA campus)
Westwood Boulevard • Westwood, California

Chad Everett played Dr. Joe Gannon on the popular TV series *Medical Center* from 1969–1976. While on the show it was called "University Medical Center," this building that was shown each week is actually the UCLA Medical Center.

Melrose Place
4616 Greenwood Place • Los Angeles, California

The main apartment building where the characters lived, loved, and fought is in the Los Feliz area of Los Angeles, at 4616 Greenwood Place. The ad agency was at 5750 Wilshire Boulevard. The hangout bar called "Shooters" is actually a small restaurant called "Fellini's," and is located at 6810 Melrose Avenue.

Mork and Mindy
1619 Pine Street (just a few blocks from the Boulder Mall)
Boulder, Colorado

This was the exterior for the house used in the late '70s and early '80s for the popular *Mork and Mindy* TV program. The show, featuring Robin Williams and Pam Dawber, focused on an alien who lands in Boulder, Colorado.

The Munsters
Universal Studios Hollywood • 100 Universal City Plaza
Universal City, California • 800-777-1000

The house from *The Munsters* (address in the show, 1313 Mockingbird Lane) is one of the most memorable in TV history. And it has an interesting history itself. When *The Munsters* finished production in 1966, Universal continued to use the house, though it was stripped of its gate, landscaping, and some of the building adornments.

By the late 1970s it had been painted yellow and was even featured in the short-lived NBC series, *Shirley*, starring Shirley Jones. Then Universal converted the house into a Cape Cod-style structure for use as a neighboring house to Jessica Fletcher's abode on *Murder, She Wrote* by removing the building's remaining gothic touches (a wraparound porch was added, as well). The house remains on the lot today in that state, though it's been painted gray.

Murder She Wrote
Blair House Inn • 45110 Little Lake Street • P.O. Box 1608
Mendocino, California • 800-699-9296

Murder She Wrote fans will recognize this gracious 1888 Victorian residence as the home of TV sleuth Jessica Fletcher (Angela Lansbury). Located in charming Mendocino Village, Blair House Inn is renowned for its stunning ocean views, cozy featherbeds, serene atmosphere, and remarkable construction of clear heart redwood.

Newhart
The Waybury Inn • 457 East Main Street
Historic East Middlebury, Vermont • 800-348-1810

"Chosen by a Hollywood set designer as the quintessential New England inn," the Waybury Inn earned a place in TV history thanks to the popular sitcom. Although only its exterior appeared on the show, the 1810 country inn (called Stratford on *Newhart*) now displays star-autographed photos and props from the show, and sells T-shirts that say "Stratford Inn."

Northern Exposure
Roslyn Cafe • Roslyn, Washington

This was the first TV show to shoot entirely on location in (central) Washington, although the real-life Roslyn (population during filming: 875) was supposed to be the fictional Cicely, Alaska. You can't miss the whimsical mural featuring a camel painted outside the Roslyn Cafe (in the show, a woman named Roslyn was said to be a co-founder of Cicely).

The Odd Couple
1049 Park Avenue • New York, New York

"On November 13th, Felix Unger was asked to remove himself from his place of residence. That request came from his wife. . . ." For TV viewers, this was the location where Felix arrived, "The home of his childhood friend, Oscar Madison. Sometime earlier, Madison's wife had thrown him out, requesting that he never return." The apartment was used both in the show's opening sequence as well as for various establishing shots. The brilliant ABC series ran from 1970–1974.

Ozark

Netflix's hit show, the Georgia-filmed Ozark, features the story of a Chicago financial advisor involved with money laundering. After a business deal with a drug cartel goes south, he and his family escape to the Missouri Ozarks so that he can pay back his former boss. Jason Bateman produces and stars as Marty alongside Laura Linney, Julia Garner, and Jordana Spiro. The popular, gritty drama was filmed throughout the state of Georgia (Not in the Ozarks!), and many locations can be found there.

Château Elan
100 Rue Charlemagne Drive • Braselton, Georgia

This luxury resort was used during production to represent the home of the drug kingpin, "Navarro." This estate is a resort and also a winery that serves as a popular vacation destination year-round.

J.D.'s On The Lake
Canton, Georgia • 6979 Bells Ferry Road • Canton, Georgia

Located near Lake Allatoona where more lake scenes from *Ozark* were filmed, fans can dine at J.D.'s On The Lake and enjoy knowing that the restaurant served as the set for "The Blue Cat Lodge." The interior even features the original sign used during filming.

Lake Lanier
Gainesville, Georgia

Lake Lanier, just north of Atlanta, has been featured for years during the filming of the show. The reservoir is used to represent the Lake of the Ozarks in Missouri where the storyline takes place.

Piedmont Park
1320 Monroe Drive NE • Atlanta, Georgia

This iconic park in Atlanta stood in for Chicago's "Great Lawn" during Season 4 of filming. The urban green space is popular for hosting large festivals and events such as Music Midtown.

Starlight Drive-In
2000 Moreland Ave. SE
Atlanta, Georgia

This historic drive-in movie theater was featured in the third season during a scene in which the character Ruth has to make a cash drop. This iconic spot still operates as an outdoor film venue and flea market.

The Ozzie and Harriet Show
1822 Camino Palmero Drive • Hollywood, California

On their classic TV sitcom, the Nelsons (Ozzie, Harriet, Ricky, and David Nelson) lived at the fictitious address of the 822 Sycamore Road. But you can find the actual house located above Hollywood Boulevard, one half a mile east of Grauman's Chinese Theatre.

The Rockford Files
28128 Pacific Coast Highway • Malibu, California

29 Cove Road was the fictional address of Jim Rockford's beach side trailer in the *Rockford Files*. It was really parked on the beach behind the Sandcastle restaurant at Paradise Cove off of Pacific Coast Highway, north of downtown Malibu.

Partridge Family
Warner Bros. Studio Ranch • 3701 West Oak Street • Burbank, California

The Partridge home façade was located on the 40-acre back lot of this Warner Bros. ranch. It often doubled as the residence of the Kravitzs on the *Bewitched*. The Partridge home eventually met its end when it was bombed during the filming of the movie *Lethal Weapon*. The adjacent garage where the Partridge Family rehearsed their music still exists.

Also at the Warner Bros. ranch was the main house from *Bewitched*. The Stephen's residence is still visible on the lot at the corner of North Kenwood and West Streets. Thankfully, it barely survived an episode of the sitcom *Home Improvement* when Tim Taylor set it on fire.

Petticoat Junction
Railtown 1897 State Historic Park • 5th and Reservoir Streets
Jamestown, California (south of Sonora on California Highway 49)
209-984-3953

Petticoat Junction was one of a number of successful rural comedies to emerge

emerge in the 1960s. First seen in September of 1963, *Petticoat Junction* centered around Kate Bradley, who ran the Shady Rest Hotel, located in the farming valley of Hooterville. Kate's three beautiful daughters, Billie Jo, Bobbie Jo, and Betty Jo were seen in the opening sequence of each show flipping their petti-

coats over the rim of a giant tower, located here at this charming park.

Many other TV shows and movies were shot here, and Petticoat Junction's Engine No. 3 is also on display in the roundhouse. Trains run seasonally; call ahead for schedules.

Peyton Place
Gilmanton, New Hampshire • 603-267-6700

In the 1950s, the tiny town of Gilmanton was made reluctantly famous, or infamous, thanks to the late Grace Metalious, author of the notorious book *Peyton Place*. The novel, supposedly based on this rural community where the author lived, touched off the largest scandal in the area's history. It contained salacious tales of overt sex and adultery, hot stuff in 1956, and went on to sell over a million copies (as well as spawning a successful TV series and two movies).

Metalious died at age 39 from liver damage brought on by too much drinking. Today, the town still has no formal acknowledgement of what brought them so much international attention.

Rivera, Geraldo
Basement of the Lexington Hotel Chicago • 2135 South Michigan Avenue Chicago, Illinois

In 1986, a nationally broadcast television special *The Mystery of Al Capone's Vault* was hosted by Geraldo Rivera—and it became the highest rated television special in history. Unfortunately, Rivera was unable to discover anything in the vaults, though he did fire a submachine gun into the walls of the second floor gymnasium where Capone's bodyguards used to work out.

When Al Capone moved into the Lexington Hotel in 1928, he rented the entire fourth floor and most of the third. He lived in #430, a six-room suite, and was living here in 1931 when he was convicted of tax evasion. The hotel was torn down in 1997.

Saturday Night Live

8-H Saturday Night Live • 30 Rockefeller Plaza • New York, New York
212-664-3056

"Live, from New York, it's Saturday Night!" was first yelled by Chevy Chase on October 11, 1975. The show was called *NBC's Saturday Night* because the name *Saturday Night Live* was already taken by Howard Cosell's show on ABC. Further mocking his show, the cast was dubbed the "Not-Ready-For-Prime-Time Players" after Cosell's own "Prime-Time Players."

George Carlin hosted the first show. The musical guests (there were two that night) were Janice Ian and Billy Preston. Andy Kaufman also made an appearance, mouthing the words to the Mighty Mouse theme. The first ever sketch was called "The Wolverines," and it involved writer Michael O'Donoghue teaching nonsense English phrases to John Belushi (playing an Eastern European immigrant).

Studio 8-H was originally painted the colors of autumn—maestro Arturo Toscanini's favorite. The Great NBC Symphony performed here, along with such favorite radio shows as Fred Allen's Town Hall Tonight. Toscanini's original podium now resides in the 8-H announcer's booth.

Seinfeld

Pendant Plaza

600 Madison Ave. (Southwest corner of Madison and 55th Street)
New York, New York

As most *Seinfeld* fans should know, this is the publishing company where Elaine worked for much of the show.

Soup Kitchen International

259A West 55th Street (north side of
the street between 8th Avenue and
Broadway) • New York, New York
212-757-7730

This is the home of the infamous "Soup
Nazi."

Tom's Restaurant ("Monks")

2880 Broadway at 112th Street
New York, New York • 212-864-6137

The famous "Monk's" is actually
Tom's Restaurant. This diner made
pervious history by being the subject
of Suzanne Vega's hit song, "Tom's
Diner." While the interior looks
nothing like it did on the show, there
is *Seinfeld* memorabilia on the wall.

The Westway Diner

614 9th Avenue (between 44th and 43rd Streets)
New York, New York • 212-582-7661

This diner may very well be the inspiration behind Monk's, rather than
Tom's Restaurant. It is at this establishment that Larry David and Jerry
Seinfeld came up with the idea for a show about nothing.

Sex and the City

Various locations around New York City
The feisty, racy, and very popular HBO series starring Sara Jessica Parker featured many real locations around New York City. Remember these?

Art Gallery
141 Price Street

The Louis K. Meisel Gallery is where the filming was done for the gallery where Charlotte worked.

Cupcake Bakery
401 Bleeker Street

Magnolia Bakery is where Carrie and Miranda memorably devoured cupcakes.

Jimmy Choo
645 Fifth Avenue (in the Olympic Tower)

This fashionable boutique is one of Carrie's favorite shoe stores.

O'Neal's Speakeasy
174 Grand Street

O'Neal's Speakeasy is where scenes from Scout, the show's popular bar, were shot.

The Sopranos

The wildly popular HBO show about gangland New Jersey features many places located in and around the Garden State:

Bada Bing

Satin Dolls • 230 State Highway Number 17 • Lodi, New Jersey
201-845-6494

Satin Dolls is the real name of the club used for scenes that take place at the Bada Bing strip club in *The Sopranos*. Satin Dolls is a gentleman's club located in Lodi, New Jersey on Route 17. Some of the girls that dance at the club are the same girls that are in *The Sopranos*.

Joe's Bake Shop

Ridge Road (corner of Jauncey Street) • North Arlington, New Jersey

In episode eight of the first season, Christopher Moltisanti (Michael Imperioli) replicates a *Goodfellas* scene by shooting a baker in the foot. The scene takes place at Joe's Bake Shop in North Arlington.

Pizzaland

260 Belleville Turnpike North Arlington, New Jersey

You can see Pizzaland on *The Sopranos* during every opening scene as Tony Soprano drives home.

Satriale's Pork Store

101 Kearny Avenue • Kearny, New Jersey

In the pilot episode of *The Sopranos*, the pork store scenes were shot at Centanni's in Elizabeth, New Jersey. For subsequent episodes, location scouts found this former auto parts store in Kearny, and transformed it into the exterior of Satriale's.

Some sites seen during *The Sopranos'* opening credits:

- The ceiling of the Lincoln Tunnel heading west to New Jersey. Tony is driving north and drives up the helix to Route 3 West.
- The New Jersey Turnpike sign at Secaucus.
- The "Cash-Only" lane entrance to NJ Turnpike at 16W is clearly visible. (NOTE: this view is no longer the same since the state converted to the automated Easy Pass system.) Tony Soprano (played by actor James Gandolfini) takes a ticket.
- The Goethals bridge, viewed from northbound truck lane side of the New Jersey Turnpike.
- View looking east from the New Jersey Turnpike extension (between exits 14 and 14C in Jersey City) going eastbound towards the Holland Tunnel to New York.
- The Carteret tank farms as viewed from the southbound New Jersey Turnpike between exits 13A and exit 12.
- Sacred Heart Basilica Cathedral, Newark, New Jersey (the Pope spoke here during a visit to the United States).

The Staircase
1810 Cedar Street • Durham, North Carolina

This is writer Michael Peterson's former house, featured in the popular Netflix docuseries *The Staircase*. The home was also a fictional set in the 1990 movie *The Handmaid's Tale*. However, it's more well-known as the site of the notorious death of Peterson's wife that was the focus of the true crime series, which followed Peterson's legal case for years after he was accused of murdering his wife.

Stranger Things

The Netflix hit series is an intoxicating homage to the 1980s that blends references from everything from The Goonies *to* E.T. the Extra-Terrestrial, Alien, Twin Peaks, *and beyond. The synth-heavy retro '80s soundtrack adds to the mix, and of course, there are places to visit related to the show, which in general is shot around the greater Atlanta area.*

Downtown Hawkins
Jackson, Georgia

Throughout the entire series, downtown Jackson, which is located approximately 50 miles south of Atlanta, serves as the town of Hawkins. This is where some of the show's main characters, including Joyce Byers (Winona Ryder) and Bob Newby (Sean Astin), worked at Melvald's General Store. Local businesses love the attention from the fans that visit. At

Lucy Lu's Coffee Cafe, you can find a "Stranger Drinks" menu. Popular beverages include the Sheriff Hopper, a hazelnut and vanilla coffee drink, and the Demogorgon, a frappé with blood-red food coloring named after the monster that rampages through Hawkins. Melvald's General Store is at 4 Second Street; and a block away, the Butts County Courthouse and Probate Court Building was used for Hawkins Library.

Hawkins Community Pool
2000 Lakewood Ave. SE • Atlanta, Georgia

In Season 3, the character Billy works as a lifeguard and flirts with older women at the fictional Hawkins Community Pool. The location is a very real community pool, South Bend Pool, and it's open from Tuesday through Saturday and is $5 for everyone ages six and up, though the fee has been waived in recent years because of COVID.

Hawkins Laboratory
Emory University
Briarcliff Campus—Building A
1256 Briarcliff Rd. NE
Atlanta, Georgia

This old academic building serves as the foreboding Hawkins Laboratory in the series. Once the mansion of a Coca-Cola co-founder, the 2017 horror film *Rings* was also shot here.

Starcourt Mall
Pleasant Hill Road corridor • Duluth, Georgia

In *Stranger Things*' third season, the gang discovers that the new, popular Starcourt Mall is actually a secret Russian base. In real life, Starcourt Mall is Gwinnett Place Mall in Duluth, Georgia, which closed down a few months before filming began after years of struggling to attract new tenants (it was built in 1984). A strange fact: Five months before filming for the third season began, a brutal murder took place in a vacant Subway within the abandoned mall's food court. You can't go inside today, but it makes for a great selfie.

Stone Mountain Park
1000 Robert E. Lee Boulevard • Stone Mountain, Georgia

The vast (more than 3,200 acres) Stone Mountain Park is Georgia's most-visited and popular attraction. Located 15 miles east of Atlanta, it's open year-round and offers many outdoor activities. Most of the exterior wooded scenes for *Stranger Things* were shot here. The railroad tracks that run through the park are shown in the first season, as the gang walks with Eleven in the woods. In Season 2, Dustin and Steve bond over girl advice in the forest as they hunt for "demodogs."

Superman
Los Angeles City Hall • 200 North Spring Street
Los Angeles, California

This famous building served as *The Daily Planet* building in the *Superman* TV series starring George Reeves. This building's image was also on Joe Friday's police badge in the series *Dragnet*.

77 Sunset Strip
8524 Sunset Boulevard • West Hollywood, California

Remember the old TV series *77 Sunset Strip*? If you do, you'll no doubt remember "Dino's Lodge." While it was indeed an actual building, it was torn down in 1989. Return to the address today and you'll find that a plaque has been laid into the sidewalk, marking the spot made famous on the show, which starred Byron Keith, Edd Byrnes, and Efrem Zimbalist Jr., among others.

The Tonight Show
Hudson Theatre • 145 West 44th Street • New York, New York • 212-789-7583

This legendary theatre has changed ownership many times and each new owner has added to its colorful history. The CBS Radio Playhouse broadcast from here in the 1930s and '40s. In 1950, NBC turned the theatre into a television studio. On September 27, 1956 the first nationwide broadcast of *The Tonight Show* starring Steve Allen came from the Hudson Theatre. Barbara Streisand made her television debut on the *Jack Paar Show*, also broadcast from the Hudson.

Saved from demolition by public outcry, it became part of the Macklowe Hotel in 1990. The Hudson Theatre was granted landmark status for both its interior and exterior features in 1987. Now called the Millennium Broadway, Millennium Conference Center, Restaurant Charlotte, and Hudson Theatre, it is fully restored and renovated with the technical capabilities of a production studio.

The Walking Dead

The Walking Dead *is a popular post-apocalyptic horror television series based on the comic book series of the same name by Robert Kirkman, Tony Moore, and Charlie Adlard. The series premiered on October 31, 2010 on AMC. To date, it has been nominated for several awards, including the Golden Globe Award for Best Television Series—Drama and the Writers Guild of America Award for New Series. Shot throughout the Atlanta area, there are many locations to visit related to the show.*

Main Street
Grantville, Georgia

The show has breathed much-needed life into the little town of Grantville, where so much action in the show takes place. They even offer *Walking Dead* tours on the weekends, and the town's reputation as a *Walking Dead* primary filming location brings in many tourists from all over the world.

Rick's House
817 Cherokee Ave. SE • Atlanta, Georgia

In the pilot episode, this was Rick's first stop upon waking up to the zombie apocalypse. In real life, it was unoccupied at the time the first season was being filmed. Now, it's been remodeled and inhabited, so please respect the current occupants.

Terminus
793 Windsor Street Southwest • Atlanta, Georgia

This is the abandoned rail yard where the community known as "Terminus" lived. Some trivia: "Terminus" was an early name for the city of Atlanta, because it was the end of the Western and Atlantic railroad line.

Westside Reservoir Park
Johnson Rd. and Donald Lee Hollowell Highway • Atlanta, Georgia

The survivor's camp where Rick is reunited with Lori and Carl in Season 1 was located at this pretty park, where camping is definitely allowed.

Wild Wild Country
Wasco County Courthouse • 511 Washington St. • The Dalles, Oregon

Netflix's smash hit 2018 documentary *Wild Wild Country* focused on the Rajneeshpuram, the cultish community that moved into Wasco County, Oregon in the 1980s. Several landmarks seen in the documentary still remain today, including the Wasco County Courthouse, which was one site of the Rajneeshpuram's 1984 bioterrorist attack. The Rajneeshees purposely contaminated salad bars at several local eateries with salmonella in an attempt to keep locals from voting in the upcoming election, where Rajneeshees were hoping to win a seat in the Wasco County Circuit Court. They also spread the bacteria around various surfaces in The Dalles, including door knobs and urinal handles. Over 750 people fell ill, with nearly 50 victims needing hospitalization, but thankfully no one died from the poisoning.

CHAPTER NINE

ART AND LITERATURE

American Gothic
Burton and Gothic Streets • Eldon, Iowa • 319-335-3916

In August of 1930, artist Grant Wood was visiting this small town in the southern part of Iowa when he stumbled upon a house that would eventually make him famous. Grant Wood imagined a farmer and his spinster daughter standing in front of the 1880's, five-room house built in a style known as "Carpenter Gothic." He sketched his idea on brown paper and had someone take a photograph of the house so that he could work out his vision when he returned home.

The now-famous painting, which glorified and satirized rural Americans, may be the most parodied work of art ever. The model for the farmer's daughter in the picture was Grant's sister, Nan Wood Graham. The model for the farmer was Dr. B.H. McKeeby, the family dentist. Although not open to the public, visitors are welcome to view the house from the outside as Grant Wood did in 1930 when its unusual Gothic window inspired him.

The State Historical Society of Iowa owns and preserves the American Gothic house. It is listed on the National Register of Historic Places. Grant Wood had been born on a farm near Anamosa, Iowa and grew up in Cedar

Rapids. Though he lived and worked around the world, he always maintained a strong bond to Eastern Iowa. He died in February 1942.

Children's Literature

Charles M. Schulz Museum
2301 Hardies Lane • Santa Rosa, California • 707-579-4452

Based in the area where *Peanuts* creator Charles M. Schulz worked for so many years, the charming Charles M. Schulz Museum (opened in 2002) features Schulz's business and personal papers, original comic strips and drawings, a library with a large collection of *Peanuts* books in several languages, many photographs, memorabilia, and special exhibits related to the great artist and thinker. Schulz was first published by Robert Ripley in his *Ripley's Believe It or Not!*

The *St. Paul Pioneer Press* published his first regular comic strip, *Li'l Folks*, in 1947. (It was in this strip that Charlie Brown first appeared, as well as a dog that resembled Snoopy). In 1950, he approached the *United Features Syndicate* with his best strips from *Li'l Folks* and *Peanuts* made its first appearance on October 2, 1950. This strip became one of the most popular comic strips of all time.

Peanuts ran for nearly 50 years without interruption and had appeared in over 2,600 newspapers in 75 countries. In November 1999, Schulz suffered a stroke, and later it was discovered that he had terminal colon cancer. Schulz announced his retirement on December 14, 1999, at the age of 77. The last original strip ran on February 13, 2000. Schulz had died at 9:45 P.M. the night before in Santa Rosa, California of a heart attack.

As part of his will, Schulz had requested that the *Peanuts* characters remain as authentic as possible and that no new comic strips based on them be drawn. To date his wishes have been honored, although reruns of the strip are still being syndicated to newspapers.

The Dr. Seuss National Memorial Sculpture Garden
The Quadrangle (State and Chestnut Streets)
Springfield, Massachusetts

You'll find the Dr. Seuss National Memorial Sculpture Garden at the Quadrangle in Springfield, Massachusetts, the city where Theodore Seuss Geisel was born and which many believe inspired much of his magical work from *The Lorax* to *The Cat in the Hat.*

Goodnight Moon
Main Street • Greenville, South Carolina

If you have kids, odds are you've read the classic, simple, charming book *Goodnight Moon* (probably over and over again). Here in Greenville, the book is uniquely celebrated thanks to a local high school student who wanted to do something good for the community. A bronzed sculpture of the book and one mouse are mounted on the fountain in front of the Hyatt Regency hotel and the other eight mice are installed along a nine-block stretch of Main Street between the Hyatt and the Westin Poinsett hotels. The artist who created the work is Zan Wells, and by finding the mice, you also get a chance to explore Greenville's Main Street.

The Little Red Lighthouse
178th Street and the Hudson River • New York City, New York
212-304-2365

DIRECTIONS: From Lafayette Place at West 181st Street, take steps, footpath, and footbridge over the highway, down to the park and south to the lighthouse.

The Jeffrey's Hook lighthouse, erected in 1880 and moved to its current site under the George Washington Bridge in 1921, has become famous as the children's literary landmark, *The Little Red Lighthouse.*

The story of the lighthouse in Fort Washington Park was popularized by the children's book *The Little Red Lighthouse and the Great Gray Bridge*, written by Hildegarde H. Swift with illustrations by Lynd Ward, published in 1942. In this fictional account of Jeffrey's Hook lighthouse, the structure was presented as a symbol of the significance of a small thing in a big world.

Make Way for Ducklings
Public Garden • Boston, Massachusetts

DIRECTIONS: The Public Garden is bordered by Arlington, Boylston, Charles, and Beacon Streets. The ducklings are on the northeast corner of the park.

In Robert McCloskey's 1941 classic children's book *Make Way for Ducklings*, Mr. and Mrs. Mallard are looking for a place to live. Every time Mr. Mallard finds a place, Mrs. Mallard says it is not a good place to raise a family. They finally decide on a place in Boston along the Charles River. Mrs. Mallard has eight ducklings and decides to leave the Charles River site and settle in the Boston Commons. Today in the lovely and historic Public Garden, you'll find bronze statues of the ducklings, depicting them just as they are in the book. (They were created in 1985.)

There is another tribute to the book like this one in a park in Moscow, Russia—a gift from the children of the United Stated to the children of Russia.

Mary Had a Little Lamb
72 Wayside Inn Road • Sudbury, Massachusetts

This is the original Redstone School, used to teach the children of District Number Two on Redstone Hill in Sterling from 1798 to 1856. When the building was moved here to Sudbury, where it sits today near Longfellow's Wayside Inn, it was used in their public school system to teach grades one through four from 1927 to 1951. It is now a small museum, and is used to demonstrate early American rural schooling traditions.

But, it holds an even more important place in American history. This is the building where Mary Tyler (1806–1889) went to school followed by her little lamb. Here are the first 12 lines of the famous verse, which are said to be written by John Roulstone:

Mary had a little lamb,
Its fleece was as white as snow,
And every were that Mary went,
The lamb was sure to go.

It followed her to school one day;
That was against the rule;

It made the children laugh and play;
To see the lamb at school.

And so the teacher turned it out;
but still it lingered near;
And waited patiently about;
Till Mary did appear.

The schoolhouse is located adjacent to the historic Wayside Inn in Sudbury, and just down the road from a famous farmhouse where Babe Ruth lived back when he played for the Boston Red Sox.

Mother Goose
Granary Burial Ground • Park and Tremont Streets
Boston, Massachusetts

The author of *Mother Goose's Rhymes* is said to lie in a grave here marked "Elizabeth Foster Goose." She lived in colonial times here in Boston and entertained her grandchildren with rhymes and chants that she remembered from her own childhood. It is said that Thomas Fleet, her son-in-law, made a collection of these rhymes and put them in a book called *Songs for the Nursery* or *Mother Goose's Melodies*. The Granary Burying Ground is also the site of the graves of Paul Revere and John Hancock. It is one of the most historic burial grounds in all of the United States and a must-visit when in Boston.

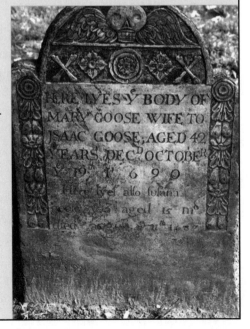

412   It Happened Right Here 📍

Grandma Moses Schoolhouse

Bennington Museum • 75 Main Street • Bennington, Vermont • 802-447-1571

This historic schoolhouse, actually attended by Grandma Moses and other members of her family in Eagle Bridge, New York, was moved to the grounds of the excellent Bennington Museum in 1972. Today, the schoolhouse features exhibitions recording the life and achievements of the artist Anna Mary Robertson Moses (1860–1961), who became known to the world as Grandma Moses, one of America's most noted folk artists.

Artifacts and documents discuss her life, the universal fame she gained, and more. Today, visitors can even watch Moses herself paint and hear her discuss her extraordinary life by viewing a classic 1955 Edward R. Murrow interview with Moses for his legendary CBS television show *See It Now*. At age 100, she illustrated an edition of *The Night Before Christmas* and the book was published after her death. Grandma Moses died on December 13, 1961. She lived to be 101 and in the last year of her life, incredibly, she painted 25 pictures.

Hemingway, Ernest

Aunt and Uncle's Home

3629 Warwick Boulevard • Kansas City, Missouri

This is where Hemingway's uncle Alfred Tyler Hemingway and aunt Arabell lived in 1917. Alfred Tyler used his pull with editor Henry Haskell to get Ernest a job writing at *The Kansas City Star* newspaper. Though Hemingway lived at a nearby boarding house (once located at 3733 Warwick), he would often visit this house for dinner with his relatives.

Birthplace

339 North Oak Park Avenue • Oak Park, Illinois

Ernest Miller Hemingway was born at 8:00 A.M. on July 21, 1899, here in the family home built by his widowed grandfather, Ernest Hall. Hemingway was the second of Dr. Clarence and Grace Hall Hemingway's six children. He had four sisters and one brother. He was named after his maternal grandfather Ernest Hall and his great uncle Miller Hall.

Today at the home you can explore displays featuring rare photographs of Hemingway, his childhood diary, letters, early writings, and other memorabilia. Exhibits and videos at the museum focus on his first 20 years in Oak Park, and its impact on his later works. There is also a great gift shop.

A Farewell to Arms
1021 West Cherry Street • Piggott, Arkansas (about 90 miles northwest of Memphis, Tennessee) • 870-598-3487

Hemingway visited here many times between 1927 and 1940. After all, he was at that time married to Pauline Pfeiffer, daughter of Piggott residents Paul and Mary. They actually owned this house and the red barn in the back, which they converted into a writing studio so Hemingway had a place to write. It was here that he composed *A Farewell to Arms* and most likely fragments of the seven other books he wrote while married to Pauline.

The property came under the administration of Arkansas State University at Jonesboro in 1997. The Red Barn is now a Hemingway Museum and the Pfeiffer House is a literary conference center so that visiting scholars can study Hemingway in a place where he lived and wrote. Both the home and the barn studio were named to the National Historic Register in 1982.

On a cinematic note, Piggott is also where famed director Elia Kazan shot much of his dark, 1957 classic *A Face in the Crowd*, starring Andy Griffith and Patricia Neal.

For Whom the Bell Tolls
Sun Valley Lodge • Sun Valley, Idaho

Ernest Hemingway wrote part of *For Whom the Bell Tolls* in Room 206 at this classic four-story lodge in the village center. He first visited this area in the fall in 1939, joined by writer Martha Gellhorn who would become his third wife. He nicknamed his suite here "Glamour House," and had a temporary bar and bookshelves installed. (Hemingway even mentions Sun Valley in Chapter 13 of *For Whom the Bell Tolls*.)

Hemingway Home and Museum
907 Whitehead Street • Old Town Key West, Florida • 305-294-1136

Ernest Hemingway lived and wrote here for more than 10 years. The house was built in 1851 by Asa Tift, a marine architect and salvage wrecker, and became Ernest Hemingway's home in 1931. Today, the cozy abode still contains the furniture that "Papa" and his family used, and the cats that prowl the home and grounds are actually descendants of the cats he kept while he lived in the house.

The building where Hemingway had his studio was originally a carriage house; his studio was on the second floor. Today a stairway has been erected from the patio on the ground floor for tourists to gain access to the second floor writing studio. Incredibly, the studio remains precisely as it was back then—Hemingway's Royal typewriter, Cuban cigar-maker's chair, and the
mementos he collected are all still in place. It was within this studio where he crafted *Death in the Afternoon*, *Green Hills of Africa*, *To Have And Have Not*, *For Whom The Bell Tolls*, and many of his most-famous short stories, such as "The Snows of Kilimanjaro" and "The Short, Happy Life of Francis Macomber."

Hemingway's Suicide
East Canyon Run Boulevard • Ketchum, Idaho

Ernest Hemingway died here on July 2, 1961 (he and his wife, Mary, had moved here in 1959). Mary Hemingway first reported that her husband had accidentally shot himself while cleaning his gun. However, the official cause of death was then listed as suicide. (It was here that Hemingway finished his book, *For Whom the Bell Tolls*.)

Though the house is not regularly open to the public, on rare occasions there are opportunities to visit. The Hemingway Memorial, located in a grove of aspens and willows overlooking Trail Creek, features a bronze bust of the writer. Hemingway's gravesite, along with Mary's, is located in the Ketchum Cemetery. Other Hemingway-related sites in Ketchum include Michel's Christiania on Sun Valley Road (where the author had his last dinner on July 1, 1961), and Whiskey Jacques, a bar at 309 Walnut Avenue North.

The Kansas City Star
1729 Grand Boulevard • Kansas City, Missouri

As a reporter here at *The Star*, Hemingway was responsible for covering fires, crimes, the General Hospital, and whatever was happening at Union Station. Inside the lobby here at *The Star*, a World War I service plaque near the main entrance displays Hemingway's name (16th from the top, in the first row). The Nobel Prize-winning writer is also remembered in a vestibule display, as well as through the paper's Hemingway Writing Award, a national contest for high school journalists.

L.C. Bates Museum
Good Will-Hinckley School, Route 201 • Hinckley, Maine • 207-453-4894

It's something no true fan of Ernest Hemingway should miss—a blue marlin caught by the author when he was in the midst of writing *The Old Man and the Sea*. That item is one of many ephemeral treasures within this small, offbeat museum located on the campus of a school for disadvantaged children. Closed in the 1950s  and then re-opened as is, this dusty, musty archive also includes minerals, stuffed birds, assorted fossils, and many other obscure items.

The Muehlebach Hotel
Southwest corner of 12th Street and Baltimore Avenue
Kansas City, Missouri

When working late on a story or if he was simply too tired to take the long trolley car home, Hemingway would crash in a bathtub in the Muehlebach's pressroom, using towels for a mattress. (In the novel, *Across the River and into the Trees*, Hemingway glorified the beds he slept on in this historic hotel during the winter of 1917.)

Riviera Apartments
229 Ward Parkway • Kansas City, Missouri

Back when it was called Riviera Apartments, Ernest and Pauline Hemingway awaited the arrival of their second son, Gregory Hancock. He was delivered via cesarean section by Dr. Guffey on November 12, 1931. To say thank you, Hemingway gave the doctor an original manuscript of *Death in the Afternoon*. (Which the doctor sold for $13,000 in 1958.)

Villa De Cubero
State Road 124 at mile marker 14 • Cubero, New Mexico • 505-552-9511

The small community of Budville was named after H.N. "Bud" Rice, who opened an automobile service and touring business here in 1928. The Villa de Cubero, built in 1937, once operated as a famous roadside inn. It played host to many celebrities over the years, including Ernest Hemingway while he was writing *The Old Man and the Sea*. The motel closed in the

1980s, but the Villa De Cubero is still open as a grocery store and gas station. The actual room used by Hemingway still stands, and is used today as a storage space (and visible to tourists who ask the management to see it).

Windemere Cottage
Lake Grove Road/Walloon Lake • Near Petoskey, Michigan

It was here at this remote cottage in the woods that Ernest Hemingway spent most of his summers until the age of 21, and where he learned to hunt and fish and to first write serious fiction. Windemere, still owned by the Hemingway family, is closed to the public.

Kerouac, Jack

Jack Kerouac Commemorative Statue
A few hundred yards from Kearney Square • Lowell, Massachusetts

Lowell honors its native son with a beautiful memorial featuring the opening passages from Kerouac's five "Lowell novels," as well as passages from *On the Road*, *Lonesome Traveler*, *Book of Dreams*, and *Mexico City Blues* inscribed on eight triangular marble columns. Created by Houston artist Ben Woitena and dedicated on June 25, 1988, the artful creation is located on the site where a 12-story brick and concrete warehouse once stood—a building Kerouac described as "the great gray warehouse of eternity." Jack Kerouac died in Orlando, Florida in 1969 at the age of 47.

On the Road
29 Russell Street (between Hyde and Eastman Streets, south side of the street) • San Francisco, California

The phrase "The Beat Generation" was first used by writer Jack Kerouac in 1948. (John Clellon Holmes introduced the phrase to the wider public in 1952 in an article he wrote in the *New York Times Magazine* called "This Is the Beat Generation.") In 1958, noted San Francisco columnist Herb Caen coined the term "Beatnik." But of course Jack Kerouac came to epitomize "The Beat Generation" to the world.

A poet, a writer, a wanderer, a traveler, a storyteller, he traversed the country and the world, combining with Allen Ginsberg, Neal Cassady, and William S. Burroughs to produce some of the most radically timeless and inventive literature of the 20th century. He is certainly most famous for 1957's *On the Road*, written at this house (in the attic) in only three weeks. (Other works of note include: *The Dharma Bums*, *The Subterraneans*, *Desolation Angels* and *Big Sur*.) Jack Kerouac had arrived at this house, the home of his friends Neal and Carolyn Cassidy, in 1951, and it was also here where the three formed a well-documented love triangle.

Pollard Memorial Library

401 Merrimack Street • Lowell, Massachusetts • 978-970-4120

A popular Kerouac haunt (when it was known as the Lowell Public Library) in the 1920s and '30s, this is where the writer would, as he detailed in *Maggie Cassidy* and *Vanity of Duluoz*, skip school "at least once a week" to read Shakespeare, Victor Hugo, William Penn, and scholarly books on chess. "It was how I'd become interested in old classical-looking library books," he writes in *Maggie Cassidy*, "some of them falling apart and from the darkest shelf in the Lowell Public Library, found there by me in my overshoes at closing time."

O'Keeffe, Georgia

Georgia O'Keeffe Museum

217 Johnson Street • Santa Fe, New Mexico • 505-946-1000

The Georgia O'Keeffe Museum in Santa Fe, New Mexico opened to the public in July 1997, 11 years after the death of O'Keeffe. Since then, the museum has welcomed more than 1,700,000 visitors from all over the world. The museum's permanent collection of O'Keeffe paintings, drawings, and sculpture is the largest in the world. Throughout the year, visitors can see a changing selection of at least 50 of these works. In addition, the museum presents special exhibitions that are either devoted entirely to O'Keeffe's work or that combine examples of her art with works by her American modernist contemporaries.

Home and Studio
County Road 164 • Abiquiu, New Mexico • 505-685-4539

The home and studio of the artist Georgia O'Keeffe (1887–1986) in Abiquiu, New Mexico (approximately 50 miles northwest of Santa Fe), is one of the most important artistic sites in the southwestern United States. Georgia O'Keeffe's stark paintings of cattle skulls bleached by the desert sun are familiar to all. From 1949 until her death in 1984, O'Keeffe lived and worked here at Abiquiu.

The buildings and their surroundings, along with the views they command, inspired many of her paintings and continue to provide great insight into her vision. The home and studio are maintained by the Georgia O'Keeffe Foundation, and are open to the public. Tours are available of O'Keeffe's home in Abiquiu for groups of 16 or less, by appointment only. The Georgia O'Keefe Foundation recommends making reservations at least six months in advance and requests a $20 per person donation.

Lawrence Tree
Kiowa Ranch • 20 miles north of Taos, New Mexico (off of Route 522 near San Cristobal) • 505-776-2245

"The big pine tree in front of the house, standing still and unconcerned and alive . . . the overshadowing tree whose green top one never looks at . . . One goes out of the door and the tree-trunk is there, like a guardian angel. The tree-trunk, the long work table and the fence!"–D. H. Lawrence

Under this mammoth pine tree, author D.H. Lawrence (*Women in Love* and *Lady Chatterley's Lover*) would spend his mornings writing at a small table.

In 1929, artist Georgia O'Keeffe came to Taos and during her visit spent several weeks here at the beautiful and remote Kiowa Ranch. While here, she painted the stately pine, which still stands today. O'Keeffe wrote that she would lie on the long weathered carpenter's bench under the tall tree staring up past the trunk, up into the branches and into the night sky.

That image is captured in her now world-famous oil painting, *The Lawrence Tree*, which is currently owned by the Wadsworth Atheneum in Hartford, Connecticut. Today, visitors can see the tree and the rest of what remains of the ranch, including a shrine where D.H. Lawrence's ashes are interred. Note: this is an isolated area with no facilities to speak of; the shrine and its environs are open during daylight hours.

Poe, Edgar Allan

Collapse Site
100 Broadway • Baltimore, Maryland

The circumstances surrounding Edgar Allan Poe's death remain a mystery even today. What's known is this: after a visit to Norfolk and Richmond for lectures, Poe was found drunk and wearing tatters outside a Baltimore tavern (reports vary on exactly where the tavern was located—many believe it was Ryan's Saloon on Lombard Street). How he arrived in that condition is not known. Had he been robbed? Had he simply gone on a bender? Was he experiencing some form of mental attack? It may never be clear. However, Poe was in fact taken unconscious here, to Washington College Hospital where he died on Sunday, October 7, 1849, several days after arriving. He was just 39 years old.

The original building that once held the hospital is completely intact, but it has been converted into apartments. Two markers have been placed in memory of the great writer. Poe is buried not far from here in the yard of Westminster Presbyterian Church, located at Fayette and Greene Streets in West Baltimore. His gravesite has regularly been visited by someone who has left a half a bottle of cognac and roses since 1949. Another nearby Poe landmark in Baltimore is the Poe House located at 203 Amity Street. Poe lived here for several years in the early 1830s with his aunt, among others. It was during this time in Poe's life that he decided to write short stories instead of poetry.

Edgar Allan Poe House
West 84th Street and Broadway

This is the "Edgar Allan Poe Street." At one time, Edgar Allan Poe lived at a broken-down farmhouse located smack in the middle of Broadway. It was here that he wrote "The Purloined Letter" (the last Dupin tale), "The Oblong Box," and "Thou Art the Man." Obsessed by a true murder case in New York, Poe twisted its events to form the two latter tales. Two plaques dedicated to Poe detail more of his life here; they are located on the northern buildings on either side of Broadway.

Edgar Allan Poe House II
532 North Seventh Street • Philadelphia, Pennsylvania • 215-597-8780

This small brick house (now connected to 530 North Seventh Street) was home to Edgar Allan Poe from 1838–1844. During the entire six years that Poe lived in Philadelphia, he attained his greatest success as an editor and critic, and he published some of his most famous tales, including, "The Gold Bug," "The Fall of the House of Usher," "The Tell-Tale Heart," and "The Murders in the Rue Morgue." Of his several Philadelphia Poe homes, this is the only one that survives. The site became part of the National Park System on November 10, 1978.

Poe Park
Grand Concourse at Kingsbridge Road • Bronx, New York
718-881-8900

The tiny Poe cottage in the Bronx was the last home of Edgar Allan Poe. Set in a tiny park on the (once grand) Grand Concourse, it is the only house left from the old village of Fordham. In 1846, Poe and his wife

Virginia leased the house for $100 a year. Virginia, who was 13 when she married her first cousin in 1836, had tuberculosis and was in failing health when Poe decided that the Bronx country air might help her feel better. Sadly, Poe was penniless despite his literary success, having lost his savings in a magazine venture that went bankrupt. Virginia's mother, who lived with them, had to forage in neighboring fields to feed the family.

During this difficult period, Poe wrote many soon-to-be-famous poems including "The Bells," "Eureka," and "Annabel Lee." Virginia finally died in 1847; and Poe himself died two years later during a trip to Baltimore. Their cottage was saved from destruction in the 1890s by the Shakespeare Society and moved from its original location on the other side of Kingsbridge Road in 1913. Today, the Bronx County Historical Society operates the house.

Virginia Home
3321 Monument Avenue • Richmond, Virginia

This house/museum is the oldest known dwelling within the original city of Richmond, dating back to before the Revolutionary War. Edgar Allan Poe lived nearby early in his career, and the Poe Museum features the life and work of the great writer by documenting his accomplishments with pictures, relics, and more, all focusing on his many years in Richmond. Established in 1921, the Poe Museum is only blocks away from Poe's first Richmond home and his first place of employment, the *Southern Literary Messenger*.

Steinbeck, John

John Steinbeck's Birthplace and Boyhood Home
132 Central Avenue • Salinas, California • 831-424-2735

The beautifully restored Victorian house where John Steinbeck was born on February 27, 1902 is now a charming restaurant. It also includes the Best Cellar Gift Shop, a treasure trove of Steinbeck books (including first

editions), Steinbeck House cookbooks and individual recipes, and wonderful gift items. You can also tour the home and view family heirlooms, precious mementos, and photographs.

John Steinbeck's Cottage
425 Eardley Avenue (between Spruce and Pine Streets)
Pacific Grove, California

Steinbeck bought this cottage early in 1941 and lived here briefly with Gwen Conger, who later became his second wife. He wrote parts of *The Sea of Cortez* and *The Forgotten Village* here before moving to New York City in the summer of 1941.

John Steinbeck Home
16250 Greenwood Lane • Monte Sereno, California

In May 1936, John and Carol Steinbeck purchased this 1.639 acre plot of land in what was then Los Gatos, California (now Monte Sereno). Carol designed a 1,452 square foot home, which was built in the summer of 1936. This small, one-story wooden structure was to become the first home owned by Steinbeck, and to protect his privacy, Steinbeck built an eight-foot grape stake fence around the property. At the entrance gate he personally placed a carved wooden plaque which read "Arroyo del Ajo" or "Garlic Gulch."

While living in this house, Steinbeck completed his classic *Of Mice and Men* and wrote another literary landmark, *The Grapes of Wrath*. While living here he also entertained many notable guests, but as other homes began to sprout up in the area, the Steinbecks decided to move to regain some privacy. They sold this house in September 1938, and in December 1989 it was added to the National Historic Registry.

Steinbeck Family Cottage
147 11th Street (between Lighthouse and Ricketts Row)
Pacific Grove, California

Built by John Steinbeck's father for use as a summer home, this pretty cottage features a pine tree in the yard that Steinbeck planted himself as a child. In 1930, Steinbeck brought his wife, Carol, here to live with him (where they got by on a $25-per-month allowance provided by John Steinbeck, Sr.). Steinbeck worked with his dad to remodel the cottage and eventually Steinbeck even added a fish pond to the property.

After leaving the cottage, Steinbeck returned in the fall of 1932 when his mother suffered a stroke, eventually dividing time between this cottage and the family home in Salinas. During this period, he worked on parts of *The Red Pony*, *The Pastures of Heaven*, *Tortilla Flat*, and *In Dubious Battle*. Steinbeck also began to write his classic *Of Mice and Men* at this cottage, but eventually moved out to Monte Sereno to escape the attention that his growing fame brought.

Warhol, Andy

Andy Warhol Museum
117 Sandusky Street • Pittsburgh, Pennsylvania • 412-237-8300

There's no place else like it—more than 3,000 objects and ephemera from Andy Warhol's extensive personal archive are on display for the first time in the U.S. The museum is housed in a renovated, seven-floor warehouse building and features more than 500 works of art, drawn from its extensive collections of works by Andy Warhol in all media, as well as from its huge archives and a collection of works by other artists. Warhol's films are screened continuously at the museum, and of course, the gift shop is phenomenal.

Andy Warhol Preserve
Off Route 27 (a half mile east of the intersection with East Lake Drive)
Eastern Tip of Montauk, Long Island, New York

In 1972, Warhol bought a home here on the farthest reaches of Montauk with his friend, film director Paul Morrissey. Between 1972 and 1987, Warhol entertained everyone from Liz Taylor, John Lennon, and Liza Minnelli out here. The Rolling Stones rehearsed for their 1975 tour of the America's here, and on August 6, 1977, the artist celebrated his 49th birthday here. After Warhol's death in 1987, Morrissey donated 15 acres of the property to The Nature Conservancy to create the Andy Warhol Preserve in honor of the artist.

The Factory(s)
Much of Warhol's myth, mystique and style was developed over the years at the various "Factory(s)" he presided over in New York City—the studio/ hangouts that served as a magnet for the glittering underground in New York, and that would influence so much of Warhol's work. These are the various locations where the Factory(s) existed:

Factory I · 231 East 47th Street • New York City, New York

The Factory started here in 1964 on the fifth floor of a building beneath an antiques store called "The Connoisseur's Corner." A photographer by the name of Billy Name who crashed at the Factory painted the Mid-Hudson with an industrial silver paint that ultimately became the trademark of the Factory look.

Factory II · 33 Union Square West • New York City, New York

After a couple of years, Factory I was torn down and so Warhol moved his colorful circus here to Union Square. It was at this location that Warhol began shooting films. In 1968, a woman named Valerie Solanas shot and almost killed Warhol here. While working at this Factory, Warhol also came up with the idea to make celebrity portraits his mainstay.

Factory III · 860 Broadway · New York City, New York

The Factory moved here in 1974, just around the corner from Factory II. From here, Warhol continued to paint and produce celebrity portraits. By now, he was also very busy in running *Interview* magazine. Today, there is a Petco store on the site.

Factory IV · 158 Madison Avenue · New York City, New York

Ten years later, 1984 saw the last incarnation of the Factory here at an old Con-Edison substation between 32nd and 33rd Streets. Warhol had just several years to live at this point.

New York Hospital-Cornell Medical Center
525 East 68th Street · New York City, New York

Andy Warhol checked into this hospital on Friday, February 20, 1987 under the alias "Bob Robert." Routine gall bladder surgery was performed on February 21, and then the artist was taken to a private room located on the 12th floor of Baker Pavilion. At 4:00 A.M. the next day, Warhol's blood pressure was recorded as "stable," but at 5:45 A.M. Warhol turned blue and his pulse became very weak before ceasing. Though the hospital staff tried for 45 minutes to resuscitate him, Andy Warhol was pronounced dead at 6:21 A.M. on February 22, 1987. He was just 58 years old. Andy Warhol is laid to rest at St. John Divine Cemetery in Bethel Park, Pennsylvania.

Residence
57 East 66th Street • New York City, New York

In 1974, Warhol purchased this six-story townhouse for $310,000. Warhol paid the full amount upfront so he wouldn't have to deal with a mortgage. He lived here for the rest of his life and a plaque on the side of the pretty home states that it was the home of "famous pop artist Andy Warhol." In 1988, the Warhol Estate auctioned off some ten thousand items belonging to the artist, and it netted a record $30 million dollars—the single largest collection ever handled by Sotheby's.

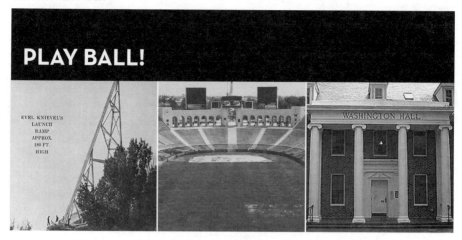

CHAPTER TEN

PLAY BALL!

Aaron, Hank

Fulton County Stadium • Lakewood Station • Atlanta, Georgia

Who can forget the sight of Aaron rounding the bases on April 8, 1974 in Atlanta, while those goofball fans chased him near shortstop and were pushed away by the new homerun king himself? Aaron hit the homerun off of the Dodgers' lefthander Al Downing in the fourth inning of the Braves' home opener against Los Angeles.

After the ball left Aaron's bat, Dodger centerfielder Jimmy Wynn and leftfielder Bill Buckner made a run, with Buckner even climbing the wall for it. Nevertheless, the ball made it into the Braves' bullpen after striking a billboard that said, "Think of it as money."

The ball was rounded up by Braves reliever Tom House, who quickly ran the ball in to Aaron at home-plate. The blast resulted in a game-delaying celebration, in which Aaron spoke to the crowd and hugged his dad. Aaron would go on to rack up 755 homers in his career, still the Major League record. The ballpark has since been torn down, but part of the retaining wall remains.

Ali, Muhammad

St. Dominick's Arena (now called the Central Maine Civic Center)
190 Birch Street • Lewiston, Maine • 207-783-2009

On May 25, 1965, in a small community arena in Lewiston, Maine, the re-match took place between Cassius Clay (who by now had changed his name to Muhammad Ali) and former champion Sonny Liston. The bout had originally been scheduled for November 16, 1964, but several days before the fight it was discovered that Ali had a hernia. Due to the operation, the fight had to be postponed seven months.

Despite the buzz surrounding the match, only 2,434 people (about half-ca-pacity) found their way to St. Dominick's Arena on fight night. The bout lasted just over a minute and a half; Ali threw only six punches before Liston went down. Liston was hit by a so-called "phantom-punch" that many of the spectators had not even seen. Seeing Liston on the canvas, Ali refused to go to the neutral corner but stood over Liston yelling: "Get up and fight, sucker!" That image of a scowling Ali has become one of sports' most famous snapshots.

Babe Ruth and Walter Johnson Game

Brea Bowl • St. Crispen Avenue and Napoli Drive • Brea, California

On October 31, 1924, Babe Ruth and Walter Johnson played a barnstorming game here that has become a solid part of the area's folklore. Sponsored by the Anaheim Elks Club, it was a homecoming for Johnson of sorts in that he grew up in the neighboring oil town of Olinda. Nearly 5,000 people turned out for the event at the Brea Bowl field, incredible given that nearby Anaheim's total population back then was just 2,000. Ruth's team won, 12–1, and the day was capped by two Ruth home runs (one of which supposedly traveled 550 feet). Remarkably, this game was documented by an 18-year-old named George E. Outland, who over the years carried on his hobby of photographing base-ball players (and eventually getting may of his shots signed by the players). A poster promoting the event touts it as the "only game in Southern California where Johnson and Ruth oppose each other." Today, the site of the old Brea Bowl is a quiet neighborhood. Just two blocks away, at 227 North Brea Boulevard, there's an auto repair company. The old garage that still stands at the site is where all of the players got dressed for the game after getting off the nearby train. From here, they marched down to the nearby field.

Babe Ruth Plaque
Intersection of Cooper and Hickory Streets • Delanco, New Jersey

The athletic field here was dedicated July 4, 1922 and has been in continuous use as a baseball venue in Delanco since that time. A small historical marker here commemorates the largest sporting event in Delanco history, the day George Herman "Babe" Ruth came to Delanco to play an exhibition game. The marker reads: "On July 1, 1924, Babe Ruth hit a home run on this Athletic Field in a game between Delanco and the Burlington County All-Stars. Over 5,000 baseball fans attended this historical baseball game. Babe Ruth, who was playing for the New York Yankees in 1924, received special permission to play an exhibition game in the tiny town of Delanco, New Jersey. It was widely advertised and the event became the largest in Delanco history. The Pennsylvania railroad ran extra trains and newspapers estimated that 5,000 people attended. Babe Ruth played for the Delanco team and the Burlington County All-Stars were engaged to oppose them. Ruth's homer came in the fifth inning. He 'socked it a terrific thump and the pellet sailed far and away over the fence in right field, for the first time in the history of Delanco Park.' 'It gave Delanco a 4-2 lead that was thereafter not disputed,' according to a newspaper account."

The town has celebrated Babe Ruth Day frequently since 1994 when former mayor, Dick Mueller, established the event by proclamation.

Babe Ruth's First Professional Home Run
Gillespie Street (near the North Carolina Department of Transportation building) • Cumberland County • Fayetteville, North Carolina

The historic marker here commemorates Babe Ruth's first home run in professional baseball. In March of 1914, the Baltimore Orioles, offered free lodging by the Baltimore-born owner of the Lafayette Hotel, traveled to Fayetteville for spring training. That season's Orioles team featured an 18-year-old

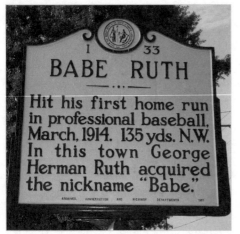

phenom pitcher named George Herman Ruth. During an Orioles intrasquad game at the old Cape Fear Fairgrounds, Ruth clobbered a ball out of the park and into a lake, marking his "unofficial" first home run as a professional player. The ballpark has long been gone and replaced by a local Department of Transportation building. But the marker was erected in 1951, thanks to the persistence of Maurice Fleishman, a 1914 bat boy who witnessed the historic blow. The ceremony at the marker's dedication was attended by former Philadelphia A's manager Connie Mack and Babe Ruth's wife, among other notables.

Babe Ruth's Longest Home Run?
Kirby Park • Wilkes-Barre, Pennsylvania

Two days after the 1926 World Series, Babe Ruth arrived at Kirby Park for an exhibition game and smacked a ball 650 feet, according to members of Wilkes-Barre's city government. The City of Wilkes-Barre built a permanent display in Kirby Park honoring Ruth's prodigious Pennsylvania poke. The sign's headline reads: "The Longest Home Run in Competitive Baseball History."

Bartman, Steve
Wrigley Field • 1060 West Addison Street • Chicago, Illinois

For years, Aisle 4, Row 8, Seat 113 was a tourist attraction at Wrigley Field. When the lower grandstands were reconfigured before the 2017 season, that seat number was changed to Section 2, Row 8, Seat 108. Now, it's still an attraction.

The Steve Bartman incident was a controversial play that occurred during a baseball game between the Chicago Cubs and the Florida Marlins on October 14, 2003, here at Wrigley Field. The incident occurred in the eighth inning of Game 6 of the National League Championship Series with Chicago leading 3-0 and holding a three-games-to-two lead in the best-of-seven series.

Marlins batter Luis Castillo hit a fly ball into foul territory in left field. Cubs outfielder Moisés Alou pursued the ball and leapt near the fence in an attempt to make the catch. Along with other spectators seated against the wall, Cubs fan Steve Bartman reached for the ball, but he deflected it, disrupting Alou's potential catch. The umpire judged the play not to be fan interference. If Alou had caught the ball, it would have been the second out in the inning, and the Cubs would have been just four outs away from winning their first National League pennant since 1945.

Instead, the Cubs endured an on-field meltdown. Pitcher Mark Prior threw a wild pitch to walk Castillo and allow Juan Pierre to reach third base. After a run-scoring single to cut the Cubs' lead to 3-1, Cubs shortstop Alex Gonzalez mishandled a ground ball that could have resulted in an inning-ending double play. The Cubs ultimately allowed eight runs in the inning, and lost the game 8-3. They also had another opportunity to win the series in Game 7 at Wrigley Field the next day, but they were eliminated by the Marlins. In the moments following the play, Cubs fans shouted insults and threw debris at Bartman. For his safety, security was forced to escort him from the ballpark. Minutes after the game, his name and personal information were published online, necessitating police protection at his home. He faced further harassment from fans and the media after the Cubs' loss in the series, as he was scapegoated for the continuation of the team's then-95-year championship drought. Bartman apologized for the incident and stated his desire to move past it and return to a quiet life. Many Cubs players came to his defense, emphasizing that their performance was to blame for their loss. In 2011, ESPN produced a documentary film exploring the subject as part of its *30 for 30* series. Titled *Catching Hell*, the film drew comparisons between the Bartman incident and Bill Buckner's fielding error late in Game 6 of the 1986 World Series, and explored the incident from different perspectives.

The actual ball was eventually procured by a Chicago lawyer and sold at an auction in December 2003. Grant DePorter purchased it for $113,824.16 on behalf of Harry Caray's Restaurant Group. On February 26, 2004, the ball was publicly detonated by special effects expert Michael Lantieri.

In 2005, the remains of the ball were used by the restaurant in a pasta sauce. While no part of the ball itself was in the sauce, the ball was boiled and the steam was captured, distilled, and added to the final concoction.

Today, the remains of the ball are on display at the Chicago Sports Museum, while further remains are amid various artifacts at the restaurant itself.

Baseball
Elysian Fields • 11th and
Washington Streets
Hoboken, New Jersey

Frank Sinatra's birthplace is also the place where the first recorded baseball game was played on June 19, 1846 when Alexander Cartwright's Knickerbockers lost to the New York Baseball Club by a score of 23 to 1. The game was held at the Elysian Fields, in Hoboken, New Jersey. A plaque at 11th and Washington Streets in Hoboken commemorates the game.

Basketball
782 State Street • Springfield, Massachusetts • 413-788-1444

Dr. James Naismith invented basketball on a cold, autumn day in 1891. He was the physical education instructor at the International YMCA Training School (now Springfield College) at Springfield, Massachusetts. Baseball had just finished up, and football was still a few weeks away. The athletes needed a sport to keep them in superb condition, and since it was too cold to train outside, Naismith had to think up a new indoor activity.

He remembered a game he played as a child called "Duck on a Rock."

Changing a few rules around, he came out with the sport "Basketball." It was played with two peach baskets and a soccer ball, and 12 of the 13 rules Naismith created are still basic to the game. Today, a McDonald's near campus occupies the exact site of the "Naismith Gym." Inside are photos and some information describing the location's history.

Bias, Len
Howard Hall • University of Maryland • College Park, Maryland
301-314-7484

This is the dorm where college basketball star Len Bias died on June 19, 1986. Just two days earlier, the Maryland forward (the Atlantic Coast Conference player of the year) had been selected by the NBA's Boston Celtics (who had the second pick of the draft). Autopsy tests revealed traces of cocaine were in his system, and the resulting investigation led to charges against three people who admitted using drugs with Bias on the day of his death. This controversy prompted the resignation of Maryland coach Lefty Driesell.

The Birth of the Curse
Griffith Park—Harding Golf Course • 4730 Crystal Springs Drive
Los Angeles, California

Did you know that the site of the "Birth of the Curse" is just 10 minutes from Dodger Stadium? It's located at the 18th hole on the Harding municipal golf course at Griffith Park—where Miller Huggins tracked down Babe Ruth in the winter of 1920 to have him sign the contract that brought him to the Yankees. And yes, there is even a plaque to mark where it all happened.

The sale of Babe Ruth from the Boston Red Sox to the New York Yankees is still arguably one of the most important transactions in baseball history. It was the start of a decades-long dynasty for the Yankees and the beginning of an 86-year World Series drought for the Red Sox, which came to be known as "The Curse of the Bambino." Harry Frazee was the owner of the Boston Red Sox, a franchise that was deeply in debt. Frazee needed cold hard cash and was willing to sell his star player to the Yankees to get it. Jacob Ruppert, the owner of the Yankees, had a different problem. Ruppert was making a small fortune selling beer during Yankees games, but Prohibition was about to put an end to that. So, Ruppert would have to find another way to keep fans coming to the games, and he believed signing Babe would be the answer. But there was just one problem: Nobody knew where Babe had gone, and Ruppert needed to close the deal fast before Frazee or Babe could change their minds. So, Ruppert sent the team's manager, Miller Huggins, unsigned contract in hand, on a search for the man of the hour with orders to get Babe's signature on that contract. Huggins questioned and cajoled anyone he could find that might have a clue as to Babe's whereabouts. And soon, with a promising lead, Huggins was on a fast train heading west.

Hollywood at the dawn of the 1920s was an "open" city and with Prohibition becoming official in a matter of days, the clubs, bars, and saloons swelled with patrons having their last legal sip of alcohol. Huggins arrived to Hollywood in the midst of all of that. He knew Babe was in town, but where in town? This is where the story becomes a bit apocryphal—no one knows for sure how Miller Huggins found Babe, but there are numerous theories as to how it came about. Regardless, Huggins did find him here, on the 18th fairway of a golf course in Griffith Park. Imagine for a moment the sight of Babe preparing his swing, when off in the distance he sees Miller Huggins, running toward him, waving the contract and yelling his name. Some say Babe signed the contract just to get Huggins off his back so he could finish his round of golf. The actual signing took place at the clubhouse at the Griffith Park golf course. It still stands today, 98 years after the day Babe became a Yankee. There's a plaque here commemorating that historic moment in 1920.

Black Sox Courthouse
54 West Hubbard Street • Chicago, Illinois

"Say it ain't so, Joe." It's become one of baseball's most famous historic catch phrases, supposedly uttered by a devastated kid as the disgraced Joe Jackson entered this one-time courthouse. It became known as the "Black Sox" scandal when several members of the Chicago White Sox conspired to lose the 1919

World Series to the Cincinnati Red Stockings.

Despite their acquittal, Baseball Commissioner Judge Landis permanently banned all of those players from the game. Jackson, one of the greatest players of all-time, had a series batting average of .375 that year and played error-free defense. However, he still received the same lifetime banishment from Judge Landis which is what keeps him from the Hall of Fame. The scandal created huge headlines and made a nation of fans feel betrayed.

This building, which housed the Cook County Criminal Courts for 35 years, was the site of many other legendary trials, including the Leopold and Loeb murder case.

Bonds, Barry
BALCO • 1520 Gilbreth Road • Burlingame, California

This is the former home of the infamous BALCO "sport nutrition center." The Bay Area Laboratory Co-operative (BALCO) was a San Francisco Bay Area business which supplied anabolic steroids to professional athletes, including baseball stars Barry Bonds and Jason Giambi, and track star Marion Jones (among others). Despite a phenomenal baseball career, Bonds was a central figure in baseball's steroids scandal. He was indicted in 2007 on charges of perjury and obstruction of justice for allegedly lying to a grand jury during the federal government's investigation of BALCO. After the perjury charges were dropped, Bonds was convicted of obstruction of justice in 2011, but the conviction was overturned in 2015. During his 10 years of eligibility, he did not receive the 75 percent of the vote needed to be elected to the National Baseball Hall of Fame. Some voters of the Baseball Writers' Association of America stated they did not vote for Bonds because they believed he used performance-enhancing drugs.

"Brothers All Are We" Marker
Intersection of Main Greeting and South Greeting Roads
Springfield, Massachusetts

In 1934, the American Legion Post 21 baseball team forfeited an opportu-

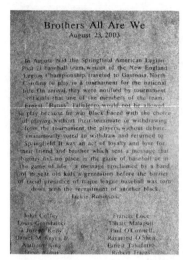

nity to win a national championship when they unanimously voted to withdraw from the Eastern Sectional Baseball Tournament in Gastonia, North Carolina because their black teammate, Ernest "Bunny" Taliaferro, would not be allowed to play. It was an act of loyalty and love for their friend and brother which sent a message that bigotry has no place in the game of baseball or in the game of life; a message proclaimed by a band of 16-year-old kids a generation before the barrier of racial prejudice of major league baseball was torn down with the recruitment of another black player, Jackie Robinson. A stone marker to honor the team and their coaches has been placed in a small plaza near the baseball stadium in Forest Park, where they played their home games. The monument is inscribed with the names of the Post 21 players and is entitled "Brothers All Are We."

Chamberlain, Wilt

Hersheypark Arena
100 West Hershey Park Drive
Hershey, Pennsylvania
717-534-3911

It's arguably the NBA's most unbreakable record: 100 points in a single game, set by Philadelphia Warrior Wilt Chamberlain on March 2, 1962. The Warriors trained in Hershey and thus returned each season to play several games there for local fans. On this wintry night before just over 4,000 people (about half the gym's capacity), Chamberlain did the unthinkable in this arena that still stands in the world's chocolate capitol. The final score was Philadelphia over the New York Knicks, 169–147. The next night when

these two teams played each other in New York, Chamberlain was "held" to just 54 points.

Decker, Mary

Los Angeles Memorial Coliseum • 3911 South Figueroa Street
Los Angeles, California

Mary Decker had hoped to run both the 1,500 and 3,000 meters at the Los Angeles Olympics in 1984, but withdrew from the 1,500 because the events overlapped. So her hopes were staked on the longer race, in which her rivals included Zola Budd, the diminutive South African controversially granted British citizenship earlier in the year. At the 1,700-meter mark, the two runners bumped into each other twice in the space of a few strides and then Decker tripped on Budd's right leg, her spikes digging deeply into Budd's heel.

Budd ran on, eventually limping home seventh, but Decker fell forward onto the infield, her only hope of a medal erased. Later, a distraught Decker refused to accept Budd's apology, and the image of Decker breaking down became synonymous with the event. Since the 1984 Olympics, the running track has been removed from the Coliseum.

Dempsey, Tom

Tulane Stadium • Aron Student Residences at Stadium Place
(intersection of McAlister Drive and Willow Street) • Tulane University
New Orleans, Louisiana • 504-865-5724

On November 8, 1970, New Orleans Saints placekicker Tom Dempsey prepared to kick a 63-yard field goal in the closing seconds of a game against the Detroit Lions. If he made it, it would be the longest field goal in NFL history. The Lions were up 17 to 16 and so Dempsey was the Saints' last chance. Adding to the drama was the fact that Dempsey's kicking foot was deformed to the point that he only had half a foot. Incredibly, Dempsey put it through the goalposts, making history and winning the game for the Saints. The images of the kick remain some of the most memorable in NFL history.

To date, the record stands as the longest, though Denver's Jason Elam tied the record in 1998. Tulane Stadium was the home field of the New Orleans Saints and the Sugar Bowl, as well as playing host to three Super Bowls. Torn down in 1980, there is not a single piece of the stadium remaining. However, three plaques that used to be on

the stadium's walls remain, now placed at what once was the northeast corner of the stadium.

Dempsey, Jack/Gene Tunney

Soldier Field • 425 East McFetridge Drive • Chicago, Illinois • 312-747-1285

Dempsey vs. Tunney II at Soldier Field in Chicago produced a gate of $2.65 million, a record that stood for 50 years. A hugely hyped rematch (Jack Dempsey had lost the first fight), the fight did not disappoint. In the seventh, Dempsey caught Gene Tunney with a long right and followed up with a left hook to the chin. For the first time in their two contests, Tunney was on his back foot and soon he was on the canvas, dropping hard after a four-punch flurry to his head.

Thus began boxing's fabled "long count." Dempsey—who would later ask what a neutral corner was—failed to back away from Tunney as the then-new rule dictated. Referee Dave Barry took several seconds to convince him to do so, but only after half-pushing Dempsey in the right direction did Barry turn back to Tunney and begin his count. He reached nine before a shaken (but clearly lucid) Tunney regained his feet.

Afterwards, Tunney would insist that he could have gotten up earlier. Either way, he managed to stave off Dempsey for the rest of the round and recovered to box his way to another points victory. He would retire unbeaten as a heavyweight, a record only Rocky Marciano has duplicated.

First Louisville Slugger

118 S. First St. • Louisville, Kentucky

In May 2017, a historical marker was unveiled to commemorate the site where

J.A. "Bud" Hillerich made the first Louisville Slugger bat for Pete Browning 133 years earlier. In 1884, Bud Hillerich skipped work at his father's woodworking shop to root for the Louisville Eclipse major league baseball team. Pete Browning, one of baseball's greatest hitters of the time, broke his bat that day. Hillerich offered to go back to his father's shop to make Browning a brand new bat. The next day, Browning got three hits with the bat Hillerich made for him, and a Louisville legend was born. The historical marker was sponsored by the Louisville Slugger Museum and Factory and the Kentucky Historical Society.

First Professional Baseball Game
333 South Clinton Street • Fort Wayne, Indiana

In 2017, a monument here at Headwaters Park was placed to mark the location of the first professional baseball league game played between the Fort Wayne Kekiongas and the Cleveland Forest Citys on May 4, 1871. Fort Wayne defeated Cleveland 2-0. The marker here reads: "KEKIONGA BALL GROUNDS 1869–1871. The first major league baseball game, now called the first game in a professional league, was played here May 4, 1871. Kekionga whitewashed Cleveland 2-0 in what was then acclaimed the greatest game ever played. It remained the lowest score in the five-year history of the National Association. The grounds were located between Elm, Mechanics, Fair, and Bluff Streets. Kekionga moved here in 1869 from its former grounds east of Calhoun between present-day Wallace and Williams Streets. In May 1870, the team improved the grounds with a fence and grandstands. The central grandstand, the Grand Duchess, was modeled after its namesake in Cincinnati. On November 5, 1871, all structures were destroyed by fire and never rebuilt."

First West Coast Night Game
Alameda Street between 7th and Palmetto • Los Angeles, California

Incredibly, there was a minor league night game in Los Angeles on July 2, 1893, even though Major League Baseball did not feature one until 1935. It occurred at old Athletic Park, very near to the spot where a Greyhound bus terminal and a McDonald's stand today. The game was between the Los Angeles Seraphs (soon to be "Angels") and the Stockton River Pirates. Los Angeles won, 5-2.

Flutie, Doug
The Orange Bowl • 1501 NW 3rd Street • Miami, Florida

Doug Flutie, the 5-foot-9 Boston College quarterback already was considered a lock for the Heisman Trophy when, on November 23, 1984, he led the Eagles against Miami in the Orange Bowl (the annual game was moved to Pro Player Stadium in 1996). The Hurricanes led the Eagles 45–41, having gone ahead with 28 seconds remaining. But Flutie made the most of those remaining seconds.

Two passes and 22 seconds later, the ball was a couple of yards beyond midfield; time for just one more play. Flutie dropped back, scrambled, then launched the ball. Three receivers and three defenders were bunched together as they arrived at the goal line. Receiver Gerard Phelan drifted back a couple of yards away from them as the ball sailed toward the pack. Defensive backs Darrell Fullington and Reggie Sutton leaped to deflect the ball—which sailed over their fingertips and into Phelan's arms. Touchdown, making it Boston College 47, Miami 45 in one of football's wildest finishes.

Gaedel, Eddie
Sportsman's Park • Area bounded by Dodier Street, Spring Street, Sullivan Avenue, and Grand Avenue • St. Louis, Missouri

One of the most publicized stunts in baseball history happened on August 18, 1951 when 3-foot-7-inch tall, 65-pound Eddie Gaedel popped out from a 7-foot tall birthday cake between games of a Browns-Tigers doubleheader. Legendary Browns owner Bill Veeck hatched the idea in part to boost attendance.

Gaedel, wearing a Browns uniform with the number 1/8, pinch hit in the first inning for Frank Saucier. Veeck had instructed the diminutive Brownie to crouch low, and not swing his toy-like bat. Due to the tiny strike zone, he walked in his only plate appearance. Tiger manager skipper Red Rolfe protested, but Gaedel had a legitimate contract for the game. Sportsman's Park no longer stands, but the field (part of the Matthew Dickey Boy's Club on North Grand Avenue) is still there.

Gathers, Hank
Gersten Pavilion • Loyola Marymount University • 7900 Loyola Boulevard Los Angeles, California • 310-338-2700

March 4, 1990: As a junior the previous season, Loyola Marymount forward Hank Gathers was the NCAA's leading scorer and rebounder. But early in the

1990 season, he blacked out during a game. Doctors cleared him to play again, placing him on medication to regulate his arrhythmia—an erratic heartbeat.

Against Portland in the semifinals of the West Coast Conference tournament played at Loyola, the 6-foot-7 Gathers slammed home a dunk, enthusiastically high fived a teammate and trotted back to midcourt. Suddenly, he put his hands on his knees and crumpled to the floor. Going into convulsions, he rolled over and got to his hands and knees before collapsing again.

Gathers was given cardiopulmonary resuscitation on the court and on his way to the hospital. But while relatives and teammates waited outside the emergency room, Gathers was pronounced dead. Hank Gathers was just 23, and the chilling images of Gathers collapsing were shown for days following the tragedy.

"Glory Days"
Miller Stadium • 5908 Jackson Street • West New York, New Jersey

For his 1985 "Glory Days" video, Bruce Springsteen used Miller Stadium in West New York for the baseball scenes. Babe Ruth and Lou Gehrig played an exhibition game here in 1931. The ballpark is used primarily by Memorial High School and the New Jersey Amateur Baseball League.

Harris, Franco
Three Rivers Stadium • 300 Stadium Circle • Pittsburgh, Pennsylvania

The "Immaculate Reception" refers to Franco Harris' miraculous 60-yard touchdown catch that gave the Pittsburgh Steelers a 13-7 victory over the Oakland Raiders in the 1972 AFC Divisional Playoffs. Down 7-6, with just over a minute left, the Steelers' Terry Bradshaw fired a pass downfield to half-back John Fuqua, who was nailed hard by Raiders defender Jack Tatum just as the ball arrived. It hit one of the players and bounced in the air and, luckily for the Steelers, into the hands of rookie running back Franco Harris.

After his "immaculate reception," Harris ran 42 yards to score with five seconds left, giving the Steelers an improbably 13-7 victory. It's still one of the most miraculous finishes in the history of sports.

The Home Run That Changed Baseball
Whittington Park • 870 Whittington Avenue • Hot Springs, Arkansas

Cap Anson, manager of the Chicago White Stockings (now the Chicago Cubs), first brought his team to Hot Springs all the way back in 1886. Known for its thermal waters, nightlife, and hotel systems, Hot Springs was the ideal place for spring training. The 1886 season marked the first arrival of a baseball team in the area, much less a well-known team from the North. But what Anson did for the area was establish a little-known program and grow an empire. Today, the state created the Historic Hot Springs Baseball Trail which marks the steps and gathering spots and tells the stories of baseball legends. The trail has 31 stops, including this one.

Built in 1909 as the Boston Red Sox training center, Whittington Park was also used by the Cincinnati Reds and Brooklyn Dodgers.

On St. Patrick's Day 1918, Red Sox pitcher Babe Ruth was throwing in a spring training game in Hot Springs at Whittington Park. The team needed someone to bat, and Ruth, not yet considered a powerhouse hitter, launched one over the fence, out of the park, across the street, over a wall, and into the farthest pond of the neighboring Hot Springs Alligator Farm. That moment all but changed the trajectory of Babe's career. Nobody ever imagined a baseball could be hit so far. Some modern experts place the distance at 573 feet on the fly. Whittington Park is gone, but home plate is marked on the parking lot where it used to be and a historical marker has been erected across the street outside the alligator farm wall. There's also a sign inside the still-existing gator farm where the ball landed. The marker reads: "Ruth trained here nine times and became a very familiar face around Hot Springs. He hiked the mountains, took the baths, played golf, patronized the casinos, and visited the racetrack. On March 17, 1918 (St. Patrick's Day), he launched a mammoth home run from Whittington Park that landed on the fly inside the Arkansas Alligator Farm. It has been measured at 573 feet, baseball's first 500-foot-plus drive."

(The home plate outline is in the far northwest corner of the large parking lot on the north side of Whittington Ave., directly across from the plain-looking Hot Springs Family Church building. The historical marker is further east, on the south side of Whittington Ave., outside the wall of the Arkansas Alligator Farm.)

Huntington Avenue Grounds

Left field (NW), Huntington Avenue; third base (SW), Bryant (Rogers) Street, now Forsyth Street; first base (SE), New Gravelly Pt. Road and New York, New Haven and Hartford Railroad tracks; right field (NE), New Gravelly Pt. Road • Boston, Massachusetts

Before the 1912 opening of Fenway Park, Huntington Avenue Grounds was home to the Boston Red Sox. In fact, it was their very first ballpark. Built for $35,000 in 1901, Huntington Avenue Grounds originally seated only about 9,000 fans. However, there was room for thousands more (albeit via standing room) beyond ropes in the outfield and in the huge foul territory. With just a single entrance (and one turnstile), the simple structure was home field to the team known as the Boston Americans, who won their first game played here

on May 8, 1901, defeating Connie Mack's A's, 12–4, behind the pitching of Cy Young. Nearly three years later, on May 5, 1904, Young tossed the first perfect game in American League history when he stopped the A's, 3–0, here. In use for only 11 years, Huntington Avenue Grounds is notable because of what is

conveyed on a plaque that sits near the original spot of home plate: Dedicated in 1993, the inscription reads: "On October 1, 1903 the first modern World Series between the American League champion Boston Pilgrims (later known as the Red Sox) and the National League champion Pittsburgh Pirates was played on this site. General admission tickets were fifty cents. The Pilgrims, led by twenty-eight game winner Cy Young, trailed the series three games to one but then swept four consecutive victories to win the championship five games to three." Now located on the campus of Northeastern University, there is also a life-size statue of Cy Young located near where the pitcher's mound used to be (in the Churchill Hall Mall). Additionally, there is a World Series Exhibit Room in the nearby Cabot Physical Education Center with memorabilia from the 1901–1911 Red Sox teams and a plaque attached to the side of the building marking where the left-field foul pole stood.

Irving, Julius
McNichols Arena • 1635 Bryant Street • Denver, Colorado • 303-640-7300

At the ninth ABA All-Star Game on January 27, 1976, during halftime, the era of the Slam Dunk contest was ushered into our culture. And Julius Irving, "Dr. J," created and perfected the mother of all dunks—his famous court-length, take-off-from-the-foul-line-and-throw-it-down showstopper. While the contest has certainly lost some of its luster over the years, this circus-like highlight is what set the entire slam-dunk-as-entertainment train in motion. The arena closed after the Nuggets and Avalanche moved to the Pepsi Center and was demolished in 2000 to make space for a parking lot surrounding Empower Field at Mile High.

Johnson, Magic/Larry Bird
Special Events Center at the University of Utah (now the Huntsman Center) • University of Utah • 1825 East South Campus Drive Front Salt Lake City, Utah

The NCAA tournament, which began the decade with a 25-team field, had expanded to include 40 teams by 1979, and the championship game featured Indiana State and Michigan State. Leading unbeaten Indiana State was Larry Bird (fifth-year senior, Player of the Year, and already a first round draft pick of the Boston Celtics). The Spartans were led by Magic Johnson, just a sophomore, but a six foot, nine inch point guard—unheard of at the time.

Michigan State won the game by 11 as Magic outscored Bird, 24-19 in the most watched NCAA game in history. A year later, Bird was the NBA's Rookie of the Year and Magic, who entered the 1979 draft as an underclassman, helped lead the Los Angeles Lakers to the world championship.

Jordan, Michael
Delta Center • 301 West South Temple • Salt Lake City, Utah • 801-325-2000

This was Bob Costas' call: "Here comes Chicago—17 seconds, 17 seconds from game 7 or from championship number 6. Jordan—open—Chicago with the lead!" That shot over Byron Russell, at that point the "last shot" of Jordan's remarkable career, gave the Bulls a victory over the Utah Jazz, and the Bulls' sixth NBA championship in eight years. The image of Jordan canning the shot is still one of the most enduring in the NBA. Since then, the actual piece of floor was taken up, auctioned off, placed in pieces of collectable cards, etc.

King, Billie Jean/Bobby Riggs
Houston Astrodome • 8400 Kirby Drive • Houston, Texas

On September 20, 1973, Billie Jean King raised women's tennis to new heights with her "Battle of the Sexes" victory over the outspoken chauvinist Bobby Riggs. Riggs, the 55-year-old hustler who had challenged King to a best three sets out of five match, had vowed there was no way a woman could beat him. And if King did, he promised to jump off a bridge somewhere in California—that never happened. King rolled to an easy 6-4, 6-3, 6-3 straight sets victory, and Riggs was so tired, he could barely speak.

It happened in front of the largest crowd ever to watch a tennis match (30,472), with a television audience estimated at 40 million, and with viewers tuned in via satellite in 36 foreign countries. The Houston Astrodome was the world's first air-conditioned, domed, all-purpose stadium. Constructed in the early 1960s, it was the home of the Houston Astros from 1965-1999.

Knight, Bobby

Assembly Hall at Indiana University • 1001 East 17th Street
Bloomington, Indiana • 866-IUSPORT

On February 23, 1985, Knight's Hoosiers were playing the Purdue Boilermakers at home. While Purdue's Steve Reid was attempting to shoot free throws, the notorious hothead Knight tossed a chair across the court, nearly hitting the people in the wheelchair section across the way. Knight was ejected from the game and suspended for one game by Big Ten Commissioner Wayne Duke. Knight issued a statement apologizing for the incident, but the image of the toss came to define the coach's always intense, sometimes violent tendencies he's showed through much of his career.

Knievel, Evel

Snake River Canyon • Twin Falls, Idaho • 203-733-3974

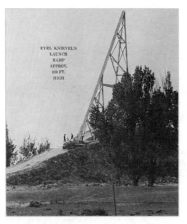

EVEL KNIEVEL'S LAUNCH RAMP APPROX. 100 FT. HIGH

DIRECTIONS: A mile north of town on US-93, south of the I-84 freeway. The jump site can be seen from the Twin Falls Visitors Center at the south end of the Perrine Bridge.

This is the site of Evel Knievel's ill-fated attempt to jump the Snake River Canyon on a rocket-powered motorcycle on September 8, 1974. Although the rockets did not perform as required, the daredevil jumper still floated by parachute to safety.

There's a large parking area and a visitor center at the south foot of the delicate Perrine Memorial Bridge, and it's well worth stopping to see the remains of his launch pad (a triangular pile of dirt, on private property a mile or so east of the bridge) or the stone monument that calls him "Robert 'Evel' Knievel—Explorer, Motorcyclist, Daredevil."

Maravich, Pete

First Church Of the Nazarene of Pasadena
3700 East Sierra Madre Boulevard • Pasadena, California 626-351-9631

On January 5, 1988, basketball great "Pistol Pete" Maravich joined Dr. James Dobson's 7:00 A.M. basketball scrimmage at this church gymnasium. Moments after telling Dr. Dobson he felt great, Pete collapsed, went into seizure, and died of congenital heart failure. Just 40 years old, the scrappy, former NBA All-Star was famous for his droopy socks and mop-top hairdo. In college, Maravich averaged 44.2 points a game at LSU, leading the nation in scoring three times, then played 10 years in the NBA, where he was the top scorer in 1977.

Mazeroski, Bill

Forbes Field • 230 South Bouquet Street (at the intersection of Sennott and Bouquet) • Pittsburgh, Pennsylvania

Bill Mazeroski was the first player to end a World Series with a home run, and the image of his shot clearing both the head of Yogi Berra and the red brick outfield wall at old Forbes Field is one of baseball's best (as is the sequence of Mazeroski then rounding the bases and getting mobbed at homeplate).

In the 1960 Fall Classic, the Yankees had rallied with two runs in the top of the ninth to tie the game 9–9. Mazeroski led off the ninth and hit a 1–0 slider over the left field wall to give Pittsburgh a 10–9 victory and a World Series title. Today, Forbes Field is gone, but you can still cross homeplate where Mazeroski got mobbed. It sits encased in plastic near its original location in a hallway of the University of Pittsburgh.

Miracle on Ice

Olympic Regional Development Authority • 218 Main Street • Lake Placid 518-523-1655

"Do you believe in Miracles?" It's thought by many to be the greatest moment in sports history, one that may have even helped end the Cold War. All thanks to the rag-tag group of college players that shocked the world by beating the Russians before going on to win the gold medal at the 1980 Winter Games in Lake Placid.

The United States was the seventh seed in the 12-team tournament and had lost to the Soviet team, recognized as the best hockey team in the world, 10-3, in an exhibition match at Madison Square Garden just 13 days before. But the Americans reached the medal round with a 4-0-1 record.

Playing in front of a boisterous home crowd, Team U.S.A. fell behind early, but Mark Johnson scored a goal to tie the game, 2-2, just before the end of the first period. The Soviets took a 3-2 lead into the third period, but Johnson scored again to tie it up. Team captain Mike Eruzione scored the game-winning goal with a wrist shot later in the third period, and goalie Jim Craig stood on his head, making 39 saves as the team held on to beat the unbeatable, 4-3.

Just two days after the emotional victory, the team scored three third-period goals to beat Finland, 4-2, for the gold. Today at the rink, a museum can be found which honors both the 1980 and the 1932 Games that were both played here.

Munson, Thurman
Akron-Canton Airport • 5400 Lauby Road NW • North Canton, Ohio

On August 2, 1979, Thurman Munson, superstar catcher for the New York Yankees, died in a plane crash. The 32-year-old was practicing takeoffs and landings in his new twin engine Cessna Citation jet at the Akron-Canton airport. Something went wrong, causing the jet to clip a tree and fall short of the runway on a landing attempt. The plane then burst into flames, killing Munson who was trapped inside, and injuring two other companions.

The entire Yankee team attended his funeral in Canton, Ohio. Lou Piniella and Bobby Murcer, who were Munson's best friends as well as teammates, gave moving eulogies. That night, the Yankees beat the Baltimore Orioles 5-4 in New York with Bobby Murcer driving in all five runs.

Namath, Joe

The Miami Touchdown Club • 3785 NW 82nd Avenue, Suite 111
Miami, Florida • 305-477-1815

The Jets were given little chance of winning Super Bowl III against the Baltimore Colts in 1969. After all, the AFL Champions had been beaten decisively by the NFL Champions in the first two Super Bowls, and many experts did not think the Jets were as strong as the Kansas City and Oakland teams that lost in Super Bowls I and II. Writers and bookmakers alike all predicted a blowout for the Colts.

But none of this fazed Jet Quarterback Joe Namath. In fact, at a Super Bowl week awards dinner at this private club, Namath stunned both experts and fans with his now famous boast: "The Jets will win on Sunday, I guarantee you." True to his words, on Super Bowl Sunday, "Broadway Joe" completed 17 of 28 passes for 206 yards and the inspired Jets made big defensive plays to stun the Colts 16–7, completing one of the biggest upsets in sports history.

Polo Grounds Lights

5999 East Van Buren Street • Phoenix, Arizona

Phoenix Municipal Stadium was built in 1964 and is currently the home to the Arizona State Sun Devils baseball program. It is the former spring training home to the Oakland A's, having played their home games there from 1984 to 2014. The San Francisco Giants also played at the ballpark during spring training in 1964. The stadium's light poles are the original light poles that were installed at the Polo Grounds in New York City in 1940. They served Polo Grounds until 1964, when the stadium was demolished. Horace Stoneham, the Giants' owner whose club started spring training at the previous iteration of the Phoenix Municipal in 1947, had the poles shipped here.

Riegels, Roy

Rose Bowl • 1001 Rose Bowl Drive • Pasadena, California • 626-577-3100

This is what legendary announcer Graham McNamee screamed as he broadcast the 1929 Rose Bowl game between Georgia Tech and California. "Am I crazy? Am I crazy? Am I crazy? Am I crazy?" What was he seeing? Roy Riegels of the California Bears had snagged a football fumbled by Georgia Tech. He caught it on the first bounce, got spun around and, seeing daylight, sprinted toward the goal line 64 yards away. However, he was headed the wrong way!

Teammate Benny Lom chased Rie-
gels half the length of the field, shouting
at him to turn around. It wasn't until he
had almost crossed the goal line, with
Lom pulling at him, that Riegels under-
stood and tried to reverse direction. But
it was too late. Georgia Tech gang-tack-
led him at the one-yard line.

Robinson, Jackie
Ebbets Field • Area bounded by Sullivan Place, Bedford Avenue,
Montgomery Street, and McKeever Place • Brooklyn, New York

April 15, 1947 was the day that Jackie Robinson played his first game for the
Brooklyn Dodgers, the first time a black man had appeared in a Major League
baseball game. He went hitless, but did score the winning run.

That season, the 28-year-old rookie played first base, the only position
open on the Dodgers (he would move back to second base the next year). The
new position was easy compared to all he had to endure—taunting and a near
rebellion by some of his teammates, black cats thrown on the field, and many
other threats. Despite the pressure, he kept his temper under control.

One poignant moment at this first game happened when Dodgers' shortstop Pee Wee Reese, a native of Louisville, draped an arm over Robinson's
shoulder, a quiet expression of support that spoke volumes.

Ron Necciai's 27 Strikeout Game
DeVault Memorial Stadium • 1501 Euclid Avenue • Bristol, Virginia

On May 13, 1952, 19-year-old Bristol right-hander Ron Necciai struck out 27
Welch hitters in a nine-inning no-hitter that put the Appalachian League on
the baseball map. Necciai, a Pirates farmhand, faced 31 batters—walking one,
hitting another, and losing two outs when his catcher dropped a third strike
and a fielder committed an error. One out was recorded on a ground ball.
Necciai's remarkable feat gained national attention and prompted Branch
Rickey to say, "There have been only two young pitchers I was certain were
destined for greatness. . . . One of those boys was Dizzy Dean. The other is Ron
Necciai." Rickey was only half right. Necciai was 4-0 at Bristol with 109 strikeouts and allowed only 10 hits in 43 innings. He was 7-9 with 172 strikeouts

in 126 innings when he moved up to Burlington of the Carolina League before finishing his 1952 season at Pittsburgh, where he struggled to a 1-6 record and 7.08 ERA in 54 innings. After that 1952 season, physical problems took a toll on Necciai and his stock tumbled quickly. But a baseball that Necciai threw in his memorable 1952 game remains on display at the Baseball Hall of Fame in Cooperstown, and a commemorative marker at DeVault Memorial Stadium honors his monumental pitching

performance. DeVault is the current home of the Bristol White Sox, a Chicago affiliate in the Appalachian League, but the original park where Necciai tossed his no-hitter is gone. The original ballpark, located about a mile from the current park at Gate City Highway and Catherine Streets, was torn down in the 1960s and is now the current location of a dairy.

Ruth, Babe

Final Baseball Game • Hanmer & George Streets, off Franklin Ave.
Hartford, Connecticut

Originally, this ballpark was home to the Eastern League's Hartford Senators, the Hartford Blues of the National Football League, and included a 1/5-mile dirt oval for motorsports. Initially named Clarkin Field from 1921-1927, it was renamed for former Connecticut Governor and First President of the National League, Morgan Bulkeley, in 1927. The park played host to Hartford's various minor league baseball teams such as the Hartford Chiefs, Hartford Senators, Hartford Laurels, and Hartford Bees of the Eastern League between 1921 and 1952. Lou Gehrig, Jim Thorpe, Leo Durocher, Hank Greenberg, Warren Spahn, and Johnny Sain all played for these teams at one point in their careers. When the Boston Braves moved to Milwaukee at the end of the 1952 season, Hartford's minor league team was relocated. But on September 30, 1945, true history was made here when George Herman "Babe" Ruth Jr. played in a charity game for the Savitt Gems of the Greater Hartford Twilight Baseball League. At 50 years of age, Ruth entered the game as a pinch-hitter and grounded out to the opposing pitcher. The ballgame was Babe Ruth's final appearance of his playing career. Bulkeley Stadium fell into disarray and was demolished in 1955. The location of the stadium is currently a nursing home, Ellis Manor. A historical plaque was dedicated there in 1998 near the former location of left field. There's also a home plate marker near the facility's main entrance, and across from the reception desk inside Ellis Manor is a wall of fame honoring the memory of Bulkeley Stadium.

Site of Baseball's First Perfect Game

Current site of Becker College • 61 Sever Street • Worcester, Massachusetts

In 1880, the Worcester Agricultural Fairgrounds was located here, and the fairgrounds field was home to the National League's Worcester team. On June 12, 1880, it was here that Worcester's Lee Richmond tossed the first perfect game in major league history. In the last season in which the pitching distance was 45 feet, Richmond mowed down Cleveland, 1-0. Just five days later, Providence's John Montgomery Ward pitched a perfect game against Buffalo. Incredibly, the third perfect game in National League history did not occur until 1964, when the Phillies' Jim Bunning accomplished the feat against the Mets. The spot where the Worcester marker sits today—in front of Becker's Main Academic Building—is where fans entered the park.

Trevino, Lee

Cog Hill Golf & Country Club (Dubsdread Course) • 12294 Archer Avenue Lemont, Illinois • 630-257-5872

At the 1975 Western Open, golfers Lee Trevino, Jerry Heard, and Bobby Nichols were all struck by lightning. All three men survived, and Trevino went on to win the 1984 PGA Championship and have a record-setting career on the Senior PGA Tour. But this one incident prompted brand new safety standards in weather preparedness at PGA events. Still, four spectators were killed by lightning during the 1991 U.S. Open at Hazeltine National in Chaska, Minnesota.

True Birthplace of Baseball?

Park Square • Pittsfield, Massachusetts

In May 2004, officials and historians in this western Massachusetts city released a 213-year-old document that they believed is the earliest written reference to baseball. The evidence came in a 1791 bylaw that aims to protect the windows in Pittsfield's new meeting house by prohibiting anyone from playing baseball within 80 yards of the building. That bylaw reads, "For the Preservation of the Windows in the New Meeting House, no Person, an Inhabitant of said Town, shall be permitted to play at any Game called Wicket, Cricket, Baseball . . . or any other Game or Games with Balls within the Distance of Eighty Yards." This was the first known mention of the national game in American history. The discovery was all thanks to diligent research by the esteemed baseball historian, John Thorn, the official historian of Major League Baseball.

Tyson, Mike/Evander Holyfield

MGM Grand Hotel • 3799 Las Vegas Boulevard • South Las Vegas, Nevada 800-929-1111

On June 28, 1997, during Holyfield-Tyson II, with 40 seconds left in the third round, Evander Holyfield stepped away from Mike Tyson and began jumping up and down. He turned away from Tyson, and Tyson charged, pushing him in the back before the ref could intervene and notify both corners that Tyson would be docked two points for biting. The replay clearly (and graphically) showed that Tyson had bitten a chunk out of Holyfield's right ear.

Tyson was warned that another foul would cost him the bout. A few seconds later, Tyson spit his mouth guard out and bit Holyfield's *left* ear. Then the fight was stopped and Tyson was disqualified. He attempted to charge Holyfield's corner, but succeeded only in punching one of the security guards. Fortunately, the chunk of ear was found and taken to a hospital, where it was sewn back onto Holyfield.

Washington, Kermit/Rudy Tomjanovich

The Forum • 3900 West Manchester Boulevard • Inglewood, California 310-419-3100

On December 9, 1977, during a game between the Houston Rockets and the Los Angeles Lakers, Rocket all-star Rudy Tomjanovich was rushing to help his teammate Kevin Kunnert, who was in the midst of a tangle first with Kareem Abdul-Jabbar and then with Kermit Washington.

Tomjanovich ran up right behind Washington, who turned and delivered a nearly fatal right-hand punch to Tomjanovich's face, knocking him to the floor. Tomjanovich's skull was dislocated and spinal fluid leaked from his brain. The punch remains one of the most horrifying video clips in sports (or any) history.

Tomjanovich had five operations, and missed the remainder of the season, while Washington served a 60-day suspension. Neither player's careers were ever the same, though Tomjanovich went on to a successful coaching career. Washington's term as a player ended in disgrace soon after the punch.

Woods, Tiger
Intersection of Hawthorne Blvd. and Blackhorse Rd.
Rolling Hills Estates, California

Golf legend Tiger Woods was involved in a single-car wreck on February 23, 2021. Woods had been staying at a resort in ritzy Rolling Hills on the Palos Verdes peninsula after hosting The Genesis Invitational tournament. The Los Angeles County Sheriff's Department issued a statement after Woods was "extricated from the wreck with the 'jaws of life' by Los Angeles County firefighters and paramedics" after his vehicle had flipped over several times. The car "sustained major damage" and Woods' manager later told *Golf Digest* that he "suffered multiple leg injuries." The California native was the only passenger in the car. Woods had been speeding as fast as 87 miles per hour, more than 45 miles per hour faster than the legal speed limit, before his 2021 Genesis GV80 SUV crashed. At the hospital afterward, a rod was inserted to stabilize Woods' tibia and femur bones, while a combination of screws and pins were used to stabilize injuries to the bones of his foot and ankle. No official cause was ever determined for the crash.

Index by State

Alabama, 34, 96, 97, 115, 116, 117, 127, 245, 358

Alaska, 231, 263

Arizona, 8, 27, 64, 158, 204, 224, 364, 451

Arkansas, 13, 90, 94, 95, 347, 356, 413, 444

California, 7, 9, 11, 12, 13, 14, 16, 17, 18, 22, 23, 24, 31, 33, 34, 36, 39, 42, 43, 44, 45, 46, 47, 48, 49, 50, 51, 52, 54, 55, 56, 61, 62, 69, 70, 74, 83, 84, 85, 87, 88, 112, 126, 135, 142, 143, 152, 154, 155, 156, 159, 160, 161, 167, 168, 172, 173, 174, 175, 176, 177, 181, 182, 183, 189, 190, 194, 196, 197, 199, 202, 203, 205, 206, 207, 208, 209, 210, 211, 212, 214, 216, 217, 218, 220, 221, 222, 223, 224, 225, 226, 227, 228, 230, 231, 232, 233, 234, 235, 236, 238, 239, 242, 244, 245, 247, 248, 249, 250, 251, 252, 253, 254, 255, 258, 259, 260, 261, 263, 264, 265, 266, 267, 269, 274, 275, 276, 277, 278, 279, 282, 283, 284, 285, 286, 290, 291, 292, 293, 294, 295, 296, 298, 304, 307, 308, 309, 310, 311, 320, 321, 322, 323, 324, 325, 326, 330, 331, 332, 334, 335, 337, 338, 339, 341, 342, 344, 345, 348, 350, 352, 353, 354, 359, 364, 365, 368, 369, 371, 373, 374, 375, 376, 378, 379, 380, 381, 382, 383, 384, 385, 386, 387, 390, 391, 392, 395, 404, 408, 417, 422, 423, 424, 430, 435, 437, 439, 441, 442, 448, 451, 455, 456

Colorado, 70, 141, 149, 178, 188, 253, 313, 346, 385, 391, 446

Connecticut, 24, 57, 79, 87, 179, 310, 386, 453

Delaware, 252, 342

Florida, 53, 84, 104, 125, 146, 147, 175, 176, 177, 190, 195, 212, 231, 233, 237, 241, 247, 280, 306, 308, 335, 345, 355, 356, 360, 414, 442, 451

Georgia, 28, 29, 31, 41, 71, 110, 116, 189, 193, 252, 256, 262, 291, 353, 360, 393, 394, 402, 403, 405, 406, 429

Hawaii, 382

Idaho, 109, 150, 267, 268, 413, 414, 448

Illinois, 22, 52, 65, 73, 85, 107, 108, 122, 126, 148, 153, 156, 183, 185, 186, 217, 234, 246, 261, 298, 306, 307, 324, 396, 412, 432, 436, 440, 454

Indiana, 15, 17, 18, 64, 72, 82, 95, 261, 330, 349, 441, 448

Iowa, 162, 199, 213, 246, 255, 341, 407

Kansas, 81, 86, 200, 262

Kentucky, 25, 64, 70, 102, 103, 106, 162, 440

Louisiana, 143, 204, 222, 236, 324, 332, 333, 334, 439

Maine, 66, 124, 200, 415, 430

Maryland, 123, 187, 245, 274, 420, 435

Massachusetts, 20, 26, 36, 37, 38, 39, 40, 65, 84, 92, 93, 98, 105, 118, 128, 129,
    130, 132, 144, 145, 146, 258, 264, 282, 289, 293, 362, 408, 410, 411, 417, 434,
    437, 445, 454

Michigan, 77, 105, 161, 218, 339, 369, 417

Minnesota, 90, 107, 154, 162, 227, 276, 312, 313, 314, 317, 319, 361, 389, 390

Mississippi, 72, 83, 114, 153, 221, 301, 302, 343, 345, 350

Missouri, 25, 89, 114, 120, 128, 163, 412, 415, 416, 442

Montana, 99, 164

Nebraska, 78, 81, 94, 98

Nevada, 7, 54, 60, 168, 195, 220, 233, 344, 455

New Hampshire, 184, 396

New Jersey, 19, 41, 60, 92, 100, 102, 113, 170, 171, 198, 251, 256, 316, 352, 361,
    362, 363, 367, 368, 400, 431, 434, 443

New Mexico, 44, 58, 136, 201, 254, 329, 377, 416, 418, 419

New York, 10, 11, 21, 25, 30, 32, 41, 50, 51, 53, 55, 58, 61, 63, 66, 76, 78, 79, 109,
    111, 115, 118, 121, 130, 131, 132, 134, 142, 151, 154, 156, 159, 172, 175, 176, 185,
    196, 209, 213, 215, 216, 219, 226, 229, 235, 238, 246, 256, 257, 258, 270, 276,
    279, 280, 283, 286, 291, 297, 299, 300, 303, 305, 306, 312, 313, 314, 315, 316,
    318, 319, 320, 321, 325, 326, 332, 333, 336, 339, 340, 350, 353, 356, 357, 358, 359,
    360, 366, 367, 370, 373, 378, 381, 383, 385, 387, 388, 389, 393, 397, 398, 399,
    404, 409, 421, 425, 426, 427, 452

North Carolina, 80, 138, 171, 257, 374, 386, 401, 431

Ohio, 20, 21, 35, 38, 59, 82, 88, 98, 101, 111, 133, 155, 180, 184, 251, 281, 303, 307, 322, 369, 385, 450

Oklahoma, 126, 205, 343

Oregon, 14, 63, 136, 242, 270, 271, 281, 335, 406

Pennsylvania, 28, 32, 67, 68, 69, 91, 99, 118, 134, 201, 269, 278, 281, 294, 325, 334, 343, 354, 385, 421, 424, 432, 438, 443, 449

Rhode Island, 37, 108, 238, 318, 359

South Carolina, 119, 151, 184, 303, 409

South Dakota, 161, 201, 384

Tennessee, 116, 131, 167, 200, 202, 229, 342, 344, 347, 348, 349, 350, 360

Texas, 9, 39, 42, 74, 96, 164, 165, 166, 188, 193, 215, 224, 232, 241, 251, 266, 285, 328, 329, 341, 354, 380, 447

Utah, 85, 112, 121, 150, 279, 446, 447

Vermont, 68, 392, 412

Virginia, 38, 138, 143, 170, 179, 187, 309, 348, 422, 452

Washington, 202, 270, 327, 333, 340, 385, 392

West Virginia, 20, 56, 57

Wisconsin, 75, 108, 147, 152, 157, 230, 237, 384

Wyoming, 89, 149, 180, 198

Canada, 100, 299, 316, 355, 357

Washington, D.C., 37, 40, 117, 119, 157, 168, 178, 187, 254, 297

Errata

Unfortunately, the following errors were caught too late in the publishing process to correct. We apologize and these items will be corrected in future printings of this book.

Page 142 – Bakley, Bonnie Lee
Blake was found not guilty of murder and of one of the two counts of soliciting murder on March 16, 2005. When it became clear that the jury was evenly split 11-1 in favor of an acquittal, the other count—for soliciting to commit murder—was dropped. A jury in a civil case found Blake responsible for his wife's tragic death on November 18, 2005, and they imposed a $30 million fine. At the age of 89, Blake passed away from heart illness in Los Angeles on March 9, 2023.

Page 174 – Corcoran Correctional Facility
This is the central California maximum-security prison where Charles Manson served his life sentences. He died here November 19, 2017.

Page 179 – Reagan, President Ronald
A federal judge later ordered that Hinckley be placed in a mental hospital, where he resided until being released in June 2022.

Page 220 – Lennon, John
Chapman was sentenced to 20 years to life in prison and today lives at the Green Haven Correctional Facility in Beekman, New York.

Page 307 – Disco Demolition Night
The original Comiskey Park was demolished in 1991.

Page 319 – The Ten O'Clock Scholar
Today, the site has been redeveloped into a commercial property.